CW01221265

'There are plenty of guides to Augustine's thought; the world doesn't need another. This book is something different: a companion to the reception of that thought, and to its effects on the development of particular Christian doctrines and theologians. There's nothing like it in English, and since the standard of the individual contributions is uniformly high, it is essential reading for anyone interested in what makes the West Augustinian, or in the variety of Augustinianisms there are.'

Paul J. Griffiths, *Duke Divinity School, USA*

'This impressive volume bears the fruits of the Augustine renewal of the past fifteen years. The editors have gathered together major essays of a uniformly high level. With this book, Augustinian theology as a constructive and ecumenical venture moves to the forefront of the theological scene.'

Matthew Levering, *University of Dayton, USA*

'What a wonderful volume! Pecknold and Toom have drawn together a collection that opens multiple windows onto one of the most important and complex theologians of the Western tradition. The first half of the book provides concise and powerful treatments of key themes in Augustine's thought; the second half entices us along some of the many roads that lead from Augustine to modern Christian thought. Throughout the compelling and continually generative nature of Augustine's thought shines.'

Lewis Ayres, *University of Durham, UK*

'The time is right for this book. The renewed interest in the study of theology and in the thought of the early Church that followed the Second Vatican Council has reached a certain maturity. It is, therefore, a good moment to expand the reach of each discipline by deepening the conversation between them. This *Companion to Augustine and Modern Theology* claims that it will be "useful in the hands of students seeking to bring the wisdom of Augustine to their own theological labours." It is, I think, more than that. It will also challenge theologians to examine their agreements and differences with Augustine and learn to exploit the tensions they find there in productive ways. It will challenge those who study Augustine to show how the pastoral quality of his thought keeps his theology firmly engaged with the times and situations he faced. The collection of articles found in this book are a good beginning. They deal with central themes and significant historical figures in a way that ought to stimulate both further engagement and more publications.'

Allan Fitzgerald, O.S.A., *Villanova University, USA*

'One of the most interesting recent developments in contemporary theology is a return to Augustine as theological resource. It is not too strong to say that some of the most creative modern theology is "Augustinian" in some way, predicated on a recovery and re-articulation of fundamental insights, and maybe even more importantly, a fundamental theological style that characterized Augustine. This new volume provides an indispensable tool for anyone wishing to track this renewal in theology, and also for those wishing, in their own way, to contribute to it. Somewhat unexpectedly but certainly pleasantly, one discovers in reading these essays that in attempting to develop Augustinian thinking in a modern context, one is also learning to see Augustine himself anew. The implication is that, perhaps, the only way to study Augustine in a way that does him justice is to develop his thinking in dialogue with the big theological questions of one's own time.'

John Cavadini, *University of Notre Dame, USA*

'Out of the many learned reference works on Augustine, this accessible companion stands out among them because it is both historically informed and theologically generative. In fact, by reading Augustine in conversation with important developments in Christian doctrine and in dialogue with prominent theologians, these essays provide a welcome contribution to Augustine studies and contemporary theology. I highly recommend it for students and scholars alike.'

Eric Gregory, *Princeton University, USA*

T&T Clark Companion to Augustine and
Modern Theology

Forthcoming titles in this series include:

T&T Clark Companion to the Atonement, edited by Adam J. Johnson
T&T Clark Companion to the Doctrine of Sin, edited by Keith L. Johnson and David Lauber

T&T Clark Companion to Augustine and Modern Theology

Edited by

C. C. Pecknold and Tarmo Toom

BLOOMSBURY
LONDON • NEW DELHI • NEW YORK • SYDNEY

Bloomsbury T&T Clark
An imprint of Bloomsbury Publishing Plc

50 Bedford Square	175 Fifth Avenue
London	New York
WC1B 3DP	NY 10010
UK	USA

www.bloomsbury.com
First published 2013

© C. C. Pecknold and Tarmo Toom, 2013

All rights reserved. No part of this publication may be reproduced or transmitted in any form or by any means, electronic or mechanical, including photocopying, recording, or any information storage or retrieval system, without prior permission in writing from the publishers.

C. C. Pecknold and Tarmo Toom have asserted their right under the Copyright, Designs and Patents Act, 1988, to be identified as Author of this work.

No responsibility for loss caused to any individual or organization acting on or refraining from action as a result of the material in this publication can be accepted by Bloomsbury Academic or the author.

British Library Cataloguing-in-Publication Data
A catalogue record for this books is available from the British Library.

ISBN: HB: 978-0-567-03381-9

Library of Congress Cataloging-in-Publication Data
Pecknold, C. C. and Toom, Tarmo
T&T Clark Companion to Augustine and Modern Theology/C. C. Pecknold and Tarmo Toom p.cm
Includes bibliographic references and index.
ISBN 978-0-567-03381-9 (hardcover)
2012045678

Typeset by Newgen Imaging Systems Pvt Ltd, Chennai, India
Printed and bound in Great Britain

Contents

Abbreviations ix
Editorial Introduction xii
C. C. Pecknold and Tarmo Toom

Part I: Doctrines

1 Augustine on the Triune God 3
  Luigi Gioia

2 Augustine on Human Being 20
  Michael Hanby

3 Augustine on Christ 36
  Ronnie Rombs

4 Augustine on the Church 54
  Michael Root

5 Augustine on Scripture 75
  Tarmo Toom

6 Augustine on the Last Things 91
  Morwenna Ludlow

Part II: Theologians

7 Augustine and Aquinas 113
  Frederick Christian Bauerschmidt

8 Augustine and Bonaventure 131
  Joshua C. Benson

9 Augustine and Luther 151
  Phillip Cary

Contents

10	Augustine and Calvin *Anthony N. S. Lane*	174
11	Augustine and Henri de Lubac *C. C. Pecknold and Jacob Wood*	196
12	Augustine and John Zizioulas *Will Cohen*	223

Contributors	240
Bibliography	242
Index	277

Abbreviations

ACPQ	*American Catholic Philosophical Quarterly*
ARCIC	*The Anglican/Roman Catholic International Commission*
AugStud	*Augustinian Studies*
bapt.	*De baptismo*
b. vita	*De beata vita*
BLW	*The Bondage and Liberation of the Will: A Defense of the Orthodox Doctrine of Human Choice against Pighius*
cat. rud.	*De catechizandis rudibus*
civ. Dei	*De Civitate Dei*
Comm. Rom.	*Commentarium super Epistolam ad Romanos*
conf.	*Confessiones*
cons. Ev.	*De consensu Evangelistarum*
c. Acad.	*Contra Academicos*
c. Adim.	*Contra Adimantum*
c. ep. Pel.	*Contra duas epistulas Pelagianorum*
c. ep. Man.	*Contra epistulam Manichaei*
c. Faust.	*Contra Faustum*
c. Gaud.	*Contra Gaudentium*
c. litt. Pet.	*Contra litteras Petiliani*
c. s. Ar.	*Contra sermonem Arianorum*
correct.	*De correctione Donatistarum*
CCL	*Corpus Christianorum, Series Latina*
CO	*Ioannis Calvini Opera Quae Supersunt Omnia*
CSEL	*Corpus Scriptorum Ecclesiasticorum Latinorum*
CTS	*Calvin Translation Society*
CollAug	*Collectania Augustiniana*
COR	*Opera omnia denuo recognita et adnotatione critica instructa notisque illustrata*
Cresc.	*Ad Cresconium*

Abbreviations

DSOD	*Defensio sanae et orthodoxae doctrinae de servitute et liberatione humani arbitrii adversus calumnias Alberti Pighii Campensis*
DS	*Denzinger*
dial.	*De dialectica*
div. qu.	*De diversis quaestionibus*
doc. Chr.	*De doctrina Christiana*
ench.	*Enchiridion*
en. Ps.	*Enarrationes in Psalmos*
Enn.	*Enneads*
ep.	*epistula*
ep. Jo.	*In epistulam Joannis*
ep. Ruf.	*Epistula ad Rufinum*
exp.	*Expositio*
ex. Gal.	*Expositio Epistulae ad Galatas*
f. et sym.	*De fide et symbolo*
Gen. adv. Man.	*De Genesi adversus Manicheos*
Gen. litt.	*De Genesi ad litteram*
Gn. litt. imp.	*De Genesi ad litteram imperfectus liber*
gr. et lib. arb.	*De gratia et libero arbitrio*
HeyJ	*Heythrop Journal*
HTR	*Harvard Theological Review*
Inst.	*Institutio*
IJST	*International Journal of Systematic Theology*
Io. tr. ev.	*In Ioannis evangelium tractatus*
ITQ	*Irish Theological Quarterly*
Jo. ev. tr.	*In Johannis evangelium tractatus*
JAAR	*Journal of American Academy of Religion*
JAC	*Jahrbuch für Antike und Christentum*
JECS	*Journal of Early Christian Studies*
JRE	*Journal of Religious Ethics*
JTS	*Journal of Theological Studies*
KDE	*Het Kerk- en Dogmahistorisch Element in de Werken van Johannes Calvijn*
LCC	*Library of Christian Classics*
lib. arb.	*De libero arbitrio*
LW	*Luther Werke*
mag.	*De magistro*
mor.	*De moribus*
nupt. et conc.	*De nuptiis et concupiscentia*
or.	*Oratio*
OS	*Johannis Calvini Opera Selecta*

pat.	De patientia
pecc. mer.	De peccatorum meritis
perf. just.	De perfectione justitiae hominis
persev.	De dono perseverantie
praed. sanct.	De praediestinatione sanctorum
PIMS	Pontifical Institute of Medieval Studies
PL	Patrologia latinae
Qu. Exod.	Quaestiones in Exodum
qu.	Quaestiones in Heptateuchum
RechAug	Recherches Augustiniennes
REtAug	Revue des Études Augustiniennes
retr.	Retractationes
SJT	Scottish Journal of Theology
SAOJC	Saint Augustin dans l'oeuvre de Jean Calvin
s.	Sermo
Simpl.	Ad Simplicianum
SP	Studia Patristica
spec.	Speculum
spir. et litt.	De spiritu et littera
StVTQ	St. Vladimir's Theological Quarterly
StudPat	Studia Patristica
ST	Summa Theologica
Super Rom.	Super epistolam ad Romanos
Super Sent.	Super Sententiarum
Trin.	De Trinitate
TS	Theological Studies
UR	Unitatis redintegratio
util. cred.	De utilitate credendi
VC	Vigiliae Christianae
vera rel.	De vera religione
Vita	Vita Augustini
WA	Weimar Ausgabe
ZAC	Zeitschrift für Antikes Christentum – Journal of Ancient Christianity

Editorial Introduction

The importance of Saint Augustine is difficult to overstate, but scholars keep trying. The fifth-century bishop of Hippo seems to contain the seeds of Western civilization itself. As Jaroslav Pelikan once quipped, the history of the West is but 'a series of footnotes' to Augustine'.[1] It is true, there has never been a generation that has not turned to the saint for wisdom – to learn from him, to follow or reject his path and most especially to utilize him as an authority. Every age seeks to measure itself against Augustine, to set his theology as a standard by which we may understand.

The medieval period seems especially 'Augustinian' to us. Augustine figured heavily in medieval *florilegia* of the twelfth and thirteenth centuries – and all the schools, religious orders and studia (Benedictine, Franciscan, Dominican, Augustinian) understood themselves as being faithful to Augustine. The Western medieval world cannot be divided up into those who are Augustinian and those who are not. It can only be divided up into different kinds of Augustinians. In the late medieval and early modern period, we can see the desire to catalogue the teachings of Augustine systematically. In the fourteenth century, Bartholomew of Urbino authored a massive study, *Milleloquium veritatis S. Augustini*, which included more than 1,000 alphabetically ordered keywords which offered the sayings of Augustine on the selected topics. Altogether, it cites about 15,000 passages from Augustine's works. And in the fifteenth century, Pope Nicholas V commissioned a project which included collecting the works of Augustine and which became the basis of the Vatican Library. In the next, sixteenth century, almost 500 editions (reprints included) of Augustine's works were published by both Protestants and Catholics. Among these 500 editions were no fewer than 16 *opera omnia* editions.[2]

---

[1] Jaroslav Pelikan, *The Christian Tradition: A History of the Development of Doctrine, vol. 1: The Emergence of the Catholic Tradition (100–600)* (Chicago: University of Chicago Press, 1975), p. 330.

[2] Arnoud S. Q. Visser, *Reading Augustine in the Reformation: The Flexibility of Intellectual Authority in Europe, 1500–1620* (Oxford Studies in Historical Theology; ed. D. C. Steinmetz; New York: Oxford University Press, 2011), p. 5.

Editorial Introduction

The diversity of medieval Augustinianism, as well as the place of Augustine during the Protestant Reformations, perhaps makes us all the more attentive to the history of his reception today. What seems different today is our awareness that one must not only understand Saint Augustine, but one must also be aware of how he has been read – indeed, how important it is to recognize which tradition of reading Augustine shapes us. Today there are also multiple projects, completed or under way, that demonstrate this ongoing fascination with how the 'seeds' of Augustine have grown in different kinds of soil. What is genuinely new is this attentiveness to the reception of 'Augustine through the Ages' as well as an attentiveness to how we receive his teaching today. A contemporary theologian simply cannot proceed without recognition of the sometimes complementary and sometimes rival ways in which he has been read over time. This volume brings together Augustine scholars, medieval historical theologians and contemporary systematic theologians to reflect on Augustine's influence on central doctrines of Christian faith, as well as his influence on prominent theologians in the medieval, early and late modern periods.

The present volume has been inspired by two projects of reception in particular. The first is the enormously helpful *Augustine through the Ages: An Encyclopedia*, published in 1999 under the able editorial leadership of Allan D. Fitzgerald, O.S.A. The approximately 900-page encyclopaedia made available to students a windfall of learning about Augustine's life, his writings and his thought. It tended to treat his reception topically rather than with reference to figures, yet throughout there is a heightened pitch of attention to the manifold complexity of Augustine's reception among different theological schools. It continues to be the best single-volume encyclopaedia for understanding Saint Augustine. With the exception of Phillip Cary, we have avoided drawing upon the same group of scholars who produced *Augustine through the Ages*, and we have tried to make our thematic and theological focus distinct from the work of encyclopaedia. A new set of contributors, both senior and junior, were asked to perform a different but related task – one that might be of special use to contemporary theologians. Contributors were not asked to be comprehensive, but to invite students to ongoing conversations with Augustine that they might join through their own research and writing.

The second influence was the *After Augustine* project, led by Karla Pollmann, which proposed a reception history on a massive scale – four projected volumes surveying the reception history from 430–2000. While the prospect of a comprehensive reception history is deeply attractive to us as scholars, we wondered if there was now more reason than ever to produce something at the more modest end of the spectrum. We wanted to produce a *handbook*, a volume that would not be quite so exhaustive, but that would nevertheless be useful in the hands of students seeking to bring the wisdom of Augustine to their own theological labours.

Editorial Introduction

This companion to *Augustine and Modern Theology*, then, is something less than an encyclopaedia or a comprehensive reception history. But it is something more than a collection of essays. Perhaps it is fruitful to think of the present volume as a series of conversations with Saint Augustine. In 1969, Joseph Ratzinger stated, 'I have developed my theology in a dialogue with Augustine, though naturally I have tried to conduct this dialogue as a man of today'.[3] Theologians throughout the history of Latin Christianity have considered dialogue with Saint Augustine to be essential to their formation. We see this companion as an aid to the formation of the theologian, whether they are just beginning as a fellow traveller on the way of grace, or whether they are returning to him like an old friend. As Augustine's biographer Possidius once wrote, 'No one can read what he [Augustine] wrote on theology without profit' (*Vita* 31). Similarly, one might say that for us, writing theology in conversation with Augustine is never without profit either.

We have set aside, in equal measure, a representative complex of doctrines and theologians that have benefited from Saint Augustine's influence. The priority of God in all things is axiomatic in Augustine's work, and so Luigi Gioia leads our doctrinal essays on the Triune God. The distinction between God and creation that Augustine never failed to illumine, especially in his teaching on *creatio ex nihilo*, encourages us to put in the second place Michael Hanby's essay on the crown of creation, namely the human person. Here Augustine's teaching on the person as the *imago Dei* is treated in a way which fully engages the contemporary challenges. Ronnie Rombs essay on Christ and Michael Root's essay on the church together form the centre of the first half of the volume because for Augustine Jesus Christ is the one true Mediator of God and humanity, and the church is the Body of Christ on pilgrimage to the City of God. Since Augustine first comes to understand Scripture through the faith of the church, it seems fitting that Tarmo Toom's essay on Augustine and Scripture should follow, for it is by the church's *regula fidei* and most especially the *regula caritatis* that he thinks the theologian can read the Bible most profitably. Finally, to Morwenna Ludlow goes a concluding essay on eschatology in the doctrinal part of this volume. In this way, readers might find a structural similarity with the second half of Augustine's *City of God* – wherein he promises to tell of the origins, histories and destinies of the two cities – the famous *exitus-reditus* structure. Our intention is to give students a set of essays that forms them to follow Augustine's custom of habitually ordering all things to the praise and glory of God.

---

[3] Joseph Ratzinger, 'Glaube, Geschichte und Philosophie. Zum Echo auf *Einfuehrung in das Christentum*', *Hochland* 61 (1969), p. 543. The English translation is from Aidan Nichols, *The Theology of Joseph Ratzinger* (Edinburgh: T&T Clark, 1988), p. 27.

Editorial Introduction

After immersing readers in the teaching of Augustine, the second half of this volume pays close attention to a representative set of theologians who exemplify the diversity and depth of the reception of Augustine. Our selections here are ecumenical in three ways.

First, within the Catholic reception of Augustine, there have been internal philosophical and theological debates throughout the modern period that find their roots in thirteenth-century scholasticism. Here we have provided students with an essay on Saint Thomas Aquinas and Saint Bonaventure. The continuities and discontinuities between them are difficult to address without reference to Saint Augustine, and each of these essays ably show why each is an 'Augustinian', but also why that description is also so problematic. The *doctores ecclesiae* establish for us paradigmatic medieval exemplars for what constitutes a truly rich and profitable conversation with Augustine today.

Second, within the Protestant reception of Augustine, and also key to the Catholic Reformation as well, are the two premier Protestant theologians, Martin Luther and John Calvin. The essays by Phillip Cary and Anthony Lane present these seminal theologians as drinking deeply from the wells of Augustinian wisdom, and demonstrate that any conversation with Augustine today that does not attend to how Protestants turned to read the bishop of Hippo for reform and renewal have cut themselves off from a great conversation indeed.

Third, our two final theologians, Henri de Lubac and John Zizioulas, represent the ecumenical, Catholic and orthodox significance of conversing with Augustine. It is true that Cardinal de Lubac and Zizioulas are theologians whose work is centred in Catholic and Orthodox theology respectively, but it is also true that the ecumenical significance of each of these theologians has been dramatic. De Lubac's work has always been described as 'Augustinian Thomist', yet it has attracted Catholic, Orthodox and Protestant readers alike. C. C. Pecknold and Jacob Wood examine how we might best understand Henri de Lubac as an Augustinian in the tradition of Giles of Rome. Will Cohen takes on one of the most difficult tasks in contemporary orthodox theology today: re-reading Augustine as a friend of the Orthodox faith.

None of these essays, of course, substitute for reading Saint Augustine yourself. Today, we have access to 5 million words penned by Augustine. Possidius once mentioned that, by the grace of God, books and pamphlets came from Augustine's pen in a constant flow (*Vita* 7). It takes 48 modern volumes in English to print everything which is extant from the bishop of Hippo in the soon-to-be completed series *Augustine for the 21st Century* (New City Press). No wonder that in one of his sermons (*s.* 302), Augustine pleads with his congregation, 'Let me be, let me not have to endure all that, don't let anyone force me to. Look, as a little concession to me, give me a holiday from this business. I beg you, I beseech you!'

Editorial Introduction

The etymology of the word 'companion' might literally be conveyed as *com-panis*, 'with bread'. Its first known use is, appropriately, in the thirteenth century – precisely when so many theological schools were formed in conversation with Augustine. In one sense, it is the works of Saint Augustine that we consider 'the bread', his 5 million words can nourish and renew theology in the twenty-first century just as it has before. Yet given the theological importance of the Eucharist as sacrifice in *City of God* 10, and given the ecumenical significance he gives to the Eucharist as the sacrament of the church's unity, the 'bread' which this volume accompanies might be understood as the same bread that the bishop points to when he preaches that no matter how many loaves there are on the church's altars, there is only 'one bread' constituting the one body of Christ (*s.* 229A.1). We hope that this *companion* to Augustine and modern theology points students not only to a timely conversation with Saint Augustine himself, but also draws students near to the heart of the church.

C. C. Pecknold and Tarmo Toom
Feast of St. Teresa of Avila
The Catholic University of America
Washington, DC

Part I
Doctrines

1 Augustine on the Triune God

Luigi Gioia

A useful pointer to the structure, aim and content of Augustine's *De Trinitate* is disclosed in book 8, that is just halfway through the treatise: 'But we must put some limits to repetition', says Augustine, 'and beseech God as devoutly and earnestly as we can to open our understandings and temper our fondness for controversy (*contentio*), so that our minds may be able to perceive the essence of truth without any mass, without any changeableness.'[1] *Contentio* (polemics), refers to the first 7 books of the treatise, whereas books 8–15 are described as an attempt to climb to the contemplation of the truth of God and of the mystery of the Trinity (an anagogy), based on a progressively refined analysis of the activity of human mind according to triadic patterns matching the formal content of the confession of the mystery of the Trinity (exemplarity).

I. Polemics

Polemics is the literary genre virtually all Trinitarian treatises adopted during the fourth and fifth centuries, as it appears from most of their titles: *Against the Arians*[2] or *Against Eunomius*.[3] They usually consisted in more or less elaborate reviews of a set of scriptural passages 'Arians'[4] exploited to

---

[1] Augustine, *Trin.* 8.1 (p. 268). Each quotation of the *De Trinitate* is followed by the page number of the critical edition of the Latin text, without referring each time to the volumes 50 and 50/A of the *Corpus Christianorum Latinorum* in which it can be found. English translation: *The Trinity* (trans. Edmund Hill; *The Works of Saint Augustine: A Translation for the 21st Century*; New York: New City Press, 1991).

[2] Cf. for example Athanasius, Hilary of Poitiers, Marius Victorinus, Phoedabius.

[3] For example Basil of Caesarea and Gregory of Nyssa.

[4] While Hill vaguely assumes that these 'Arians' are 'Arian metaphysicians of the fourth century, the chief of them being Eunomius' (p. 49), Barnes identifies them with Latin Homoians Augustine would have known during the 380s in Milan: 'Augustine's time in Milan corresponded with the peak of Homoian strength'; 'in 385 Justina and the pro-Homoian court in Milan made the faith of Rimini and Constantinople 360 legal in their city'; M. R. Barnes, 'The Arians of Book V and the Genre of *De Trinitate*', *JTS* 44 (1993), pp. 185–95 (p. 189). Thus, Barnes does not agree with the hypothesis of Augustine's 'intellectual distance from the Arian controversy' (p. 193) and finds that the arguments refuted in books 5–7 can be those of Palladius and Maximinus (p. 190). He also notices that the doctrines ascribed to Arius in book 6 'are all doctrines to be found in the three Western

argue for the inferiority of the Son and of the Holy Spirit with regards to the Father. Augustine too follows this tradition and roughly distributes the analysis of disputed scriptural quotations between New Testament (book 1 and the first half of the book 2) and Old Testament (second half of the book 2 and book 3).

For the New Testament, he begins by adopting the classical anti-'Arian' hermeneutical principle based on Philippians 2: in his 'form of God (*forma dei*) Christ is equal to the Father; in his form of a servant (*forma serui*) he is inferior to the Father'.[5] When Scripture seems to affirm the inferiority of Christ, it refers to his humanity (*forma serui*), whereas when the equality between the Son and the Father are clearly stated, Scripture is talking about his divinity (*forma dei*). Very soon, however, Augustine takes his leave from received anti-Arian patterns, to let his theological genius freely take the upper hand. This traditional rule does not satisfy him: the relation between the humanity and the divinity in Christ is more than a simple question of the attribution of his actions to either of his two natures. A far more sophisticated hermeneutical principle is required to underpin the daring formulas he favours: 'crucified God' (*deus crucifixus*)[6] and 'humility of God' (*humilitas dei*).[7] At the beginning of book 2, he observes that some scriptural passages, although referring to the divinity of the Son, seem to imply some sort of subordination from the Father – not to talk about the Holy Spirit who seems dependent on both Father and Son. The carefully chiselled formulas of the Nicene Creed offer the ideal framework for the interpretation of these passages: although equal to the Father, the Son is 'God from God' (*deus de deo*) and 'light from light' (*lumen de lumine*).[8] In the same way, the Holy Spirit is

---

anti-Arian texts . . . Augustine knew: Hilary's *De Trinitate*, Victorinus' *Aduersus Arianum* and Ambrose's *De Fide*' (p. 185). The same argument is developed in a later article by the same M. R. Barnes, 'The Visible Christ and the Invisible Trinity: Mt 5.8 in Augustine's Trinitarian Theology of 400', *Modern Theology* 19 (2003), pp. 329–55. The vicissitudes of the Arian community in Milan in the 380s and of their conflict with Ambrose in 385–86 are described in M. Meslin, *Les Ariens d'Occident. 335–430* (Paris: Editions du Seuil, 1967), pp. 44–58. We are inclined to agree with Barnes as to the really polemical (and not just literary or instrumental) nature of the controversy against 'Arians' in the *De Trinitate* and think that Augustine would not have lingered as long as he did in the discussion of their logical and ontological categories had this not been necessary to determine the best way of confuting them. At the same time, to avoid the drawbacks of an overindulgent taxonomy which has all but helped to clarify the Trinitarian controversy in the early church, the safest option is to adopt Augustine's own terminology and refer to his opponents as 'Arians'. This term shall always appear in inverted commas because for Augustine, as for his predecessors, it had become the label for virtually any position at variance with what in the end became the mainstream orthodox confession of the mystery of the Trinity.

[5] Augustine, *Trin.* 1.14 (pp. 44–6), summed up again in 2.2 (p. 81).
[6] Ibid.,1.28 (p. 69).
[7] Ibid., 4.4 (p. 164); cf. 8.7 (p. 276) and 13.22 (p. 412).
[8] Ibid., 2.2 (p. 82).

God but 'he proceeds from the Father' (*a patre procedit*).[9] In other words, what appears to be subordination in reality indicates 'direction' in the relation between the divine persons: only the Father is 'God' without qualification; the Son is 'from God', *de deo*; the Holy Spirit is *a deo* or *ex deo*. Father, Son and Holy Spirit, however, are equally 'God'.[10] To bear this second hermeneutical rule out, a solid and extensive scriptural foundation is then unfolded under the heading of 'missions' (*missiones*). Careful analysis of the New Testament shows that the Son is said to have been sent (in Latin *mittere*, hence 'missions') only with the incarnation, the Holy Spirit only at Pentecost,[11] whereas the Father is never said to have been sent. This means that Son and Holy Spirit manifest their personal identity only with the incarnation and at Pentecost, whereas the Father reveals himself precisely as the one who is not sent, who does not appear, that is, that can be known, can be reached only through the Son and the Holy Spirit. The equality of the divine persons, then, must account for the difference in their self-manifestation, through the elaboration of a theology of revelation focused on divine action in the process by which we come to know God or, rather, as Augustine is fond of repeating, we come to be known by God.[12]

Anti-'Arian' polemics is carried on through the long discussion on the theophanies of the Old Testament in books 2 and 3. 'Arians' had referred the divine attributes of immutability (Wis. 7.27) and invisibility (1 Tim. 1.17–8 and 6.15–6)[13] only to the Father on the pretext that whenever God manifested himself in the theophanies of the Old Testament it had been through the Son. The Son would be 'visible in himself' (*uisibilis per se ipsum*) because even before the incarnation he could appear to mortal eyes[14] and, as a result, he is not God in exactly the same sense as the Father is God. A detailed analysis of God's manifestations in the Old Testament was necessary to oppose this view and argue that, if we adhere closely to what Scripture says, it is often impossible to attribute them to any of the three persons in particular.[15] Only on the basis of the full revelation of the identity of divine persons in the New Testament, it is possible to conjecture which of them might have acted in specific Old Testament instances.[16] Such view is by no means the symptom of a modalistic tendency of his Trinitarian

---

[9] Ibid., 2.5 (p. 86).
[10] Augustine's fundamental standpoint is that there cannot be any intermediate being between God and his creatures: 'For every substance that is not God is a creature, and that which is not a creature is God' (Augustine, *Trin.* 1.9 [p. 38]). Hence, the Son and Holy Spirit are either creatures or they are God.
[11] Augustine, *Trin.* 2.11 (p. 95).
[12] Ibid., 9.1 (p. 292).
[13] Ibid., 2.14 (p. 99).
[14] Ibid., 2.15 (p. 101).
[15] Ibid., 2.18 (pp. 103–05).
[16] Ibid., 2.18, 26 (pp. 103 and 114–15).

thought,[17] but simply flows from the obvious fact that revelation of the Trinity only occurred with the incarnation and Pentecost. The Old Testament offers hints of God's identity and action which start to make sense only in the light of the New Testament, and therefore cannot be safely ascribed to one of the divine persons in particular. Moreover, theophanies of the Old Testament happened 'by means of the creature made subject to him' (*per subiectam creaturam*),[18] because (and this is the crucial theological point Augustine intended to make) Father, Son and Holy Spirit are *equally* invisible.[19]

Anti-'Arian' polemics also accounts for the turn the argument of the treatise takes in books 5–7. Second-generation 'Arians' (sometimes called 'Eunomians') had developed a set of polemical arguments based on logical and ontological categories and designed to disprove the 'consubtantial' (*homoousios*) which had slowly become the watchword of Nicene orthodoxy.[20] Thus, these three books scrutinize the formula elaborated during the Trinitarian controversy: *mian ousian treis hypostaseis*, translated in Latin as *unam essentiam tres substantias* ('one essence, three substances').[21] The first half of book 5 discusses the use of essence (*ousia*),[22] and the second half that of person (*persona*, the Latin word chosen instead of the more equivocal 'substance' to translate the Greek *hypostasis*).[23] The argument seems then to move away from this point, but in reality the Trinitarian formula remains in the background and comes to the surface again in the middle of book 7 to be examined until the end of the same book.[24]

This anti-'Arian' polemical framework is crucial to the theological evaluation of this long discussion on substance. Ontological vocabulary of substance or accidents and the distinction between what is said substantially (*ad se*) and what is said relatively (*ad aliquid*) of God are inherited from the 'Arians' and force those who want to oppose their views to argue along the same lines.[25] Since 'Arians' use these categories to argue for the diversity of substance

---

[17] Cf. K. Rahner, 'Remarks on the Dogmatic Treatise *De Trinitate*', in *Theological Investigations* (trans. K. Smyth; vol. 4; Baltimore: Helicon Press, 1966), pp. 80–82 and C. Gunton, 'Augustine, the Trinity and the Theological Crisis of the West', in *The Promise of Trinitarian Theology* (Edinburgh: T&T Clark, 1991), pp. 30–55 (p. 42). The latter also attributes Augustine's treatment of the Old Testament theophanies to 'anti-Incarnational Platonism' (p. 34) and to 'a spiritualising tendency' which 'by losing the mediatorship of the Word at once distances God from the creation and flattens out the distinctions between the persons of the Trinity' (p. 35).

[18] Cf. Augustine, *Trin.* 2.35 (p. 126).

[19] Augustine, *Trin.* 3.21 (p. 150).

[20] Cf. R. Vaggione (trans. and ed.), *Eunomius: The Extant Works* (Oxford Early Christian Texts; Oxford: Oxford University Press, 1987).

[21] Augustine, *Trin.* 5.10 (p. 217).

[22] Ibid., 5.3–9 (pp. 207–16).

[23] Ibid., 5.10–17 (pp. 216–27).

[24] Ibid., 7.7–12 (pp. 255–67).

[25] 'Arian' positions are quoted three times in *Trin.* 5.4 (pp. 208–09) and 5.7 (pp. 211–12).

between Father and Son, pro-Nicene polemists need to determine an alternative orthodox way of using vocabulary of substance and accidents and the distinction *ad se/ad aliquid* when it is applied to God.[26] The outcome of the argument is that each person is the 'substance' – that is, God – and that the three together are 'the one substance' – that is, the one God. Yet within the unity of this substance there is a 'direction' (*de deo*),[27] which is the same point the second scriptural hermeneutical rule explained above was meant to illustrate.

The discussion on person is also unfolded in the same wave-like form. In book 5, once he has dealt with essence (*ousia*), Augustine takes up hypostasis (*hypostasis*),[28] quickly replaced by what had become its Latin equivalent, person. Only with deep reluctance, he resorts to an ontological category to encompass what is common to Father, Son and Holy Spirit. He famously declares: 'We say three persons, not to affirm that, but so that we are not reduced to silence',[29] and spends the rest of the section devoted to person trying to determine the content of this term. The driving question is *Quid tres?* ('Three what?'). The determination of the content of the notion of person calls for the examination of the properties (*proprietates*) of Father, Son and Holy Spirit. Since the most problematic property (*proprium*) is that of the Holy Spirit, a large section of book 5 deals with this point.[30] The issue of the property of each person is taken up again in book 6, with a quotation of Hilary of Poitiers and Augustine's evaluation of it.[31] Finally, the question is resumed in the middle of book 7 through a relentless criticism of the application of some metaphysical categories to the mystery of the Trinity.[32]

II. Exemplarity and Anagogy

As the polemical section is gradually brought to its conclusion, some literary devices are deployed to prepare the transition to the second half of the treatise. Towards the end of book 7, while pursuing his criticism of logical and ontological categories applied to the Trinity, Augustine engages in a last censure of the use of 'person' in Trinitarian theology through the review of scriptural passages that refer to God's triunity.[33] To talk about God, Scripture uses sometimes both singular and plural pronouns and sometimes only plural pronouns. However, if the plural is attested in Scripture in connexion with relative names like Father

---

[26] Augustine, *Trin.* 5.3–9 (pp. 207–16).
[27] Ibid., 7.1–3 (pp. 244–50).
[28] Ibid., 5.10 (p. 217).
[29] Ibid.: *dictum est tamen tres personae non ut illud diceretur sed ne taceretur.*
[30] Augustine, *Trin.* 5.12–17 (pp. 218–27).
[31] Ibid., 6.11–12 (pp. 241–43).
[32] Ibid., 7.7–12 (pp. 255–67).
[33] Ibid., 7.12 (pp. 265–67).

and Son, we never find the plural of non-relative names (like person) applied to God, that is, we never find Father, Son and Holy Spirit designated as three 'something(s)' in the way we do when talking about three 'persons'. Now, one of the scriptural passages talking about God in the plural listed in the course of this argument is the well-known sentence from Genesis, 'Let us make man in our image, after our likeness' (1.26). Rather unexpectedly, instead of being offered a simple discussion on the significance of this sentence for Trinitarian vocabulary, we run into a catechesis on the meaning of the image of God which in fact anticipates and very effectively sums up everything Augustine is going to say on the same topic in books 12–14 and more generally in the second half of the *De Trinitate*. According to this catechesis, we are created not simply in the image of the Son, but of the whole Trinity. The reason for this assertion is not just the tenuous textual argument that 'let *us* make' and '*our* image' are in the plural, although this point certainly plays a role in this claim. On the contrary, the refusal to confine the model for the image to the Son alone depends on the same reasons put forward to deny the attribution of the theophanies of the Old Testament to the Son alone in the first four books of the *De Trinitate*. The Son's equality with the Father means that *he is equally invisible by nature* and cannot therefore be an 'image' properly speaking any more than the Father or the Holy Spirit. Scripture says that we are created in the *image* of God precisely to stress the distinction between simple likeness (*similitudo*) and equality with God. Only the Son is 'equal to' (i.e. *imago*) God; we are only 'in the image' (*ad imaginem*) of God. Furthermore, the main reason for the assertion that we are 'to the image' of the Trinity simply is that God *is* Trinity.[34]

This transition anticipates the inquiry into the 'essence of truth' of the second half of the treatise announced in the sentence we quoted at the beginning,[35] that is the shift from a polemical to a speculative exploration of the Trinitarian mystery, conducted through the help of the exemplary character of the image of God. Scriptural claim that God is our creator and made us in his image implies that something, in what we are, must reflect the identity of our maker and exemplar and should therefore allow us to know him as if through a mirror. Similarities between the image and the Trinity are discovered by looking at the human self in the light of the formal aspects of the confession of the mystery of the Trinity summed up at the beginning of the book 9, namely the unity of an equal essence and the triad of persons related to each other (crucial to the interpretation of this strategy is that the analogy is established not between the self *and God the Trinity*, but between the self and formal aspects *of the confession* of the mystery of the Trinity).[36]

---

[34] Ibid., 7.12 (p. 266): *Deus autem trinitas*.
[35] Augustine, *Trin.* 8.1 (p. 268).
[36] Ibid., 9.1 (p. 293).

Thus, we encounter a real unity of essence when the triad of 'lover, what is being loved and love' conjured up at the end of book 8,[37] is applied to the mind (that is to the 'self'): the loving mind (*mens amans*) and the love it loves itself are 'one spirit, not two beings but one being; and yet they are two . . . and these are called two things relatively to one another'.[38] However, on the basis of Augustine's leading postulate of the inseparability between knowledge and love, nothing can be loved which is not known already. The mind can love itself only because it simultaneously knows itself,[39] thus leading to the following triad: 'mind (loving itself), self-knowledge and self-love', that is three elements relative to each other and yet constituting only one substance.[40] This triad meets the formal requirements of equality, consubstantiality, inseparability belonging to the orthodox confession of the unity of the Trinity,[41] even though, whereas self-knowledge and self-love are relative terms (*ad aliquid*), the mind is an absolute term (*ad se*).[42] Thus, in the course of book 10, almost incidentally, a new element is introduced, self-memory which, by the end of the same book, replaces the mind in the new triad of 'memory, intelligence and will'.[43] The elements of this triad are relative to each other in a perfectly symmetrical way.[44]

With book 11, the line of exemplarity is supplemented by an anagogical strategy: starting from realities nearer to our everyday experience, readers (unflatteringly dubbed as *tardiores*[45]) are gradually helped to climb from easily intelligible triads highlighted in sensorial experience to the more ethereal triad of the mind and finally to the ineffable mystery of God's triunity (always from a formal point of view). We are thus presented with the triads of 'the thing we see, the actual sight and the conscious intention' (*res, intentio animi et uisio*)[46] and 'memory, internal sight and will' (*memoria, interna uisio et uoluntas*).[47] These triads too are checked against the formal characteristics of the confession of the Trinitarian mystery and the analysis of their inadequacies helps to refine the search and to introduce to the next step.[48]

---

[37] Ibid., 8.14 (pp. 290–91).
[38] Ibid., 9.2 (p. 295).
[39] Ibid., 9.3 (pp. 295–96).
[40] Ibid., 9.5 (p. 298). Therefore Augustine does not leave behind the triad of love of book 8 to replace it with a new one. In reality, we are still in the triad of love, even though, on the basis of the inseparability between knowledge and love, Augustine shows that it necessarily includes self-knowledge as well.
[41] Augustine, *Trin.* 9.8 (pp. 300–01).
[42] In Trinitarian terms, this triad would correspond to 'God, the Son and the Holy Spirit'.
[43] Augustine, *Trin.* 10.17 (pp. 329–30).
[44] Ibid., 10.18 (pp. 330–31).
[45] Ibid., 10.19 (p. 332).
[46] Ibid., 11.2 (pp. 334–36).
[47] Ibid., 11.7 (pp. 341–43).
[48] Ibid., 9.5 (pp. 297–98) and 9.7 (pp. 299–300).

In books 12–14, however, Augustine's interest shifts elsewhere and while the theme of the image of God still acts as a catalyst for the inquiry, the formal relation of exemplarity between creator and creature are kept alive only through sometimes-awkward summaries at the end of each of these books.[49] Only in book 15, the exemplar and the anagogical lines regain the upper hand and reach their outcome. Some characteristics of the exemplar can indeed be traced back through the mirror represented by the image of God in us. In particular, the inner life of the Trinity can be expressed in the same way as the inner life of the mind, namely in the light of the triad of 'mind, self-knowledge and self-love'.[50]

A puzzling – and revealing – trait of this outcome needs to be noticed. One of the driving motives behind the passage from the first to the second triad in book 10 was precisely the latter greater conformity to the formal aspects of the confession of the mystery of the Trinity: with regards to the first triad (mind, self-knowledge and self-love), Augustine had noticed that whereas self-knowledge and self-love are relative terms, 'mind' is an absolute term; this meant that, translated into Trinitarian formulas, it would have to be rendered not as 'Father, Son and Holy Spirit', but as '*God*, Son and Holy Spirit'. This was why, in the course of book 10, he had elaborated the second triad of memory, intelligence and will,[51] three elements, that is, perfectly symmetrical with each other and thus indeed corresponding to the exact formal portrait of the relations between Father, Son and Holy Spirit.[52] Why, then, when the time finally came to lead the exemplary and anagogical lines to their outcome in book 15, he chose the less suitable of these triads from the formal viewpoint, namely 'the mind, and the knowledge it knows itself with, and the love it loves itself with'?[53]

If the exemplary and anagogical approaches to the theme of the image of God had been Augustine's main epistemological tool in the *De Trinitate* – as we have assumed so far – such inconsistency would be unjustifiable and disappointing. As it is, however, this somehow casual stance with regards to the very formal requirements he had set for himself proves that their significance in the unfolding of his doctrine of the image of God is not as crucial to the project he pursues in the *De Trinitate* as generation of scholars have assumed. However extensively spread out throughout the second half of the *De Trinitate* it might be, the exemplary and anagogical strategies are only one facet of a much larger and deeper approach to the theme of the image of God with regards to knowledge of the Trinity, which still needs to be identified.

---

[49] Cf. Augustine, *Trin.* 12.25 (pp. 379–80) and 13.26 (pp. 418–20).
[50] Augustine, *Trin.* 15.10 (p. 474).
[51] Ibid., 10.17 (pp. 329–30).
[52] Ibid., 10.18 (pp. 330–31).
[53] Ibid., 15.10 (p. 474).

III. Mystagogy

The truth of the matter is that the polemical, exemplary and anagogical threads unfolded so far act like something of an outer shell for a deeper and more important core of the argument of the treatise. The *De Trinitate* aims not only at the elucidation of the Trinitarian dogma but also at participation in the life of the Trinity and thus orchestrates a mystagogical strategy encapsulated in the following sentences: 'For the fulness of our happiness, beyond which there is none else, is this: to enjoy (*frui*) God the Trinity in whose image we were made',[54] and 'When we say and believe that there is a Trinity, we know what a triad is because we know what three are. *But this is not what we love* ... What we love is not a triad but the Trinity that is God. So what we love in the Trinity is what God is'.[55]

This mystagogical strategy, although already detectable in books 1–3, is clearly declared only in book 4, where the apparently detached and neutral exposition of the Trinitarian mystery unveils its deeper existential urgency and its epistemological relevance. If books 1–3 had already argued for the dependence of the doctrine of the Trinity on God's self-manifestation, book 4 reveals that this is the consequence of a fundamental soteriological point, namely the identity between God's self-revelation and the reconciliation accomplished through Christ in the Holy Spirit. The exposition of the Trinitarian mystery needs to take into account incarnation and soteriology, needs to talk about sin, Christ's sacrifice, faith and love. In its simplest terms, the argument goes as follows: if God made himself known to us, it was because we were unable to know him by ourselves. Our inability to know God is the consequence of our separation from him and from the happiness (*beatitudo*) and truth which can only be found in him.[56] This sinful situation is variously described as pride (*superbia*), despair (*desperatio*),[57] covetousness (*cupiditas*)[58] and blindness (*mentes caecatae*).[59] Through his self-manifestation, God wanted to persuade us of what sort of people we are that he loves (*quales dilexerit nos*), that is, of our sinful condition and our need for his love, and of how much he loved us (*quantum nos diligeret*), so as to heal simultaneously our pride and our desperation.[60]

IV. Theology of Revelation

The claim underlying this turn in the argument is that exposition of Trinitarian doctrine can only be an echo of God's own self-exposition and cannot even

---

[54] Ibid., 1.18 (p. 52).
[55] Ibid., 8.8 (pp. 278–79), translation modified.
[56] Augustine, *Trin.* 4.2 (p. 161).
[57] Ibid.
[58] Ibid., 4.4 (p. 163) and 4.12 (p. 177).
[59] Augustine, *Trin.* 4.4 (p. 163).
[60] Ibid., 4.2 (p. 161).

for a moment, even provisionally, make abstraction from the consequences of our sinfulness on knowledge of God. In other terms, without Christ's soteriological and epistemological mediation, in the Holy Spirit, no knowledge of God, no union with God, no exposition of the Trinitarian mystery is conceivable. Hence the controversy of a good portion of book 4 against any form of soteriological or epistemological mediation other than Christ's and even more vehemently against the pretension of those who thought they did not need any mediation at all.[61]

In this context, the discussion on missions we have sketched above appears to be much more than an exegetical nicety and is brought to fruition. The nature of Son and Holy Spirit's sendings (or missions) can only be grasped in the light of their purpose. The sinfulness which prevents us from knowing God is summed up in the covetousness (*cupiditas*) which weighs us down or turns us outside ourselves in an immoderate love for sensible and mutable realities, which Augustine calls *temporalia*, 'temporal realities'. Therefore, in the incarnation of Christ, God decided to purify us through these same *temporalia* which had become the occasion of our sin.[62] In Christ's mission, that is, the incarnation, God the Trinity makes himself known to us and bridges from his side the abyss between his immutability and our mutability, his invisibility (i.e. his unknowability) and our need of mediation of sensible realities.[63] The mission of the Holy Spirit at Pentecost is entirely linked to that of the Son at the incarnation. In fact, since the humanity of Christ is not revelatory as such, God makes himself known through love (*dilectio*), that is, through the action of the Holy Spirit.[64]

Only with the incarnation, with Christ's sacrifice on the cross, his Resurrection and the sending of the Holy Spirit, do we have a revelation of inner-Trinitarian life. Only then, does the way God acts correspond to what he is in the deepest possible way. This is what Augustine means when he says that 'to be sent' means 'to be known', 'to be perceived'[65] and that 'just as being born means for the Son his being from the Father, so his being sent means his being known to be from him'.[66] In this way, a properly Trinitarian doctrine of revelation takes shape that squares the circle of the knowledge of an essentially invisible God and of the manifestation in time and through temporal realities of an essentially immutable God.[67] Only from his own side can the

---

[61] Argument against purification through *teletas* in *Trin.* 4.13–19 (pp. 178–87) and against the auto-purification of philosophers in 4.20–24 (pp. 187–93).
[62] Augustine, *Trin.* 4.24 (pp. 191–93).
[63] Ibid., 4.25 (p. 193–94).
[64] Ibid., 4.29 (pp. 199–201).
[65] Ibid., 4.28 (p. 198).
[66] Ibid., 4.29 (p. 199).
[67] Cf. Ibid., 2.14 (pp. 98–9), quoting Wis. 7.27 for immutability and 1 Tim. 1.17–8 and 6.15–6 for invisibility. See also Augustine, *Trin.* 2.9 (p. 92); 2.25 (p. 114); 3.21 (p. 150).

invisible and immutable God make himself known: since God is invisible, that is unknowable, no one can know him unless he reveals himself through Christ in the Holy Spirit; since God is immutable, the act through which he comes towards us is always a grace, is always free, is always the consequence of his name of *misericordia*.[68]

In the same way, the unity, equality and inseparability of Father, Son and Holy Spirit are the ground of the uncompromisingly divine character of revelation and reconciliation. The invisible Father does not cease to be invisible and unknowable (Augustine says 'not sent') in the act through which he makes himself known. This paradox explains why the revelatory role of the Son as well is not a function of his inferiority, nor yet of his difference from the Father, but precisely of his unity, inseparability and equality with him: he is revelation – or 'teaching' – as he is Son[69], that is, 'God from God'. What shields Augustine's Trinitarian doctrine from any theistic understanding of divine attributes – invisibility, immutability, simplicity, unity, equality, inseparability – is that these are postulated not on the basis of an abstract notion of divinity, but on the basis of the nature of revelation and reconciliation. Augustine does not start from a unitary notion of divine nature characterized by these attributes and then tries to see how it can be understood in a Trinitarian way. On the contrary, he starts from the properly speaking *divine* character of Christ's work of revelation and reconciliation through the Holy Spirit: God (the Father) can *only* be known and loved through God (the Son and the Holy Spirit) because he is invisible, unknowable and immutable; the Father can *really* be known and loved through the Son and the Holy Spirit because the Three are inseparably and equally one God.

V. Worship

So far we have sketched something of the objective side of the mystagogical strategy at work in the *De Trinitate*, that is the identity between revelation and reconciliation and between God's inner-Trinitarian identity and his action in the history of salvation, through the sending of the Son (God from God) in the incarnation and the sending of the Holy Spirit (God proceeding from the Father and the Son and linking the Father and the Son) at Pentecost. This mystagogy, however, also has a subjective side played by the doctrine of the image of God and encompassed under the heading of *sapientia*, that is, 'wisdom': 'Man's wisdom, true wisdom, is in accordance with God and is the true and principal worship of him . . . God himself is supreme wisdom; but the worship

---

[68] Cf. s. 6.5 (*CCL* 41, p. 64).

[69] *Trin.* 2.4 (pp. 84–5). The same idea is expressed in the fact that he teaches from the Father *natiuitas ostenditur*, that is, it shows that he is from the Father (2.3 [p. 84]).

of God is man's wisdom'.⁷⁰ Wisdom enshrines the only form of relation and knowledge that suits God, that is, worship. The sentence just quoted could then be rendered as follows: 'We know God as he should be known by worshipping him; we worship God by knowing him as he should be known'. What is, then, the link between the doctrine of the image of God and wisdom, that is proper knowledge of God, proper relation with God?

In the light of Augustine's doctrine of creation, as it is developed especially in the *De vera religione* (390–91), the *De genesi ad litteram* (401–14) and question 51 of the *De diversis quaestionibus* (388–96), it appears that 'image' implies much more than the simple relation of exemplarity (i.e. of 'analogy') between human beings and God.⁷¹ Indeniably, the exemplary dimension belongs to the image as to all other created beings. But the image is above all that through which we are in relation with our Creator. To be 'in the image' means to have an immediate link with God, that is, that there is a dynamic or, more exactly, a *Trinitarian* relation of origin and of end between us and our Creator.⁷² A great deal of secondary literature on the *De Trinitate* seems to miss the relational aspect of the image almost completely and to take for granted that its epistemological status consists mainly

---

⁷⁰ Augustine, *Trin.* 14.1 (p. 421).

⁷¹ Cf. J. E. Sullivan, *The Image of God. The Doctrine of St. Augustine and Its Influence* (Dubuque, IA: Priory Press, 1963), p. 16: 'Such expressions indicate that the relation of origin implies more than pure exemplarity. Ordinarily it would seem to include something of efficient causality, though this would not be verified in the case of that Image who is the Son of God.' Cf. also G. Ladner, 'St. Augustine's Reformation of Man to the Image of God', in *Augustinus Magister. Congrès International Augustinien Paris, 21–24 septembre 1954* (vol. 2; Paris: Etudes Augustiniennes, 1954), pp. 874–75: 'How little St. Augustine's concept of the divine image in man is exhausted by that of similitude, can be seen in his work *On the Trinity*.' Cf. Augustine, *Trin.* 11.8 (p. 344).

⁷² The proper meaning of *image* appears very clearly when it is applied to the Son, as compared to *likeness* and *equality*: 'In God . . . the conditions of time do not obtain, for God cannot be thought of as having begotten in time the Son through whom he has created the times. Hence it follows that not only is [the Son] his image, because he is from [God], and the likeness, because the image, but also the equality is so great that there is not even a temporal distinction standing in the way between them' (*div. qu.* 74 [CCL 44/A, p. 214]). If the Son is perfectly equal to the Father, what does the notion of 'image' add to that of 'equality'? Augustine explains that '[the Son is] his image, because he is from [God]' (*imago eius sit, quia de illo est*), thus drawing the attention on the main characteristic of the image as distinguished from equality and likeness. *The image is not intended primarily to stress exemplary relation* – although always implying it, since every image is a likeness too –, *but the relation of origin*, 'because he is from [God]' (*quia de illo est*). This is exactly the main feature of a definition of the image of God in human beings formulated in a passage from the unfinished book on *De Genesi ad litteram imperfectus liber*: 'And God said, "Let us make man in our image and likeness". Every image is like that of which it is an image, but not everything which is like something is also its image. Thus, because in a mirror or in a picture there are images, they are also like. But if the one does not have its origin from the other, it is not said to be the image of the other. For *it is an image only when it is derived from the other thing*' (*Gn. litt. imp.* 16.57 [CSEL 28/1, pp. 497–98]).

if not exclusively in its exemplary character: these commentators only see the image as that which in us is *like* God.[73] On the contrary, the image is first of all that which allows us to be *in relation* of knowledge and love with God or, better, that which allows us to *enjoy* (*frui*) God, to worship God.

As we have seen, two main triads emerge from the long argument spread out through books 9–14 of Augustine's *De Trinitate*: (1) mind, self-knowledge and self-love[74]; (2) self-memory, self-knowledge and self-love.[75] We have also noticed that Augustine seems at first to consider the latter triad a formal improvement over the former.[76] However, both triads play a role when Augustine leads his argument to its conclusion in books 14 and 15. It could be argued that there are two conclusions to the *De Trinitate*, virtually independent from each other: (1) the exemplary and anagogical lines culminate in book 15, as we have seen above, with the following sentence: 'So there [in God] we have a trinity, namely Wisdom and its knowledge of itself and its love of itself. We found a similar trinity in man, namely the mind, and the knowledge it knows itself, and the love it loves itself with'[77]; (2) the mystagogical approach to the image, which sees in it that through which we are in *relation* with God the Trinity, reaches its climax in book 14, and particularly in this passage: 'This triad of the mind is not the image of God because the mind remembers and understands and loves itself, but because it is also able to remember and understand and love him by whom it was made. And when it does this it becomes wise . . . Let it worship the uncreated God, by whom it was created with a capacity for him and able to participate in him.'[78]

However, if the devising of triadic patterns in the structure of human mind made sense within the exemplary logic culminating in book 15, what role does it fulfil with reference to the mystagogical strategy which comes to fruition in book 14? Three main answers can be given to this question.

First of all, from the mystagogical viewpoint, a triadic structure for the mind ('self-memory, self-knowledge and self-love') becomes a way of explaining how our rationality can function properly and fulfil its dynamism: (1) our mind must be present to itself, which corresponds to self-memory[79] and (2) we

---

[73] For example, E. Gilson, *Introduction à l'étude de saint Augustin* (Paris: Vrin 1943), pp. 286–98.
[74] Augustine, *Trin.* 9.5 (p. 298).
[75] Ibid., 10.19 (p. 332).
[76] Ibid., 10.17, 18 (pp. 329–31).
[77] Ibid., 15.10 (p. 474).
[78] Ibid., 14.15 (pp. 442–43), translation modified.
[79] Augustine, *Trin.* 14.7 (p. 429): 'The mind knows nothing so well as what is present to it, and nothing is more present to the mind than itself'; 14.8 (pp. 431–42): 'But when it [the mind] is not thinking about itself, it is indeed not in its own view, nor is its gaze being formed from itself, and yet it still knows itself by being somehow its own memory', and 14.8 (p. 432): the mind 'was already known to itself in the way that things are known which are contained in the memory even when they are not being thought about'.

must love ourselves properly in order to know ourselves properly, since love and knowledge are inseparable ('self-knowledge' and 'self-love').

Then, the necessity for our mind to have a triadic structure and to be spontaneously aware of this is a way of describing the actual sinful and dysfunctional state of our rationality and to explain why we are not only unable to know God, but also to know ourselves and everything else adequately. Books 10–12 in particular can be summarized as follows: (1) even if we never cease to be self-memory (that is self-knowledge), we are no more aware of this, because we do not know that we know ourselves[80]; (2) this is caused by the corruption of our love (covetousness as opposed to charity), seeing that love and knowledge are inseparable and mutually conditioning.[81]

Finally, talk of a triadic structure of our mind is instrumental to exploring how the image goes from 'capacity' of God to 'participation' in God,[82] that is *how we come to knowledge of God*, how we become wise, how we enter into the only proper creaturely and epistemological relation with God which consists in worship. For Augustine, already in general epistemological terms, that is with regards to objects we would normally consider within our reach,[83] no real knowledge is possible unless we love ourselves properly through the right hierarchy between using and enjoying (*uti* and *frui*) and unless we are aware of ourselves and of our actual condition of sinfulness.

On the basis of such an ethically (and theologically) loaded epistemology, going even further in counter-intuitional grounds, Augustine develops at

---

[80] Augustine, *Trin*. 14.8 (p. 430): 'What do we know, if we do not know what is in our own mind, seeing that whatever we know we can only know it with the mind?'; 14.8 (p. 431): 'how it [the mind] can not be in its own view when it is not thinking about itself, seeing that it can never be without itself, as though it were one thing and its view another, I cannot really fathom'; 14.9 (p. 434): 'we do not know that we know' and 'anyone who is unable to see these things even when he is reminded of them and has his attention drawn to them, is suffering from great blindness of heart and sunk very deep in the darkness of ignorance, and needs very special aid from God to be able to attain true wisdom'.

[81] Cf. the example of the child who cannot think himself because of covetousness in 14.7 (pp. 429–30); 14.18 (pp. 445–46): 'The human mind is so constructed that it never does not remember itself, never does not understand itself, never does not love itself . . . The man who knows how to love himself loves God; and the man who does not love God, even though he loves himself, which is innate in him by nature, can still be said quite reasonably to hate himself . . . By forsaking the one above itself with regard to whom alone it [the mind] could keep its strength and enjoy him as its light . . . it became weak and dark, with the result that it was miserably dragged down from itself to things that are not what it is and are lower than itself by loves that it cannot master and confusions it can see no way out of'.

[82] Augustine, *Trin*. 14.6, 11, 15 (pp. 428, 436, 443).

[83] For Augustine, no object can straightforwardly be said to be 'within the reach of our knowledge' independently from our relation with God, that is from the necessity to be enlightened by God and for our ability to know to be restored through the conversion of our love from covetousness to charity through Christ's salvific action.

length the strain imposed on the definition of knowledge when the 'object' becomes all-pervasive both ontologically and ethically, that is when the 'object' is he by whom we have been created; in whom we have life, movement and being[84]; who is truth as he is our light and our good[85]; who is the very basis of our ability to know and love; who is more intimate to ourselves than we ourselves are[86]; who is more known to ourselves than we ourselves are[87]; in whom alone we are destined to find happiness, wisdom, eternal life; who is the fulfilment of what we have been created for.

The triad of memory, knowledge and love and everything it entails had been devised precisely to prepare the reader to grasp the whole scope of the answer to the question of 'how do we know *such a God?*': (1) to know *this* God is first of all *to 'remember' him*, that is to become aware that he is at the very source of our being, that he is our light and our good, even when we turn away from him and we become blind to this truth which should be more evident to us than everything else; (2) to know *this* God is *to love him* and love ourselves in him, since knowledge and love are inseparable, since he is love and since love comes with its own evidence which is irreducible to any other thing known[88]; (3) to know *this* God, we need *to be rescued from the sinful condition* which prevents us not only from knowing him, but even from knowing ourselves and from the right knowledge and enjoyment of everything else. Thus, far from placing ourselves in a neutral position, knowledge of God, more than any other human activity, requires the full thankful and humble acknowledgement of our total dependence on God.

Even though we never cease to be self-love, self-knowledge and self-memory, separation from God reverses the dynamism of our created being: 'The man who knows how to love himself loves God; and the man who does not love God, even though he loves himself, which is innate in him by nature, can still be said quite reasonably to hate himself when he does what is against his own interest.'[89] This situation is caused by sin,[90] and therefore can only be re-established by God's salvific action.[91] The Christology, the soteriology and the doctrine of the Holy Spirit of the *De Trinitate* flow together in the last part of book 14, where the Trinitarian action of renewal and reformation of the image of God in us is developed through making explicit the latter's fundamental dynamic nature.

---

[84] Augustine, *Trin.* 14.16 (pp. 443–44).
[85] Ibid., 8.2–5 (pp. 269–74).
[86] *Conf.* 3.11 (*CCL* 27, p. 33).
[87] *Trin.* 8.12 (p. 286).
[88] Cf. the argument of *Trin.*, book 8.
[89] Augustine, *Trin.* 14.18 (pp. 445–46).
[90] Ibid., 14.21 (p. 449).
[91] Ibid., 14.18 (p. 446), translation modified.

Creatures of the Creator revealed in the incarnate Christ and in his Holy Spirit, we are constituted by a threefold fundamental dependence on him, and we are continuously called to fulfil our existence through adhesion to God the Father, through God the Son and God the Holy Spirit. This relation is exemplified by the way the image of God stretches towards its intended aim. This way is constituted by memory, knowledge and love, in their fundamental inseparability. Thus, Augustine states: 'We said about the nature of the human mind that if it is all contemplating truth it is the image of God . . . Now the more it reaches out toward what is eternal, the more it is formed thereby to the image of God.'[92] The same dynamism of the image of God is formulated in terms of love: 'For man's true honour is God's image and likeness in him, but it can only be preserved when facing him from whom its impression is received. And so the less love he has for what is his very own the more closely can he cling to God.'[93] The dynamic nature of the image is not only located in its growth, in its fulfilment or in its renewal, but already in its preservation (*custoditur*). The very existence of the image of God is constituted by a movement going from the creative act of God to the vision of God: *ad ipsum a quo imprimitur*.[94] This movement is constituted by love (*dilectio*) and, because of the consequences of sin, it requires the overcoming of covetousness.

Thus, both ontologically and ethically, we are in the image of God, that is, we are inscribed in a dynamic relation with the Lord who constantly keeps us in being and calls us both to fulfil our nature (ontological or creaturely level) and to overcome the consequences of our sinful state through becoming himself the object of our knowledge and love (ethical level). The same Lord who rescues us from the tendency towards nothingness resulting from our contingent created nature, also rescues us from our covetousness resulting from our sinful condition. In Augustinian terms, just as it is impossible to envisage epistemology apart from God, so it is impossible to define our identity without God or to consider the image *of God* as a property handed over to us which could be, even only in principle, managed in isolation from its source. For this reason, rather than image 'of God', it would be more appropriate to talk of image 'from (and obviously 'towards') God'.

We can therefore conclude that the *understanding* of the Nicene orthodox confession of the mystery of the Trinity is not the primary aim of the *De Trinitate*. For Augustine, knowing God the Trinity means rather being *introduced* into the fullness of relation with the Father, through the Son, in the Holy Spirit. The image of God the Trinity in us, that is our fundamental threefold

---

[92] Augustine, *Trin.* 12.10 (pp. 364–65). The same idea of *extensio* can be found in 9.1 (pp. 292–93).
[93] Augustine, *Trin.* 12.16 (p. 370).
[94] Ibid.

dependence on him, reaches its fulfilment when this dependence in being, knowledge and love becomes conscious and is converted into *worship*, that is, ac-knowledged, thankful dependence. At heart, this worship, that is, the acknowledgement of this dependence, consists in love, in *dilectio*. But love is inseparable from knowledge, and therefore worship consists in remembering or rather, in *being reminded of God* and in being given, in Christ through the Holy Spirit, the possibility of *knowing and loving* the Father.

For Further Reading

For a more developed version of the argument of this essay and a full bibliography see Gioia, Luigi, *The Theological Epistemology of Augustine's De Trinitate* (Oxford University Press: Oxford 2008).

The best critical evaluation of secondary literature on Augustine's *De Trinitate* is offered by Kany, Roland, *Augustins Trinitätsdenken. Bilanz, Kritik und Weiterführung der modernen Forschung zu 'De trinitate'* (Studien und Texte zu Antike und Christentum 22; Mohr Siebeck: Tübingen 2007).

A decisive renewal in the interpretation of the *De Trinitate* was inaugurated by some seminal essays by Williams, Rowan, 'Sapientia and the Trinity. Reflections on *De Trinitate*', in *Mélanges T. J. van Bavel, Collectanea Augustiniana* (ed. B. Brunner; Leuven: Leuven University Press, 1990), pp. 317–32.

— 'The Paradoxes of Self-Knowledge in the *De Trinitate*', in *Augustine: Presbyter factus sum, Collectanea Augustiniana* (ed. J. T. Lienhard; New York: P. Lang, 1993), pp. 121–34.

— 'De Trinitate', in *Augustine through the Ages: An Encyclopedia* (ed. A. D. Fitzgerald; Grand Rapids, MI: Eerdmans, 1999), pp. 845–51.

In the wake of Rowan Williams, the most insightful recent monography is Ayres, Lewis, *Augustine and the Trinity* (Cambridge University Press: Cambridge 2010).

2 Augustine on Human Being

Michael Hanby

'The Christian revelation of the unity of the human race', according to Benedict XVI, 'presupposes a *metaphysical interpretation of the "humanum" in which relationality is an essential element*.'[1] Consequently, the Pope calls for 'a deeper critical evaluation of the category of relation' in order to arrive at an understanding adequate to the mystery of the person, who is at once existentially unique – 'the incommunicably proper existence of a spiritual nature', as Richard of Saint Victor put it – *and* constitutively related to God and to all others in God.[2] Such an understanding is necessary not only to understand the truth of the *humanum*, but also to resist the forces of atomization and reduction, forces at once cultural and technological, that put the human future at risk by threatening to render humanity impotent in the face of its own political and technical machinery.

At first glance, Saint Augustine seems like an unlikely ally in this evaluation. His 'invention of the inner self' has been credited with paving the way for Cartesian subjectivity and modern individualism more generally, notions of the self for which 'ontological solitude' is always prior to relation.[3] Following in the footsteps of Olivier du Roy, generations of scholars have accused Augustine and his so-called psychological analogy of the Trinity of marginalizing Christology and undermining relationality both within the Trinity and here below by elevating the unity of the divine substance over the distinction of persons.[4] Those who oppose the 'nuptial' or 'familial' analogy for the Trinity advanced by John

---

[1] *Caritas in Veritate* 55 (emphasis original).
[2] Richard of Saint Victor, *Trin.* IV.6.
[3] See Phillip Cary, *Augustine's Invention of the Inner Self: The Legacy of a Christian Platonist* (Oxford: Oxford University Press, 2000); Stephen Menn, *Descartes and Augustine* (Cambridge: Cambridge University Press, 1998); Charles Taylor, *Sources of the Self: The Making of Modern Identity* (Harvard: Harvard University Press, 1989), pp. 127–42.
[4] Olivier De Roy, *L'Intelligence de la Foi en la Trinité selon Saint Augustin. Genèse de sa Théologie Trinitaire jusqu'en* (Paris: Études augustiniennes, 1966). For a thoroughgoing criticism of Du Roy's influential work, see Lewis Ayres, *Augustine and the Trinity* (Cambridge: Cambridge University Press, 2010), pp. 20–41. See also Luigi Gioia, *The Theological Epistemology of Augustine's* De Trinitate (Oxford: Oxford University Press, 2008), pp. 6–23.

Paul II in his *Theology of the Body*, which does articulate a relational anthropology, often do so on grounds first ploughed by Augustine.[5] In an important lecture advancing a relational and existentialist notion of the human person, even Joseph Ratzinger, who wrote his dissertation on Augustine and is typically numbered among the 'Augustinians' of Vatican II, followed du Roy in blaming Augustine's 'psychological doctrine of the Trinity' for a flawed 'substantialist' understanding of the person and for weakening a Trinitarian understanding of the God-world relation in the Western Church. As he began to advance his relational and existentialist notion of the human person in an important lecture in the 1970s. He would revise this judgement in a later version of the lecture.[6] More recent scholarship, initiated by Rowan Williams and spearheaded by Michel René Barnes and Lewis Ayres, appears to be concurring with this revision, especially when it comes to the Trinitarian side of the equation.[7]

In this essay, I wish both to extend the revision of received opinion about Augustine initiated by Cardinal Ratzinger and others and to take up the call by Benedict XVI to develop 'a metaphysical interpretation of the "humanum" in which relationality is an essential element'. This is more of a speculative than an exegetical enterprise. Nevertheless, by rooting these speculations in the texts of Augustine, notably *De Trinitate* and the *Confessions*, I wish to show that the grounds for understanding the human person on terms

---

[5] Perhaps the most polemical assessment is offered by Kerr, who opines of 'nuptial mysticism', 'It is not in our rationality but in sexual difference that we image God – in our genitalia, not in our heads, so to speak' (Fergus Kerr, *Twentieth-Century Catholic Theologians: From Neoscholasticism to Nuptial Mysticism* [Oxford: Blackwell, 2007], p. 94). For an account of this analogy compatible and even complementary with the Augustinian triad, see Angelo Cardinal Scola, *The Nuptial Mystery* (trans. by Michelle K. Borras; Grand Rapids: Eerdmans, 2005).

[6] See Joseph Ratzinger, 'Concerning the Notion of Person in Theology', *Communio* 17 (Fall 1990), pp. 439–54 (p. 454). Indeed Ratzinger's interpretation was always more nuanced than this. Though he faults Augustine for a 'decisive mistake' when he 'projected the divine persons into the interior life of the human person and affirmed that intra-physic processes correspond to these persons', he also credits Augustine for advancing a relational notion of person in treating of the divine persons in *De Trinitate*, for distinguishing between substance and relation, and for transposing the theological affirmation of personhood into anthropology (Ratzinger, 'Concerning the Notion of Person in Theology', pp. 443–47). Augustine develops his treatment of the substance-relation distinction in *Trin.* V.

[7] See Rowan Williams, '*Sapientia* and the Trinity: Reflections on the *De trinitate*', in *Collectanea Augustiniana: Mélanges T..J. Van Bavel* (ed. B. Bruning et al.; Leuven: Leuven University Press, 1990), pp. 317–32; Ayres, 'Remember That You Are Catholic (*serm.* 52.2): Augustine on the Unity of the Triune God', *JECS* 8 (2000), pp. 39–82; 'The Christological Context of *De Trinitate* XIII: Towards Relocating Books VIII–XV', *AugStud* 29 (1998), pp. 111–39; Barnes, 'Exegesis and Polemic in Augustine's *De Trinitate* I', *AugStud* 30 (1999), pp. 43–59; 'Re-Reading Augustine's Theology of the Trinity', in *The Trinity: An Interdisciplinary Symposium on the Trinity* (ed. Stephen T. Davis, Daniel Kendall and Gerald O'Collins; Oxford: Clarendon Press, 1999), pp. 329–55; Michael Hanby, *Augustine and Modernity* (London: Routledge, 2003).

analogous to the 'substantive relations' of the Trinitarian personae are both commendable in principle and lie deep within the tradition. Moreover, I wish to show that such an understanding does not conflict with the so-called psychological analogy or a substantialist interpretation of personhood but is rather an integral dimension of it (though carrying this point through to its conclusion would require us to amend the Aristotelian/Thomist understanding of substance, a task which is beyond the scope of this essay). This opens the door to a reintegration of the traditional and nuptial analogies for Trinity, though I cannot develop that here. Finally, I will offer a few reflections on how such an understanding militates against the endemic reductionism of our culture's most authoritative form of knowledge.

I. Paradoxical Anthropology and the *Memoria Dei*

Summing up both Augustine's doctrine of grace and the drama of his conversion in the *Confessions,* James Wetzel says, 'Those who come to the scene of their conversion expecting to encounter God for the first time arrive too late'.[8] The remark captures a paradox not only of the doctrine of grace, but also of what we would now call Augustine's fundamental anthropology. This paradox is signalled at the very outset of the *Confessions,* as Augustine asks, 'Lord, grant me to know and understand which is first, to call upon you or to praise you, and also which is first to know you or to call upon you? But how does one who does not know you call upon you?'[9]

This paradox, stated here as a question of the origin of our knowledge and desire for God, is reminiscent of the *Meno*. It stands at the beginning of Augustine's development of the 'psychological analogy' in books 8 and 9 of the *De Trinitate* and conditions all that unfolds therein. It is only by loving the good that is God, Augustine says, that the mind becomes good and able to discern truly the good of anything else. 'But who loves what he does not know?' Augustine asks. 'For it is possible something may be known and not loved: but I ask whether it is possible that what is not known can be loved; since, if it cannot, then no one loves God before he knows him.'[10] The paradoxical difficulty of loving what is utterly unknown is compounded by the fact, which Augustine will soon take pains to demonstrate, that love and knowledge mutually entail each other. Augustine responds immediately that God can be loved in faith, but he says more than that – and so deepens the paradox – first, by attempting to show how a just human being can be loved only because we

---

[8] Wetzel, *Augustine and the Limits of Virtue* (Cambridge: Cambridge University Press, 1990), pp. 190–91.
[9] Augustine, *conf.* I.1.
[10] Augustine, *Trin.* VIII.6.4.

somehow participate in the form of justice, and thus have within ourselves a knowledge of the justice that we lack, and secondly that we can begin to 'see God' in the very love by which we love the just human being.

> Let no one say, I do not know what I love. Let him love his brother, and he will love the same love. For he knows the love with which he loves, more than the brother whom he loves. So now he can know God more than he knows his brother: clearly known more, because more present; known more because more within him, known more because more certain. Embrace the love of God, and by love embrace God . . . Well, but you will say, I see love, and as far as I am able, I gaze upon it with my mind, and I believe the scripture saying, that 'God is love; and he that dwelling in love, dwelleth in God;' but when I see love, I do not see in it the Trinity. Nay, but thou dost see the Trinity if thou seest love.[11]

It is on the basis of statements such as these that Augustine is often credited (or blamed) with the 'invention of the inner self', to use Phillip Cary's phrase, which reaches its denouement in Descartes' *res cogitans*. I am more willing now than I was ten years ago to acknowledge the genuine intuition in this thesis. There is indeed something in Augustinian interiority that is unprecedented in ancient literature, something, I believe, which emerges as a function of his understanding of creation. I will try to develop this more below. But in contrast to Cartesian interiority and to those arguments which would pin Augustine with the ultimate responsibility for it, this interiority is indeed curious; for it is constituted in relation to which is other to it and which transcends it. This is evident in Augustine's argument, repeated in different forms in *De libero arbitrio*, *De Trinitate* and elsewhere, that it is the presence of eternal truth to the soul – or perhaps the soul's presence to eternal truth – that is the basis for the soul's true judgements, and it is all the more the case as Augustine identifies the Trinity with love and locates the *imago dei*, not simply as a participant in Platonic forms, but within the divine charity given in the Holy Spirit. Indeed I have argued elsewhere that Christ himself as *exemplum* and *sacramentum*, and thus as both exemplary image and giver (with the Father) of the Spirit, is the context for the unfolding of this analogy and the perfection of the image.[12] The Trinitarian and Christological

---

[11] Ibid., VIII.8.12.
[12] See Hanby, *Augustine and Modernity*, pp. 55–71. See also Ayres, 'The Christological Context of *De Trinitate* XIII', pp. 111–39; *Augustine and the Trinity*, pp. 142–70; Basil Studer, 'History and Faith in Augustine's *De Trinitate*', *AugStud* 28 (1997), pp. 7–50. Luigi Gioia has recently developed this theme further in *The Theological Epistemology of Augustine's De Trinitate*, pp. 68–124.

context is crucial not only because the Trinitarian analogy unfolds within the mediation of Christ's revelation of the Father, making visible the archetype whose image it is, but also because Christ as *sapientia* and *scientia* unites in himself the suprahistorical order of being and the order of history, the order of contemplation and the order of action, in a way that is crucial to the Augustinian understanding of the human person exemplified in the first person in the microcosm of the *Confessions* and in the macrocosm of *De civitate Dei*.[13] We will return to this point shortly. This is the context for what Rowan Williams calls the 'long digression' of *Trin.* 9–14, and it conditions all that unfolds therein.[14]

Let us first consider how the Trinitarian and Christological context of the 'psychological analogy' informs its original meaning in the *De Trinitate*. The first thing to note is that the sense in which this triad is analogous to the Trinity fits the proper sense of analogy later codified by the Fourth Lateran Council: that any likeness of the creature to God is infinitely surpassed by an ever-greater unlikeness.[15] Augustine makes this clear in numerous ways, stressing – in contrast to the human *mens*, both the simplicity and the irreducibility of the divine personae.[16] But perhaps the most important is the fact that he ultimately *denies* that the 'psychological analogy' *as such*, is constitutive of the *imago dei*: 'This

---

[13] It is true that Augustine differentiates these orders (and rightly so) and locates the *imago dei* (insofar as it can be identified with the *mens*), 'in that alone which belongs to the contemplation of eternal things' (Augustine, *Trin.* XII.4.4). Augustine is clear, however, that when 'we discuss the nature of the human mind, we discuss a single subject, and do not double it into those two which I have mentioned, except in respect of its functions'. And he is equally clear, both that *scientia* and *actio* are necessary and that Christ is the unity of the order of being and history, wisdom and knowledge. 'Therefore Christ is our knowledge, and the same Christ is also our wisdom. He himself implants in us faith concerning temporal things, he himself shows forth the truth concerning eternal things. Through Him we reach on to Himself: we stretch through knowledge to wisdom; yet we do not withdraw from one and the same Christ, "in whom are hidden all the treasures of wisdom and knowledge"' (*Trin.* XIII.19.24). We may thus conclude that Augustine's distinction between the ontological and temporal order and his association of the *imago dei* with the former only condemns the latter insofar as it ceases to be ordered to and illuminated by the contemplation of eternity. And yet, on the basis of this same Christological union of time and eternity, he is equally harsh on 'those distinguished philosophers of the heathen, who have been able to understand the discern the invisible things of God by whose things which are made . . .' because they 'philosophized without a mediator', and thus, 'placed as they were in the lowest things . . . could not but seek some media through which they might attain to those lofty things which they had understood; and so they fell upon deceitful spirits, through whom it came to pass, that "they changed the glory of the incorruptible God into an image made like to corruptible man, and to birds, and four-footed beasts, and creeping things"' (*Trin.* XIII.19.24).

[14] Williams, 'Sapientia and the Trinity', p. 323.

[15] See for example, Augustine, *Trin.* XV.21.40–23.44.

[16] Consequently, Ayres denies these mental analogies provide 'any warrant for the view that Augustine's Trinitarian theology treats the Trinity as most like a unitary self-thinking mind' (Ayres, *Augustine and the Trinity*, pp. 275–76).

trinity, then, of the mind is not therefore the image of God, because the mind remembers itself, and understands and loves itself; but because it can also remember, understand, and love Him by whom it was made.'[17]

Augustine identifies the *imago dei* in us with our participation in the life of the Trinity through love and contemplation, for which the triad of *memoria*, *intellectus* and *voluntas* is the necessary equipment. The 'greater unlikeness' between this triad and its divine archetype is evident both in Augustine's decision to make the created image a matter of participation and in his decision to place *memoria* at the font of his psychological triad, in the position roughly analogous to the Father within the Trinity. It seems to me that this is important in at least two respects. First, *memoria* is dependent in its operation on the activities of *intellectus* and *voluntas*; for we can only return in memory to what we already know, and our doing so is an expression of desire. And secondly, *memoria* is distinguished by the fact that it is not its own origin. Not only is it dependent upon *intellectus* and *voluntas*, but its movement is by definition a response to something first *given*, which is to say that it is at once self-moved *and* moved by another without opposition or conflict. *Memoria*, in other words, is implicated from the outset in just that paradoxical participation exemplified by the case of loving the just man and the dramatic movement of the *Confessions*. Its structure mirrors the structure of grace which Augustine advances against the Pelagians, where he is adamant against parcelling out discrete divine and human contributions to the good human act.[18] Moreover, the decision to feature *memoria* so prominently in the triad means, paradoxically, that the human person's likeness to God's *aseity* consists precisely in its unlikeness: it is a function of his prior relation *to* and dependence *upon* God who depends upon nothing. Second, Augustinian *memoria* is at once ontological and historical.[19] Not only does it mark the site

---

[17] Augustine, *Trin*. XIV.12.15.

[18] On the relation between the *De Trinitate* and the doctrine of grace with which it is roughly contemporaneous, see Hanby, *Augustine and Modernity*, pp. 72–105.

[19] Joseph Ratzinger, attempting to overcome modern misunderstandings of *conscientia* proposes to replace the scholastic notion of *synderesis* with *anamnesis*. In so doing, conscience acquires this status of an ontological memory in terms deeply reminiscent of Augustine. 'This means that the first so-called ontological level of the phenomenon conscience consists in the fact that something like an original memory of the good and true (they are identical) has been implanted in us, that there is an inner ontological tendency within man, who is created in the likeness of God, toward the divine. From its origin, man's being resonates with some things and clashes with others. This anamnesis of the origin, which results from the god-like constitution of our being, is not a conceptually articulated knowing, a store of retrievable contents. It is, so to speak, an inner sense, a capacity to recall, so that the one who it addresses, if he is not turned in on himself, hears its echo from within. He sees: That's it! That is what my nature points to and seeks . . . The possibility for and right to mission rest on this anamnesis of the Creator, which is identical to the ground of our existence'; Joseph Ratzinger, 'Conscience and Truth', in *On Conscience* (San Francisco: Ignatius Press, 2007), pp. 11–41 (p. 32).

of the creature's participation in an order of being that transcends him and in a relation to God that he can never escape; for this very reason it confers upon the subject an abiding unity and identity that transcends his 'point identity' at any given instance. Augustine marvels at this in the *Confessions* going so far as to say that 'this thing [memory] is the mind, and this I am myself'.[20] With it comes a certain 'all at once' transcendence *of* time, where we experience time itself as a kind of *distentio animi* that is the very mode of our distention and ultimate dissolution *in* time and the very precondition of our maintaining a substantial identity *through* time.[21] Consequently, though it is not at all clear that Augustine intends it this way, *memoria* functions not simply as a remote analogue to the Father in the mental triad of *memoria, intellectus* and *voluntas*, but as a kind of image of the Christological unification of *sapientia* and *scientia*, eternity and history.

What I wish to suggest, in other words, is that the triad of *memoria, intellectus* and *voluntas* in Augustine's thought gives us something much more complex and interesting than an anatomy of the ego, a simple account of the mind's self-presence, or a simple parallelism for the inter-Trinitarian processions. Rather for Augustine, this triad is the mysterious site of our participation, through history, in the eternity of God. It is both the site of our own irreducible personal identity, at once historical and suprahistorical, and it marks an anterior relation to him that precedes the fulfilment of his image in us. One could consider the unity and the distinction of this triad and its participation in God from the distinct vantage afforded by any one of the other members of the triad. One could consider, for instance, how *voluntas* in its particular character as a response to the self-communication of beauty is essential to the movement of *memoria* and *intellectus* and integral both to our participation, in Christ, in the unity of the Father and Son through the *donum* of the Holy Spirit and to the perfection of the *imago dei* in the self-gift of charity. I have focused on *memoria*, however, both because it makes visible the constitutive relation of creature to Creator and because the peculiar way it unites the orders of being, and history opens up new windows into the mystery of the human person.

In further developing these points, let us first note a metaphysical principle with far-reaching ramifications that seems to be implicit in what we have said so far, but which Augustine himself does not state or could probably not have articulated for himself. On an Aristotelian and Plotinian view of being or act, receptivity is regarded as an imperfection

---

[20] Augustine, *conf.* X.17.
[21] See *conf.* XI.26, 29, for this double sense of *distentio*. Cf. Hanby, *Augustine and Modernity*, p. 146, n. 88.

which compromises perfect unity and actuality.[22] By contrast – and this ranks among Christianity's greatest and most revolutionary contributions to the history of metaphysics – Augustine's identification of the Trinitarian essence with infinite love tacitly makes receptivity itself a perfection; for love is by definition the perfect coincidence of gift and reciprocity.[23] There can be no true self-donation, which is not at the same time a reception, that does not delight in the irreducible otherness of the other for its own sake. This irreducibility is implicit in Augustine's pro-Nicene assertion that the Son is all things that the Father is except that he is not the Father.[24] And I take this to be a legitimate interpretation of his claim that 'in that Trinity is the supreme source of all things, and the most perfect beauty, and the most blessed delight. Those three, therefore, both seem to be mutually determined to each other, and are in themselves infinite.'[25] It is perhaps easiest for us to imagine receptivity as a perfection in the eternal generation of the Son, who receives everything eternally from the Father and who is Son precisely in seeing the Father.[26] Nevertheless it must also be true of the Father, though he is *archē* insofar as he is only Father with the Son and insofar as he eternally receives anew from the Son the gift of love in the unity of the Spirit.[27] This irreducible otherness does not contradict the perfect unity and simplicity of the Trinity; rather it is the very form of a unity understood as infinite love. Nor does the inclusion of receptivity among the divine perfections – and the possibility that the Father might receive a 'new' gift in

---

[22] For more on this point in Aristotelian terms, see Joseph Owens, *The Doctrine of Being in the Aristotelian Metaphysics* (Toronto: Pontifical Institute of Mediaeval Studies, 3rd edn, 1978), pp. 435–73. Hankey captures the difference from Plotinus. '[F]or Plotinus, being and will do not belong to the One in an act of self-reflexion. Such an act would divide the One, placing it above and below itself, as if it received itself from itself as from another. What is true of the soul which exists from another, and needs above all to know this alterity, cannot be true of the One. There is no reflexive self-othering in the One'; Wayne Hankey, 'Stephen Menn's Cartesian Augustine: Metaphysical and Ahistorically Modern', *Animus* 3 (1998), pp. 183–210 (pp. 202–03), available at www2.swgc.mun.ca/animus/Articles/Volume%203/hankey3.pdf; accessed 8 June 2012.

[23] I do not mean to suggest that this is idiosyncratic to Augustine but rather that the doctrine of the Trinity as such has metaphysically revolutionary implications.

[24] Augustine, *Trin.* VII.1–2. On Augustine's simultaneous commitment to the unity of essence, the inseparability of operations and the irreducibility of the personae, see Ayres, *Augustine and the Trinity*, pp. 42–95.

[25] Augustine, *Trin.* VI.10.12. As I have argued elsewhere, Augustine's identification of the Son as forma or beauty of the Father and the Holy Spirit as unifying *delectatio* are critical to the convertibility of unity and difference in love. See Hanby, *Augustine and Modernity*, pp. 27–71; 'These Three Abide: Augustine and the Eschatological Non-Obsolescence of Faith', *Pro Ecclesia* 16/3 (Summer 2005), pp. 340–60.

[26] Augustine, *Trin.* II.1.3.

[27] On the Holy Spirit as *donum*, see Augustine, *Trin.* V.14.15–16.17; XV.17.27–19.33.

the Word made Flesh – compromise the impassible plenitude of the divine being.[28] To the contrary, this inclusion of difference and receptivity within the simplicity and unity of the divine plenitude actually liberates unity from its juxtaposition with multiplicity and liberates the divine being from what Thomists would call a 'real relation' to the world.[29]

This principle bears analogously on the order of creation. Substantiality in the etymological (and roughly Aristotelian) sense of standing in oneself is proportionally and not inversely related to receptivity. The greater a thing's capacity for receiving that which is not itself, the greater is its capacity for self-transcendence and the more distinct it is. I have argued elsewhere that this is essentially the principle at stake in the doctrine of grace advanced against the Pelagians, a principle that works itself out in the drama of the *Confessions* as Augustine, who was outside himself while God was within, seeks to find himself in God. The incarnation shows us that divine and human agencies are not opposed. Jesus is the New Adam precisely because he is also God. His divinity assumes his humanity; it does not absorb or negate it. Analogously, the more deeply I participate in God, the more truly I am myself, the greater my autonomy and freedom.[30] The principle, that a depth of receptivity is proportionate to the degree of 'individuation', also applies in the Augustinian hierarchy of being, living and thinking and the Aristotelian hierarchy of the

---

[28] Recognizing the irreducible otherness of the divine personae as the form of Trinitarian unity allows us to give a Balthasarian twist to Augustine's praise of the divine beauty as ever ancient and ever new. This coincidence of infinite unity and infinite difference is why the Son, in assuming flesh, can receive and offer a new gift to the Father from inside his original generation *from* the Father. And it is why from the side of God we can regard creation ex nihilo as generating a real addition to being from inside of being, a difference that is even somehow 'more' than God, without for all that compromising God's transcendent otherness or the superlative fullness and simplicity of divine being. Creation can be 'more than God' in the infinite beauty of the Son and the infinite delight of the Holy Spirit, because God is always 'more than himself', comprising all possibility in his infinite actuality, without ever being less than himself. Thus, as von Balthasar says, 'the transition from infinite freedom to the creation of finite freedoms (with all this implies) need not constitute the "ultimate paradox" of thought . . . For the infinite distance between the world and God is grounded in the other, prototypical distance between God and God' (Hans Urs von Balthasar, *Theo-Drama: Theological Dramatic Theory*, vol. 2, *The Dramatis Personae: Man in God* [trans. Graham Harrison; San Francisco: Ignatius Press, 1992], pp. 261, 266).

[29] See chapters 2 and 7 of my book, forthcoming from Blackwell, tentatively titled *No God, No Science: Theology, Cosmology, Biology* (Oxford: Wiley-Blackwell, 2013).

[30] Of course to see this one must see that freedom is ultimately an expression of my desire for the good, which cannot be fully realized so long as my desire is internally divided against itself, and this, in turn, depends upon the intrinsic goodness of being. This ultimately is why grace restores rather than negates freedom. For a fuller explanation, see Hanby, *Augustine and Modernity*, pp. 72–105; D. C. Schindler, 'Freedom beyond Our Choosing: Augustine on the Will and Its Objects', *Communio* 29 (Fall 2002), pp. 618–53.

nutritive, sensitive and rational soul.[31] A human being is at once more receptive of, integrated in, and distinct from its world than, say, a stone. It is precisely because it has a profound capacity to receive the world, because the soul is, in a way, all things, that it is able to stand over against the world, transcending its point identity, as a distinct individual, and a dramatic centre of action. This puts an interesting twist on Augustine's meditations on the nature of sin, such as we find in the famous pear-tree incident in *conf.* 2, which Augustine interprets as an unintelligible and perverse *imitatio* of divine power. If receptivity is a perfection of the divine essence understood as Trinitarian love, then part of the 'essence' of sin – improperly speaking, of course – is a *failure* of reception, a perverse *imitatio dei* which rejects the filiality of creaturehood. If this principle holds, then it follows that Augustine's 'invention of the inner self' is not opposed either to the self's constitutive relation to God or to the 'outward turn' of charity. To the contrary, the creature's relation to God discovered in the 'inward turn' is the source both of that inwardness and the charity that is the fulfilment of the *imago dei*.[32] Because it is only in charity that being, which is gift in both origin and structure, is fully true to itself.[33]

Bearing this principle in mind, let us now look more closely at the implications of Augustine's *imago trinitatis* for the meaning of the human person. Previously we observed that his decision to place *memoria* in a position within his triad roughly analogous to the Father was doubly curious. First, *memoria* is decidedly unlike the Father in that it is not its own origin. And second, inasmuch as *memoria* is both ontological and historical, it is an image both of the Father and of Christ, who unites both eternity and time, *sapientia* and *scientia*, contemplation and action in himself. The implications of this, I believe, are born out from the 'inside', as it were, in the *Confessions*.

Those who blame Augustine for the invention of the solitary ego sometimes refer to the *Confessions* as the first autobiography. This overlooks the fundamentally typological character of the work, however – a fact we can better

---

[31] Jonas makes a similar point (Hans Jonas, *The Phenomenon of Life: Toward a Philosophical Biology* [Evanston: Northwestern University Press, 2001], p. 99).

[32] With this principle, it seems to me, the foundation is laid for reconciling the 'psychological' and nuptial analogies for the Trinity. Since the question of the imago concerns not just a resemblance to God but its fulfilment in beatitude, carrying through on this reconciliation would require one to penetrate further the mutual entailment of love and knowledge and to develop further the 'ecstatic' or donative dimension of contemplative sight itself, and one would need to unfold the sacramental character of body as such and its status as a sign of the gift – and thus 'communional' structure of being. All of these things are present inchoately in Augustine, in spite of Augustine's explicit denial of the 'nuptial analogy' in *Trin*. XII.

[33] As Ladner puts it, 'Only the saint truly *is*' (Gerhart Ladner, *The Idea of Reform* [New York: Harper Torchbooks, 1967], p. 279).

appreciate if we read *De civitate Dei* as its 'macrocosmic' counterpart – and how Augustine 'makes himself an instance of the universal human story'.[34] And the peculiar genre of the work says something important about the nature of the Augustinian subject. Nevertheless, I do not wish to lose the insight inherent in calling this an autobiographical work. For Augustine's attempt to see his own life as an intelligible unity from the vantage afforded by grace, a vantage which makes his life an instantiation of universal types, does not dissolve its unrepeatable historical character and the actual relations which characterize every instance of our historical existence. Rather it brings to his recalled life history a meaning and a weight which it prospectively lacked. The Augustine recalled in the *Confessions* is at once universal *and* particular; in other words, his existence bears out the same structure implied by the *memoria dei*. His is a unique and irreducibly historical existence precisely because it is also suprahistorical, and it is from this suprahistorical vantage that Augustine can say that 'in your sight, I have become a riddle to myself'.[35]

There is of course a psychological dimension to the interiority of rational creatures capable of receiving and contemplating God and the world. But Augustinian interiority is not the self-enclosed psychological interiority of a solitary ego – participation in the universal intelligibility of being precludes that. And I would argue that Augustinian interiority is not in the first instance 'psychological', though this becomes a very complicated argument when one allows for the *intrinsic* intelligibility of being. Augustinian interiority is, for lack of a better word, existential. Creatures have an interior, first, because they are the irreducible subjects of their own being, dramatic centres of action poised between the gift at their origin and the call for their conversion in Christ.[36] The interiority of *mens* is simply the highest expression of interiority of being distributed throughout the Plotinian hierarchy of being, living and knowing.[37] And they are mysterious subjects of their own being because the

---

[34] 'The episodes in his life which he earlier chooses to narrate are illustrative of the themes he discusses at length, themes which can appear digressive and tedious if we imagine the principal interest is in giving an autobiographical account. Of course there is an apologetic element . . . But there is also a didactic thrust, and the overall perspective is on human existence and God's providence. Augustine points away from himself to God, but to do that he has to demonstrate how God has led him to appreciate the fact that true knowledge is ignorance. By doing this, Augustine makes himself an instance of the universal human story, and the work is fundamentally typological' (Frances Young, 'The Confessions of St. Augustine: What Is the Genre of This Work?' *AugStud*, 30/1 [1979], pp. 8–16). For further discussion of this point, see Hanby, *Augustine and Modernity*, pp. 144–60.

[35] Augustine, *conf*. X.34.

[36] For creation itself as a kind of *reformatio* or *conversio*, see Ladner, *The Idea of Reform*, pp. 167–85, 212–38.

[37] On Augustine's use of this triad, see Ayres, *Augustine and the Trinity*, pp. 293–96.

God who is being is interiorly present to them, indeed closer to them than they are to themselves, continually giving them to themselves. In other words, I wish to suggest that, as a consequence of the role of *memoria* in the constitution of the subject and its simultaneously historical and suprahistorical being, the Augustinian person is, in effect, 'the incommunicably proper existence of a spiritual nature', occupying an ontological vantage within the cosmos that can never be repeated. And because the infinite God, as the source of the creature's being, is closer to the creature than it is to itself, the person and indeed all creatures are, in a certain sense, *bottomless*. 'What then am I, O my God? What is my nature? A life varied and manifold and mightily surpassing measurement.'[38]

II. The Future of Memory

Now, I concede that this is something of a free interpretation of Augustine. A great deal more work would have to be done, on both exegetical and philosophical grounds, to justify this interpretation as fully Augustinian and to justify certain Augustinian assumptions – for example, the intelligibility of being – as philosophically acceptable. And I am willing to concede as well the difficulty if not the impossibility of simply rehabilitating Augustine for a contemporary understanding of the person. Nevertheless, I think Augustine offers us a window into the mystery of the human person that is important both as a sympathetic amendment to the prevailing theological anthropology that has come down to us through scholasticism *and* for a theological engagement with the view of the person perpetuated by a culture whose thought forms are governed by the reductive assumptions of modern science. I can only make brief mention of each of these things in closing; each obviously requires a great deal more work.

Let us briefly consider this, first, with respect to the inter-theological question. Within certain Thomist appropriations of Aristotle, it is commonplace to subordinate relation to substance and to treat it as an accident – even a proper accident – of that substance (the one ontological exception, of course, being the Trinity, in which substance itself is relative and relations are themselves substantial).[39] The upshot of this tends to be that communion is in no way constitutive of substances in their very substantiality but is relegated to a 'second-order' phenomenon belonging to the realm of operations – what a

---

[38] Augustine, *conf.* X.17.
[39] Joseph Ratzinger, in the aforementioned lecture, maintains that scholasticism treats the substantive relations of the Trinitarian personae as a kind of ontological exception (Ratzinger, 'Concerning the Notion of Person in Theology', p. 449).

substance 'does' according to its nature or in its freedom.⁴⁰ One can understand the hesitancy here to make relation integral to the definition of substances; indeed I would wish to concur in this and to preserve a form of the distinction between a substance and its operations, though I would also insist that it is possible to allay these concerns on Thomistic grounds.⁴¹ Nevertheless, to make relation to God constitutive of substances in an ontological schema exhausted by the substance-accident dichotomy would seem to compromise both the gratuity of their creation and the infinite difference between God and the world by making relation to God a part of the definition of their essence and converting creatures themselves into subsistent relations.

Though we haven't space here to enter in detail into the enormous anthropological, social and ecclesial implications of this understanding, one consequence is that the world's having been created has little bearing on its ontological structure – as evidenced by those Thomists for whom Thomas is thought to bring no substantial alteration to Aristotelian metaphysics – which means in turn that theological engagement with anthropological and social questions is ultimately confined to a merely moral level.⁴² Augustinian

---

⁴⁰ As Walker characterizes this position, 'But we human beings are not God. Apparently, then, we human beings must first begin to exist in ourselves – and then, only much later, if at all, go out of ourselves in a fully conscious act of loving (and being loved). It would seem, in other words, that, whatever might be true about God, in our case personal singularity cannot be constituted even partly, let alone wholly, within communion. Communion cannot be the *context* in which personal singularity arises and makes sense, but can be only the result of the action of already constituted personal singularities. Communion cannot embrace the whole arc of our personal existence, from conception on, but can only follow upon our conscious acts of love. Or, at least, so it has seemed to many' (Adrian Walker, 'Personal Singularity and the *Communio Personarum*: A Creative Development of Thomas Aquinas' Doctrine of *Esse Commune*', *Communio* 31 [Fall 2004], pp. 457–79 [p. 459]).

⁴¹ The crucial point for developing this understanding on Thomistic grounds, which Walker does in his essay and which I take up in chapter 7 of my forthcoming book, is to understand the paradoxical character of *esse* as common to all things and proper to each, and its non-subsistence character, such that it is both 'prior' to substances in making them be and posterior to substances as a kind of proper accident.

⁴² Again, Walker puts the point very well. 'Like many apparently abstruse metaphysical issues, the question of whether or not the singularity of human persons is constituted within communion has huge implications for how we understand ourselves and how we live our lives, not only as individuals, but also as cultures and communities. If, in fact, communion can only be the result of our conscious acts of love, and cannot be seen as somehow constituting consciousness itself, then such acts can no longer be strictly necessary for the integrity of our being. They become, at best, supererogatory "extras." But if conscious acts of love are just extrinsic add-ons, they are not even acts of love, for there is no love without the grateful acknowledgment that relation to the beloved is not a mere option, subject to human velleity, but is the foundation of one's very existence. In a word, if we cannot maintain that personal singularity is somehow constituted communionally even for us, then we are bound to say that our finite being, as such, is inescapably "ontologically selfish," and that redemption into the trinitarian *agape* is a redemption *from* the human condition, and not *of* it' (Walker, 'Personal Singularity and the *Communio Personarum*', pp. 459–60).

memoria implicates suprahistorical relation to God and the historical relation to everything else in the very constitution of beings – an implication, I would argue, which is profoundly consonant with the Thomist *actus essendi* properly understood – while preserving the infinite difference between God and the world. Recovering the aprioricity of this relation to God indicated by Augustinian *memoria* would help to recover the patristic sense that our being made for communion is not simply a matter of our supernatural end, but belongs to the original structure of being as such. Henri de Lubac made a virtual catalogue of this understanding.[43] It seems to me that this is simply another way of stating our earlier point that charity flows as a logical consequence from the structure of the Augustinian *mens*, properly understood.

As to the second point, we have seen that relation to God is the source and ground of the incommunicable and inexhaustible interiority of being. The mechanistic ontology which continues to govern modern science is premised precisely upon the reduction of being from act to brute facticity and the evacuation of immanence and interiority. This is largely a function of the new concept of matter, typified by Descartes' *res extensa*, which is positive and actual in its own right prior to and outside of its actualization by form, but it is important to understand that externality and measurability are the 'essential' characteristics of *all* modern conceptions of matter, despite their variations. Identifying nature primarily with matter of this sort, as we have done since the seventeenth century (German idealism notwithstanding), empties beings of their interiority, thereby making their relation to God extrinsic. God ceases to be more interior to me than I am to myself for the simple reason that I no longer *have* an interior that is not a concatenation of external surfaces. This transforms the nature of a being's unity from the indivisible self-transcending unity of a proper *per se unum* to the artificial unity of an aggregate. It reduces truth from being to utility and makes our knowledge of things identical to our capacity to predict and control them, and it reduces ontological identity to the coordinated interactions of a thing's component parts and the history of accidental causes which produced it.[44] All of this allows science to ascend to the position of first philosophy in our culture.

The contrast between the objectified, exterior view of the scientific gaze and the inside view of the human person as an incommunicable subject of being and a dramatic centre of action is captured beautifully by Thornton Wilder in his brief novel *The Bridge of San Luis Rey*.[45] The story is set in eighteenth-century Peru, when the finest bridge in all the country inexplicably

---

[43] See Henri De Lubac, *Catholicism: Christ and the Common Destiny of Man* (trans. Lancelot C. Sheppard and Sr. Elizabeth Englund; San Francisco: Ignatius, 1988), pp. 25–47.
[44] See chapter 3 of my forthcoming book.
[45] Thornton Wilder, *The Bridge of San Luis Rey* (New York: Perennial Classics, 1998).

collapses, plunging five travellers to their death in the gorge below. Brother Juniper, an eager Franciscan with a penchant for science who witnesses the tragedy, sets out to vindicate God and a just order of providence by providing a 'scientific account' of the accident that showed how the wicked were 'visited by destruction and the good called early to Heaven'.[46] His quest sends him on a rigorous analysis of the empirical facts of each victim's life, an analysis which is appallingly blind to the 'inside view' of their various sufferings available to the omniscient narrator, a view often only partially visible to the victims themselves.

The example shows us some of what is lost with the demise of Augustinian interiority and what is at stake in its recovery. When the human person and creatures more generally are emptied of the being they have by participation, their interiority becomes an epiphenomenon of the solitary ego if not altogether invisible. To turn a blind eye to this interiority is to turn a blind eye to being itself, and this in turn is to renounce a priori the claim that truth and beauty make upon our souls (and of course this is precisely what the reduction of truth to functional utility *is*). The consequences are internal as well as external. One cannot seek with great longing after the truth of one's being, as Augustine does in the *Confessions*, where it has been determined in advance that there is no such thing. As *Gaudium et Spes* teaches, when the mystery of God is eclipsed and God is forgotten, the human person becomes unintelligible.[47] This unintelligibility differs not just in degree, but in kind, from the enigma that Augustine became to himself. For it is not merely the answer to Augustine's question 'who or what am I?' that ceases to make sense, but the question itself. Man has always lost his way, Chesterton said. But modern man has lost address, and he doesn't seem all that interested in finding it.[48] And yet if we remain blind or indifferent to that love that goes behind and before us, we cannot find that love at the core of our being and cannot truly make a gift of ourselves in turn. The internal Trinity of *memoria*, *intellectus* and *voluntas* and the external charity stand and fall together.

For Further Reading

Ayres, Lewis, *Augustine and the Trinity* (Cambridge: Cambridge University Press, 2010).
Hanby, Michael, *Augustine and Modernity* (London: Routledge, 2003).
Ratzinger, Joseph, 'Concerning the Notion of Person in Theology', *Communio* 17 (Fall 1990), pp. 439–54.

---

[46] Wilder, *The Bridge of San Luis Rey*, p. 101.
[47] *Gaudium et Spes* 36.
[48] G. K. Chesterton, *What's Wrong with the World?* (San Francisco, CA: Ignatius Press, 1994), p. 53.

Schindler, D. C., 'Freedom beyond Our Choosing: Augustine on the Will and Its Objects', *Communio* 29 (Fall 2002), pp. 618–53.

Walker, Adrian, 'Personal Singularity and the *Communio Personarum*: A Creative Development of Thomas Aquinas' Doctrine of *Esse Commune*', *Communio* 31 (Fall 2004), pp. 457–79.

Wetzel, James, *Augustine and the Limits of Virtue* (Cambridge: Cambridge University Press, 1990).

Williams, Rowan, '*Sapientia* and the Trinity: Reflections on the *De trinitate*'. In *Collectanea Augustiniana: Mélanges T..J. Van Bavel* (ed. B. Bruning and M. Lamberigts; Leuven: Leuven University Press, 1990), pp. 317–32.

3 Augustine on Christ

Ronnie Rombs

There is a paradox to be faced at the outset of any study of Augustine's Christology. On the one hand Christ is ubiquitous in Augustine's writings and thought. Even before his return to the faith of his mother – 'Christ' seems to have held a fundamental and irremovable place in his thought. Recounting the influence of Cicero's *Hortensius*, Augustine would later write:

> In so great a blaze only this checked me, that Christ's name was not in it. For this name, O Lord, according to your mercy, this name of my Savior, your Son, my tender heart had holily drunken in with my mother's milk and kept deep down within itself. Whatever lacked this name, no matter how learned and polished and veracious it was, could not wholly capture me.[1]

The word *Christus* occurs almost 19,000 times in Augustine's corpus; the name *Iesus*, though somewhat less frequent is, nevertheless, to be found some 4,500 times.[2]

And yet paradoxically, Augustine seems less interested in a technical metaphysical speculation about the *Person* of Christ – that is, what most would consider 'Christology' proper. Where Augustine does turn his attention to the specific question of Christ's person, his language is certainly orthodox by the standards of Ephesus and the later Chalcedonian formula, if not somewhat unremarkable.

This disinterest is, no doubt, due in part to the historical circumstances of Augustine's theological career. Most of Augustine's theological writings were occasioned by controversy. Augustine's writings on nature and grace, for example, were occasioned by the Pelagian controversy, and his writings on the nature of the Church were driven by his engagement with the Donatists. But with respect to the great Christological controversies, Augustine's Christian life was situated during a period of relative calm. The first great phase of

---
[1] Augustine, *conf.* 3.4.8, and 7.5.7. Cf. 3.4.8; 7.9.13; *c. Acad.* 3.20.43.
[2] These figures are taken from an electronic search through the Library of Latin Texts (formerly Cetedoc). Cf. Basil Studer, *The Grace of Christ and the Grace of God in Augustine of Hippo: Christocentrism or Theocentrism?* (trans. M. J. O'Connell; Collegeville: The Liturgical Press, 1997), p. 14: Studer's count differs only slightly from mine.

Christological controversy, that is, that surrounding Apollinarianism, was already settled by the time of Augustine's conversion; the later fifth-century controversy between Nestorius and Cyril would begin only shortly before Augustine's death.

The lack of a technical Christology led to the judgement among scholars that Augustine was not an important contributor to the historical development of Christology. Not so long ago it would have been true to say – as the few studies on Augustine's Christology typically begin by pointing out – that Augustine's Christology was largely ignored by modern Augustinian and patristic scholars.[3] That trend, however, is changing; there are beginning to appear more and more studies on Augustine's Christology, though the number of studies in English continues to be quite small relative to the amount of Augustinian scholarship that is produced.[4]

One rightly wonders, then, if Augustine's 'Christology' doesn't follow the traditional lines of patristic doctrinal controversy and concern with the technical formulation of the ontology of Christ, what *was* Augustine's Christology? How did Augustine understand the Christ who was ubiquitous in his thought and writing? Anyone familiar with his writings knows that there are a handful of scriptural passages that Augustine never tired of quoting. Like a buoy or channel marker, Augustine turns time and again to Rom. 5.5 in the context of the Pelagian controversy: 'The love of God has been poured out into our hearts through the Holy Spirit that has been given to us.' In exactly the same way when Augustine thinks of Christ Jesus, 1 Tim. 2.5 is never far from his mind: 'There is one mediator between God and man, the man Christ Jesus.'[5] This verse, or part of a verse, provided what would be the centre of Augustine's thoughts about Christ, the root concept from which his Christology emerged.

A study of Augustine's Christology, then, takes a unique direction relative to other patristic (doctrinal) studies for several reasons. First, the concept 'Christ the Mediator' subtly indicates the close connection for Augustine between the person and work of Christ: soteriology is not separate from Christology

---

[3] See the major, notable exceptions: Tarsicius van Bavel, *Reserches sur la Christologie de saint Augustin* (Fribourg: Editions universitaires, 1954); Goulven Madec, *La patrie et la voie: Le Christ dans la vie et la pensée de saint Augustin* (Paris: Desclée, 1989); and Otto Scheel, *Die Anschauung Augustins über Christi Person und Werk* (Tübingen: Mohr, 1901).

[4] See, for example, Gerald Bonner, 'Christ, God and Man in the Thought of St. Augustine', *Angelicum* 61 (1984), pp. 268–94; Brian Daley, 'A Humble Mediator: The Distinctive Elements in Saint Augustine's Christology', *Word and Spirit* 9 (1987), pp. 100–17; Idem., '"The Giant's Twin Substances" Ambrose and the Christology of Augustine's "Contra Sermonem Arianorum"', *CollAug* (Leuven: Peeters, 1993), pp. 477–95; and Studer, *Grace of Christ*.

[5] *Vulgate: Unus et mediator Dei et hominum homo Christus Iesus.* See, for example, Augustine, *civ. Dei* 9.15; *ep.* 187.3; *Trin.* 1.7.14; *s.* 26D.44.

for Augustine.[6] All of the major dimensions of Augustine's Christology – each conceived in terms of 1 Tim. 2.5 – involve both the person and the work of Christ: as the Son of God who becomes Son of man, the Mediator restores the unity between God and humanity that was lost by sin. As priest and sacrifice, the Mediator redeems humanity, making atonement for our sin. As Word made flesh, the Mediator becomes our Way (*via*) through whom we find our end. Christ is the mediating source of grace, through participation in whom we are given the love of God and participation in the Spirit. As the divine Word spoken by God in the flesh of Christ, the Mediator reveals the unseen Father.

Second, this last aspect of Christ's mediation – Christ as the Mediator or Revealer of God – intersects an important trend of contemporary Christology. Certainly the integration of soteriology and Christology finds a palatable reception in contemporary Christology. But more significantly, Augustine's interest in Christ as the Word of God, uttered in the flesh, promises a fruitful engagement with at least one prominent line of Christology in the contemporary theology of such diverse thinkers as Karl Rahner, Avery Dulles and Roger Haight. Accordingly, Christ – precisely in and through his humanity, which, as we will see, the Word assumes for the sake of making God visible – gives visible (or perhaps better, *audible*) expression to that which is other, to God. In this regard, Augustine comes very close to what Rahner means by 'real symbol'. And insofar as the Christologies of Dulles and Haight build upon or engage the idea of Christ as 'symbol' of God, Augustine makes a natural and valuable interlocutor. First, however, a consideration of the doctrinal Christology that Augustine does articulate is in order.

I. An Excursus on the Doctrinal Teaching of Augustine

Augustine's preference, when he preaches or writes about the nature of the *person* of the incarnate Christ, is for bold, rhetorically antithetical formulations. Augustine can describe Christ, for example, as 'a man who is God'.[7] 'He by whom we were to be created was born of God, and He by whom we were to be re-created was born of a woman.'[8] 'The same one, God and man, man and God.'[9] In this way, Augustine's rhetoric is very similar to the way Ignatius of

---

[6] Studer, *Grace of Christ*, p. 43: 'The answer to the question of who Christ is always includes, more or less explicitly, his role in salvation. The one Christ, God and human being, is always seen also as Savior.' Cf. William Babcock, *The Christ of the Exchange: A Study in the Christology of Augustine's 'Enarrationes in Psalmos'* (Ann Arbor, MI: University Microfilms, 1972), p. 15.

[7] Augustine, *Io. tr. ev.* 4.14.

[8] Ibid., 2.16.

[9] For example, *s*. 186.1. See Aloys Grillmeier, *Christ in the Christian Tradition* (London: Mowbray, 1996), p. 408; Daley, 'The Giant's Twin Substances', 475; Idem., 'A Humble Mediator', p. 101.

Antioch described Christ in the early second century but also anticipates – as did Ignatius himself – the delicate formulation given at Chalcedon.

Nevertheless, there are a few occasions on which Augustine does turn his attention to a more precise theological consideration of the Person of Christ. *Ep.* 137 to the 'pagan' Volusianus; *ep.* 219 to Leporius, a layman who seems to have suffered from a lack of proper Christological catechesis and Leporius's retractation, his *Libellus Emendationis*, which Augustine heavily influenced, are examples. There is also *Quaestio* 80 in his *De diversis quaestionibus 83*, which takes up Apollinarianism, some 13 Christmas sermons,[10] and chapters 34–41 of his *Enchiridion*.

On these occasions, Augustine's preference is to describe the union of God and humanity in Christ according to what we might call 'dynamic formulations',[11] or '*homo assumptus* terminology'.[12] That is to say, Augustine speaks of the Word 'assuming',[13] 'associating', 'taking up'[14] or 'joining to himself'[15] a human nature.[16] When Augustine writes of human nature in this context, he seems always to mean a particular, concrete human nature or substance. Augustine will write of the 'reality', for example, 'of that human nature which he assumed but did not destroy'.[17] Augustine's expression in his *Enchiridion*, written in 421/422, epitomizes his Christological expression:

> Christ Jesus, the Son of God is both God and man: God before all ages, man in this age of ours; God because he was the Word of God . . ., man because in the unity of his person there was joined to the Word a body with a rational soul (*homo autem quia in unitatem personae accessit Verbo, anima rationalis et caro*). Accordingly, insofar as he is God, himself and the Father are one; insofar as he is man, the Father is greater than he. When he was the only Son of God, not by grace, but by nature, so that he might be also full of grace, he

---

[10] Augustine, *s.* 184–96.
[11] For example *ep.* 187.5: '. . . the human nature which God the Word *assumed* (suscepit) . . .' Studer notes the 'dynamic terms' of Augustine's formulation (*The Grace of Christ*, p. 40).
[12] So Boniface Ramsey. See *Responses to Miscellaneous Questions* (trans. Boniface Ramsey; Hyde Park: New City Press, 2008), p. 147, n. 431.
[13] For example, Augustine, *ep.* 137.2.6; 3.9: '*dicitur Verbum Dei . . . sic* assumpsisse *corups ex virgine*'; *cons. Ev.* 4.10.20: susceptione *Verbum caro factum est*.
[14] *Civ. Dei* 21.15: 'For he, abiding unchangeable, took (*suscepit*) our nature upon himself'. Cf. *div. qu.* 73.2: '. . . taking up true humanity (*verum hominem suscipiendo*) . . . when he was clothed in the humanity that he somehow united and conformed to himself and joined to his own immortality and eternity (*cum indutus est homine, quem sibi uniens quodam modo atque conformans, immortalitati aeternitatique sociaret*)'.
[15] *Ep.* 137.3.12.
[16] See *ep.* 137.9–11 for a rich series of dynamic expressions of the unity of divinity and humanity in Christ.
[17] *Ep.* 137.9.

became also the Son of man. He has himself both natures, and from these two natures is one Christ (*idemque ipse utrumque ex utroque unus Christus*).[18]

Two natures, humanity and divinity, are united in the singularity of Christ's person.[19] But such unity does not involve a co-mingling or mixture of the natures. Christ is one, Augustine explains, 'not by the confusion of nature but by the unity of person'.[20] Augustine thinks of the example of the unity of soul and body in the singular human being as an analogy for understanding how divinity and humanity – two radically different kinds of being – can possibly be united in Christ and their integrity maintained.[21] And it is the soul of Christ – as Origen had previously maintained – that is for Augustine the locus of union between the human nature and divinity in Christ.[22]

The clarity of Augustine's recognition of personal unity in Christ while preserving the integrity of both natures serves as the theological basis for a prominent doctrine of the *communicatio idiomatum* for Augustine and anticipates Chalcedon.[23] The *communicatio idiomatum*, 'exchange of properties', is the principle that what Christ accomplishes according to his divine nature can be attributed to the human because of the singularity of person in Christ – and vice versa. Hence, Augustine can have the boldness to use such expressions as 'God . . . was born', 'the crucified God', 'the God who died'.[24]

It should also be recognized that Augustine's *homo assumptus* language leaves no doubt that, for Augustine – even though Christ is the 'occasion', we might say, of the unity of two natures, or a singular person who possesses two natures – it is the Word who remains the centre of personal identity in Christ.[25] Augustine explains:

> The one who was the Son of God became the son of man by the taking on of the lower element, not by the changing of the principal one; by accepting

---

[18] *Ench.* 35. For 'two substances' see *Io. tr. ev.* 99.1.
[19] So the Augustinian formula *una persona in utraque natura* (cf. *s.* 294.9.9). *Cons. Ev.* 1.53: 'This same Wisdom of God, assum[es] into the unity of His person the (nature of) man'; *Io. tr. ev.* 108.5: 'The Word was made flesh, for the word and the man became one person'. See Basil Studer, *Trinity and Incarnation* (Collegeville, MN: Liturgical Press, 1993), p. 183.
[20] Augustine, *s.* 186.1.1.
[21] See especially *ep.* 137.11 and *Io. tr. ev.* 19.15.
[22] *Ep.* 137.2.8; 3.11; 3.12. See Eugene TeSelle's discussion of the point: *Augustine the Theologian* (New York: Herder and Herder, 1970), pp. 148–50.
[23] See, for example, Augustine, *Trin.* 1.7.14. For Augustine's influence on Chalcedon (especially through Leo the Great), see van Bavel, *Reserches sur la Christologie de saint Augustin*; J. T. Newton, 'The Importance of Augustine's Use of the Neoplatonic Doctrine of Hypostatic Union for the Development of Christology', *AugStud* 2 (1971), pp. 1–16.
[24] Augustine, *ep.* 169.2.8; *s.* 194.9; 213.4.
[25] See on this point Brian Daley, 'Christology', in *Augustine through the Ages* (ed. Allan D. Fitzgerald; Grand Rapids, MI: Eerdmans, 1999), pp. 167–68 (p. 167b).

what he was not, not by losing what he was . . . What we have to confess, therefore, is that the one who was the Son of God, in order to be born of the virgin Mary, took on the form of a servant, and became the son of man; while still remaining what he was and taking on what he was not; beginning to be that which made him less than the Father, and always remaining that by which he and the Father are one.[26]

The 'he' of Christ is the eternal Word; Augustine's Christology is a Christology from above.[27] The Son of God manifests himself – manifests divinity – through 'the lower element' or 'in what he was not' – in other words, through his humanity, which is other than or distinct from the Son of God. According to Karl Rahner, it belongs to the very nature of being itself to express itself through what is other, through what is a symbol.

II. Christ the Mediator

'But now he has so appeared as the Mediator between God and men, that, uniting the two natures in one person, he both exalted what was ordinary by what was extraordinary, and tempered what was extraordinary by what was ordinary in himself.'[28]

That 1 Tim. 2.5 uses the term *Mediator* to designate Christ represented for Augustine a felicitous coincidence with Neoplatonism. If God and humanity are to be reconciled, or, perhaps more generally conceived, if humanity is to be united with God, there must be – for the Neoplatonist in Augustine – some *thing* that stands in the middle (*in medio*), something that functions as the vehicle through which these two dissimilar things may be joined together.[29] 'All contraries', Augustine explains, 'are reduced to unity by some middle factor (*per aliquid medium*).'[30]

The inability, however, for humanity to be united with God and its need for a mediator is compounded by sin: because of our sin, humanity has become

---

[26] Augustine, *s.* 186.2.
[27] See Grillmeier, *Christ in the Christian Tradition*, pp. 408–09. The point may seem self-evident and hence tedious, but its relevance will be clearer subsequently when Augustine's Christology is considered in the modern context.
[28] Augustine, *ep.* 137.3.9.
[29] See *s.* 47.211; 121.5. Studer, *Grace of Christ*, p. 44: 'Looking at it from a more philosophical viewpoint, [Augustine] understands Christ the mediator to be "between" (*medius*) God and human-kind, and thus as one who belongs both to the creator and to creatures and who possesses both immortality and mortality and therefore can lead human beings out of the present state of transitoriness to permanent blessedness.' Cf. Daley, 'A Humble Mediator', p. 107.
[30] Augustine, *cons. Ev.* 1.53; cf. *s.* 47.12.21; *ep.* 137.9.

subject to death.[31] The mediation of Christ, then, involves the interposition of the Son 'in the middle', who brings immortality to mortality in the unity of his person. Apart from this mediating work of Christ, enmity stands between God and humanity, and sin itself, Augustine declares, can be thought of as a kind of *medium*, standing between us and God.[32] Not only is there, then, a metaphysical need for a Mediator, but also that Mediator, by the merciful grace of God, reconciles humanity to God.[33] 'We are not reconciled', Augustine explains, 'unless that which is in the midst is taken away, and something else is put in its place. For there is a separating medium (*medium separans*), and, on the other hand, there is a reconciling Mediator (*mediator reconcilians*). The separating medium is sin, the reconciling Mediator is the Lord Jesus Christ.'[34] He is 'the good Mediator who reconciles enemies',[35] humbly placing himself between God and humanity.[36]

The primary effects of sin according to Augustine are death, the liability to divine judgement, concupiscence and the darkening of the intellect. Christ's saving work as Mediator extends to all of these. Because of our sin, humankind justly drew upon itself the anger of God. And yet, unlike human anger, the fruit of divine anger was mercy:

> The anger of God is not like that of man, but the calm fixing of punishment. In this anger of his, God restrains not, as it is written, his tender mercies; but, besides other consolations to the miserable, which he does not cease to bestow on mankind, in the fullness of time, when he knew that such had to be done, he sent his only-begotten Son, by whom he created all things, that he might become man while remaining God, and so be the Mediator between God and men, the man Jesus Christ.[37]

---

[31] See *civ. Dei.* 9.15: 'Things below, which are mortal and impure, cannot approach the immortal purity which is above; and so, to remedy this condition of separation from God, a mediator is indeed needed ... We need a Mediator who is united with us in our lowest estate by bodily mortality, yet who, by virtue of the immortal righteousness of his spirit, always remains on high: not in terms of temporal location, but because of the excellence of his resemblance to God. Such a one can afford us aid which is truly divine in cleansing and redeeming us.' Cf. *Io. tr. ev.* 12.11.

[32] Ibid., 41.5.

[33] Pagans no less recognized the need for a mediator of this sort. Augustine occasionally speaks about the devil and demons as taking advantage of the pagan recognition of the need for purification and reconciliation as an opportunity to present themselves as fraudulent mediators. See, for example, *s.* 198.28. Cf. *Trin.* 13.24: Philosophers were able to 'see' divine things to a certain extent, but they did so 'without the mediator, that is without the man Christ ... They could not but look for some middle level of things, by which to reach the topmost things they understood; and in this way they fell into the hands of fraudulent demons.'

[34] *Io. tr. ev.* 41.5.

[35] *Civ. Dei* 9.15; cf. *doc. Chr.* 4.20.

[36] See, for example, *Io. tr. ev.* 53.10. See Brian Daley, 'A Humble Mediator', p. 107.

[37] Augustine, *Io. tr. ev.* 124.5; cf. *ench.* 33.

Here Augustine's Christology involves the idea of priestly mediation. 'Christ our Mediator' means Christ our priest who 'makes intercession for us'.[38] Christ represents us and makes an atoning sacrifice on our behalf.[39] As the just Mediator, Christ's sacrifice atones for sin, redeeming humanity, and saving those who put their faith in him from divine judgement.[40] Christ's mediation in this regard is perfected by the fact that as priest he offers no less sacrifice than himself, a blameless victim who takes on the sin of all, hence, making atonement for all.[41] Augustine makes the point:

> The true Mediator, the man Jesus Christ, became the Mediator between God and man by taking the form of a servant. In the form of God, he receives sacrifice together with the Father, with whom he is one God. In the form of a servant, however, he chose to be a sacrifice himself, rather than to receive it ... Thus he is both the priest who offers and the sacrifice which is offered.[42]

A subtlety in Augustine's understanding of Christ's role as Mediator comes to light in this context of atonement. Here Christ's role as Mediator lies precisely in the person who is constituted by divinity and humanity. This line of thought takes its point of departure from the equal presence of both natures in Christ and provides the conceptual and theological basis for the possibility that Christ (Mediator as the God-man) offers a blameless and just sacrifice (as divine) for us (as man).[43] This same model stands behind the metaphysical dimension of Christ's mediation: precisely as the God-man, he is *in medio* able to unite humanity with God.

This mode of conceiving Christ's mediation stands in contrast to a second mode which is conceptually distinct. 1 Tim. 2.5 (*Vulgate*) seems to emphasize the point that it is precisely as man that Christ functions as Mediator: 'There

---

[38] *Cons. Ev.* 1.3.6.
[39] *Ench.* 33: 'Wherefore the apostle says: "We were by nature the children of wrath, even as others". Now, as men were lying under this wrath by reason of their original sin, and as this original sin was the more heavy and deadly in proportion to the number and magnitude of the actual sins which were added to it, there was need for a Mediator, that is, for a reconciler, who, by the offering of one sacrifice, of which all the sacrifices of the law and the prophets were types, should take away this wrath.' Cf. *civ. Dei* 10.6.
[40] *Trin.* 4.2.4. See Patout Burns, 'How Christ Saves', in *Tradition and the Rule of Faith in the Early Church* (ed. Ronnie Rombs and Alexander Hwang; Washington, DC: The Catholic University of America Press, 2010), pp. 193–210.
[41] See Augustine, *Trin.* 4.14.19; *Io. tr. ev.* 41.5; *ench.* 41; and *qu.* 3.57.2–4 where Augustine's presentation of Christ's mediation revolves around the idea of his sacrifice on our behalf.
[42] *Civ. Dei* 10.20; cf. 10.22; 17.20. Christ is both priest and sacrifice; he is thus the Mediator through whom 'we are cleansed of sin' and 'reconciled to God'.
[43] See Daley, 'The Giant's Twin Substances', pp. 486–88.

is one mediator between God and man, the man Christ Jesus (*homo Christus Iesus*).' It is according to this mode of interpretation that Augustine explains: 'He is not . . . the Mediator because he is the Word; for, as the Word, supremely immortal and supremely blessed, he is far removed from miserable mortals. Rather, he is the Mediator *because he is man.*'[44] This second model stands behind the idea that Christ reveals God – to be considered below.

In Christ's Passion, then, not only is atonement made for sin, but also the humility and love of God are revealed.[45] Christ's mediation involves for Augustine the idea that Christ, as the revelation of divine humility and love, invites all men to participate in Christ: Christ as Mediator is *exemplum* and also *via*. As *exemplum*, Christ provides the model which we are called to imitate.[46] As *via*, or our Way, Christ offers himself as a source of grace through participation in whom concupiscence is overcome and the Christian begins to love God with the love of Christ through the outpouring of the Spirit.[47]

By the assumption of a human nature, the Word sanctifies the flesh; that is, the Word becomes a mediator of grace, pre-eminently for the humanity of Christ but also for every other person who participates in Christ.[48] Through his humanity (our *via*) we are brought to God (our *patria* or homeland): *per Christum hominem ad Christum Deum*.[49] Augustine, displaying the dexterity of his skill as rhetor and preacher, puts it mellifluously: *ad illum imus, per illum imus, non perimus* ('we are going to him, we are going by him, we do not perish').[50]

III. Christ the Mediator as Revealer of God

Although God is omnipresent,[51] because of sin, the human intellect was darkened and lost the ability to perceive God. 'By his very nativity he made an

---

[44] Augustine, *civ. Dei* 9.15; cf. *Io. tr. ev.* 82.4.
[45] *Trin.* 13.10.13; *ep.* 137.5.20. See Studer, *Trinity and Incarnation*, p. 169.
[46] Augustine, *Io. tr. ev.* 52.1–3; *Trin.* 13.17.22.
[47] See *Trin.* 4.2.4.
[48] Augustine will repeatedly make the point that Christ's humanity is itself sanctified through the grace made present in its assumption by the Word. See, for example, *s.* 67.7.
[49] *Io. tr. ev.* 13.4. Cf. *civ. Dei* 9.15: 'In redeeming us from our mortality and misery, he does not lead us to the immortal and blessed angels so that, by participating in them, we may ourselves also become immortal and blessed. Rather, he leads us to that Trinity by participating in whom the angels themselves are blessed. Therefore, when he chose to take the form of a servant, lower than the angels, so that he might be our Mediator, he remained above the angels in the form of God, being himself both the way of life on earth and life itself in heaven.'
[50] *S.* 189.4; cf. *s.* 123.3.3: '*Deus Christus patria est quo imus, homo Christus via est qua imus, ad illum imus, per illum imus* (Christ as God is our homeland whither we are going; Christ as man is our way by which we are going. To him we are going, through him we are going)'; and *civ. Dei* 11.2.
[51] See *Io. tr. ev.* 35.4, for example.

eye-salve to cleanse the eyes of our heart, and to enable us to see his majesty by means of his humility', in other words, to see his divinity by means of his humanity.[52] But, it is not merely because of sin that we are unable to 'see' God. Augustine, drawing upon a Johannine line of thought – whereby it is the Word made flesh, who comes forth from the bosom of the Father, and who alone reveals and makes known the unseen God – also attributes our lack of knowledge or vision of God to the natural limits of human being.[53] Christ knows the Father in himself; we know God by him.[54] Christ, then, Augustine (interpreting Jn 10.1–10) explains, is both 'shepherd' and 'door'.[55] 'In the form of God in which he is equal to the Father', Augustine explains, 'the Son, too, is invisible; but that he might be seen by men, he took the form of a servant, and made in the likeness of men, he was made visible'.[56] The flesh of Christ makes God visible to us.[57] Augustine uses the point for rhetorical play in his Christmas sermons. On the day (the winter solstice) that pagans celebrated

---

[52] Ibid., 2.16.12.
[53] See, for example, *cons. Ev.* 4.10.20, where Augustine subtly integrates both of these marks of human existence for the fact that we now 'walk by faith and not by sight'. Similarly, *s.* 6.1: Augustine, commenting on the theophany present through the burning bush (Exod. 3.1–14), remarks, 'After all, God's very Wisdom, through whom all things were made, would only appear to human eyes by taking on mortal flesh'.
[54] Augustine, *civ. Dei* 11.2: 'God does not speak to such a man through some corporeal creature which resonates his bodily ears by means of vibrations of the air in the space between the source of the sound and its hearer . . . Rather, he speaks by the truth itself, if anyone is able to hear him with the mind rather than with the body: he speaks to that in man which is better than every other part of him which makes him a man, and than which there is nothing better save God alone . . . But the mind itself, even though reason and intelligence dwell in it by nature, is by its dark and inveterate faults made unable not only to embrace and enjoy but even to bear his immutable light until it has been renewed from day to day, and healed, and made capable of such great felicity; and so it had first to be imbued with faith, and so purified. And in order that the mind might walk more confidently towards the truth, the Truth itself, God, God's son, assuming humanity without putting aside his Godhood, established and founded this faith, that man might find a way to man's God through God made man. For this is "the Mediator between God and man: the man Christ Jesus." For it is as man that he is the Mediator and the Way (Jn. 14.6). If there is a way between one who strives and that towards which he strives, there is hope of his reaching his goal; but if there is no way, or if he is ignorant of it, how does it help him to know what the goal is? The only way that is wholly defended against all error is when one and the same person is at once God and man: God our goal, man our way.'
[55] *Io. tr. ev.* 47.3.
[56] Ibid., 53.12; cf. 3.6.
[57] *Div. qu.* 73.2: 'He who took [true humanity] up "was made in the likeness of men" (Phil. 2.7), not for himself but for those to whom he appeared, and "he was found in *habitus* as a man" (Phil. 2.7) – that is, by having (*habendo*) humanity he was found as a man. For he could not be found by those who had an unclean heart and who were unable to see the Word with the Father unless he took up what they were able to see, and thus they could be brought interiorly to that light.'

Sol Invictus, that is, the *visible* sun, Christians celebrate the 'one who became visible for us, by whom in his *invisibility* [Mary, his virgin mother] herself was created.'[58]

The visibility of the divinity of the Son, however, is a mediated visibility. God is made visible to man in and through the very humanity of Christ. This is why, Augustine explains, those who persecuted Christ were able to do so: 'for he who was manifest as man, was hid as God; he who was manifest suffered all these things, and himself also, who was hid, arranged them all.'[59] In other words, in the one person, Christ Jesus, both divinity and humanity were present, but divinity was present through the 'manifest' humanity. The one who had 'arranged them all (*disponebat haec omnia*)' is divine, the eternal Word who is one with the Father. In another Christmas sermon, Augustine speaks of Christ in a classically Augustinian antithesis as the one 'who was himself made among all things; who is the revealer of the Father, creator of his mother'.[60]

Here, it should be noted, Augustine's conception of the precise locus of Christ's role as Mediator has shifted from the model considered earlier. According to this line of thought, it is precisely as man that Christ functions as Mediator. Through Christ's humanity, God is revealed and grace mediated to humanity.[61] Augustine makes the point, *per Christum Hominem ad Christum Deum* ('through Christ as man to Christ as God').[62] Christ is both our Way (our *via*) and our End (our *patria*).[63]

Augustine expresses this dimension of Christ's mediatorial role, not simply in terms of revealing the Father, but, given the obvious title of Christ in the prologue of John's Gospel, as the Word of God spoken in the flesh.[64] Again, the idea involves a mediated revelation through the very humanity of Jesus.

---

[58] Augustine, *s.* 186.1; cf. 190.1.
[59] *Io. tr. ev.* 119.4. See also 3.4; 3.18.
[60] *S.* 187.1.
[61] See Studer, *Grace of Christ*, 44–5. Studer sees a lack of consonance in Augustine's thinking about mediator: where Augustine stresses Christ's humanity as mediator, there is a disjunction with the antitheses (i.e. the mode that takes Christ as the God-man as its point of departure).
[62] Augustine, *Io. tr. ev.* 13.4: 'Through Christ as human being to Christ as God; through the Word made flesh to the Word that was in the beginning, God with God; from that which human beings at to that which the angels eat daily.' Cf. *s.* 261.7; *civ. Dei* 11.2; and *ep.* 137.8.
[63] *S.* 92.3. Similarly *s.* 123.3.3: 'That's the way; proceed along humility, in order to come to eternity. Christ as God is the home country (*patria*) we are going to; Christ as [human being] is the way (*via*) we are going by. It's to him we are going, by him we are going; why are we afraid of going wrong?' See especially Madec, *La Patrie et la voie*.
[64] Augustine, *s.* 185.1: 'It is called the Lord's birthday when the Wisdom of God presented itself to us as an infant, and the Word of God without words uttered the flesh as its voice.' Cf. *s.* 69.7.7; 120.3.

Here Augustine builds upon the Stoic distinction between the word or idea that is to be found within the mind of the speaker (*logos endiathetos*) and the uttered word (*logos prophorikos*). Augustine uses the analogy of human thought and speech: just as the word, first conceived in the human mind, while it goes forth in the uttered word and thus reveals or communicates the mind of the speaker, so too Christ, the Word of God, goes forth and nevertheless never abandons his divine place.[65] 'God's speaking is the Son Himself . . . the Son is the Word of God, and the Son spoke to us not His own word, but the word of the Father.'[66]

> In what way did He come but this, 'The Word was made flesh, and dwelt among us'? Just as when we speak, in order that what we have in our minds may enter through the ear into the mind of the hearer, the word which we have in our hearts becomes an outward sound and is called speech; and yet our thought does not lose itself in the sound, but remains complete in itself, and takes the form of speech without being modified in its own nature by the change: so the Divine Word, though suffering no change of nature, yet became flesh, that He might dwell among us.[67]

The humility of God is reflected in a myriad of ways in the theology of Augustine. Here it becomes manifest in the antithesis between the divine and eternal Word through whom all things are created and the infant (*infans*, literally meaning 'one who cannot speak' in the Latin) which the Word becomes for the sake of our salvation.[68] Marvellously, the Word of God is spoken to man through the very flesh of the infant, the one who could not initially speak. Ultimately, 'the Son spoke but the Father taught', Augustine explains. 'If I, since I am a man, teach him who listens to my word, the Father, too, teaches that man who listens to his Word. Seek what Christ is and you will find his Word. "In the beginning was the Word".'[69]

IV. Augustine and Modern Theology

As indicated above, two complementary, though distinct models of Christ's mediation, stand behind Augustine's Christology.[70] The former takes the unity of both natures in Christ as its point of departure; the latter takes the *humanity*

---

[65] S. 187.3–4. Cf. *Io. tr. ev.* 7.14.
[66] S. 14.7.
[67] *Doc. Chr.* 1.13.
[68] S. 190.3. Here, as often in these Christmas homilies, Augustine makes the antithetical comparison between the eternal Word the *infans* and the speechless infant he becomes.
[69] *Io. tr. ev.* 26.8.
[70] For a very lucid consideration of these two modes of thought and their development in Augustine, see Daley, 'The Giant's Twin Substances', pp. 477–95.

of Christ to be the precise locus of Christ's mediatorial role. It is with this second model that we find an important intersection between Augustine's thought and modern theology.

Drawing upon Jn 1.14, this line of Augustine's thought begins with Christ, the divine Word made flesh. Augustine can speak, as we have seen, of Christ's flesh as the utterance of God in history. Christ's humanity, which reveals the God who is otherwise invisible, mediates divinity to us and for us. It is, in other words, through the mediation of Christ as man that we come to know, to participate in and to love Christ as God. It is in precisely this sense that Augustine makes the claim: *per Christum hominem ad Christum Deum*.[71] Augustine does not use the terminology, but one immediately thinks of the concept of 'symbol' in the theology and Christology of Karl Rahner.[72] Avery Dulles and Roger Haight develop Christologies that are heavily influenced by Rahner and are grounded in the notion of 'symbol': Christ precisely through his humanity reveals, mediates – that is to say, makes present – God. Jesus, Pope Benedict XVI very recently reminds us, is the one who shows us the 'face of God'.[73]

V. Christ Jesus, Symbol of God

In his seminal essay, 'The Theology of Symbol', Karl Rahner argues that 'all beings . . . necessarily "express" themselves in order to attain their own nature'.[74] To readers unfamiliar with Rahner, such a statement is likely perplexing and obscure. What Rahner means is this: human beings, for example, are composites of body and soul. But, we are not merely the combination of two things, the way machines are collections of many parts. Rather, we are a genuine *unity in plurality*; each human being, body and soul, is a single person. How, then, are the plurality and the singularity of the person related? Drawing upon the traditional Aristotelian schema, Rahner thinks of the human soul as the act or form of the body. In other words, Rahner can write that the body is the 'expression' of the soul. In fact, the soul, because it is immaterial, must express itself in and through the body in order that it be 'here' at all. In order, then, for a person to attain or actualize his or her nature as a terrestrial creature, the soul must express itself through what is fundamentally other than itself: the body. In this way, the body functions as a symbol: the body mediates, that is to say, makes present, what is other than itself.

---

[71] Augustine, *Io. tr. ev.* 13.4.
[72] Karl Rahner, 'The Theology of the Symbol', in *Theological Investigations* IV (London: Darton, Longman, and Todd, 1974), pp. 221–52.
[73] See especially the introduction to his *Jesus of Nazareth* (San Francisco: Ignatius Press, 2008), pp. 5–8, where the pope describes Jesus in the context of Moses' prophetic role as 'mediator'.
[74] Rahner, 'The Theology of the Symbol', p. 224.

Two further points concerning Rahner's theology of symbol are important to note. First, although the symbol mediates what is other than itself, the symbol constitutes a part of the thing symbolized. In the case of the body, although the body is not the soul, it is a part of the person. Symbols in this sense (Rahner is under no illusion that there aren't other types of symbols, like words or signs, that don't participate in the same way with what they symbolize) are not merely indicators, pointing to what is not there. Symbols make present, albeit a mediated presence, the reality they participate in. Rahner will call this type of symbol a *'real* symbol'. 'The symbol is the reality, constituted by the thing symbolized as an inner moment of itself, which reveals and proclaims the thing symbolized, and is itself full of the thing symbolized, being its concrete form of existence.'[75]

Second, the symbolic nature of being is not limited to finite being, that is to say, to creatures. Divine being also is marked by plurality-in-unity and is therefore symbolic. According to the Christian faith, God, the simple and single transcendent cause, exists as a 'unity in plurality'. So Gregory of Nazianzus can declare, preaching on the topic of the Trinity, that 'unity' – that is, the unity of God – 'having from all eternity arrived by motion at duality, found its rest in trinity'.[76] According to the letter to the Hebrews, the Son is the 'reflection of God's glory and the exact imprint of God's very being' (Heb. 1.3). The Son is the Word, image and expression of the unseen Father. Augustine is cognizant of the same theological insight: in *ep.* 11, Augustine argues that it belongs precisely to the Son to be incarnate, because he is the divine Word, the eternal expression of the Father. The Father and his Word together with the Spirit is one God.

This basic understanding of the symbolic nature of being provides the basis for one prominent line of Christological thought in the twentieth century. 'If we take the term symbol in a strongly realistic sense', Avery Dulles explains, 'meaning a sign in which the thing signified is really present, Christ may be called the symbol of God par excellence'.[77] Roger Haight, likewise, builds his Christology around the concept of 'symbol': 'Jesus', Haight explains, 'is the concrete symbol of God'.[78]

The Christologies of each of these theologians – Augustine, Rahner, Dulles and Haight – can all be considered *symbolic* Christologies. And yet, there are two axes around which these Christologies fall into two quite distinct camps.

---

[75] Ibid.
[76] Gregory of Nazianzen, *or.* 29.2.
[77] Avery Dulles, *Models of Revelation* (Maryknoll, NY: Orbis Books, 1994), p. 158.
[78] Roger Haight, *Jesus Symbol of God* (Maryknoll, NY: Orbis Books, 1999), p. 14.

VI. The 'Dialectic of Symbol' and Christologies from above and below

The first 'axis', we might call it, dividing the aforementioned Christologies is what Roger Haight calls the 'dialectical character of symbols'.[79] Haight means by this that symbols are 'tensive', that there is a basic tension in a symbol: it both *is* and *is not* what it symbolizes. Rahner and Haight, however, understand the tensive or dialectical character quite differently.

According to Rahner, as we've seen, the symbol participates metaphysically in what it symbolizes: a body – while being other than the soul – belongs metaphysically to the person. And yet, the symbol is distinct – though, not separate – from what it symbolizes. To say, then, that Jesus is the symbol of God means for Rahner and for Avery Dulles that Jesus both is and is not God. What they mean by this tensive statement is that what was manifest in the life of Jesus of Nazareth was man, not God, an insight fundamental to Augustine's Christology of mediation. Nevertheless, because the human nature of Christ is a part of or a 'moment' in the greater reality of the Person of Christ, who enjoys also the fullness of the divine nature, Rahner, Dulles and Augustine would also maintain that Christ is God. And, they would insist that the statement is true in a metaphysical sense. We recall that for Augustine the Person of Christ, the subjective centre of identity, is the divine Word. Hence Rahner can make the claim: 'The Logos, the Son of the Father, is truly, in his humanity as such, the revelatory symbol in which the Father enunciates himself, in this Son, to the world – revelatory, because the symbol renders present what is revealed.'[80] According to Rahner,

> [T]he Incarnate Word is the absolute symbol of God in the world, filled as nothing else can be with what is symbolized. He is not merely the presence and revelation of what God is in himself. He is also the expressive presence of what – or rather, who – God wished to be, in free grace, to the world, in such a way that this divine attitude, once so expressed, can never be reversed, but is and remains final and unsurpassable.[81]

Here we see that for Rahner as well as for Augustine – while certainly avoiding a naive conflation of divinity and humanity in Jesus of Nazareth – the symbol can truly and hence in a metaphysically valid sense be said to

---

[79] Ibid., p. 201.
[80] Rahner, 'The Theology of the Symbol', p. 239. Similarly, Rahner explains in his *Foundations of Christian Faith* (Chestnut Ridge, NY: Crossroad Publishing Company, 1982), p. 224: 'The man Jesus must be the self-revelation of God through who he is and not only through his words, and this he really cannot be if precisely this humanity were not the expression of God.'
[81] Rahner, 'The Theology of the Symbol', p. 237.

be the thing symbolized, Christ *is* God. The humanity, Augustine would say, is not divine, but the person of Jesus is. It is through the human nature of Christ that divinity is mediated; but, the human nature of Christ exists as a 'moment', to use Rahner's expression, in the actualization of the person of Jesus who is the eternal Word. So Avery Dulles comments: 'In Christ, therefore, the manifestation and that which is manifested ontologically coincide. The man Jesus Christ is both the symbol and the incarnation of the eternal Logos, who communicates himself by becoming fully human without ceasing to be divine.'[82]

Roger Haight interprets the dialectical nature of symbols differently, that is to say, in a non-metaphysical sense. His Christology, as a result, will look quite different. Haight explains: 'The dialectical character of symbol allows one to assert contrary things about the symbol, because it is not the symbolized, and yet it makes the symbolized present.'[83] In other words, according to Haight, the symbol is not a metaphysical moment in the actualization of the thing symbolized; Haight prefers a theory of symbol revolving around the idea of representation. A religious symbol, according to Haight, is 'first of all a finite reality of this world ... It can be understood on its own terms, so to speak, prior to being a symbol. It is potentially explicable as an integral finite reality ... On the first level, then, a symbol is itself and not other than itself'.[84] For Haight, the symbol of God is not so much the human *nature* of Christ as much as the *man or person*, Jesus.[85] And, what he mediates is not divinity precisely, but the 'experience of God in history'.[86] In other words, Jesus points to what is other than himself: the transcendent God. 'On his part, Jesus of Nazareth, the human being', Haight maintains, 'pointed to something other than himself, namely, God and God's rule in history.'[87]

It might seem that here the Christologies of Haight and Augustine have approached one another: Christ is the Mediator through whom divinity is present. What we see manifest is humanity; what is present, though veiled is divinity. Nevertheless, the Christologies of Haight and Augustine diverge precisely at this point. Because of the singularity of person in Christ, according to Augustine – a person who enjoys both divine and human natures – the

---

[82] Dulles, *Models of Revelation*, p. 158.
[83] Haight, *Jesus Symbol of God*, p. 201.
[84] Roger Haight, *Dynamics of Theology* (Maryknoll, NY: Orbis Books, 1990), p. 133.
[85] Haight's 'dialectical' approach to symbol and Christology leads to problems: 'Jesus both is and is not the object of Christology ... The characterization of a symbol as a tension between two poles is also a description of how the symbol of Jesus Christ functions in religious consciousness. Christians experience a finite person in history; and they experience God in and through him' (*Jesus Symbol of God*, p. 205).
[86] *Jesus Symbol of God*, p. 14.
[87] Ibid., p. 203.

divinity that Jesus mediates, albeit through his humanity, is, nevertheless, genuinely identical with himself. In other words, it is through Christ as man that the same Christ as God is made present. For Haight, by contrast, the divinity Jesus makes present is ontologically other than himself.

Haight is cognizant of this distinction; criticizing the same tendency in Rahner's Christology to identify the person of Jesus as a divine person (i.e. as the Word incarnate), Haight suggests that such an approach compromises the authenticity of Christ's humanity:

> [A]lthough Rahner does not usually refer to Jesus as a human person, he always refers to his humanity as an integral human nature. Indeed, his description of this integral human nature is realistic. But Rahner's hypostatic union seems to be an 'enhypostatic union,' that is, Jesus' integral humanity is borne and sustained by the divine being of the Logos. Such is not the case with other human beings, so that, once again, Jesus appears different from other human beings.[88]

Haight makes the point as being apodictically wrong-headed. This criticism opens the way to the second axis upon which these Christologies divide: whether one's Christology is from above or from below. The Christologies of Augustine, Rahner and Dulles, precisely because they maintain that it is the Word who constitutes the Person of Christ are Christologies from above.

From the perspective of a postmodern context, wherein the idea of the incarnation of eternal Word of God is met with increasing incredulity, Haight points out that such a Christology from above is 'problematic'.[89] Instead, Haight adjusts his Christology in two ways: while maintaining a symbolic approach that originates with Rahner, Haight nevertheless, recasts it 'in the framework of a christology [*sic*!] from below and an Antiochene pattern of understanding the duality of Jesus' humanity and divinity'.[90] What Haight means entails more than that; he will begin with the assumption of a complete human nature in the Person of Christ. His Christology takes as its point of departure an integral human person who is Jesus of Nazareth. Such a starting position is consistent with his definition of a religious symbol: it is first and foremost to be understood integrally as a thing in this world, as some *thing* in its own right. In the case of Christ, Haight would argue that on a fundamental level, Jesus is first a human being – and only as such could he function as symbol of God.

---

[88] Ibid., p. 433.
[89] Ibid., p. 432.
[90] Ibid., p. 439.

While Augustine does not use the contemporary language of symbol, his Christology certainly manifests a basic affinity for and compatibility with it. Augustine would comfortably make the claim: Jesus is the symbol of God. He would say more: Jesus is the absolute symbol of God. But contrary to Roger Haight, Augustine would insist that there is no Jesus apart from or distinct from his role as Christ the Mediator. Jesus, the incarnate Word, is Christ the Mediator without remainder. In this sense, precisely in the relief that the Christology of Roger Haight provides to Augustine's Christology, one sees a small part of the influence of Augustine upon Chalcedon: 'one and the same Christ, Son, Lord, unique . . . not divided into two persons, but one and the same Son and only-begotten God, Word, Lord Jesus Christ.'[91]

For Further Reading

Daley, Brian, 'The Giant's Twin Substances: Ambrose and the Christology of Augustine's *Contra sermonem Arianorum*'. In *Augustine: Presbyter Factus Sum* (ed. Joseph T. Lienhard, Earl C. Muller and Roland Teske; New York: Peter Lang, 1993), pp. 477–95.

— 'A Humble Mediator: The Distinctive Elements in Saint Augustine's Christology', *Word and Spirit* 9 (1987), pp. 100–17.

Joanne McWilliam, 'The Study of Augustine's Christology in the Twentieth Century'. In *Augustine: From Rhetor to Theologian* (ed. Joanne McWilliam; Waterloo: Wilfred Laurier University Press, 1992), pp. 183–205.

Madec, Goulven, *La patrie et la voie: Le Christ dans la vie et la pensée de saint Augustin* (Paris: Desclée, 1989).

— 'Christus'. In *Augustinus-Lexikon* (ed. Cornelius Mayer and Erich Feldmann; vol. 1; Basel: Schwabe, 1986), pp. 845–908.

Scheel, Otto, *Die Anschauung Augustins über Christi Person und Werk* (Tübingen: Mohr Siebeck Verlag, 1901).

Studer, Basil, *Grace of Christ and the Grace of God in Augustine of Hippo: Christocentrism or Theocentrism?* (Collegeville, MN: Liturgical Press, 1997).

— *Trinity and Incarnation: The Faith of the Early Church* (Collegeville, MN: Liturgical Press, 1993).

— 'Die Offenbarung der Liebe des demütigen Gottes nach Augustinus'. In *Handbuch der Dogmengeschichte* (ed. Michael Schmaus; vol. 3, fasc. 2; Freiburg: Herder, 1978), pp. 156–74.

---

[91] From the definition of faith promulgated at Chalcedon. For Augustine's influence on the teaching of Chalcedon, see van Bavel, *Reserches sur la Christologie de saint Augustin*.

4 Augustine on the Church

Michael Root

Any comprehensive theological discussion of the church must address a fundamental problem: the church is confessed to be one, and yet there are many churches, existing in varying degrees of separation one from another. How is that reality to be understood? Is there one true church, surrounded by imposters? Or are the churches somehow one, despite their apparent division? Or is unity an ideal to be achieved only eschatologically, analogous to a perfect holiness in the saints to be achieved only in the Kingdom? The 'scandal of division' is not just a call for ecumenical action; it is a problem for any ecclesiology, and modern theologies of the church have addressed this problem in varying ways.

Modern Western discussions of this topic almost all share a basic feature: they are thoroughly Augustinian. This Augustinian character is less a matter of some particular answer to a disputed question and more a matter of the terms in which the question is asked and answered. On other topics – for example, grace and freedom – Augustine put forward views that have remained one powerful option in contrast to others. In discussions of Christian unity and division, however, Augustine is less one option and more the air the disputants breathe: taken for granted, invisible, yet ubiquitous. Modern Western understandings of the unity and apparent division of the church are variations on an Augustinian model.[1]

This essay will examine this Augustinian background. The primary focus will be on Augustine, particularly on the anti-Donatist writings in which his

---

[1] The Orthodox do not fit this mould, since they do not accept the decisive Augustinian starting point: a general recognition of the validity of at least some sacraments (most importantly, baptism) beyond their own communion. A good example of this alternative Orthodox outlook is the 2000 statement of the Jubilee Bishops' Council of the Russian Orthodox Church, 'Basic Principles of the Attitude of the Russian Orthodox Church Toward the Other Christian Confessions' (online at http://orthodoxeurope.org/page/7/5/1.aspx. Accessed 9 September 2012). Many of the perennial difficulties of Orthodox involvement in ecumenical discussions are rooted in their distance from the Augustinian assumptions of most Western ecumenism.

ecclesiology was developed. After an analysis of Augustine's ecumenical theology, some modern variations will be discussed.

I. An Alternative – Unity as Simple

Augustine's influence on the topic of the church does not arise from his acute formulation of what was already a consensus when he wrote. On the topic of the church, Augustine found a conceptually and institutionally fluid situation. The North African Church was riven by a dispute over the nature of the church's holiness and the conditions under which the sacraments could be rightly celebrated and received. The dispute took concrete institutional form in the Donatist schism, already 75-years old when Augustine returned to Africa in 387. The Catholic side was handicapped by the influence of Cyprian, whose legacy was revered by all, but who advocated a position like the Donatists on the central question whether heretics and schismatics could truly baptize. Augustine's arguments drew on earlier North African theologians (especially Optatus of Milevis and Tyconius, himself an odd sort of Donatist), but the resultant synthesis was new and constituted a turning point in Western ecclesiology. This new understanding can be better grasped by first outlining what preceded him and its development in Donatist theology.

When we look at ecclesiology prior to Augustine, we sometimes find a picture of church unity as simple. At least in theory, the church is completely at one with itself; its boundaries are definite, and beyond them is only non-church. Ignatius of Antioch is clear. The one church is joined to the bishop, presbyters and clergy. 'Apart from these a gathering cannot be called a church.'[2] What happens outside the church might look like the church's sacraments, but they are not. As Tertullian said, since heretics do not rightly have baptism, they do not have it at all.[3] For such a view, there is no true ecumenical problem, no division of the church nor any division of that which pertains to the church. There is only inside and outside.

As attractive as such a well-defined position might be, is one willing to say that all ecclesiastical acts carried out during a perhaps brief schism – all baptisms, anointings, ordinations – must be counted as nothing and repeated when communion is re-established? The Western end of the Mediterranean saw a vigorous debate on this question in the third century, with a focus on rebaptism.[4]

---

[2] Ignatius, *Trall.* 3, in *The Apostolic Fathers* (trans. Bart D. Ehrman; Loeb Classical Library; vol. 1; Cambridge, MA: Harvard University Press, 2003), p. 259.
[3] Tertullian, *bapt.* 15.
[4] See Everett Ferguson, *Baptism in the Early Church: History, Theology, and Liturgy in the First Five Centuries* (Grand Rapids, MI: Eerdmans, 2009), pp. 380–99.

The great councils of the fourth century (Nicaea, canon 19; Constantinople, canon 7) distinguished schismatic but Trinitarian baptisms (not to be repeated) from heretical baptisms (not true baptisms and thus to be repeated). Such a distinction became widespread, but not universal.[5] Most significant for Augustine, Cyprian and the North African Church resolutely defended the rebaptism of heretics and schismatics.[6] In none of these cases, however, were the ecclesiological implications of the varying practices thought through.

The Donatist schism, rooted in reactions to the Diocletian persecution at the beginning of the fourth century, was a complex phenomenon, with theological and non-theological factors intertwined in its history, but its theological focus was on the conditions needed for an authentic ecclesial act.[7] The minister of baptism or similar acts must not be in schism or heresy, but he also must be a *true* participant in the *true* communion of the church, that is, he must himself be worthy and the communion of which he is a part must not tolerate the unworthy. The Donatists said that the Catholic Church in Africa included *traditores* who had surrendered the church's books under persecution and were thus unworthy. The wider church beyond Africa remained in communion with the African Catholics and was thus corrupted. Only in the Donatist remnant did the true church survive; only there was true baptism or true ordination administered.

Two points should be noted about the Donatist position. First, at least some Donatist theologians not only seemed to go beyond making the status of the minister a necessary condition for an authentic ecclesial act, but also seemed to ascribe a sort of causal efficacy to that status. Petilian, a Donatist bishop whose defence of Donatist practice is quoted at length by Augustine, states in relation to baptism: 'We attend to the conscience of the giver, which cleanses that of the recipient' (quoted in *c. litt. Pet.* 2.3.6). For Augustine, this assertion fundamentally misunderstands the relation between divine and human agency in baptism (see, e.g., *bapt.* 3.11.16). As will be discussed below, issues of divine and human agency will be the hinge on which Augustine's argument turns.

---

[5] On the complexities of doctrine and practice at this time, see especially Francis J. Thomson, 'Economy: An Examination of the Various Theories of Economy Held within the Orthodox Church, with Special Reference to the Economical Recognition of the Validity of Non-Orthodox Sacraments', *JTS* 16 (1965), pp. 402–12; and Dorothea Wendebourg, 'Taufe und Oikonomia: Zur Frage der Wiedertaufe in der Orthodoxen Kirche', in *Kirchengemeinschaft – Anspruch und Wirklichkeit* (ed. Wolf-Dieter Hauschild, Dorothea Wendebourg and Carsten Nicolaisen; Stuttgart: Calwer Verlag, 1986), pp. 97–103.

[6] See Ferguson, *Baptism in the Early Church*, pp. 388–94.

[7] For a brief account of Donatism and recent discussion of Donatism, see Robert A. Markus, 'Donatus, Donatism', in *Augustine through the Ages: An Encyclopedia* (ed. Allan D. Fitzgerald; Grand Rapids: Eerdmans, 1999), pp. 284–87.

Second, Donatism makes the unity of the church as simple as possible. Various elements hold the church together: a common life in communion, shared sacraments, a shared holiness. Donatist theory and practice make the unities created by these different elements as congruent as possible. The limits of a common life in communion are the same as the limits of any unity created by common sacraments, since outside that communion there are no authentic sacraments. The borders created by a shared holiness should coincide with the borders of communion (and thus the unworthy, such as the *traditores*, cannot be within the communion) and with the borders created by shared sacraments (and thus the unworthy cannot celebrate true sacraments). Donatism represents a fully non-ecumenical ecclesiology.

II. Exterior Unity in the Sacraments

For Augustine, a central Donatist mistake was a false understanding of who does what in baptism. Obviously, there is a human actor in any baptism who says the words and carries out the actions. But who performs the action of cleansing, renewing and forgiving the baptized? Or, as Augustine asks, whose baptism is it? A kind of baptism was truly given to John the Baptist; it was his and can be rightly called 'John's baptism' (*Jo. ev. tr.* 5.6). John is the agent. The baptism which John says will come after him and which Jesus brings, however, is not 'given' to human agents in the same way. 'The Lord kept to himself the power of baptizing (*baptizandi potestatem*) and gave to his servants the ministry (*ministerium*)' (*Jo. ev. tr.* 5.7). Paul spoke of 'my gospel' and 'my mission', but never of 'my baptism' (*Jo. ev. tr.* 5.9). Thus, 'those whom the servants of the Lord were to baptize, the Lord baptized, not they. For it is one thing to baptize as minister (*per ministerium*), another thing to baptize with power (*per potestatem*)' (*Jo. ev. tr.* 5.6). John the Baptist can thus say that the one on whom he sees the dove descend (i.e. Jesus) will baptize with the Holy Spirit (Jn 1.33), and yet the Gospel then later says that Jesus' disciples and not Jesus himself baptized (Jn 4.2). The solution to this biblical crux is the recognition of the mixed agency in baptism. 'He, and not he; He by power, they by ministry; they performed the service of baptizing, the power of baptizing remained in Christ' (*Jo. ev. tr.* 5.18).

Augustine believes that the Donatists are guilty of more than a technical philosophical mistake. They have misdirected the Christian's trust, away from the infallible action of God, to whom all glory should be given, and towards the fallible human. They have made the mistake of the Corinthians whom Paul rebukes for attaching themselves to whoever baptized them (*c. litt. Pet.* 3.5.6; *Jo. ev. tr.* 10.7). Even worse, they have made the mistake of Simon Magus (Acts 8.18–24), who thought that the apostles possessed as their own the power of granting the Holy Spirit and so could give it to whom they pleased (*s*. 266.3). For the Donatists, the gifts given in baptism must remain uncertain, Augustine argued, for who can be sure that the minister of baptism is not perhaps a hypocrite, lacking the Holy Spirit and forgiveness of sins, who then, by Donatist theory, cannot give the Holy Spirit and forgiveness of sins (*c. litt. Pet.* 1.3.4)?

For Augustine, the standing of the baptizer is irrelevant to whether a true baptism has occurred. A drunkard, a murderer, even Judas himself can truly baptize (*Jo. ev. tr.* 5.18), for each is only the human instrument of the 'hidden grace, hidden power in the Holy Spirit (*occulta gratia, occulta potentia in Spiritu sancto*)' by which Christ works (*c. litt. Pet.* 3.49.59). The same holds true for the schismatic or even the heretic. If the Trinitarian formula is used in baptism, then an authentic baptism occurs. 'If we discern this [triune] name in it [baptism], we do better to distinguish the words of the gospel from heretical error and approve what is sound in them, correcting what is faulty' (*bapt.* 6.36.70; see also in the same text 4.15.23; 4.17.25; 6.17.29; 7.16.31). Even a Marcionite truly baptizes if the Trinitarian formula is used (*bapt.* 3.15.20; 7.16.31).

Thus, if a baptized heretic or schismatic seeks to enter the Catholic Church, not only is a new baptism not necessary, but also a new baptism is sinful (*ep.* 23.2), for it denies the nature of baptism and God's action within it. Even if Donatists wish to enter the Catholic Church, but have scruples whether their Donatist baptism is authentic and wish a new baptism, they are not to be accommodated (*bapt.* 5.5.5).

To say, however, that all baptism in the triune name is authentic is not to say that such authentic baptism always works salvation. For Augustine, baptism alone does not save. 'The sacrament of baptism is one thing, the conversion of the heart another; but that means salvation is made complete through the two together' (*bapt.* 4.25.33). Or, again: 'it [baptism] is of no avail for salvation unless he who has authentic baptism (*integritatem baptismi*) be incorporated into the church, correcting also his own depravity' (*bapt.* 4.21.29). If baptism is not accompanied by interior conversion, it is not redemptive.[8]

The conditions necessary for the saving reception of baptism are not found among schismatics and heretics. They have a legitimate (*legitimum*) baptism, but they do not have it legitimately (*legitime*), for they use it against the law (*bapt.* 5.6.7). They have the form of religion (*forma pietatis*), but not its strength (2 Tim. 3.5), because they lack the unity of the Spirit in the bond of peace (Eph. 4.3; *s.* 71.32). Since they are outside the unity of the Spirit, they do not receive the Spirit which works forgiveness: 'It follows that since the forgiveness of sins can only be given in the Holy Spirit, it can be given in that Church alone which

---

[8] For Augustine, the baptism of adults is still the paradigm. With infants, God's grace makes up for the conversion of heart that they lack through no fault of their own (*bapt.* 3.24.32).

has the Holy Spirit' (*s.* 71.33).[9] Those baptized within heretical communions thus are not washed by Christ's baptism and are not incorporated into his unity (*Christi baptismo non abluantur nec unitati eius incorporentur*) (*cons. Ev.* 4.6.7). Baptism received within schism not only does not save, but also it does harm, since one is receiving the good in a bad way (*s.* 266.7). The schismatic baptism will serve as testimony against those in schism (*s.* 272). Augustine is no less rigorous than the Donatists or Cyprian in his insistence that *extra ecclesiam nulla salus*; those outside the communion of the church do not obtain eternal life (*c. litt. Pet.* 2.81.178).

Surprisingly, despite the rigour of his critique of schismatic baptism, Augustine advises persons facing possible death and who can receive baptism only from a schismatic to accept Donatist baptism. As long as they receive baptism 'in a catholic spirit and with a heart not alienated from the unity of peace' and do not identify with the attitude of schism, they then receive such baptism to the soul's health (*bapt.* 6.5.7; similarly 7.52.100). This possibility is an indication that for Augustine the defect lies in the schismatic heart, not in the baptism itself.

For the modern interpreter, Augustine appears to be using a standard distinction between the validity of a sacrament and its efficacy. The logic of his response to the Donatists significantly furthers the development of such a distinction, but the modern interpreter should be careful not to import later terminology, which perhaps rounds off the edges of what for Augustine is not yet a settled matter (and I have thus avoided using the language of validity). When Augustine does move towards a more technical explanation of the defect in schismatic baptism, he makes use of a distinction between *sacramentum* and *res*: 'they possess the sign (*sacramentum*) outside the Church, but interiorly (*intus*) they do not possess the reality (*rem*) of which it is the sign (*sacramentum*)' (*correct.* 11.50). Or, partially echoing the passage already cited from 2 Tim. 3.5, he will say that schismatic have the form (*forma*) but not the fruit (*fructus*) of the sacrament (*Jo. ev. tr.* 13.16). Even with these explanations, however, one should not think that Augustine has a full theory of sacraments that he is applying to particular cases. Technical terms are not being used arbitrarily, but Augustine's language still has a somewhat ad hoc character.

What does Augustine's understanding of authentic baptism and ordination outside the communion of the church imply for an understanding of the church's unity? Most decisively, it means that the *simple* unity envisioned by the Donatists, in which the limits of unity constituted by different uniting elements all coincide, is broken. Unity becomes complex; different uniting

---

[9] In *De baptismo*, Augustine is unsure whether one who receives baptism in schism receives forgiveness, but then has that forgiveness immediately cancelled by participation in the sin of schism, or never receives forgiveness at all. Since the result is the same, Augustine feels no compulsion to settle the question and leaves it open (*bapt.* 1.12.18–19; 3.13.18).

elements will posit different boundaries. No longer must an individual or a community be either simply inside or outside; they might be inside in one sense and outside in another. The problem presented by schism and some forms of heresy is now precisely ecumenical; it concerns a division, if not in the church itself, at least a division in something truly ecclesial.

For Augustine, any social body is bound together by some 'bond of association' (*societatis vinculo*) (*civ. Dei.* 15.8.2). More specifically, every religious society has some visible sign of unity (*c. Faust.* 19.11). For the church, the sacraments are elements that bind the church into a unity. 'By a very small number of sacraments [or signs] . . . the society of the new people [the church] was bound together (*Sacramentis numero paucissimis . . . societatem novi populi colligavit*)' (*ep.* 54.1.1).

The Donatists thus are not simply unconnected with the church:

> If they observe some of the same things, in respect of these they have not severed themselves; and so far they are still a part of the framework of the Church (*ex ea parte in texturae compage detinentur*), while in all other respects they are cut off from it. Accordingly, any one whom they have associated with themselves is attached to the church in all those points in which they are not separated from it (*ex ea parte nectitur Ecclesiae, in qua nec illi separati sunt*) (*bapt.* 1.8.10).

Or again: 'Where they do not differ from us, they are not separated (*disiunguntur*) from us' (*bapt.* 1.13.21). As Augustine tirelessly repeats, he detests in the Donatists only that which makes them schismatics and heretics. Catholics should acknowledge and embrace in the Donatists their sacraments and the name of God they bear (*ep.* 61.1).

Schismatics are not the equivalent of 'pagans'; they are wandering sheep over whom the church should grieve and whom the church should seek (*ep.* 61.1). More strongly put, they are brothers and sisters: 'Bad brother, quarrelsome brother, still my brother is what you are' (*s.* 357.4).

Schism thus brings about a true division in an ecclesial reality. Augustine most often uses verbs of rend (*conscindo*) or divide (*divido*) with 'unity' as the object of the verb (e.g. *ep.* 43.8.21, 24; *Jo. ev. tr.* 13.15; *bapt.* 1.8.10). On occasion, however, he will speak of the church itself being divided by schism. 'You divide the Church by schisms, you rend the Body of Christ (*dividis ecclesiam per schismata, dilanias corpus Christi*)' (*ep. Jo.* 6.13; similarly at 6.14 and 10.10). By their quarrels, 'Christians divide the Church (*christiani Ecclesiam dividunt*)' (*Jo. ev. tr.* 13.13).

In passages such as this, Augustine lays out the foundation of the attitude that shapes an ecumenical outlook: the sense that either the church or something genuinely ecclesial has been divided and that those divided remain deeply connected despite all division. G. R. Evans in *The Church and the Churches*, an ecumenical ecclesiology from an Anglican perspective, finds in Augustine already a theology of 'partial communion'.[10] To rightly understand Augustine, however, it is important to see why Evans's reading goes one step too far.

Augustine will speak of various sorts of connections between the Donatists and the Catholic Church, but as far as I can tell, he avoids describing that connection with the decisive verbs *communico* or *participo*, the verbs that describe the communion of the church. If shared authentic sacraments create a 'partial communion', that communion is partial in not just a quantitative sense, but in a qualitative sense. The connection is not of the same *kind* or *sort* that exists in the church.

Similarly, those in schism are not, for Augustine, partially or in some sense within the church. They are wholly outside the church, despite the presence of authentic baptism. Many unworthy are in some sense in the church, but not the schismatics: '*Multi intus, quasi intus sunt; nemo autem foris, nisi vere foris*' (*ep. Jo.* 6.13). The heretic and the Catholic have one baptism but they do not have one church (*bapt.* 5.21.29). Thus, when the schismatic leaves, the church is not divided, but remains whole: 'Woe to those who are cut off! But she [the church] will remain entire (*integra*)' (*Jo. ev. tr.* 10.8).

Augustine's insistence that his Donatist opponents truly baptize, truly anoint, truly ordain, opened the door to a more nuanced and complex understanding of the unity of the church and of the relations between 'churches'. Beyond the church, there are genuinely ecclesial, even divine elements, creating 'brothers'. Nevertheless, for Augustine those ecclesial elements beyond the church do not mean that the church exists outside the church or that the church is genuinely divided. To understand that qualification, one must ask what sacraments do and how they mediate the deepest reality of unity: unity in Christ, charity and the Spirit.

III. Interior Unity in Charity, Christ and the Spirit

For Augustine, baptism (or, mutatis mutandis, ordination) is not an end in itself. Again echoing 2 Tim. 3.5, he says that 'the power of piety (*virtus pietatis*) is the end (*finis*) of the commandment [to baptize], that is, love from a pure heart and a good conscience and unfeigned faith.' The outward rite is at the service of the inward action of Christ and the Spirit, cleansing, purifying and forgiving. The water that washes the body signifies (*significat*) the action of

---

[10] G. R. Evans, *The Church and the Churches: Toward an Ecumenical Ecclesiology* (Cambridge: Cambridge University Press, 1994), p. 35. Evans discussion of Augustine on these matters runs from pages 28 to 43.

the Spirit cleansing and feeding the soul (*ep. Jo.* 6.10). This internal divine action and what it brings is the power or fruit or root or *res* (Augustine uses all these terms) of which the external action is the sacrament. The sacrament, the outward rite, achieves its end only when this inner action achieves its end in the baptized.

The gift given in baptism is more than just an effect in the baptized person. First Jn 2.27 speaks of an anointing which abides in the Christian, which Augustine connects with the anointing that occurs in baptism. The external anointing brings with it a spiritual, invisible anointing. 'The spiritual anointing is the Holy Spirit himself, of which the sacrament is the visible anointing' (*ep. Jo.* 3.5). A few paragraphs later, he expands the gift further: 'The invisible anointing is the Holy Spirit; the invisible anointing is that charity which, in whomever it is, will be like a root in him' (*ep. Jo.* 3.12). To receive and abide in the Spirit means to possess that charity which is always a divine gift and which for Augustine is the centre of the Christian life.

This charity worked by the Spirit, inseparable from the Spirit, is not simply the end or telos of the sacraments; unity in the Spirit and the Spirit's love is also the end or telos of unity in the sacraments. Unity in the sacraments is not an end in itself; unity in the sacraments is a sign and instrument of unity in the Spirit and charity. Just as, for Augustine, the Holy Spirit is, in a sense, the society of the Father and Son (*societas est quodam modo Patris et Filii ipse Spiritus Sanctus*), so the unity of the society of the church is the proper work of the Spirit (*societas unitatis Ecclesiae Dei . . . tamquam proprium opus est Spiritus Sancti*) (*s.* 71.33). What the soul is to the body, the Spirit is to the church (*s.* 267.4), vivifying it and making it a unity.

Since the indwelling of the Spirit and charity are inseparable, so unity in the Spirit and unity in charity are inseparable. Augustine can thus move back and forth between saying that the Spirit constitutes the church as one and that charity constitutes the church as one. The 'harmony of charity (*concordia caritatis*)' (*s.* 229A.2) makes the church one. The unity of the church is constituted by 'the unity of the Spirit in the bond of peace' (Eph. 4.3) and this 'bond of peace' is charity (*c. litt. Pet.* 2.32.74; this passage from Ephesians particularly underwrites for Augustine the equation of unity in the Spirit and unity in charity).

A further aspect of this unity must be noted to grasp its true depth. To receive the Spirit and charity through baptism is to enter into unity with Christ, to become a member of his body. For Augustine, this Pauline language is not mere metaphor or simile. Christ and the church relate as head and body, but head and body from a true unity. Thus when we speak of Christ, our language can be understood in three ways (*tribus modis*): we might be speaking of the eternal Son prior to the incarnation; we might be speaking of the Logos in unity with human nature; or we might be speaking 'in a certain way of the whole Christ in the plenitude of the Church (*quodam modo totus Christus, in plenitudine Ecclesiae*)' (*s.* 341.1). Christ and church together constituted 'the whole Christ, head and body (*Christus totus, caput et corpus*)' (*ev. Jo. tr.* 1.2).

The unity of church and Christ is so intimate that they can constitute a single agent, though an internally complex one. Actions of the church can be actions of Christ, so that Augustine can say that Christ is preached by Christ himself when he is proclaimed by the church (*s.* 354.1). Especially in Augustine's interpretation of the Psalms, the interpenetration of voices becomes an important hermeneutical tool. Augustine often reads the speaking voice in the Psalms as the voice of Christ. But then how is a passage such as Ps. 37(38).4 to be interpreted, where the Psalmist speaks of 'my sins', but Jesus has no sins? The speaker is 'the whole and full Christ (*plenum et totum Christum*)', here giving voice to the sins that belong not to the head but to the body (*en. Ps.* 37.6). Augustine does not efface the distinction between head and body; the head cleanses from sin, the body confesses sin (*en. Ps.* 37.6; cf. *en. Ps.* 63.1). Nevertheless, the unity of the church for Augustine is a unity of a reality internal to Christ, not merely an effect of Christ's presence, but an aspect of Christ's presence.

Unity in charity, unity in the Spirit, and unity in Christ are identical; they are all ways of speaking of unity in that which is most important, unity in the salvation which is participation in Christ and the Spirit. This unity of the church is indivisible. There is only one Spirit; Christ has only one body; charity unifies. The sacraments may be divided, like the clothes of Christ at the crucifixion divided among the soldiers. But among the garments is a seamless robe, which is not divided. It is described as woven from the top (Jn 19.23),

> [A]nd thus from (*de*) heaven, thus by (*a*) the Father, by (*a*) the Holy Spirit. What is this tunic, but charity, which no one can divide? What is this tunic, but unity? . . . The heretics could divide the sacraments among themselves, charity is not divided. What they cannot divide, they leave; it remains whole (*integra*). (*en. Ps.* 22[2].19)[11]

Unity in the sacraments is subordinate to the unity it mediates when rightly received, unity in Christ, the Spirit and charity. Unity in the sacraments can be rent, divided, and Augustine, as we have seen, used strong language for such division. The unity which is end and not means, however, is indivisible. Division in not *in* this unity, but always *from* this unity.

---

[11] The seamless tunic as the undivided unity of the church is a common theme in Augustine; see further *ep.* 23.4; *Jo. ev. tr.* 13.13.

Schismatics or heretics cannot be within this deeper unity. Decisive here is Augustine's interpretation of what lies at the heart of schism: a lack of charity. It is of the nature of charity to work unity; to reject unity is, for Augustine, to reject charity. 'He is not a partaker of the divine charity who is the enemy of unity' (*correct.* 11.50). Other causes may also be at work, but the failure of charity is always decisive. 'None would create schisms, if they were not blinded by hatred of their brethren' (*bapt.* 1.11.15). Only in unity can charity be preserved. 'Christian charity cannot be preserved except in the unity of the Church' (*c. litt. Pet.* 2.78.172). On one occasion, Augustine does seem to imply that sufficient cause might exist for separation – schism is a sacrilege, 'if there is no cause for separation (*si nulla fuit causa separationis*)' (*bapt.* 5.1.1) – but this concession seems strictly theoretical. He is relentless in his insistence that the schism is grounded in a lack of charity.[12]

This lack of charity is what blocks orthodox faith or the sacraments from being effective outside the communion of the church. Augustine typically appeals in this case to 1 Cor. 13, especially verse two: without charity, I am nothing. All who forsake unity violate charity and are thus nothing (*s.* 88.21). Correct belief is of no profit if the soundness of charity is destroyed by schism (*bapt.* 1.8.11). To refuse charity is to refuse the Spirit, and thus the Spirit is refused outside the unity constituted by charity: 'those are wanting in God's charity who do not care for the unity of the Church; and consequently we are right in understanding that the Holy Spirit may be said not to be received except in the Catholic Church' (*bapt.* 3.16.21). *Extra ecclesiam nulla salus* because *extra ecclesiam nulla caritas*.

This Pauline insistence, that all that is apart from charity is nothing, stands behind, I believe, Augustine reticence to speak of communion in the sacraments as a partial, but still genuine, communion. Shared sacraments are a real connection, but since they lack charity, 'the one thing necessary', they do not pass the decisive threshold that would constitute communion.

Only in the church as genuine communion and participation in charity, Christ, and the Spirit are faith and the sacraments effective unto salvation. Thus, when a schismatic returns to the church, the sacraments before frustrated in their intended effect now attain their goal. The limb which before was severed from the body and thus did not participate in the body's life (*s.* 267.4) now returns to the body and is taken into its life (*correct.* 9.42). Only with this return is the animosity inherent in schism replaced by the 'unity of the Spirit in the bond of peace' (*bapt.* 1.12.18).[13]

---

[12] For more examples of this assertion, see *ep.* 61.2; 298.6; *s.* 88.21; *en. Ps.* 54.19; *ep. Jo.* 1.8,12; 2.3; 7.5; 9.10; *bapt.* 1.9.12.

[13] At times, Augustine will say that participation in the communion of the church itself forgives sins; see *bapt.* 2.13.18; 3.18.23; 6.5.7.

IV. A Middle Unity: In, But Not of, the Church

So far, the picture of church unity given by Augustine has two non-congruent levels: unity in the sacraments, an external, non-salvific unity, which does not constitute a truly ecclesial body, and unity in charity, Christ and the Spirit, participation in which is redemptive and which constitutes the church. The logic of the argument, shared by the Donatists and Augustine, implied also a third level of unity.

The Donatist argument that they alone had authentic baptism and ordination intertwined moral, subjective elements and ecclesiological, objective elements. If, as Petilian contended, the conscience of the baptizer cleansed the conscience of the baptized, then a moral judgement about the state of the baptizer was a necessary part of any consideration of baptism. Since communion with the corrupt was itself corrupting, thus negating the authenticity of baptism, the Donatist rejection of Catholic baptism had also an ecclesiological element.

Augustine's counterargument about divine agency in baptism (and anointing and ordination) rejected the importance of the moral, subjective state of the baptizer. Both the hypocrite within the church and the necessarily charity-deficient schismatic outside the church can authentically baptize. The objectivity of the sacrament bears the divine action. Augustine's argument that schismatic baptism is not redemptive, however, is less ecclesiological than moral. He does not directly argue that because a baptism takes place in schism, it thus cannot be saving (an argument that would be hard to square with his acceptance of schismatic baptism in case of emergency, as long as one rejects the schismatic spirit). Rather, he argues that a schismatic baptism is not saving because schism implies a refusal of charity, and a refusal of charity blocks the saving reception of the gifts of baptism. The moral, rather than ecclesiological, failure of the schismatic is the immediate cause of the breakdown in sacramental efficacy.

Schismatics are not the only persons who receive baptism but refuse charity, of course. Within the Catholic communion, many are similar. They are baptized, but remain essentially carnal.[14] Like the schismatics, they too are not redeemed. With them also, the sacraments do not attain to their end. Augustine regularly equates the situation of the 'carnal Catholic' with that of the schismatic. The carnal Catholic is outwardly, bodily, joined to unity (*in eius unitate corporaliter mixti*), but in fact separated by an evil life (*per vitam pessimam separantur*), just like the schismatics (*bapt* 1.10.14). The carnal Catholic has no real communion with the redeemed. 'There is no fellowship (*participatio*) between

---

[14] The carnal do not include those who are advancing spiritually, but are still weak and fall back on occasion (*bapt*. 1.15.24).

righteousness and unrighteousness, not only without, but also within the Church . . . There is no communion (*communio*) between light and darkness, not only without, but also within the Church' (*bapt.* 4.13.20).

The carnal Catholic who does not truly love can no more receive Christ and the Spirit than does the schismatic. As a result, the carnal Catholic does not belong to that unity in Christ which is the authentic unity of the church. Those who bodily mingle with Christ's sheep, but have a false heart, do not belong to the church; they are not within the society of the Spirit (*s.* 71.32). The church is incorrupt, pure and chaste; the avaricious, thieves and usurers do not belong to her (*non ad eam pertinent*) (*bapt.* 4.2.2). If one does not depart from iniquity, one may name the name of Christ, but one does not belong to his Kingdom (*s.* 71.4).

The schismatic and the carnal Catholic, however, are not on the same footing in all respects. The carnal Catholic is in the visible communion of the church in a way the schismatic is not. Augustine adopts the language of 2 Tim. 2.20 to describe the place of the carnal Catholic: 'In a great house there are not only vessels of gold and silver, but also of wood and earth; some unto honor and some unto dishonor.' Following Cyprian, Augustine takes the 'great house' to be the church. The two sorts of vessels are two ways of belonging to the house (*bapt.* 4.12.19). The houses subsists in the good and faithful, bound together by the unity of the Spirit. The good and faithful *are* the house, just as they *are* the body of Christ. The 'others' may be said to be *in* the house, but they do not belong to its structure (or constitution), nor to its fellowship of fruitful and peaceful righteousness (*Alios autem ita dico esse in domo, ut non pertineant ad compagem domus, nec ad societatem fructiferae pacificaeque iustitiae*) (*bapt.* 7.51.99). The carnal and the spiritual both belong to the church, but in different senses. The spiritual are *in* the church and they *are* the church; the carnal are *in* the church, but they *are not* the church. One might say that the spiritual are in and of the church, while the carnal are in but not of the church, although this is not Augustine's typical phrasing.

Augustine does not, however, give a detailed description of this middle unity, the unity of the visible communion of the church. Neither the controversies of his time nor the inner conceptual exigencies of his theology required him to do so. His references to the Eucharist as the 'sacrament of unity', however, makes clear that this visible fellowship is realized in a commonly celebrated Eucharist (e.g. *s.* 272). 'The supper of the Lord is the unity of the body of Christ' (*correct.* 6.24). This unity has an inner aspect, constituted when the sacrament of unity achieves its end, true unity in Christ, and an exterior aspect, communing bodily, *corporaliter*, in the Eucharist. When Augustine says that some are in the church, but are not the church, he is referring to those who receive the Eucharist (and thus are within this common life) but are not truly regenerate. They do not share in righteous deeds, but they do share in

Christ's altar (*non factis eorum, sed altari Christi communicant*) (*ep.* 43.8.21). The Eucharist is the focus of a more comprehensive common life, for example, a shared episcopate. The Catholic and Donatist communities in Augustine's Africa were competing groups of bishops, but they are competing in that they constitute separate Eucharistic communities.

For Augustine, then, there are not two, but three levels of unity: a unity constituted by common sacraments, a unity constituted by visible communion in the Catholic Church, and a unity constituted by true communion in charity, Christ and the Spirit. Schismatics participate only in the first form of unity; they are neither in nor of the church, but they are in a real but limited sense brothers and sisters through baptism in a way Pagans are not. Carnal Catholics belong to the first two unities, but not the third; they are in the church, but they cannot be said to be the church. Spiritual Catholics belong to all three unities; only of them can it be said that they are the church, the Body of Christ, the spotless Bride. These three unities thus form three concentric circles, each within the other. Most importantly, the redeemed are all (at least after the incarnation) among the communion of the baptized[15] and within the communion of the church.

V. An Invisible Church?

The distinction between the outward, visible communion of the church, including both the inwardly spiritual and the inwardly carnal, and the true communion of those in charity, Christ and the Spirit, including only the inwardly spiritual, gives rise to one of the most important questions in the interpretation of Augustine's ecclesiology, a question of profound historical importance for the history of the theology of church unity and division. What is the relation of the outward, visible communion to the interior, spiritual communion and what is the ecclesial status of each?

Augustine has two ways of identifying the referent of the term 'church'. Sometimes, he uses 'church' to refer to the outward communion constituted by the visible life of the church. This body is the 'great house' of 2 Tim. 2.20 referred to above, in which there are noble and ignoble vessels. It is the field of the Lord, where both wheat and tares grow until the final harvest (*c. litt. Pet.* 2.46.108). It is the threshing floor of the Lord, where wheat and chaff are both to be found (*s.* 88.19). Inevitably, this church is a *corpus permixtum* and must remain so until the divine winnower comes to separate the wheat and the chaff in the final judgement (*correct.* 2.47.110). Augustine's language in his argument with the Donatists only makes sense if this visible body is 'church'

---

[15] For Augustine, a catechumen is not yet redeemed; salvation only comes with baptism (*bapt.* 4.21.29).

in a strong sense. It is this visible body which the Donatists have left and, having done so, have left the church; it is from the visible body that they are demonstrably in schism. The vast majority of the time, when Augustine is speaking of the church, he means this visible, mixed body.

Nevertheless, Augustine will at other times insist that only the communion of the spiritual is truly the church. Properly speaking, the good are the body of Christ (*boni, qui proprie sunt corpus Christi*) (*c. Faust.* 13.16). A distinct set of biblical terms describing the church applies to this body alone. It alone is the spotless Bride of Christ, without stain or wrinkle (Eph. 5.27; *bapt.* 5.27.38). It alone is the house built on the rock (Mt. 7.24; *bapt.* 6.24.44). It alone is the 'one perfect dove' (Cant. 6.9; *bapt.* 4.3.5).[16]

Unlike membership in the external communion of the church, membership in this 'one dove' is invisible. In this life, we cannot see who truly has a repentant heart (*s.* 71.21). The evil may *appear (videntur)* to be within, but they are severed from the invisible bond of charity (*bapt.* 3.19.26). 'They appear to be in the Church, but they are not (*videntur esse in Ecclesia, sed non sunt*)' (*bapt.* 4.3.5).

Alternatively, Augustine will understand this membership eschatologically. The church which is the spotless Bride is made up of the elect who will be manifest on the Last Day. Christ's 'enclosed garden' (Cant. 4.12; another term for the church comprised only of the regenerate) is made up of 'the number of the just persons who are called according to his [God's] purpose, of whom it is said "The Lord knows those that are his" (2 Tim 2.19)' (*bapt.* 5.27.38). In Augustine's later writings, the eschatological perspective will become more prominent. In the *Retractationes*, the church with spot or wrinkle is less the present hidden church of the regenerate than the future church of glory (*retr.* 2.18). Even prior to the Pelagian controversy, however, Augustine will occasionally identify true church membership with the number of the elect who will appear as such on the Last Day (*Jo. ev. tr.* 26.15). Just who constitutes this number is unknowable, not just because regeneration is not always indicated by outward behaviour, but also because we cannot know who may either convert or fall away prior to death (*bapt.* 5.27.38).

Does Augustine have a twofold or double concept of the church: an external, visible church, constituted by the church's total life and also an interior, invisible church, united only by charity, Christ and the Spirit? As noted, Augustine's language can suggest such a duality and some interpreters have understood his ecclesiology along such lines.[17] The discussion above should

---

[16] When Augustine invokes one of these biblical terms, he often brings in others, for example, *bapt.* 4.10.17; 5.27.38.

[17] Most forcefully, Hermann Reuter in the nineteenth century. See Hermann Reuter, *Augustinische Studien* (Gotha: F. A. Perthes, 1887).

show, however, that Augustine is speaking of only one church, but a church with interior and exterior aspects; a visible, exterior life in the service of a common union with Christ and the Spirit in charity. Each side can be prioritized from different angles. On the one hand, Augustine holds that there is normally no entrance into the internal fellowship except through the external. For Augustine, Jn 3.5 – 'Unless one is born of the water and the Spirit, he cannot enter the Kingdom of God' – admits of exception only through an external obstacle that makes baptism impossible (*bapt.* 4.22.30). The external, sacramental fellowship of the church is the necessary medium of salvation. On the other hand, as noted, the internal fellowship is the end, the telos, of the external fellowship. This spiritual unity is what truly matters and in the future it, and it alone, will be the church in glory.

As Yves Congar notes, the external and internal aspects of the church relate for Augustine as *sacramentum* and *res*. The *sacramentum* exists for the sake of the *res*, but, with few exceptions, the *res* is available only through the *sacramentum*.[18] The *sacramentum* is not infallibly effective; it can fail to attain its end of renewal and in such a case, the recipient of the sacrament is not truly incorporated into the church as the communion of salvation. Thus, the church as the Body of Christ exists within the church as an external communion.

Adolf Harnack argued that Augustine's understanding of the visible church was 'full of self-contradictions'. Augustine combined but did not integrate elements pushing towards visibility and invisibility. Harnack attributed these internal tensions to Augustine's need to defend church practice.[19] Harnack is right that Augustine's language is not always consistent. His ecclesiological writings were occasional, usually prompted either by the concrete argument with the Donatists or by the exegetical pressures of explaining particular texts. He wrote no ecclesiological equivalent of *De Trinitate*. Nevertheless, as the above analysis has tried to show, his ecclesiology, while complex, is internally consistent and embodies a coherent vision of the church as a social body in the world which, through God's work in and through that body, fosters a spiritual reality that transcends this world and which will survive this world.

VI. Augustine and Ecumenism

Augustine's three levels of unity – unity in common sacraments, unity in a shared, visible communion and unity in Christ, the Spirit and charity – create

---

[18] Yves Congar, *Die Lehre von der Kirche: Von Augustinus bis zum Abendländischen Schisma* (Handbuch der Dogmengeschichte, III,3c; Freiburg: Herder, 1971), p. 5. See similarly Stanislaus J. Grabowski, *The Church: An Introduction to the Theology of St. Augustine* (St. Louis: Herder, 1957), p. 239.

[19] Adolf Harnack, *History of Dogma* (trans. Neil Buchanan; vol. 5; Boston: Little, Brown and Company, 1902), p. 163.

the template for an ecumenical outlook, in contrast to the simpler ecclesiology of the Donatists. This ecumenism is limited. One might say that it represents a pure 'ecumenism of return'. On the one hand, the Catholic Church (including at his time, of course, both the Western and Eastern churches) is the one church, within whose limits is to be found the communion of true saints. To this body all who claimed the name of Christian must return. On the other hand, beyond the church, among the schismatics and heretics, are to be found some of the elements that constitute the unity of the church – authentic sacraments and (at least if heresy is avoided) the true faith. These elements belong to the church, not to the schismatics, even when the schismatics administer them (*bapt.* 1.10.14), but that reality calls out more strongly for the church to reach out and reclaim what is its own. The church has a responsibility to seek out and correct these erring brethren precisely because they are in fact brethren.

Augustine's behaviour and language bears out this ecumenical attitude. The vigour of his theological argument with the Donatists can obscure his concrete action in seeking out forums for ordered and minimally polite conversation with the Donatist leaders.[20] He was initially reluctant to use state force to compel union (*correct.* 1.7.25) and, when he did come to support such action, insisted that this be done out of concern for those whose salvation the Donatist leaders endangered (*correct.* 1.6.23). He was in favour of bending disciplinary practice to permit reconciling Donatist clergy to exercise their ministry in the Catholic Church. 'This [permission] should not be (*Hoc non fieret*)', but to graft in a broken branch, one must cut, inflict a wound on, the mother tree so that it can receive the branch (*fit aliud vulnus in arbore, quo possit recipi*) (*correct.* 10.44). Normal discipline must be broken for the sake of peace and unity.

Almost no one today proposes an ecumenical theology precisely like Augustine's. How then can one say that his theology constitutes the air that much modern ecumenical theology breathes? The answer lies in the way Western ecumenical theology remains structured by the questions Augustine asks and the concepts he uses to answer those questions. Most notably, modern ecumenical theologies continued to be structured by the three levels or circles of unity Augustine posited. They depart from Augustine on concrete questions of how to understand the significance and interrelation of these unities.

One of the most important of modern ecumenical texts is *Unitatis redintegratio*, the Decree on Ecumenism of the Second Vatican Council.[21]

---

[20] Geoffrey Grimshaw Willis, *Saint Augustine and the Donatist Controversy* (London: S.P.C.K., 1950), pp. 36–92.

[21] Latin text and English translation in Norman P. Tanner (ed.), *Decrees of the Ecumenical Councils* (London: Sheed & Ward, 1990), p. 910. References will be given in parentheses within the text, with section number indicated. The English translation will be altered to more closely reflect the original Latin.

The ecumenical theology of the text is, in most ways, thoroughly Augustinian. There is only one church (§1). The unity of this church cannot be destroyed and is to be found in the Catholic Church (§4). The Dogmatic Constitution on the church, *Lumen gentium*, had already spoken of the communion of this church as both internal and external, 'a visible assembly and a spiritual community (*coetus adspectabilis et communitas spiritualis*)'.[22] As with Augustine, however, it is affirmed that 'some and even most of the elements and goods which together build up and vivify that Church can exist outside the visible limits of the Catholic Church' (§3). These include a valid baptism (§22).

The decisive variation from Augustine comes in relation to the effect of that baptism. For Augustine, baptism outside the communion of the church is authentic, but the gifts of baptism are not there received because schism implies a rejection of charity that blocks baptism's effect. A common baptism thus does not create a genuine communion between Catholic and schismatic for they do not share in the inner reality, the *res*, of baptism. This blanket assertion of a lack of charity is not obvious and becomes more difficult to maintain as second and third generations simply inherit division (and Augustine, despite his usual unqualified statements, himself occasionally qualifies his condemnation).[23] UR explicitly denies that all in non-Catholic communities are guilty of the sin of schism: 'those born into these separated communities and instructed (*imbuuntur*) in the faith of Christ cannot be accused of the sin of separation, and the Catholic Church embraces them as brothers, with respect and affection' (§3). Such baptism brings rebirth to divine life and incorporation into Christ (§22). Thus, a real, even if imperfect, communion exists between the Catholic Church and the truly baptized beyond its limits (§3). What Augustine does not quite assert – a true partial communion beyond the limits of visible communion – is now affirmed.

If these communities have not only valid, but also efficacious sacraments, can their communal lives be without ecclesial significance? Are they more than 'schisms', but in some sense 'church'? They do, after all, grant access to the communion of salvation (§3). In line with earlier tradition, UR recognizes the Orthodox Churches as church (§14)[24] and sees the communities that emerged from the Reformation in the West as 'ecclesial communities', communities

---

[22] In Tanner, *Decrees of the Ecumenical Councils*, p. 854, par. 8.

[23] For example: 'But though the doctrine which men hold be false and perverse, if they do not maintain it with passionate obstinacy, especially when they have not devised it by the rashness of their own presumption, but have accepted it from parents who had been misguided and had fallen into error, and if they are with anxiety seeking the truth, and are prepared to be set right when they have found it, such men are not to be counted heretics' (*ep.* 43.1.1). This passage is quoted by Aquinas, *ST* II-II, q. 11, a. 2, ad. 3; cf. Augustine, *c. litt. Pet.* 2.97.221.

[24] The tradition for this recognition is given in the references listed in note 19 to chapter 1 of UR.

whose lives bear an ecclesial significance, even if they cannot be said to be church in the full sense (§22).

This variation on Augustine's scheme means that the distinctions among the three circles of unity begin to blur, though the basic structure remains. What does the real, but imperfect communion of the Catholic Church with those within the circle of authentic sacraments, but outside the circle of visible communion, imply? Does the truly regenerate member of an ecclesial community have a closer communion with the interior communion of the Body of Christ than does the unregenerate Catholic? For a theologian such as Yves Congar, whose theological work influenced UR, 'the personal case of the good dissident is plainly better than that of the bad Catholic, though both, in truth, are in an abnormal and irregular situation'.[25] Vatican II carefully avoids saying whether or not a faithful member of a non-Catholic community is a 'member' of the church.

UR's variation on Augustine derives from a shift on one central question: the efficacy of non-Catholic sacraments. Its ecumenism is more vigorous, for the ecumenical problem is deepened. Beyond the visible communion of the Catholic Church are to be found efficacious sacraments, genuine Christians, and communities with a true ecclesial character (in the case of the Orthodox, the church in its essentials). The ecumenical call becomes compelling.

A second, more radical variation on Augustine's ecumenical theology is more typical of much recent ecumenism, especially in Protestant circles. If efficacious sacraments and true Christian communities exist beyond the limits of any one church body, then the church as true spiritual communion becomes more closely tied to the presence of common sacraments (the first, non-ecclesial circle of unity found in Augustine) and separate from the visible communion of a common Eucharist and church life that constitute a distinct church (the second circle of unity for Augustine). The circles of unity are concentric, but their order is changed and the visible communion fragmented. The largest circle is constituted by common faith and sacraments. Within and smaller than that circle (since word and sacrament do not always work saving faith) is the circle of those united with Christ, who thus make up the one, indivisible church. Within that circle are then a variety of smaller circles of unity, constituted by a common church life, most notably a common Eucharist.

What Augustine held together as two aspects of the church, visible and spiritual, become discrete realities. As noted above, Augustine most often uses term 'church' to refer to the visible communion, existing as a *corpus permixtum*, but will also use the term to refer only to the true spiritual communion in Christ, to which alone are reserved certain theological predicates.

---

[25] Yves Congar, *Divided Christendom: A Catholic Study of the Problem of Reunion* (London: Geoffrey Bles, 1939), p. 235.

For this more Protestant ecumenical perspective, however, Augustine's less than consistent language becomes a systematic distinction. The visible and the spiritual pull apart, so that the spiritual communion in Christ is no longer the end achieved by the means of visible communion, the *res* attached to the visible sacramental communion, but becomes a relatively independent reality, which the visible communion only imperfectly realizes or expresses.

An example of such an outlook is the statement on unity from the 1961 New Delhi Assembly of the World Council of Churches. The assembly states: 'We believe that we share in this unity in the Church of Jesus Christ, who is before all things and in whom all things hold together.' A spiritual unity exists in which they participate, despite division. This unity seeks visible expression: 'We believe that the unity which is both God's will and his gift to his Church is being made visible as all in each place who are baptized into Jesus Christ and confess him as Lord and Saviour are brought by the Holy Spirit into one fully committed fellowship . . .'[26] The ecumenical quest begins in an existent spiritual unity and then seeks expression in the life of visible communion.

While the end result is different from Augustine's refusal to find the church outside its visible communion, the questions and concepts are still recognizably Augustinian. The analysis begins in the recognition of authentic sacraments beyond one's own communion. Like *UR*, these sacraments are seen as not only valid, but also efficacious in the full sense. That recognition is radicalized into a recognition of a spiritual unity which is the true spiritual unity of the church and of multiple, equally authentic churches. The result is a separation of the church as spiritual communion in Christ and the Spirit from the church as shared life in a single visible communion. The ecumenical task so to bring the divided life of the church as visible, exterior communion into line with the reality of the ultimately undivided unity of the church as inward, spiritual communion.

V. Conclusion

Ecumenical theology always has an ecclesiological element, for the goal is always a closer approach to the unity Christ intends for those who love him. A greater self-consciousness about the assumptions that govern how we think about the church and its unity is thus a significant ecumenical desideratum. Awareness of the Augustinian background of much of our thought about the church and its unity will make us more sensitive to the possibilities and limits of the standard models of ecumenical theology. By seeing how different ways of thinking of ecumenism are variations of a shared background in Augustine,

---

[26] Michael Kinnamon and Brian E. Cope (eds), *The Ecumenical Movement: An Anthology of Key Texts and Voices* (Geneva: WCC Publications, 1997), p. 88.

Catholics and Protestants can more clearly perceive what they do and do not share in their basic beliefs about the ecumenical task. Most especially, a sensitivity to these Augustinian assumptions can foster a deeper engagement with the Orthodox, who do not share those assumptions. East and West need to mutually challenge one another within a common pursuit of a deeper and more faithful understanding of the church. In that quest, careful thought about Augustine is an absolute necessity.

For Further Reading

Congar, Yves, *Divided Christendom: A Catholic Study of the Problem of Reunion* (London: Geoffrey Bles, 1939).

Evans, Gillian R., *The Church and the Churches: Toward an Ecumenical Ecclesiology* (Cambridge: Cambridge University Press, 1994).

Grabowski, Stanislaus J., *The Church: An Introduction to the Theology of St. Augustine* (St. Louis: Herder, 1957).

Hofmann, Fritz, *Der Kirchenbegriff des Hl. Augustinus, in seinen Grundlagen und in seiner Entwicklung* (Münster: Antiquariat Th. Stenderhoff, 1978).

Sagovsky, Nicholas, *Ecumenism, Christian Origins, and the Practice of Communion* (Cambridge: Cambridge University Press, 2000).

Van Bavel, Tarsicius J., 'Church'. In *Augustine through the Ages: An Encyclopedia* (ed. Allan D. Fitzgerald; Grand Rapids: Eerdmans, 1999), pp. 169–76.

5 Augustine on Scripture

Tarmo Toom

> You, my dear and revered brother, if you wish to be truly informed about these matters . . . take the trouble of reading Augustine's own tracts.
>
> (Prosper of Aquitaine, *ep. Ruf.* 18)

I. Augustine's Way into Scripture

Augustine was aware of Christianity and its Scripture since his childhood (*c. Acad.* 2.2.5; *ep.* 137.3; cf. 2 Tim. 3:15, but see *conf.* 3.4.8), yet he lacked interest in these things. At the age of 19, he picked up Scripture once again, but to his disappointment, he discovered only contradictions and a mass of dubious, even offensive stories. He confesses, 'I was not in any state to be able to enter into [the Scriptures], or to bow my head to climb its steps' (*conf.* 3.5.9). Bishop Augustine assessed that the young Augustine had been 'a bitter and blind critic [who was] barking at the Scriptures' (*conf.* 9.4.11). Indeed, having refined his taste for eloquence (Cicero!), the adolescent Augustine remained deeply disturbed by the stylistic 'unworthiness' (*indignitas*) of the Word of God (*conf.* 3.5.9).

After becoming a Manichean 'hearer' (*auditor*), Augustine came to share his sect's interest in the writings of Paul.[1] Manicheans rejected the Old Testament though. Faustus says in his *Capitula*, 'I do not mix Christian newness with Hebrew oldness' (Augustine, *c. Faust.* 8.1), and adds, 'The testimonies of the Hebrews contribute nothing to the Christian Church [i.e. to the Manichean *ecclesia*]' (*c. Faust.* 13.1). Manicheans were disturbed by such things as the shameless behaviour of the Old Testament patriarchs and anthropomorphic descriptions of God. So was Augustine (*util. cred.* 16.13). Moreover, Manicheans accepted only the 'purified' gospels[2] and the letters of Paul. In

---

[1] R. J. Teske, 'Augustine, the Manichees and the Bible', in *Augustine and the Bible* (ed. P. Bright; The Bible through the Ages 2; Notre Dame: University of Notre Dame Press, 1986), pp. 208–21; M. Cameron, *Christ Meets Me Everywhere: Augustine's Early Figurative Exegesis* (Oxford Studies in Historical Theology; ed. D. C. Steinmetz; Oxford: Oxford University Press, 2012), pp. 251–63.

[2] That is, purified from the alleged 'interpolations' which did not confirm the doctrines of Mani (Augustine, *c. Faust.* 11.2). However, Manicheans were unable to produce any manuscripts of the un-interpolated gospels or letters, which clearly showed that they were just making up their theories about interpolation-free originals (*mor.* 1.29.61).

addition, they also rejected the book of Acts,[3] the 'misleading' genealogies of Jesus and some other parts of the New Testament. Augustine later assesses, 'You [i.e. Manicheans] attack the Scriptures of the New Testament as falsified and corrupted . . . and blame many things in those books in which you approve some things' (*c. Faust.* 32.8).

Augustine's eventual flirtation with scepticism brought about a slow realization that, in fact, his Manichean understanding of Scripture as well as the church's teaching was just wrong. He realized that 'the books of the church' did not contain the absurd teachings that he thought they did (*conf.* 6.11.18). The young wisdom-searcher began to wonder and 'with avid intensity . . . seized the sacred writings of your Spirit and especially apostle Paul' (*conf.* 7.21.27; cf. *c. Acad.* 2.2.5).

Moreover, soon Ambrose demonstrated how to read Scripture for spiritual benefit and how to overcome contradictions in texts with the help of figurative interpretation (*conf.* 5.14.24; 6.4.6; cf. *doc. Chr.* 3.5.9–3.25.35). Augustine discovered a new and wonderful way of reading the Word of God. The former arrogant critic of style, who was moving 'from snobbish disdain to unrestrained admiration',[4] now said about Scripture, 'The surface meaning lies open before us and charms the beginners. Yet the depth is amazing, my God, the depth is amazing' (*conf.* 12.14.17; cf. *en. Ps.* 105.35).[5] 'Holy Scripture . . . speaks in such a way as to mock proud readers with its heights, terrify the attentive with its depths, feed great souls with its truth and nourish little ones with sweetness' (*Gen. litt.* 5.3.6).

Immediately after his ordination (391), Augustine took time off in order to study Scripture (*ep.* 21). After all, his future duty was to be a '[preacher] of Your word' (*conf.* 11.2.2). Roughly by the time Augustine began his ministry as a bishop, he had already commented twice on the book of Genesis and Apostle Paul's letter to Romans, once on Jesus' sermon on the Mount, Paul's letter to Galatians and had begun his mammoth commentary on the Psalms.[6] Later, and next to his sermons, polemical writings, and other exegetical works, he added a 12-book literal commentary on the book of Genesis, a set of selected exegetical questions on the Heptateuch, a study on the agreement of the four evangelists, over hundred sermons on the Gospel

---

[3] The book of Acts said nothing about the Holy Spirit being Mani (Augustine, *c. Adim.* 17.5; *c. Faust.* 19.31).

[4] K. Froehlich, '"Take Up and Read": Basics of Augustine's Biblical Interpretation', *Interpretation* 58/1 (2004), pp. 5–16 (p. 5).

[5] See T. Finan, 'St. Augustine on the "*mira profunditas*" of Scripture: Texts and Contexts', in *Scriptural Interpretation in the Fathers: Letter and Spirit* (ed. T. Finan and V. Twomey; Dublin: Four Courts, 1995), pp. 163–99.

[6] *Expositio epistulae ad Galatas* is Augustine's only commentary on the *entire* biblical book (*retr.* 1.24). *Enarrationes Psalmos* skips a few Psalms.

of John and finally an anthology of the moral precepts in Scripture called *Speculum*.[7]

II. What Scripture Is and What It Is about

What Scripture is believed to be determines the way it is approached. Hence, it is important to consider Augustine's dynamic doctrine of Scripture,[8] which has to be reconstructed from numerous statements in various treatises.

Augustine was convinced that God spoke (and speaks) in and through Scripture. The convictions that God spoke, communicated and expressed concern (Heb. 1.1–2) were bold convictions in the light of the prevailing (Neo–) platonism of the time. Furthermore, the conviction that God spoke through a sensible, material medium seemed strange and even somewhat degrading for the intelligible, spiritual God. Nevertheless, Augustine's Christian faith affirmed both the 'speaking God' as well as the usefulness of material means, such as human languages and written texts for human comprehension of this 'speaking God'.

For Augustine, Scripture is a unique case of God's communication with the humankind and, as such, it is supposed to be perceived as a means in the larger context of economy.[9] Scripture addresses the postlapsarian humankind which is preoccupied with the sensible realm and thus needs to be attended to through what is sensible (i.e. what can be seen and heard) (*vera rel.* 30). In the communicative process of semiosis,[10] Scripture functions as a system of sensible, referential linguistic signs.[11] At the same time, the words of Scripture

---

[7] There are two early catalogues of Augustine's writings: his own *Retractationes* and Possidius's *Indiculum*. In addition, a sixth-century monk Eugippius compiled a 1,000-page anthology of the writings of Augustine, which was organized according to the order of canonical books of the Bible. Later something similar, but in a lesser scale, was also compiled by Bede and Florus of Lyons, until in the seventeenth century, David Lenfant put together his massive *Biblia Augustiniana*. Anne-Marie La Bonnardière's seven-volume *Biblia Augustiana* (Paris: Études augustiniennes, 1960–75) is a modern, critical and chronological study of Augustine's citations of Scripture.

[8] For the distinction between a doctrine and a theology of Scripture, see F. Watson, 'Hermeneutics and the Doctrine of Scripture: Why They Need Each Other', *IJST* 12/2 (2010), pp. 118–43 (pp. 122–23). I have used the designation 'Scripture' (singular), except in citations, in order to highlight its theological status as God's continuous communication vis-à-vis 'the Scriptures' (plural) as a collection of ancient religious texts.

[9] For Augustine, Scripture was a 'second-order' revelation; that is, not unimportant, but secondary to *the* revelation in the incarnated Son of God. Cf. *The Bible: Its Authority and Interpretation in the Ecumenical Movement* (Geneva: WWC, 1980), p. 47; *Scripture and Tradition: Lutherans and Catholics in Dialogue* (ed. H. C. Skillrud, J. Francis Stafford, Daniel F. Martensen; Minneapolis: Augsburg, 1995), par. 5.

[10] Semiotics is involved whenever any kind of information about something is communicated through sensible, mediating signs (Augustine, *dial.* 5; *doc. Chr.* 2.1.1).

[11] That is, words are sensible signs (*signa*), whether written or spoken, which point beyond themselves to things or intelligible realities (*res*).

are also the 'divinely given signs' (*signa divinitus data*) which reveal the will of God (*doc. Chr.* 2.2.3; *conf.* 12.23.32; cf. Eph. 1.9) as well as direct one's attention from the sensible realm to the intelligible realm (Augustine, *mag.* 8.24.150; 10.35.170; 11.36.1; cf. Rom. 1.20). However, words as signs do not only reveal but they also obscure and veil the realities to which they refer (Augustine, *c. Acad.* 3.17.39; *div. qu.* 9; *doc. Chr.* 2.10.15). After all, the actual words in Scripture are but conventional signs in human languages, given deliberately by human beings.[12] This means that God's Word is mediated through human words (all words are human words!) as well as that such mediation often sets its own impediments to the process of communication.[13]

Hence, while trying to understand what Scripture is, one has to take into consideration two factors: the divine Word and the human words.[14] Augustine kept these two factors together with the help of his orthodox Christology (*Jo. ev. tr.* 19.15; 27.4; *s.* 137.3.9; 186.1). According to *doc. Chr.* 1.13 and *Trin.* 15.20, just as the Word of God became flesh (Jn. 1.14), the divine speech also assumed a sensible medium (i.e. audible speech or visible text) in order to communicate the divine will to human beings (Augustine, *doc. Chr.* 2.5.6; *Jo. ev. tr.* 13.4). The perceptible humanity of Christ is a sign which communicates his divinity, and the readable/audible words of Scripture are the signs which communicate that which God has in mind. Moreover, and although this analogy, too, is not exact,[15] just as the incarnated God has two natures in one person, the divine Word and the human words constitute the one Scripture. Such analogy provides a balanced view of Scripture.[16]

So, on the one hand, Scripture is the divine speech.[17] As such, 'the Scriptures are holy, they are truthful, they are blameless' (*s.* 23.3).

---

[12] For conveying both the intentionality and conventionality of word-signs, Augustine employs the designation *signa data*.

[13] See T. Toom, 'Augustine on the "Communicative Gaps" in Book Two of *De doctrina Christiana*', *AugStud* 34/2 (2003), pp. 213–22.

[14] For comparison, *Dei Verbum* contends that, in Scripture, God 'employed human agents' (pp. 11–12), 'their powers and faculties' (p. 12) as well as their 'language[s]' (p. 13), for revealing himself and his will to humankind. Cf. the Preface to *The Interpretation of the Bible in the Church* (Pontifical Biblical Commission, 1993), and ARCIC *Authority I* (1979), p. 2.

[15] Augustine does not enhypostasize the 'letter' into the divine person. Although he uses the adjective 'divine' (*divina*) to speak about Scripture (e.g. *en. Ps.* 8.7, 10.10; *ep. Jo.* 3.1), he urges nevertheless, 'We must not equate this Word with our own words' (*f. et sym.* 2.3).

[16] The word 'balanced' does not mean that the divine and human aspects are perfectly equal entities, although they are equally important entities. Rather, it attempts to prevent a postulation of a one-sided view. The orthodox Christology, too, is an 'asymmetrical Christology'.

[17] Augustine uses the phrases *verbum Dei* and *sermo Dei* interchangeably (e.g. *s.* 4.31; 5.1). *Catechism of the Catholic Church* 104 reminds one that Scripture should be accepted 'not as a human word but as what it really is, the word of God' (1 Thess. 2.13).

First, as the divine speech, Scripture is holy (e.g. *en. Ps.* 103[1].9; *ep. Jo.* 2.1). To be holy means to be reserved for a special divine purpose and be rejuvenated by the *Holy* Spirit (*en. Ps.* 45.8). The notion of 'sanctification', which concerns the divine use of created realities, may be particularly helpful in perceiving Scripture as the means of the divine speech.[18]

Second, because the God of truth is the primary 'author' of Scripture,[19] its message is true (Ps. 119.160; Jn. 17.17). 'Lord, surely your Scripture is true, for you, being truthful and Truth itself, have produced it' (*conf.* 13.29.44; cf. *Gen. litt.* 4.34.53).[20] 'Have [the Scriptures] deceived us on any point, have they made any prediction that misled us, in that things turned out differently? No, indeed!' (*en. Ps.* 39.28).[21]

Third, Scripture is 'blameless' in what it asserts (Ps. 12.6; Prov. 30.5). 'Of these [i.e. the canonical Scriptures] alone do I most firmly believe that the authors were completely free from error' (Augustine, *ep.* 82.1.3).[22] Augustine did not have a favourite theory about inspiration, although he was quite sure about the fact that God spoke in a special way through the canonical writings.

---

[18] J. Webster, *Holy Scriptures: A Dogmatic Sketch* (Current Issues in Theology; ed. I. Torrance; Cambridge: Cambridge University Press, 2003), pp. 17–30.

[19] The Latin word *auctor* is of late provenance and of a wide semantic field. Arguably, it was not applied to God in connection with Scripture before Augustine (B. Vawter, *Biblical Inspiration* [London: Hutchinson, 1972], p. 25; cf. Augustine, *en. Ps.* 104.27). The first conciliar statement about God's 'authorship' of Scripture is *Statua Ecclesia Antiqua* of the fifth century (*DS*, 325). *Dei Verbum* in turn calls God the 'author/originator' (*auctorem*) of Scripture (11). Cf. Leo XIII, *Providentissimus Deus* 1, 23; Vatican I, *De revelatione*; *The Gift of Scripture* 14–15, 23; *The Interpretation of the Bible in the Church* II, B1; *Scripture and Tradition*, par. 7; *Catechism of the Catholic Church* 105.

[20] To be precise, for Augustine, the Truth (with a capital 'T') is a larger category than the true meanings of Scripture (Augustine, *conf.* 12.24.33–25.34; *doc. Chr.* 3.27.38). Augustine just could not equate Truth with something that exists in the human language, be this the biblical Hebrew, Greek or Latin! He found Jerome's favourite notion *Hebraica veritas* inadequate precisely because, by appealing to it, Jerome seemed to identify truth with a linguistic phenomenon (i.e. with the Hebrew text of Scripture).

[21] There was a controversy about the absolute truthfulness of Scripture between Augustine and Jerome (Augustine, *ep.* 28, 40, 71, 73, 82; *ex. Gal.* 15.6–11, 1.2.11–14; Jerome, *ep.* 102, 106, 112, 115). This controversy led Augustine to a convinced assertion: 'If we admit in that supreme authority even one polite lie, there will be nothing left of these books' (*ep.* 28.3.3; cf. *pat.* 26.22).

[22] *Dei Verbum* 11, too, uses the phrase 'without error' (*sine errore*) (cf. Vatican I, *De revelatione*, Pius XII, *Divino Afflante Spiritu* 21), but not the word 'inerrant' which has gained a particular meaning among fundamentalists. While previous proposals for *Dei Verbum*, Forms A to C, did employ the word 'inerrant' in their titles, Form D dropped it (R. Bieringer, 'Biblical Revelation and Exegetical Interpretation According to *Dei Verbum* 12', in *Vatican II and Its Legacy* [ed. M. Lamberigts and L. Kenis; Bibliotheca Ephemeridium Theologicarum Lovaniensium 166; Leuven: Leuven University Press, 2002], pp. 25–58 [p. 36]). For the denominational differences about the issue of inerrancy, see 'Report on Sacred Scripture' (Southern Baptists-Roman Catholic Conversations, 1999).

T&T Clark Companion to Augustine and Modern Theology

One of his oft-used phrases was indeed 'the divinely inspired Scriptures' (e.g. *civ. Dei* 11.3; *ep.* 147.7; cf. the *divinitus inspirata* of 2 Tim. 3.16). Augustine can even say that God 'dictated' his words to human co-authors (Augustine, *en. Ps.* 62.1; *cons. Ev.* 1.35.54; *s.* 299B.3),[23] but the verb *dictare* must not mean passive instrumentality and should not be filled, anachronistically, with the narrow dogmatic meaning that it acquired later.[24] The verb *dictare* can also be rendered as 'charge, direct, urge, incite'.[25]

In addition and fourth, Augustine mentions 'the perfect clarity of scriptural expressions' (*ep.* 82.2.6; cf. Ps. 119.130) as well as 'the most plain and clear utterances of the apostles' (*cat. rud.* 18.68). He wrote enough exegetical treatises on seeming contradictions (e.g. *De consensu Evangelistarum, Locutionum in Heptateuchum*) to know that Scripture was sometimes anything but clear. Yet, his point is that Scripture can be trusted as a clear and secure guide in faith, morals and salvation (*doc. Chr.* 2.9.14; *pecc. mer.* 2.59).[26] He further contends that at least some things in Scripture are said with ultimate clarity (*ep.* 137.5.18), and these clear passages function as a hermeneutical key to the more obscure ones. 'Instances from the plainer passages are used to cast light on the more obscure passages' (*doc. Chr.* 2.9.14; cf. 2.6.8; 3.27.38–28.39; *cat. rud.* 18.68; *civ. Dei* 11.19; *c. Adim.* 17.5; *c. Faust.* 12.7; *en. Ps.* 10.8).

The belief that Scripture is, above all, the divine speech has some important implications. To mention two: (1) everything said in Scripture matters and (2) no one can exhaust its meaning(s).

First, whatever else inspiration might mean for Augustine, it means that Scripture is spiritually 'useful' (2 Tim. 3.16). He asserts that the biblical events 'were not recorded under the guidance of the Holy Spirit for nothing' (*ex. Gal.* 40.7). Rather, the words of Scripture, all of them, are 'useful signs' (*signa utilia*) (*doc. Chr.* 3.8.12). Augustine reiterates, 'No detail [in the Scriptures], therefore is pointless, everything has a meaning' (*Jo. ev. tr.* 24.6; cf. *c. Faust.* 22.96). His conviction that the divine Spirit secured the occurrence of particular words in Scripture inevitably led to such a conclusion.

Second, the riches of Scripture are inexhaustible. Augustine admits that even in his old age, he was 'still daily making progress in discovering their treasures'; he was still making progress, because 'so many things . . . veiled under manifold shadows of mystery remain to be inquired' (*ep.* 137.3). Texts

---

[23] Cf. the Council of Trent, *Sacrosancta oecumenica*; Leo XIII, *Providentissimus Deus* 5, 20; Vatican I, *De revelatione*.

[24] One should consider the fact that while writing to Jerome, who was neither an apostle nor a bishop, Augustine mentions nevertheless the words that the Spirit had 'dictated' to Jerome (*ep.* 82.1.2).

[25] A. D. R. Polman, *The Word of God According to St. Augustine* (Grand Rapids: Eerdmans, 1961), p. 45.

[26] Cf. *Dei Verbum* 11; 5th Plenary of the Lutheran-Orthodox Joint Commission (1989), B13.

have many true meanings (e.g. *conf.* 12.13.16–22.31; *en. Ps.* 118[5].2; *ex. Gal.* 13.6–7; 17.1–2) and therefore, it is impossible to figure out all the true meanings as well as to arrive at the one and the only true meaning.[27]

After all these considerations, one should realize that it is one thing to eagerly collect statements which speak very highly about Scripture – and these are virtually endless in Augustine's writings – and another to fit these statements into the framework of his philosophy of language and linguistic signification.

Thus, on the other hand, the truly human aspect of Scripture needs to be acknowledged as well. Augustine definitely affirms the human agency in the writing and translating Scripture. In order to communicate, '[God] employed the ministry of mortal men and made use of mortal instruments' (*en. Ps.* 103[1].8; cf. *civ. Dei* 18.41).[28] This means that God's Word is a humanly mediated word (Preface to *De doctrina Christiana* 6; cf. 2 Pet. 1.21) and, despite being inspired, Scripture retains the limitations of human words and languages – ambiguity, obscurity, vagueness, temporality and mutability.[29] Words as signs (*signa*) have only an approximate correspondence to the things (*res*) they signify. That is, the signs are never identical with the things signified, for otherwise they would cease to be signs. Consequently, the very perception of words as signs has its own important implication to Augustine's doctrine of Scripture.

In addition, although it is certainly possible to express true statements about God in human language, linguistic expressions nevertheless prove to be inadequate for speaking about God.[30] 'What has anyone achieved in words when he speaks about you?' (Augustine, *conf.* 1.4.4). Human words and languages are part of the created world, part of the finite reality, which come

---

[27] Augustine also postulates a set of hermeneutical controls, such as *caritas* and *regula fidei*, which help to avoid relativity and to discern between legitimate and arbitrary meanings. For him, there are interpretations which are clearly inadequate (*c. ep. Man.* 6; *Gen. adv. Man.* 7.8; *util. cred.* 14.31).

[28] Augustine uses 'the ablative for the work of the Holy Spirit and the preposition *per* for that of biblical authors' (Polman, *The Word of God According to St. Augustine*, p. 51). Cf. 'Theology Today: Perspectives, Principles, and Criteria' 8, International Theological Commission 2011 at: www.vatican.va/roman_curia/congregations/cfaith/cti_documents/rc_cti_doc_20111129_teologia-oggi_en.html, which quotes Augustine's *civ. Dei* 17.6 and urges to understand 'the Word of God in the human words of the holy Scriptures'.

[29] 'Every word is ambiguous' (Augustine, *dial.* 9). At times, the words are also obscure and difficult to understand (*conf.* 11.2.3; *c. Faust.* 19.31; *doc. Chr.* 2.6.7; *en. Ps.* 35.1; 54.22; 68[2].1). Worse still, sometimes 'even the obscurity is not evident' (*en. Ps.* 118 prologue), which makes it especially hard to understand Scripture properly. For the reasons why some things in Scripture are said in an obscure way, see *conf.* 11.2.3; *doc. Chr.* 2.6.7; *en. Ps.* 103(2).1; *ep.* 55.21; 137.18; *s.* 60A.

[30] P. van Geest, *The Incomprehensibility of God: Augustine as a Negative Theologian* (Late Antique History and Religion; ed. H. Amirav et al.; Leuven: Peters, 2011).

short of the infinite God the Creator in a very fundamental way. God's 'magnificence has surpassed the words of all the Scriptures, because it surpasses and stretches beyond the proclamations of all words and tongues' (*en. Ps.* 8.8). Even though Scripture is authoritative, holy, true, blameless and clear, it inevitably 'shares the limitations of the human condition', because it exists in a linguistic form.[31]

Consequently, in *doc. Chr.* 1.39.43, Augustine surprises many by saying that those who have a good grip on theological virtues 'have no need of the Scriptures except for instructing others'. This notorious statement is actually a logical outcome of a combination of an understanding of Scripture as a system of signs, *uti/frui* distinction,[32] and the words of the Apostle Paul about love in 1 Cor. 13. There are things which are to be used and left behind (Augustine, *doc. Chr.* 1.4.4; *Jo. ev. tr.* 2.2–3; cf. Plotinus, *Enn.* I.6.8), and things which are to be enjoyed eternally. Compared with *caritas* which 'abides', Scripture 'passes away' (1 Cor. 13.13).[33] It 'passes away', because everything that exists in language and is sensible is thereby also finite, transitory, contingent. After all, Scripture is a soteriological means, something to be 'used', and not the *res*, something to be 'enjoyed'. It is *not* that Augustine is throwing the Bible out of the window. He only argues that the Bible is not the ultimate object of worship and enjoyment. God is! This is the reason why those who already 'enjoy' God, no longer need Scripture.

The statement in *doc. Chr.* 1.39.43 is not an accidental, one-time slip of the tongue of Augustine, because at about the same time that he finished book 4 of *De doctrina Christiana*, he wrote, 'All the Scriptures – which were lit for us like lamps in the night of this world's age so that we might not remain in darkness – [will] be removed from our midst. With all these taken away, lest they should go on shining as though we needed them . . . [we behold the] true and brilliant Light' (*Jo. ev. tr.* 35.9).

Once again, this is to say that Scripture belongs to the 'temporal dispensation' (*dispensatio temporalis*) (*doc. Chr.* 1.35.39) (i.e. the divine economy), and that 'the usefulness of the temporal dispensation itself is temporary'.[34]

Arguably, Augustine's Platonic conviction was that the lower sensible things (e.g. words) cannot really have an effect on the higher intelligible

---

[31] P. Bright, 'St. Augustine', in *Christian Theologies of the Scripture: A Comparative Introduction* (ed. J. S. Holcomb; New York: New York University Press, 2006), pp. 39–59 (p. 46).

[32] Augustine, *div. qu.* 30; *doc. Chr.* 1.3.3–4.4. The eternal and unchangeable God alone is to be enjoyed (*frui*), while everyone and everything else – in fact, the whole created reality – is to be used (*uti*).

[33] In Mt. 5.18, the evangelist says that the Law will be around 'until heaven and earth disappear' and 'until everything is accomplished'. Mk. 13.31 makes a stronger claim.

[34] P. Cary, *Outward Signs: The Powerlessness of External Things in Augustine's Thought* (Oxford: Oxford University Press, 2008), p. 138.

realities.[35] If such conviction is absolutized, then Scripture cannot reveal much about God and it should perhaps be ignored altogether! Yet and despite Augustine's basic Platonic stance, he also affirms the usefulness of the sensible things and is convinced that Scripture reveals God, the *signa* reveal the *res* (*gr. et lib. arb.* 2; *s.* 12.4).[36] In *c. Faust.* 19.16, Augustine reaffirms at least the lasting, beneficial effect of Scripture and other sensible *signa*: 'All these take place and pass away; they sound and pass away. Yet the power that works through them remains constant, and the spiritual gift that is signified by them is eternal.' Therefore, Scripture as the Word of God can also be said to 'abide forever' (Isa. 40.8), although, in the eternal presence of the Word, words are no longer needed (Augustine, *conf.* 13.15.18).[37]

Finally, what is Scripture about? In order to understand what a sign signifies, one has to have some knowledge of the thing signified. Therefore, before Augustine offers some guidance to future exegetes in *De doctrina Christiana* (books 2 and 3), he discusses the overall reference of Scripture (book 1). The reference, that which Scripture is all about, the *res*,[38] is God's salvific activity in the incarnated Christ. Augustine prefers to define the reference of Scripture even more succinctly – it is the double love of God and neighbour (Mt. 22.37–40). 'What is the highest reach of God's Scripture? The precept of charity!' (Augustine, *cat. rud.* 4.8; *doc. Chr.* 1.35.39; *en. Ps.* 103[2].3; 140.2). God is love and therefore, God's Word is about love. Everything in Scripture has to be interpreted in accordance with this insight (*div. qu.* 68.6; *doc. Chr.* 1.36.41; 40.44).

III. The Canon and the Unity of Scripture

Augustine recommended the reading of the whole Scripture (*doc. Chr.* 2.8.12) and the memorization of as much of it as possible (*doc. Chr.* 2.9.14). However, the problem is that there was no uniform understanding yet of what the 'whole Scripture' was. 'Augustine never saw a Bible',[39] that is, a one-volume codex of the whole Bible. In the fourth century, the designation 'Scripture' did not yet denote a universally agreed upon and closed collection of inspired

---

[35] Ibid., 7; cf. Augustine, *mag.* 10.33.115.
[36] Cary, *Outward Signs*, pp. 43, 87.
[37] Here the analogy with the two natures of Christ breaks down. Rather than being abandoned, the body/flesh of Christ is resurrected, transformed and divinized. Languages, however, do cease to exist (*Jo. ev. tr.* 22.2). True, in *Jo. ev. tr.* 19.18, Augustine also states that 'the slave form will pass away'. Yet, he does not mean that the humanity of Christ ceases to exist. See *Trin.* 1.8.15, *c. s. Ar.* 37 and Cameron, *Christ Meets Me Everywhere*, pp. 228–31.
[38] See H.-J. Sieben, 'Die "res" der Bibel: Eine Analyse von Augustinus, *De doctr. christ.* I-III', *REtAug* 21 (1975), pp. 72–90.
[39] J. J. O'Donnell, 'Bible', in *Augustine through the Ages: An Encyclopedia* (ed. A. D. Fitzgerald; Grand Rapids: Eerdmans, 1999), pp. 99–103 (p. 99).

writings.[40] Therefore, the recommendation 'to read them all' was ambiguous and Augustine had to explain that by 'all' he meant only 'those pronounced canonical' (*doc. Chr.* 2.8.12).[41]

For Augustine, the canonical Scripture has 'the highest normative authority' (*conf.* 12.16.23; cf. *civ. Dei* 11.3; *c. Faust.* 11.5; *ep.* 82.2.5; 148.4.15). 'I have learned to yield ... respect and honor only to the canonical books of Scripture' (*ep.* 82.1.3). No other writings – not even those of the esteemed bishop Cyprian or the proceedings of the Council of Carthage – measure up the authority of the canonical Scripture (*Cresc.* 2.31, 38; *ep.* 93.10.35–6; 28*.3).

The bishop of Hippo was right in the middle of the church's attempts to find a consensus about which sacred writings were canonical. He participated in the Council of Hippo (393) and the Council of Carthage (397), both of which discussed the question of the canon.[42] Augustine provides his list of canonical books in *doc. Chr.* 2.8.13,[43] which diverges from modern versions only by the order of some writings. He organizes the 44 books of the Old Testament (LXX) according to what is history (or narrative) (*historia*) and what is prophecy (*prophetia*).[44] As far as the 27 books of the New Testament are concerned, the most significant feature is the placement of the book of Acts right before the book of Revelation. Augustine also points out that individual churches have their own final lists which do not always agree with each other (*doc. Chr.* 2.8.12). Evidently, there was still some indeterminacy about the precise list of canonical books.[45]

Above all, there was the difference between the Hebrew and the Greek canons. In *De doctrina Christiana*, Augustine makes no mention of this difference, but in his later writings, he is clearly aware of it (*civ. Dei* 17.20 and *c. Gaud.* 1.31.38). Nevertheless, he gives priority to the Septuagint as the traditional

---

[40] For what can be known about the Bible in Roman Africa in the beginning of the fifth century, see P.-M. Bogaert, 'Les bibles d'Augustin', in *Saint Augustin et la Bible. Actes du colloque de l'université Paul Verlaine-Metz (7–8 avril 2005)* (ed. G. Nauroy and M.-A. Vannier; *Recherches en literature et spiritualité* 15; Bern: Peter Lang, 2008), pp. 17–36 (pp. 17–28).

[41] Cf. Canon 36 of the *Breviarium Hipponense* (CCL 149). For the would-be apocrypha, see Augustine, *civ. Dei* 18.38 and *ep.* 237.

[42] CCL 149, pp. 21 and 43. The earliest known Latin conciliar list of the canon of Scripture comes from the year 382, when Pope Damasus held a council in Rome. For other lists, see Jerome, *ep.* 53; Rufinus, *exp.* 37; Innocent I, *ep.* 'Consulenti tibi'; and Junillus, *Inst.* 1.3–6.

[43] This list is repeated in Cassiodorus, *Inst.* 1.13.1.

[44] For various divisions of the Old Testament canon, the number of books and the closure of the canon, see A.-M. La Bonnardière, 'The Canon of Sacred Scripture', in *Augustine and the Bible*, pp. 26–41; G. Dorival, 'L'apport des Pères de l'Église à la question de la clôture du canon de l'Ancien Testament', in *The Biblical Canons* (ed. J.-M. Auwers and H. J. De Jonge; *Bibliotheca Ephemeridum Theologicarum Lovaniensium* 163; Leuven: Leuven University Press, 2003), pp. 81–110; and E. L. Gallagher, *Hebrew Scripture in Patristic Biblical Theory: Canon, Language, Text* (Supplements to Vigiliae Christianae 114; Leiden: Brill, 2012), esp. pp. 85–104.

[45] Augustine himself had to justify his use of the book of Wisdom and its inclusion in the canon (*civ. Dei* 17.20; *Simpl.* 1.2.20; *praed. sanct.* 14.27–28).

Bible of the Christian Church (*spec.* 22).[46] What complicates matters is that the designation 'Septuagint' does not necessarily imply the endorsement of a fixed table of contents of the Bible. The few extant complete Septuagint manuscripts, along with lists of the Old Testament books, confirm that LXX copies did not circulate with identical contents and sequence of books.[47]

Speaking about the unity of Scripture, Augustine believes that if the canonical Scripture is rightly understood, everything in it coheres beautifully. 'Peace reigns in the Scriptures, everything is in agreement, there are no contradictions at all' (*Jo. ev. tr.* 19.7; cf. *conf.* 13.15.16; *Gen. litt.* 5.8.23; *s.* 82.9).[48] Although Scripture addresses human beings in many words and through several human authors, Scripture as such is the 'one single utterance of God (*unus sermo Dei*)' (*en. Ps.* 103[4].1).[49] The Scriptures as a single text 'speak the truth and do not say things that in any way contradict one another, as long as a reader approaches them piously, reads them humbly, and asks not with the mind of a heretic that leads to quarrels but with a believing heart that produces edification' (*c. Faust.* 3.5; cf. *ep.* 82.1.3). The conviction that everything in Scripture coheres is consistent with the understanding of Scripture as the divine speech.

In order to demonstrate this unity and coherence of Scripture,[50] Augustine has to be rather resourceful.[51] One should consider the well-known figurative explanations of the creation story in *Confessions*, book 12, where Augustine has to match the creation account in Genesis 1 with the rest of Scripture (i.e. Ps. 112.4; Sir. 1.18; and Wis. 11.17). In his *Expositio epistulae ad Galatas*, too, Augustine is working hard to reconcile various texts: Apostle Paul swears (Gal. 1.20), which violates Jesus teaching in Mt. 5.33–7; he rebukes Peter publicly, which is contrary to what Jesus said in Mt. 18.15 ('show him his fault when the two of you are alone'); he calls Galatians 'fools' (Gal. 3.1), when, in Mt. 5.22, Jesus says not to do so.[52]

---

[46] Originally the Septuagint designated merely the Pentateuch (*Letter of Aristeas* 30, 46; Philo, *Vita Moysis* 2.38). Later, and especially among Christians, it became an umbrella term covering a variety of Greek translations of the books of the Old Testament which were made during the three centuries before the Common Era.

[47] M. Hengel, *The Septuagint as Christian Scripture: Its Prehistory and the Problem of Its Canon* (trans. M. E. Biddle; Edinburgh: T&T Clark, 2002), pp. 57–74.

[48] Even when something in Scripture seems contradictory, the Holy Spirit has allowed this for particular predetermined purposes (Augustine, *cons. Ev.* 2.21.52).

[49] 'The word [mentioned in Ps. 119:105] . . . is the word contained in all the holy scriptures' (*en. Ps.* 118[23].1).

[50] *Dei Verbum* 12, too, mentions 'the coherence of the Scriptures as a whole'.

[51] For the various ways in which Augustine solves the seeming contradictions between the gospels, see his *De consensu Evangelistarum* and C. Harrison, '"Not Words but Things": Harmonious Diversity in the Four Gospels', in *Augustine: Biblical Exegete* (ed. F. van Fleteren and J. C. Schnaubelt; Bern: Peter Lang, 2001), pp. 157–73 (pp. 159–62).

[52] These cases are pointed out by E. Plumer, *Augustine's Commentary on Galatians: Introduction, Text, Translation, and Notes* (Oxford Early Christian Studies; ed. G. Clark and A. Louth; Oxford: Oxford University Press, 2003), pp. 92–3.

Arguably because of the Manicheans's rejection of the Old Testament, Augustine gives special attention to the harmony between the Old and New Testaments. The two Testaments are 'in mutual accord' (*en. Ps.* 67.19; cf. *en. Ps.* 56.1; *ep.* 166.11); both speak 'with one mouth' (*c. Faust* 11.6; cf. *en. Ps.* 49.4; 100.13). After all, there has to be a harmony between the two Testaments, because 'both were written by one God' (*c. Adim.* 7.4; cf. 16.3; *ex. Gal.* 24.15; *util. cred.* 3.9; *vera rel.* 17.33).[53] Augustine even maintains rather optimistically that the harmony between the Old and New Testament is 'so complete that there remains no point of disharmony' (*util. cred.* 3.9)!

At the same time, he gives certain hermeneutical priority to the New Testament as the revelation of the meaning of the Old. 'In the Old Testament, there is a veiling of the New, and in the New Testament, there is a revealing of the Old' (*cat. rud.* 4.8; cf. *civ. Dei.* 16.26; *c. Adim.* 16.3; *c. Faust.* 12.11; *cons. Ev.* 1.1; *en. Ps.* 118[21].3; 105.36; *Jo. ev. tr.* 48.9; and *Qu. Exod.* 2.73). Put differently, the New Testament provides the theological perspective to 'unlock' the meaning of the Old. More precisely, 'Our Lord's cross was like a key for opening what was locked away . . . may these hidden things be unveiled' (*en. Ps.* 45.1).[54] Augustine's deep and traditional conviction that both Testaments are about Jesus Christ[55] justifies such hermeneutical prioritizing of the New (*civ. Dei* 20.4),[56] as well as Christological reading of the Old Testament (*en. Ps.* 3.1; 9.4; 21.2),[57] and the fact that the Hebrew Bible is considered a legitimate part of Christian Scripture. Indeed, it is all about Christ – 'Christ meets and refreshes me everywhere in those books' (*c. Faust.* 12.27).

IV. The Translations and the Text(s) of Scripture

Although Scripture is a canonized collection of texts, it does not mean that the wording of these texts is canonized. Therefore, one still has the problem of finding out what exactly the biblical text might have been for Augustine.

---

[53] The Council of Trent, *Sacrosancta oecumenica*, affirms that 'God is the author of both [Testaments]'. Cf. Leo XIII, *Providentissimus Deus* 14, Vatican II, *Dei Verbum* 14–16, 4th Plenary of the Lutheran-Orthodox Joint Commission (1987), 6; *Scripture and Tradition*, par. 9.

[54] 'The mystery of Christ offers the key to interpretation of all Scripture' (*The Interpretation of the Bible in the Church* II, B3).

[55] Lk. 24.27; Jn. 5.46; Rom. 5.14; 1 Cor. 10.11. Augustine contends that the Old Testament events 'prefigure things to come in some way, and are always to be referred to Christ and his church'(Augustine, *civ. Dei* 16.2).

[56] Cf. *The Gift of Scripture* 36; *Catechism of the Catholic Church* 129.

[57] Cf. Augustine's prosopological exegesis of the Psalms (e.g. *en. Ps.* 34[1].1). Cf. *The Gift of Scripture* 18.

As is evident from *doc. Chr.* 2.15.22, Augustine was mostly interpreting the text of *vetus Latina*. The pre-Vulgate Latin texts were not uniform.[58] Augustine remarked that 'the variations found in the different codices of the Latin text are intolerably numerous' (*ep.* 71.6). After all, there were such annoying things as 'lying manuscripts' (*cat. rud.* 13.41). Furthermore, Augustine complained, 'Whenever in the early days of the faith a Greek codex came into anybody's hand ... he rushed in with a translation' (*doc. Chr.* 2.11.16). Thus, to assess and revise the existing Latin translations was an urgent need indeed.

Augustine was adamant that the Septuagint translation 'has the greatest authority' (*doc. Chr.* 2.15.22; cf. *ep.* 28; *civ. Dei* 18.42–3) and therefore, it should be used for checking the variety of Latin translations (*civ. Dei* 15.13; *doc. Chr.* 2.11.16). He pointed out that these were the New Testament writers who made a choice between the Hebrew and Greek versions of Scripture and they clearly preferred the latter. 'The church has received the Septuagint as if it were the only translation' (*civ. Dei* 18.43). In fact, Augustine took the legend of the Septuagint very seriously – that is, he considered it a miracle that the 70 translators had came up individually with exactly the same text (*civ. Dei* 15.11; 18.42; *doc. Chr.* 2.15.22; cf. Philo, *Vita Moysis* 2.37–40). He also mentioned a *theological* reason for the superiority of the Septuagint: 'Whatever is found in the Septuagint but not in the Hebrew texts is something which the same Spirit chose to say through the translators rather than through the prophets' (*civ. Dei* 18.43; cf. *civ. Dei* 15.23; *cons. Ev.* 2.66.128; *doc. Chr.* 2.15.22).

However, it should be clarified that Augustine had no wooden position on the untouchability of the Septuagint text. He seems to have opened up towards *Hebraica veritas* in time.[59] Namely, he eventually accepted the usefulness of the text *iuxta Hebraeos* in his *ep.* 82 – not for liturgy, but for arguing with Jews. Somehow 'both [the Greek and Hebrew Scriptures] are one, and both divine' (*civ. Dei* 18.44; cf. *civ. Dei.* 15.14) and contribute to a more profound understanding of the Word of God.

Although Augustine did not know Hebrew, he had a copy of a Latin translation of the Hebrew Bible. Despite his requests, he never saw Jerome's (new) Latin translation of the Septuagint though.[60] Augustine did not particularly like Jerome's attempt to substitute the LXX with a Latin translation from the Hebrew text in the first place. He might have had Jerome in mind,

---

[58] E. Schulz-Flügel, 'Der lateinische Bibletext im 4. Jahrhundert', in *Augustin Handbuch* (ed. V. H. Drecoll; Tübingen: Mohr Siebeck, 2007), pp. 109–14.

[59] J. Lössl, "A Shift in Patristic Exegesis: Hebrew Clarity and Historical Verity in Augustine, Jerome, Julian Eclanum and Theodore of Mopsuestia', *AugStud* 32/2 (2001), pp. 157–75 (pp. 157–63).

[60] Jerome's excuses for not sending his new translation to Augustine can be found in his *ep.* 134.

when he (ironically) spoke about a single(!) scholar correcting the work of the 70: 'It would not be right or proper for any one person, however expert, to think of correcting a version agreed by so many experienced scholars' (*doc. Chr.* 2.15.22).

The bottom line is that because Augustine either used various versions of the *vetus Latina*, translated the text himself or quoted from memory, the same scriptural passage is almost always cited a little differently. Consequently, it might be impossible to establish *the* form of the biblical text that he used.

V. Augustine's Doctrine of Scripture and Modern Theology

In modern theology, there are many echoes of Augustine's doctrine of Scripture and even more echoes of the interpreters and mediators of Augustine's doctrine of Scripture. Apart from compilations of Augustine's works by Prosper of Aquitaine, Eugippius, Bede and Florus of Lyons, a medieval Augustinian Bartholomew of Urbino put together the *Milleloquium Sancti Augustini*. This opus consisted of alphabetically arranged entries of approximately 15,000 passages from Augustine's works. Then, during the sixteenth century, almost 500 editions (reprints included) of Augustine's works were published by both Protestants and Catholics. Among these 500 editions were no fewer than 16 *opera omnia* editions.[61] Adding later grand projects, such as the volumes of Augustine's works in *Patrologia Latina* and in various critical editions, one must conclude that Augustine's works and ideas have been easily accessible for modern readers.[62]

However, there have been various modern developments of thought which have moved away from that which Augustine believed about Scripture.[63] Among these tone-setting factors has been the recent dominance of the historical-critical methodology, especially some presuppositions of this methodology which concern the philosophy of meaning. Advances in textual criticism, in turn, have made Augustine's preference of the Septuagint a mere patristic oddity. His Platonic convictions have been deemed as flawed and his optimism about the unity, truthfulness and clarity of Scripture, too, has caused the raising of many modern eyebrows.

---

[61] A. S. Q. Visser, *Reading Augustine in the Reformation: The Flexibility of Intellectual Authority in Europe, 1500–1620* (Oxford Studies in Historical Theology; ed. D. C. Steinmetz; New York: Oxford University Press, 2011), p. 5.

[62] In premodern times, Augustine was known primarily in the Western Church. In the East, and apart from occasional quotes of Augustine in *florilegia*, his works were translated into Greek only after Planoudes's pioneering translation of Augustine's *De Trinitate* in 1280s.

[63] M. C. Legaspi, *The Death of Scripture and the Rise of Biblical Studies* (Oxford Studies in Historical Theology; ed. D. C. Steinmetz; Oxford: Oxford University Press, 2010), pp. 3–26.

Nevertheless, there are definitely some features in Augustine's doctrine of Scripture which have either carried the day or which are currently finding an increasing appreciation.[64] Without trying to be exhaustive and without claiming that Augustine has any monopoly on these topics, one can mention a few.

First, semiotics.[65] Augustine was the first to focus primarily on *linguistic* signification,[66] and the first to apply the insights from the ancient accounts of linguistic signification extensively to the task of interpreting Scripture.[67] The idea that scriptural words signify theological realities continues to be employed as a way of thinking about the Bible.[68]

Second, Christological analogies (incarnation, the two natures) are still used to comprehend what Scripture as such is.[69] While some people are rather enthusiastic about these analogies,[70] others are much more cautious.[71]

Third, the continuous spiritual usefulness of Scripture, which does not relegate God's revelation simply or exclusively to the past, has received a lot of attention in various recent publications. 'Spiritual usefulness' involves the rediscovery of the benefits of figurative interpretation,[72] the priority of the divine intention in determining the meaning(s) of the text[73] and the renewal of interest in the theological interpretation of Scripture,[74] as well as interest in how human words function as 'divine words'.

In modern times and for many, Scripture has unfortunately become a mere set of classical texts to be studied mostly as history and/or literature. What is

---

[64] Some of these features, which have been reaffirmed in modern documents, have been provided in footnotes. For general overview, see A. Dulles, 'Scripture: Recent Protestant and Catholic Views', *Theology Today* 37/7 (1980), pp. 7–26.

[65] By semiotics I mean Augustine's *scientia signorum* and not merely structuralism as does *The Interpretation of the Bible in the Church* I, B3.

[66] G. Manetti, *Theories of the Sign in Classical Antiquity* (trans. C. Richardson; Advances in Semiotics; ed. T. A. Sebeok; Bloomington: Indiana University Press, 1993), p. 157.

[67] B. D. Jackson, 'The Theory of Signs in St. Augustine's *De doctrina Christiana*', *RÉtAug* 15 (1969), pp. 9–49.

[68] *Dei Verbum* 2. Unfortunately, the footnotes in the given document do not identify Augustine as the author of this idea. See also 'Thinking in Signs: Semiotics and Biblical Studies' (ed. D. Patte; *Semeia* 81, 1998).

[69] *Dei Verbum* 2, 13; *The Gift of Scripture* 13, 16, 23; *Catechism of the Catholic Church* 101.

[70] The 4th Plenary of the Lutheran-Orthodox Joint Commission (1987) claims that Scripture 'is not simply speech from or about God but the hypostatic Word of God incarnate' (3)!

[71] Webster, *Holy Scriptures*, pp. 22–3.

[72] *Divino Afflante Spiritu* 26–7; *The Gift of Scripture* 20.

[73] Since *Dei Verbum* promoted greater openness to the historical-critical methodology, perhaps the human authorial intention was given a higher significance in constituting the meaning of a text (12) than Augustine would have allowed. See T. Toom, 'Was Augustine an Intentionalist? Authorial Intention in Augustine's Hermeneutics', *StudPat* 54 (2012).

[74] For example, a recent ecumenical conference on theological interpretation of the Scripture at Regent College, Vancouver, Canada (16–17 September 2011).

needed, however, is something like Augustine's own rediscovery of Scripture. That is, *the Scriptures* have to become *Scripture* (i.e. a special case of God's communicating activity) for us once again before some of Augustine's convictions about the Word of God can begin to resonate anew with us.

For Further Reading

Bright, Pamela (ed. and trans.), *Augustine and the Bible* (The Bible through the Ages 2; Notre Dame: University of Notre Dame Press, 1986).

De Margerie, Bertrand, *An Introduction to the History of Exegesis 3: Saint Augustine* (trans. P. de Fontnouvelle; Petersham, MA: Saint Bede's Publications, 1991).

Holcomb, Justin S. (ed.), *Christian Theologies of the Scripture: A Comparative Introduction* (New York: New York University Press, 2006).

La Bonnardière, Anne-Marie, *Biblia Augustiana* (7 vols; Paris: Études augustiniennes, 1960–75).

Loewen, Howard J., 'The Use of Scripture in Augustine's Theology', *SJT* 34 (1981), pp. 201–24.

Polman, Andries D. R., *The Word of God According to St. Augustine* (Grand Rapids: Eerdmans, 1961).

6
Augustine on the Last Things

Morwenna Ludlow

All modern Western theology lies in Augustine's shadow. This is no less true with regard to eschatology, but it is surprisingly difficult to find sustained and specific engagements with his eschatological ideas. There are, I think several reasons for this. First, the method of much twentieth-century eschatology challenges Augustine's whole way of doing eschatology. Even though Augustine is not always so certain in all of his pronouncements as some of his readers think, the last four books of the *City of God* do appear to set out the 'last things' with clarity and a fair degree of certainty. But the 'eschatological turn' in the twentieth century tends to make such eschatological pronouncements as uncertain and difficult to grasp as shadows. Second, Augustine's theology is viewed by some theologians as a *dark* shadow, a somewhat sinister presence which presents intractable problems for theodicy and human freedom.

Nevertheless, some modern theologians have grappled with Augustine's eschatology and the way in which they have done so is illuminating both of their own theology and of Augustine's own. Yet here again there are surprises. One of the most striking aspects of Augustine's *City of God* – and indeed of much of his thought – is his ability to combine a comprehensive overview with a detailed focus on many particular aspects of the human condition. One might suspect that the broad sweep of eschatology has been more attractive to modern theologians, partly because the genres of modern systematic theology and philosophy of religion are more attuned to study of big questions and overarching structures, but also because modern theological and philosophical writers are often perplexed by Augustine's exposition of the details. However, as I will show, in fact some of the most *direct* recent engagement with Augustine's eschatology has been precisely with those aspects which appear to the modern reader to be the most rhetorical, detailed, imaginative, excessive and even incredible.[1] In this essay, I will address both aspects of

---

[1] These are all concepts which the commentators examined in Part II use to characterize Augustine's discussion of the resurrection body.

Augustine's eschatology and its modern reception, first attending to its 'broad sweep' – the idea of the two cities and their 'proper ends' (Parts I and II) – and secondly looking at one particular aspect, that is, his defence of the resurrection of the body (Parts III and IV).

I. The Two Cities and Their 'Proper Ends': Augustine

Augustine introduces the *City of God* as a defence of that 'most glorious' city. While he describes the aim of books 1–10 as the refutation of 'the objections of the ungodly' to the worship of the one true God, he consistently says that the second part of the work has a threefold object: to set out the 'origin and progress and merited ends (*debitis finibus*) of the two cities – that is, of the earthly and the heavenly – which, as we have said, are in this present world mixed together and, in a certain sense, entangled with one another'.[2] This object Augustine carries out in books 11–14, 15–18 and 19–22 respectively. For obvious reasons, our focus here will be on the merited ends of the two cities, but some attention to the origins and progress is also necessary.[3]

In particular, books 12–14 are crucial for understanding Augustine's eschatology, for it is here that Augustine sets out his theology of the creation and Fall of humankind. A key principle is that humanity is one, because all human individuals derive from the first man Adam (e.g. *civ. Dei* 12.22). This is not a fellowship based on 'natural likeness' (*naturae similitudine*), nor a merely biological unity; rather it is perfect society: God intended humans to be 'bound together by kinship in the unity of concord, linked by the bond of peace' (*cognationis necessitudine in unitatem concordem pacis uinculo conligandum*).[4] Because of this unity, when the first humans sinned, 'they were then punished by death in such a way that whatsoever sprang from their stock should also be subject to the same penalty'.[5] This death – the 'first death' – consists in the 'death of the whole man': not only physical mortality (when body abandons soul), but also the death of the soul ('when God forsakes it').[6] It also leads to the sundering of the 'bond of peace' – the fragmentation of human society which is illustrated by Augustine in many ways throughout the *City of God*, but especially with the concept of the lust for power.[7]

---

[2] Augustine, *civ. Dei* 11.1; c.f. *civ. Dei* 1.35; 10.32; 11.1; 15.1; 18.1; 18.54; 19.1.

[3] For an introduction to the *City of God*, see especially Gerard O'Daly, *Augustine's 'City of God': A Reader's Guide* (Oxford: Oxford University Press, 1999); this has some particularly helpful comments on structure: pp. 67–73.

[4] Augustine, *civ. Dei* 14.1; c.f. Eph. 4.3.

[5] Augustine, *civ. Dei* 13.3.

[6] Ibid., 13.2.

[7] 'Princes are as much mastered by the lust for mastery (*dominandi libido*) as the nations which they subdue are by them' (*civ. Dei* 14.28).

But, Augustine writes, the first death should properly be followed by hell, the 'second death' of the book of Revelation.[8] As he states at the beginning of book 14, all 'would have been driven headlong, as their due punishment (*poena debita*), into that second death to which there is no end, had not some of them been redeemed by the unmerited grace of God'.[9] There are three aspects of this doctrine of election (God's choice of the saved) that need to be drawn out. First, Augustine believes that those people whom God will redeem have been chosen by God from all eternity: he has predestined them to salvation.[10] Second, those whom he has chosen do not deserve their fate: rather, it is by divine grace alone that they are selected from humanity which is 'deservedly and justly condemned'.[11] Third, although the fullness of that grace is still to be worked out, God's plan of salvation is already being mediated – for God's chosen people – through Christ's life, death and Resurrection and subsequently through Christ's reign on earth in the Church.[12] It is this which Augustine identifies with the millennium (Rev. 20.1–7). Although the Church is *not* identical to the Kingdom or City of God in its historical, institutional form (not everyone in the Church will necessarily be saved), Augustine seems to see the Church as a symbol of the City of God on earth, however imperfect a symbol it is.

So, according to Augustine, current human society is disharmonious because of the effects of the Fall. Furthermore – because God has chosen some to be saved – human society is fundamentally divided between 'two cities'. The City of God comprises those whom God has chosen to save and whom he gives the grace to live as humans ought to live. 'The one [city] is made up of men who live according to the flesh, and the other of those who live according to the spirit. Each desires its own kind of peace, and, when they have found what they sought, each lives in its own kind of peace.'[13] At the end of book 14, Augustine expresses the same idea through the concept of love: the earthly city being characterized by 'love of self' and the heavenly by 'love of God'.[14]

While books 10–14 deal with the origins of humankind (when humans lived in prelapsarian peace), books 15–18 treat the conflicted present situation.

---

[8] Rev. 2.11; 20.6; 20.14; 21.8.
[9] Augustine, *civ. Dei* 14.1; cf. 14.26: 'He does not now choose them for their merits . . . he chooses them by grace'.
[10] *Civ. Dei* 14.26. In *civ. Dei* 22.24, Augustine refers to 'those who are predestined to death' as well as those 'predestined to life', suggesting a theory of double predestination – but whether Augustine held consistently to this view is disputed: see O'Daly, Augustine's 'City of God', p. 231 for helpful brief note on the relevant literature.
[11] Augustine, *civ. Dei* 22.1.
[12] For this non-millenialist reading of Revelation, chapter 20, see the comments of O'Daly, *Augustine's 'City of God'*, p. 212.
[13] Augustine, *civ. Dei* 14.1.
[14] Ibid., 14.28.

Book 19 discusses teleology, that is, the question of proper ends in general (according to various philosophical theories) and, more specifically, the proper ends of human society.[15] In the light of Augustine's claim that the end of each city is a 'kind of peace', a large portion of this book is an analysis of peace itself. Augustine holds that the two cities are so currently 'entangled and mingled with one another' that separation is necessary for their ultimate peace.[16] Thus the discussion of peace leads directly to book 20's discussion of the divine judgement which brings the separation and thus that peace about. There follows Augustine's discussion of hell in book 21 (much of which is given up to the defence of the idea that an eternal punishment can be visited on embodied humans) and of heaven in book 22 (much of which analyses the concept of resurrection). In sum, then, Augustine's discussion of the 'ends' of the two cities in *City of God* 19–22 asserts that they are: merited, eternal, brought about by God (the act of judgement/separation) and are constituted by two opposed ways of living in society (according to love of self or of love of God).

II. The Two Cities and Their 'Proper Ends': Modern Theologians

As I suggested above, twentieth-century theology presented several challenges to Augustinian eschatological method.[17] First, although Augustine interpreted the millennium as the present reign of Christ on earth in the heavenly City (in form of the Church), he also clearly looked forward to the future eschatological consummation of that heavenly City. By contrast, an important trend in early mid-twentieth-century eschatology radically questioned the future orientation of Christian eschatology. This was not only a response to traditional eschatologies with their promise of a future heavenly Kingdom, but also to 'liberal' theologies of the nineteenth century, which took an evolutionary view of the present world, interpreting the Kingdom of God as the gradual ethical progress of humanity on earth (both of which views could be seen as having Augustinian antecedents).[18] Dialectical theology boldly asserted that in the New Testament eschatological language was not about the future, but denoted the urgency of the Gospel. Rudolf Bultmann, for example, stressed a radically realized eschatology with an emphasis on the believer's

---

[15] See O'Daly, *Augustine's 'City of God'*, pp. 197–210.

[16] See Augustine, *civ. Dei* 1.35 and 18.54.

[17] No scholarly work that I am aware of specifically and systematically relates modern eschatology to Augustine's theology; however, Brian Hebblethwaite, *The Christian Hope* (Oxford: Oxford University Press, rev. edn, 2010) is a very helpful guide to the broader theological concerns underlying it. See also, Jerry R. Walls (ed.), *The Oxford Handbook of Eschatology* (Oxford: Oxford University Press, 2008).

[18] See for example Hebblethwaite, *The Christian Hope*, pp. 105–10 and 125–27.

present existential relationship with the divine. 'The judgment of the world', he wrote, 'is not a cosmic event that is still to happen but is the fact that Jesus has come into the world and issued the call to faith.'[19] Karl Barth's conviction that Jesus Christ is 'the eternal, decisive, act of God in history' meant that, to the extent that his eschatology has a future focus, it is a hope for humanity's final understanding of the full scope of God's salvation in Christ – not the future completion of that salvation.[20]

Even less radical theologians guarded against the danger of appearing to 'predict' the end times. Karl Rahner, for example, while asserting belief in 'an eschatology which . . . really is still to come in a very ordinary, empirical sense of the word time', also warned that 'God has *not* revealed to man the day of the end', and that humans can only understand the future out of their present experience of salvation.[21] Even though Augustine might have agreed with those two principles, it is difficult to find in the *City of God* the kind of restraint Rahner advocates! Nevertheless, one could read Rahner's analysis of 'salvation history' and 'profane history' as a response (in a somewhat existential mode) to Augustine's 'two cities'. Similarly, when other theologians, Protestant and Catholic, grappled with how to interpret Christianity's present state 'between the times', they were in a sense answering Augustinian questions – although they, like Rahner, rarely cite Augustine directly.[22]

A closer correspondence with Augustinian themes can be found in more political responses to his idea of the *saeculum* – the period after Christ's incarnation but before the consummation of the kingdom at the eschaton. Again the mode of engagement is critique rather than appropriation and criticism has focused on two closely related aspects in Augustine. First, as we have seen, Augustine asserts the 'mixed' character of the present age: even though God reigns in the Church in the world, the heavenly City coexists with the earthly. Furthermore, even the heavenly City in the present age cannot be regarded as pure. The problem is that this theory, when added to a hope for

---

[19] Rudolf Bultmann, *New Testament and Mythology and Other Basic Writings* (ed. and trans. Schubert Ogden; London: SCM, 1984), p. 19.

[20] Hebblethwaite, *The Christian Hope*, pp. 128–33. See also Colin Gunton, 'Salvation', in *The Cambridge Companion to Karl Barth* (ed. John Webster; Cambridge: Cambridge University Press, 2000), pp. 143–58 (p. 146): 'We could go further and say that Barth is above all a theologian of the resurrection, rather than of the incarnation or cross – a feature of his thought which gives it a strongly realized eschatology. Whatever may still be to come is chiefly the outworking of that eschatological salvation which is realized here.'

[21] Karl Rahner, 'The Hermeneutics of Eschatological Assertions', in *Theological Investigations* (vol. 4; London: Darton, Longman & Todd, 1960), Theses 1 and 3, p. 326, pp. 329–31; cf. Morwenna Ludlow, *Universal Salvation: Eschatology in the Thought of Gregory of Nyssa and Karl Rahner* (Oxford: Oxford University Press, 2000), pp. 136–50.

[22] See, for example, Hebblethwaite's comments on attempts to give proper weight to both the present and future dimensions of salvation by Emil Brunner, von Balthasar, Reinhold Niebuhr and others in his *The Christian Hope*, pp. 136–38, 144 and 156.

the future separation of the cities, later led all too easily to political quietism: if the *saeculum* is inevitably imperfect and if God's judgement is what will bring perfection, then what is there to do in the meantime but endure? Although their object is Catholic theology in general, rather than Augustine in particular, this is one of the fundamental critiques made by Catholic liberation theologians.

Second, however, theologians have attacked the identification of the Church with the heavenly City. Augustine, of course, intended this move as a critique of those Christians who associated God's reign on earth with the future indulging of bodily desires: it was itself, therefore, a critique grounded on a theological conception of what makes a good human society. For Jürgen Moltmann, however, Augustine's view had its own danger: 'Because Augustine . . . viewed the Thousand Years' empire as already realized in the church now, in antithesis to the earthly empire which will perish, he was bound to conclude that the visible church with its judicial priests and its hierarchical order was the kingdom of God.'[23] Even though Moltmann recognizes that the church-Kingdom association in Augustine is not absolute (until the eschaton), he fears its 'inherent trend towards theocracy'.[24] Again, the identification of the Kingdom with any particular political form is a major criticism made by liberation theology.[25]

A third, more positive and yet more complex response to Augustine's notion of the *saeculum* can be found in the thought of John Milbank. The last chapter of Milbank's *Theology and Social Theory* is, among other things, a sustained reading of the *City of God* – with especial focus on book 19 and the notions of peace and violence.[26] Milbank points out that Augustine asserted an ontology based on a *fundamental* concept of peace – fundamental because it is a peace which is not predicated on the ordering or 'making good' of a pre-existing chaos. (Thus, Augustine emphatically argues for a doctrine of creation out of nothing, rather than the ordering of a primeval unformed matter which could be read as the bringing of peace out of chaos.) In terms of Augustine's account of the history of human salvation, then, peace is not the cure for a prior state of violence, but an original state which has been lost and which must be restored. Milbank takes this narrative and makes it fundamental to

---

[23] Jürgen Moltmann, *The Coming of God: Christian Eschatology* (London: SCM, 1996), p. 181.
[24] Ibid.
[25] See for example Hebblethwaite, *The Christian Hope*, pp. 160–63.
[26] John Milbank, *Theology and Social Theory: Beyond Secular Reason* (Oxford: Blackwell, 1990), pp. 390–92. For a helpful (and mostly descriptive) survey of Milbank's reading of Augustine, see Michael J. Hollerich, 'John Milbank, Augustine and the "Secular"', in *History, Apocalypse and the Secular Imagination: New Essays on Augustine's* City of God (ed. Mark Vessey, Karla Pollmann and Allan D. Fitzgerald; Bowling Green, OH: Bowling Green State University Press, 1999), pp. 311–26.

Augustine on the Last Things

his ontology – but, in keeping with Milbank's theological method, this is an ontological narrative and (in keeping with much recent eschatology) Milbank is seemingly not committed to Augustine's literal temporal sequence of past fall – present salvation – future consummation.[27]

There are two interesting consequences of Milbank's reading of Augustine. First, Milbank has a strong emphasis on peaceful human community as something to be striven for now.[28] He thus avoids the criticism of political quietism, but is perhaps more vulnerable to the critique that he has reduced to the merely teleological concepts which are both teleological *and eschatological* in Augustine (the 'proper end' of the *City of God* is both the right ordering of their desires to the God as their end *and* the eschatological fulfilment of the City). Or perhaps he is rather critiquing a strictly chronological or temporal concept of eschatology which has an excessive focus on the future. Second, although Milbank is quite cautious about stating this, he strongly hints that the concept of divine punishment is incompatible with the notion of an Augustinian hell – not just because of the problem of conceiving of a 'future' state of punishment, but because Augustine's 'account of a legitimate, non-sinful, "pedagogic" coercion violates this ontology [of peace], because it makes some punishment positive, and ascribes it to divine will'.[29]

Modern eschatology, then, finds it difficult to deal with the relentless future orientation of Augustine's eschatology: it is as if moderns have either lost the self-confidence to speculate on the future aspect of humanity's 'proper end' (or ends) or – to put it more positively – have gained the self-confidence radically to critique such a future-oriented eschatology as Augustine's. The exception to this rule is an ongoing discussion in the philosophy of religion which brings eschatology directly to bear on the question of theodicy. Perhaps most famously, John Hick used Augustine as the inspiration for an 'Augustinian theodicy' which was the foil to his preferred 'Irenaean' theodicy.[30] When addressing the question of whether either theodicy can account for the coexistence of human suffering with a good omnipotent God, he focuses on human experience before death; however, there clearly are eschatological questions raised by his answer. For example: surely there are some people whose experience of life is so dreadful (or so

---

[27] Indeed, he has been criticized precisely for this failure: 'Radical Orthodoxy's misconceptions about ontological peace radically and mistakenly elevate history over nature and revelation and, in so doing, render history theologically incomprehensible' (Todd Breyfogle, 'Is There Room for Political Philosophy in Postmodern Critical Augustinianism?' in *Deconstructing Radical Orthodoxy: Postmodern Theology, Rhetoric and Truth* [ed. Wayne Hankey and Douglas Hedley; Aldershot: Ashgate, 2005], pp. 31–47 [p. 35]).

[28] Milbank, *Theology and Social Theory*, pp. 398–422 (the section on 'Counter-Ethics').

[29] Milbank, *Theology and Social Theory*, pp. 418–22, quotation on pp. 419–20.

[30] John Hick, *Evil and the God of Love* (Basingstoke: Macmillan, 1977).

short) that it is not justified by any 'soul-making' they experienced? Hick's thesis seems to be calling out for a universalist doctrine of salvation, which is in fact what he provided.[31] But it is not just that the rejection of hell is offered as a solution to the problem of evil; as Marilyn Adams points out, 'the problem of hell' *is* 'a problem of evil for Christians' – it is part of the suffering that needs to be justified in the face of a loving God.[32] Adams's answer is to argue clearly and forcefully for a doctrine of universal salvation: only that can meet the demand that a theodicy justify the suffering of each individual – not just of humanity as a whole.[33] Although Adams does not engage directly with Augustine in any detail, she is clearly responding both to Hick and to philosophers of religion coming from a Reformed tradition, for whom Augustine – as read through Calvin – is an éminence grise. Although she is clearly rejecting Augustine's notion of a number of elect rescued from a larger *massa damnata*, she asserts that her 'brand of universalism offers all the advantages of Augustine's and Calvin's *sola gratia* approaches' because 'it makes our salvation utterly gratuitous and dependent on God's surprising and loving interest in us'.[34] Interestingly, both Hick and Adams seem to assume a continued temporal existence after death which is in tension with the direction of most recent theological eschatology.

III. Human Particularity: Augustine on Resurrection Bodies

For this aspect of Augustine's eschatology, we shall turn to a more detailed look at Augustine's *City of God*, book 22. Here, Augustine presents his readers with an astonishingly rich and determined defence of the resurrection body against its detractors. These 'learned and wise people' and 'distinguished philosophers' appeal to, for example, Cicero, Plato, Varro and Porphyry.[35] However, Augustine's eschatology of the body is also developed against Manichees – who longed for the escape of the body from the taint of the world – and those Christians whom Augustine feared were headed in too dualist a direction: Julian of Eclanum and the Pelagians.[36] Furthermore, just as Augustine uses Origenistic universalism as a rhetorical counterargument to

---

[31] For example in John Hick, *Death and Eternal Life* (London: Collins, 1976), chapter 13.
[32] This quotation is from the title of Marilyn McCord Adams, 'The Problem of Hell: A Problem of Evil for Christians', in *God and the Problem of Evil* (ed. William L. Rowe; Oxford: Blackwell, 2001), pp. 282–309 (p. 282).
[33] This is the implication of the arguments of Adams, 'The Problem of Hell', pp. 285 and 299.
[34] Adams, 'The Problem of Hell', p. 305.
[35] Augustine, *civ. Dei* 22.4.
[36] Paula Fredriksen, 'Beyond the Body/Soul Dichotomy: Augustine on Paul against the Manichees and the Pelagians', *RechAug* 23 (1988), pp. 87–114.

his own conception of eternal hell in the *City of God*, he seems also implicitly to place Origen's alleged interpretation of the 'spiritual' resurrection body as an counterpoint to Augustine's own exegesis of 1 Cor. 15.44–6.

Book 22 begins and ends with descriptions of the 'eternal blessedness of the City of God' (*civ. Dei* 22.1), where all those who make up the body of that City will enjoy 'full, certain, secure and everlasting felicity' (*plena certa, secura sempiterna felicitas* [*civ. Dei* 22.30]). But whereas the book closes with an attempt to articulate the *quality* of that beatitude, Augustine begins with emphasizing its *quantity*: while God is eternal in the sense of transcending time, God's Kingdom is eternal in the sense that it will have no end. Furthermore, the City will not persist through the constant replacement of its mortal constituents, like an earthly city or like an evergreen tree which flourishes despite the continual shedding and growing of individual leaves; rather, 'all the citizens of that city will be immortal' (*civ. Dei* 22.1).

Since God's promise for eternal punishment or reward depends on resurrection, Augustine summarizes the main objections to the resurrection (*civ. Dei* 22.4) and he deals with each in turn. Rhetorically, the book is presented as a defence of a disputed doctrine, but Margaret R. Miles correctly notes that in fact Augustine's 'acknowledged fantasy of the resurrection in book 22 and in his sermons . . . seems to be for the purpose of enabling and encouraging belief, not convincing philosophical opponents'.[37] Perhaps this is why it stresses the guarantee of the general resurrection: 'This may once have been incredible; but behold: the whole world now believes that the earthly body of Christ was received up into heaven. Learned and unlearned men alike believe in the resurrection of his flesh and his ascension into heavenly habitations . . .' (*civ. Dei* 22.5). If it is by the Resurrection of Christ that humans will be fully 'conformed to [his] image', then it is crucial that the earliest disciples witnessed his Resurrection.[38] The ascension here is significant, for it distinguishes Christ's eternal Resurrection from that of Lazarus or others raised by the first disciples.[39] Thus, the eternity of the City of God is underwritten by Augustine's consistent emphasis on 'the resurrection of Christ, and *His ascension into heaven with the flesh in which He rose again*'.[40]

---

[37] Margaret R. Miles, 'Sex and the City (of God): Is Sex Forfeited or Fulfilled in Augustine's Resurrection of Body?' *JAAR* 73/2 (June 2005), pp. 307–27 (p. 315) (reprinted in Margaret R. Miles, *Rereading Historical Theology: Before, during and after Augustine* [Eugene, OR: Cascade Books, 2008], pp. 165–85).

[38] Brian Daley, *The Hope of the Early Church* (Peabody: Hendrickson, 2003; Cambridge: Cambridge University Press, 1st edn, 1991), p. 142, citing Rom. 8.29; Augustine, *Trin.* 14.18.24 and *s.* 243.3.

[39] *Civ. Dei* 22.5: see *Augustine, The City of God against the Pagans*, R. W. Dyson (ed. and trans.) (Cambridge Texts in the History of Political Thought; Cambridge: Cambridge University Press, 1998) translator's note 21 on p. 1115.

[40] Augustine, *civ. Dei* 22.5; see also 22.8; 22.7; 22.10.

Chapter 12 tackles a dilemma: either people will all be resurrected with a body like that of Christ (in which case some will be shorter in the resurrection than in their earthly lives, abrogating the promise that 'not a hair of your head will perish': Lk. 21.18), or the resurrection will not be one of equal conformity to Christ (denying the promise that 'all of us [will] come to the unity of the faith and of the knowledge of the Son of God, to maturity, to the measure of the full stature of Christ' [Eph. 4.13]). Augustine's answer is tentative, but his best guess is that 'everyone will receive back his own size: the size which he had in youth, if he died an old man, or that which he would have had, if he died before attaining it' (*civ. Dei* 22.15). Thus 'the measure of the full stature of Christ' refers not to an ideal physical height, but to an ideal age – or the body of Christ, the 'full stature' of which will be reached when all the members are added to Christ, its head.[41]

In chapter 17, Augustine again rejects the idea of absolute physical equality in the resurrection, making his famous comment that 'both sexes are to rise', but that 'there will be no lust, which is now the cause of confusion' (*civ. Dei* 22.17):

> Vice will be taken away from these bodies, therefore, and nature preserved. And the sex of a woman is not a vice, but nature. They will then be exempt from sexual intercourse and childbearing, but the female parts will nonetheless remain in being, accommodated not to the old uses, but to a new beauty, which, so far from inciting lust, which no longer exists, will move us to praise the wisdom and clemency of God . . .[42]

This principle – that God will remove that which deforms or corrupts the body, while (miraculously) not removing any of the body's substance – runs throughout the following four chapters. Whatever the deformity is, whether it caused by a part which is missing or too large or too small, God will make bodies beautiful again. Nothing will be lost and there will be 'no deformity, no infirmity, no heaviness, no corruption' (*civ. Dei* 22.20). In chapter 21, Augustine explains why bodies will no longer excite lust: they will be perfectly under the command of the spirit: that is why Paul called them 'spiritual bodies' (see 1 Cor. 15.44).[43] (Thus, 'spiritual' does not denote the transformation of bodies into immaterial substance.)

---

[41] *Civ. Dei* 22.15; see also 22.18.
[42] *Civ. Dei* 22.17.
[43] Thus, 'spiritual' does not denote the transformation of bodies into immaterial substance; 'spiritual' bodies contrast with bodies post-fall which are not under the control of the spirit. See O'Daly, *Augustine's 'City of God'*, p. 157 and Augustine, *civ. Dei* 14.15–19.

The notion of the body's beauty is illuminated by an excursus on the ills and blessings of this life, Augustine explaining that a body ideally exhibits a perfect unity:

> Even leaving aside the necessary function of [the human body's] parts, there is a necessary congruence between them all, a beauty in their mutual arrangement and correspondence, such that one does not know whether the major factor in their creation was usefulness or beauty. Certainly, we see that no part of the body has been created for the sake of usefulness which does not also have something to contribute to its beauty.[44]

It is no coincidence that the emphasis on use and beauty echoes what Augustine said about women's bodies in the resurrection (*civ. Dei* 22.17, quoted above): Augustine here reprises this theme, explaining that in the resurrection, all the members of the body will be released from their earthly uses, instead contributing to the beauty and *harmonia* of the resurrection body. But Augustine seems to imply that, far from becoming useless, the body's members now take on a new usefulness, first by becoming something whose beauty other people can enjoy properly for the first time and, secondly, rendering praise to God through their beauty and its mutual enjoyment: 'the time is coming when we shall enjoy each other's beauty without any lust: an enjoyment which will specially redound to the praise of the Creator'.[45]

Augustine then turns to the theme of the eschatological vision and grapples with the biblical promise that 'then we will see face to face' (1 Cor. 13.12). He quickly asserts that God's 'face' is his 'manifestation',[46] and that the saints will see God *in* their bodies, but, as he admits, 'whether they will see him *by means of* the body's eyes . . . that is no small question'.[47] Augustine's answer is, simultaneously, that the saints will not *need* bodily eyes to see God,[48] yet that those eyes will have a new function in the heavenly City, when they are – like the rest of the body – entirely subject to the spirit. Thus their eyes will see incorporeal things.[49]

IV. Human Particularity: Reading Augustine's Remarks on Resurrection Bodies

Augustine's discussion of the resurrection is surely intended to portray a body at perfect peace: the physical counterpart of the soul that has 'found

---

[44] *Civ. Dei* 22.24.
[45] Ibid.
[46] Ibid., 22.29.
[47] Ibid.
[48] Ibid.
[49] Ibid.

its rest' in God.[50] However, there are tensions in Augustine's account which have attracted the attention of scholars influenced by feminist criticism and theology – not just because of Augustine's famous comment on women's resurrection bodies, but because '(the) body' has been a particular locus of modern feminist debate and because the tensions in Augustine's account usefully point to significant tensions in cultural and theological attitudes to bodies, both present and future. In what follows, I discuss three very different approaches to reading Augustine on resurrection bodies. None should be seen as comprehensively representative of these women's work or feminist scholarship as a whole: rather I am using them as indicative of the kinds of readings Augustine's provocative text can generate from modern thinkers.[51]

Virginia Burrus's reading of *City of God* 22 attends to the difficulty of tying up the loose ends of Augustine's text.[52] She probes the excessive quality of his prose, focusing in particular on what she calls the 'carnal' or 'fleshly excess' found in Augustine's representation of resurrection bodies.[53] She reads *City of God* not just as an apologetic text, seeking to defend the doctrine of the resurrection, but as an exercise in early Christian imagination, an imagination which steps in when experience or reason fails: when it comes to eschatological concepts like the resurrection, Augustine must try to 'imagine the unimaginable'.[54] She draws attention to Augustine's lists of improbable feats of bodily control in *City of God* book 14 and of amazing miracles of healing in book 22: his treatment of these themes as a springboard for the imagination is already excessive in its detail, but emphasizes that these phenomena stretch the mind: 'if the miracles of this world exceed the capacity of the mind, so too do the miracles of the world to come.'[55]

Moving from the excessive quality of Augustine's detailed descriptions of such bizarre and wonderful phenomena, Burrus then investigates his discussion of a particular problem of 'excess' in the resurrection: if it is the case that 'not a hair of your head will perish' (Lk. 21.18) Augustine asks, 'What reply shall I now make concerning the hair and nails?'[56] Burrus highlights the tension

---

[50] *Conf.* 1.1.1.
[51] I prefer not to label the work of these three women in the traditional categories of the academy (e.g. 'philosopher', 'historian', 'theologian' or 'practical theologian/ethicist'), since in each case their work spans all of those disciplines.
[52] Virginia Burrus, 'Carnal Excess: Flesh at the Limits of Imagination', *JECS* 17/2 (2009), pp. 247–65.
[53] Set alongside other examples of carnal excess in Platonic, Talmudic and Christian ascetic traditions.
[54] Burrus, 'Carnal Excess', p. 252. Burrus acknowledges the influence of the analysis of the Christian 'corporeal imagination' by Patricia Cox Miller, to whom Burrus's paper is dedicated.
[55] Burrus, 'Carnal Excess', p. 254.
[56] Augustine, *civ. Dei* 22.19.

in Augustine's reply: Augustine rejects a 'heavenly egalitarianism' in which God will equalize everyone to the height of the tallest giant, but insists that any body parts cut off in life will be reincorporated into the resurrection body.

> He does so despite his continued attraction to the notion that resurrected bodies will preserve their original (or potential) mature height: 'there may be some addition to the stature as a result of this' he confesses (22.20). Even when a limit has been set at a Christlike thirtysomething, the body still exceeds.[57]

Thus, Burrus argues, 'stasis' is not the key to Augustine's resurrection theology (as Caroline Walker Bynum suggests); rather, his portrayal of resurrection reflects an incarnational theology in which the body is the site of transcendence not because of what it statically *is*, but of what it *becomes*.[58] For Burrus, then, materiality paradoxically exceeding itself in the resurrection body is not a challenge to the notion of transcendence, but is the epitome of transcendence:

> The incarnational and the apophatic – similarly, imagination and the unimaginable – converge at their extremes in Augustine's thought. This is nowhere more evident than in his (dramatically and productively failed) attempts to *imagine* resurrected bodies. Resurrected bodies are transcendent not because they are static or weightless, as Bynum suggests, but because they are the *most embodied*.[59]

In this reading, she challenges the common association of apophaticism with the rejection or at least the downplaying of materiality.[60]

Margaret R. Miles's reading is also situated in the context of contemporary intellectual developments – in her case, Freudian and post-Freudian analyses of human sexuality. Just as Burrus started from a paradox raised by Augustine's meticulous imagination (resurrection bodies' hair and nails), so also Miles begins from an 'incredible' aspect of Augustine's 'detailed and frankly imaginary picture of the resurrection': human bodies with sexual difference, yet without lust.[61] If Augustine recognized sexual difference in the resurrection, but ruled out sexual lust, intercourse and procreation, is there in his theology any space for 'an implicit sexuality free from the constraints and damages of present sexuality'?[62]

---

[57] Burrus, 'Carnal Excess', pp. 254–55.
[58] Burrus, 'Carnal Excess', p. 256, citing Caroline Walker Bynum, *The Resurrection of the Body in Western Christianity 200–1336* (New York: Columbia University Press, 1995), pp. 95, 97, 99.
[59] Burrus, 'Carnal Excess', p. 256.
[60] Ibid., p. 247.
[61] Miles, 'Sex and the City (of God)', pp. 308 and 314.
[62] Ibid., p. 309.

Miles's warns that 'sexuality' is a notion deriving from nineteenth-century psychology and that, therefore, 'the concept of sexuality as an intimate feature of who a person *is* was not part of Augustine's conceptual repertoire'.[63] But she argues that some of Freud's other ideas might be more relevant, notably his reconfiguration of sexuality as to do with more than biological function and as involving more than genital activity.[64] Post-Freudians have picked up on these latter ideas, while rejecting Freud's idea that sexuality is necessarily central to the human self. Drawing various strands of this scholarship together, Miles concludes that 'sexuality can be pictured as social rather than individual, as *part*, rather than essence of the self, as gendered rather than universal, and as embedded in social assumptions and arrangements rather than isolated'.[65]

But with regard to Augustine, the question of sexuality and function cannot be dispensed with easily, because of a key aspect of his anthropology – that is, the way he 'classified all features (including the genital organs) of present bodies as either for "use" or for "beauty"'.[66] Although Augustine thinks that bodies are *already* beautiful (see *civ. Dei* 22.24), in heaven this beauty will persist, while various uses of the parts of the body will cease.[67] In particular, the use of the sexual organs will cease, so that there will only be 'enjoyment of one another's beauty for itself alone'.[68] Miles hints that this enjoyment could be construed as an implicit sexuality, one from which procreational function has disappeared, but in which 'pleasure has been retained'.[69] That this cannot be reduced to a merely intellectual pleasure Miles argues with careful reference to Augustine's account of vision as 'a kind of touch'.[70]

It is important to be clear that although Miles does claim that 'Augustine did not deny, and even suggested, that a quality and value we name as "sexuality" will be a feature of resurrected "spiritual" bodies',[71] she is in fact more interested in making a proposal that goes beyond that:

> A post-Augustinian resurrection sexuality emerges from the insights of Freud and his followers, an extension of Augustine's fantasy, but not

---

[63] Despite the keen attempts of some scholars to place sexuality at the core of their reading of Augustine (she is particularly scathing about Peter Brown): Miles, 'Sex and the City (of God)', pp. 309 and 310, n. 2.
[64] Miles, 'Sex and the City (of God)', p. 311.
[65] Ibid., p. 314.
[66] Ibid., p. 316.
[67] Ibid., pp. 317–19.
[68] Ibid., p. 320. Quotation from Augustine as cited by Miles: she cites *civ. Dei* 22.24, but I can't find the exact quotation in the text and her construal of it is slightly difficult to reconcile with Augustine's assertion that 'we shall enjoy each other's beauty without any lust: an enjoyment which will specially redound to the praise of the Creator'.
[69] Miles, 'Sex and the City (of God)', p. 325.
[70] Ibid., pp. 323–24.
[71] Ibid., p. 310.

incompatible with it. Challenging *both* Augustine's narrow conception of sex (as sexed bodies and acts) and modern usage (despite Freud and his critics) by which 'sexuality' is used to refer to genitally organized activity, a sexuality of eternally blissful sensuality can be imagined.[72]

But what, one might ask, is the point of reflecting on the sexuality of resurrection bodies? Miles's reply is that 'the value of imagining ideal sexualities is that only then can one begin to make "good sex" now'.[73] Because sexuality is (at least in part) socially constructed, it is liable to the distortions and violence caused by, for example, economic need or inequalities in power. One of those social constructions is Augustine's definition of female sexuality in terms of procreation. While acknowledging that Augustine's theology has contributed to Western cultural attitudes to embodiment that are far from desirable, Miles contends that 'a more accurate understanding of Augustine on physicality and sexuality offers the possibility of beginning to dismantle attitudes toward bodies that continue to fund economic injustice, ecological irresponsibility, and oppression based on race, class, and sexual orientation'.[74] On the other hand, she suggests, Augustine's attempt to imagine bodies who peacefully enjoy each others' beauty – a state which 'invites evaluation as "uninteresting"' from a modern perspective – might challenge modern readers whose conceptions of sexuality are easily dominated by 'elaborate and unrealistic media depictions'.[75]

My final selection also takes a political and ethical look at the same Augustinian idea (that resurrection bodies will have sexual differentiation without their sexual organs being used for sexual activity) but applies this much more directly to a very specific 'problem case' – that of those people with intersex or disorders of sex development (DSD) conditions.[76] Like Miles, Cornwall makes the point that speculations about resurrection bodies have theological interest not just in the realm of eschatology, but because they reveal (and can actively promote) certain evaluations of human bodies here and now: 'Eschatology affects lived attitudes here and now'.[77] Portrayals of resurrection bodies attempt to propound an ideal redeemed body and from the perspective of disability studies, 'any attempt to propound a universalized, idealized

---

[72] Ibid., p. 324. Similarly, Miles's conception of 'distributed' sexuality, which I have not had time to discuss here, is proffered as a challenge to both Augustine (for whom sexuality became a 'centrepiece . . . due to its intractability') and Freud (for whom it was 'the "key" to selfhood').
[73] Miles, 'Sex and the City (of God)', p. 325.
[74] Ibid., p. 309.
[75] Ibid., p. 324.
[76] Susannah Cornwall, *Sex and Uncertainty in the Body of Christ: Intersex Conditions and Christian Theology* (Oakville, CT: Equinox, 2010).
[77] Ibid., p. 184.

redeemed version of the body as able, as sexed, and so on, should therefore be subjected to a scrutiny which is critical at the very least'.[78] Do they *implicitly* suggest that people with impaired bodies are further away from redemption, or are less in the image of God than others?[79] Second, the concept of the resurrection body raises really tricky questions about healing: while many people might welcome the chance eschatologically to cast off a physical impairment,[80] others might view 'healing' (when construed as conforming everyone to a supposed ideal norm) as a threat to their personal identity: would a person with a severely impaired body even be recognizable as the same person if they were fully healed?[81] Third, eschatology affects not just how people regard their fellows with impairments, it also affects how they treat them. Here Cornwall follows the kind of theological critiques of quietist eschatology mentioned above: 'A belief that bodies will be "fixed"[82] after death sometimes makes it too easy to dismiss the struggles faced currently, but an attitude that human beings might be co-redeemers with Christ encourages doing everything possible to eradicate enforced discommodity and promote inclusion.'[83]

It is in this context that Cornwall examines Paul's and Augustine's visions of resurrection bodies. Her question is not so much 'are they correct?', but – given the 'tantalising vagueness and uncertainty surrounding what resurrected perfection will entail' – what their visions say about how the church presently values human bodies.[84] In this light, Augustine's pronouncements might appear to be less than helpful, for he seems quite clear that people will be resurrected either male or female.[85] However, there are certain aspects of his thought in the *City of God* which Cornwall sees as productive for further reflection. First, Augustine denies that sexual difference is an imperfection (specifically, he denies that the sex of *women* is a vice). If the difference between women and men is good, 'the question is whether this [principle] can be extended to other characteristics beyond dichotomous sex'.[86] Indeed, as we have seen, Augustine consistently denies that resurrection bodies will be exactly the same, rejecting the view that all will attain the precise height of Christ. Cornwall draws attention to what one might call Augustine's 'social' reading of Eph. 4.13: the idea, that is that the full stature of Christ is reached

---

[78] Ibid., p. 175.
[79] Ibid., p. 184.
[80] Ibid., p. 178.
[81] Ibid., p. 183.
[82] That is, 'made good' (not 'static').
[83] Cornwall, *Sex and Uncertainty*, p. 183.
[84] Ibid., p. 184.
[85] Augustine discusses hermaphrodites, but as Cornwall states, 'within the medical paradigm of his time he would have deemed them "truly" one sex with extra material from the other added on' (Cornwall, *Sex and Uncertainty*, p. 190).
[86] Cornwall, *Sex and Uncertainty*, p. 190.

when all members of the body of Christ come together under Christ, their head (*civ. Dei* 22.15; 22.18). Perhaps then, Cornwall suggests, 'stature' is here closer to 'status' – the recognition and acceptance of all members full personhood – with the result that 'physical "perfection" in the resurrection body is less significant than right relationship and the eradication of inequity in bodies'.[87]

Second, Augustine argues that some present human bodies have lacks which will be made good in the resurrection. Might God, then, supply in the resurrection what is currently lacking to a person with physical impairments? Could God restore to humans with intersex/DSD conditions parts of their body which were surgically removed to 'normalize' them?[88] However, not all intersex conditions can be healed (even in theological speculation) by the making good of missing parts or the rearrangement of existing parts.[89] Here Cornwall turns to Augustine's vision of the martyrs for a more radical notion of healing: the idea that it is precisely the parts which were involved in their martyrdom that are most glorified in heaven suggests that perhaps 'the body parts which have proven most troublesome in the present realm either in themselves or because of the negative attention they have solicited will also be the body parts most celebrated . . .'[90]

Third, in Augustine's vision of the eschaton, bodies and their parts are released from a narrowly functional use. Hence, for Cornwall, the importance of Augustine's claim that sexually differentiated bodies will be enjoyed without causing lust is that, finally, women's bodies will be released from their traditional functional 'justification' in terms of procreation. But if that is the case, then 'atypically sexed bodies' are also released from 'procreative sexed norms': released from by being judged by what they are not, or cannot do, they are finally free to be who they are before God.[91] But this is not the only release. Rejecting an analysis of lust as purely psychological, in favour of interpreting it in sociopolitical terms, Cornwall writes that Augustine's imagined resurrection proffers a hope that finally humans will be able to relate to one another and enjoy each other's beauty without the 'lust to perfect, correct, regulate, manage, dominate and homogenise'. They will be free from the 'lust to know definitively what constitutes a good body'.[92]

Finally, Cornwall is very cautious in her suggestions: her approach is one of testing ideas, rather than 'specify[ing] what resurrection bodies will be like'.[93]

---

[87] Ibid.
[88] Ibid., pp. 188–89.
[89] Ibid., p. 191.
[90] Ibid., p. 192.
[91] Ibid.
[92] Ibid.
[93] Ibid., p. 189.

The main reflection she draws from the fathers is not an exact image of the resurrection body (a merely biological definition of body) but an understanding that embodiment is inextricably linked to temporality and that, therefore, what will be restored will be a 'redeemed body *story*' (a social as well as biological definition).[94] In this context, eschatological healing is fundamentally a condition in which 'the pain and prejudice attached to a particular physical configuration will melt away without thereby erasing either the beauty of that specific configuration, or the genealogical importance of the life lived in this body in its joy and woundedness'.[95]

V. Conclusion

In the last section, I have argued that the very tensions in Augustine's account of resurrection bodies have been theologically productive: Miles and Cornwall both use the paradox of bodies with sexual organs liberated from sexual reproduction or lust to ask questions about how humans define and evaluate sexuality. For Cornwall, Augustine also raises the question of whether the 'perfection' of bodies lies in their physical completeness (e.g. in the replacement of members) or in the healing of a whole history of an embodied life. This tension between materiality and temporality is also evident in Burrus's suggestion that Augustine defines bodily wholeness in such a temporal way (the resurrection of the body and its parts over its whole lifetime) that the resurrected body both is identical with and exceeds or transcends its earthly self. All three readers draw out the implications of their reading of Augustine for wider theological questions beyond the resurrection of the body.

The theologians we investigated in Part II also found Augustine good 'to think with'. For many, the broad sweep of Augustinian eschatology – the temporal movement of salvation history from 'origin' to 'progress' and 'merited ends'; the contrast between the temporality of this life with the eschaton which is both future and eternal; the absolute distinction between heaven and hell – has been a framework to be rejected. But whether it is defended or jettisoned, the sheer scope of Augustine's eschatology demands rigorous attention. For some, the tensions in Augustine's concept of the two cities, the *saeculum* and the eschaton provoke them to give their own constructive answers to the question of the relationship between God's salvation and human history. But, as we have seen, sometimes Augustine's theology is regarded not so much as full of productive tension, but is viewed – a bit like his earthly city – as riven against itself. In these cases, as we have seen, theologians ultimately criticize Augustine's eschatology, not by rejecting it outright, but rather by

---

[94] Ibid., p. 188.
[95] Ibid., p. 189.

identifying a theology which not only promises an ontology of peace and the gratuitousness of salvation, but which also ascribes eternal retributive punishment to the divine will. Here, the implications of these readings reach right into the heart of theology: the question of the nature of God. Thus, whether one's concern is human justice, theological method or fundamental doctrine, Augustine's eschatology – whether one likes it or not – deserves not to be treated as the quaint musings of a different age, but as material which merits serious theological engagement.

For Further Reading

Adams, Marilyn McCord, 'The Problem of Hell: A Problem of Evil for Christians'. In *God and the Problem of Evil* (ed. William L. Rowe; Oxford: Blackwell, 2001), pp. 282–309.

Daley, Brian, *The Hope of the Early Church* (Peabody, MS: Hendrickson, 2003; Cambridge: Cambridge University Press, 1991).

Fredriksen, Paula, 'Beyond the Body/Soul Dichotomy: Augustine on Paul against the Manichees and the Pelagians', *RechAug* XXIII (1988), pp. 87–114.

Hick, John, *Evil and the God of Love* (Basingstoke: Macmillan, 1977).

Milbank, John, *Theology and Social Theory: Beyond Secular Reason* (Oxford: Blackwell, 1990).

O'Daly, Gerard, *Augustine's 'City of God'* (Oxford: Oxford University Press, 1999).

Part II
Theologians

7 Augustine and Aquinas

Frederick Christian Bauerschmidt

In Sint-Pieterskerk in Leuven, Belgium, there is a painting of Saint Augustine and Saint Thomas Aquinas by Pieter-Jozef Verhaghen (1728–1811), a late follower of Reubens, in which Augustine is pointing to a place in a book he is holding, possibly the Scriptures or one of Augustine's own works, and Thomas is peering intently at the place Augustine is indicating and writing diligently in the book he himself is holding. While hardly a masterpiece of Flemish painting, or even one of Verhaghen's own better works, it is interesting in the harmonious relationship it depicts between the two doctors of the Church, as well as Augustine's tutelage of Thomas, which indicates not only Thomas's debt to Augustine, but even a certain subservience: it is clear who is the teacher and who is the student. The relationship depicted is particularly striking because in modern, post-Vatican II Catholic theology, Augustine and Thomas have come to serve as rhetorical 'tropes' – symbolic stand-ins – for distinct and even opposed styles of theological reflection.[1] Specifically, 'Thomas' serves as a marker for an attitude of optimistic openness to the modern world while 'Augustine' stands for all who are pessimistically disposed to that same modern world.

As will probably come as no surprise, this rhetorical use of the names 'Augustine' and 'Thomas' does scant justice to the complexity of the actual theology of these two writers and the debt that Thomas owes to Augustine. Moreover, if one compares recent uses of these names as tropes to earlier ones, one sees that they have not always functioned as metonyms for pessimism and optimism, and that confusing earlier rhetorical deployments of Augustine and Thomas with later one's can lead to misleading ways of mapping the territory of contemporary Catholic theology. Moreover, the terms themselves are something less than value-neutral descriptions and as such seem to me ultimately neither helpful in understanding the current theological terrain, nor for imagining how Augustine and Thomas might serve as useful resources for theologians today.

---

[1] For this particular use of the term 'trope', see Hayden White, *Tropics of Discourse: Essays in Cultural Criticism* (Baltimore: The Johns Hopkins University Press, 1978).

I. Thomas the Augustinian

No Western Christian theologian escapes the influence of Augustine, and the depth of Thomas's debt to Augustine is widely recognized among historical theologians.[2] Servais Pinkaers notes that in the *Secunda Pars* of the *Summa Theologiae*, for example, Thomas cites Augustine 1,630 times, slightly more often than he cites Aristotle (1,546) and far more often than he cites Gregory the Great, who comes in a distant third (439).[3] In Thomas's commentary on the Gospel of John, we find an almost continual stream of citations from Augustine's own *Tractates* on John. But Thomas's Augustinianism goes beyond what can be quantified by totalling up citations.

Some of Augustine's influence on Thomas might be characterized as 'philosophical'. Though interpreters of Thomas disagree on how best to understand the Neoplatonic elements in his thought – whether as grace notes in an essentially Aristotelian world view or as the key to a distinctive synthesis of Platonism and Aristotle – what is clear is that Augustine, along with Dionysius the Areopagite, is a significant source of those elements.[4] Notions such as divine ideas and the blending of Aristotelian causality with Platonic participation are part of Thomas's inheritance from Augustine. At the same time, because Thomas must deal with the flood of Aristotelian and quasi-Aristotelian texts that entered the West in the twelfth century, he in many ways lives in a vastly different philosophical world than Augustine – not least because it is a world in which a distinction between 'philosophy' and 'theology' is beginning (but only beginning) to be comprehensible.

On many doctrinal points, Thomas uses Augustine in ways that are unsurprising for a medieval Catholic theologian. For example, in his treatment of the Trinity, he follows virtually all Western theologians in using Augustine's 'psychological analogy' of human memory, reason and will.[5] However, Thomas uses Aristotle's understanding of 'immanent operations' to enrich and refine Augustine, arguing that, just as reasoning produces an idea that is itself not 'outside' the mind, so too the Word proceeds from the Father without being 'outside' of what it is to be God, thus making the analogy arguably

---

[2] See the essays collected in *Aquinas the Augustinian* (ed. Michael Dauphinais, Barry David and Matthew Levering; Washington, DC: Catholic University of America Press, 2007), especially the introduction.

[3] Servais-Theodore Pinkaers, 'The Sources of the Ethics of St. Thomas Aquinas', in *The Ethics of Aquinas* (ed. Stephen J. Pope; Washington, DC: Georgetown University Press, 2002), p. 17.

[4] Wayne Hankey, however, argues that the Proclian Neoplatonism of Dionysius is a more significant influence on Thomas than the Plotinian Neoplatonism of Augustine. See *God in Himself: Aquinas' Doctrine of God as Expounded in the Summa Theologiae* (Oxford: Oxford University Press, 1987).

[5] See Augustine, *Trin.* 10.

more dynamic than it is in Augustine.[6] At the same time, Thomas modifies Aristotle, for whom an immanent operation is in no sense productive of anything, in an Augustinian direction by arguing that, at least in a Trinitarian context, the immanent operation of the Father issues in the divine Word, who is a distinct person within God.[7]

Perhaps even more indicative of Thomas's debt to Augustine than his adoption of and engagement with Augustinian commonplaces are the theological points at which he takes a distinctively Augustinian position over and against the prevailing Western medieval consensus.

One example is Thomas's account of the sacraments, in which he continues the rehabilitation, begun by Peter Lombard, of Augustine's theology of sacraments as belonging to the category of 'sign'. This view of sacraments, which can be found in various places in Augustine's writings,[8] fell under a something of a cloud in the High Middle Ages, in part because of the use to which it was put by Berengar of Tours in his Eucharistic theology. Berengar's view was that if the Eucharist is, as Augustine said, a sign of Christ's body, then it could not be the reality of Christ's body, since a sign (*signum*) is by definition distinct from the thing (*res*) to which it refers.[9] Lombard sought to retrieve the Augustinian theology of sacraments as signs of grace by supplementing it with the notion of sacraments as causes of grace: in addition to being signs, sacraments were also causes.[10] This supplementation presumably would banish the spectre of Berengar for sacramental theology. Thomas's insight was that the Augustinian theology of sacramental signs did not need supplementation by a theology of sacramental causality, but rather simply the clarification that it is by virtue of their signification that sacraments are causes: *sacramenta significando causant*.[11] Sacraments are not two kinds of things – signs and causes – but rather a particular *kind* of sign: one that brings about an effect and is not simply a pointer to something else. Thus Thomas can affirm, even more strongly than Lombard, the sign-character of sacraments without compromising their causal efficacy.

An even clearer example of Augustine's influence on Thomas is the way in which his views on grace developed over the course of his life. In his earlier writings, Thomas follows the prevailing theological view of his day that one can

---

[6] See Aquinas, *ST* 1.27.
[7] See Gilles Emery, *The Trinitarian Theology of Saint Thomas Aquinas* (trans. Francesca Aran Murphy; Oxford: Oxford University Press, 2007), pp. 58–9.
[8] See, for example, Augustine, *civ. Dei* 10.5; *cat. rud.* 26.50.
[9] This was at least what Berengar was understood by his opponents to be saying. See Lanfranc of Canterbury, *De corpore et sanguine Domini adversus Berengarium* 20.
[10] Peter Lombard, *Sententiae* 4.1.4.
[11] Aquinas, *De Veritate* 28.2–12.

dispose oneself to the reception of God's grace by doing what is within one's capacity to do, and to such a one, God will not deny grace.[12] It was through reading Augustine's later writings on grace that Thomas came to see that such a view was inadequate, leading him to modify his views such that even one's preparation to receive sanctifying grace must itself be a work of God's grace.[13] Just as Thomas uses Aristotle's notion of immanent operations to enrich Augustinian Trinitarian theology, here Thomas affirmed this Augustinian position on grace by means of the Aristotelian understanding of the need for matter to be properly disposed to receive a form, thus using Aristotle to help him articulate a *more* Augustinian position than he had held previously.

These two examples must suffice to bolster the claim that, while Thomas did not feel compelled to follow him in all matters, Augustine remained a determinative influence upon Thomas, so much so that Thomas is fruitfully understood as representing one strand of the medieval Augustinian heritage, as much as Bonaventure or Henry of Ghent.[14] This claim also seems to run against the grain of modern Catholic tropes that divide the theological world up into Augustinians and Thomists. But what if the division between Augustine and Thomas is not a material one between specific theological conclusions, but rather a 'formal' one, a difference in fundamental attitude? This would seem to be the implicit claim of those who invoke Augustine and Thomas as rhetorical tropes. If we look at the way one set of early twentieth-century Catholic thinkers used the terms 'Augustinian' and 'Thomist', it may help us critically to evaluate more recent uses of those tropes.

II. The Restless Heart and the Scientific Mind

The term 'Augustinian' is not a medieval term and first appears in the seventeenth century as an adjective associated with the Order of Saint Augustine. The first use in English of 'Augustinianism' to identify a theological position was in 1830, when it was used to describe, interestingly enough, the theology of grace in Thomas Aquinas.[15] The fact that the term arrives so late upon the scene, and was at times used to characterize Thomas's position over and against others, indicates that even when the terms 'Augustinian' and 'Thomist' have been used, they have not always been used in the same way.

In the first part of the twentieth century, one way of figuring the Augustine-Thomas distinction was as a distinction between a theology flowing

---

[12] See *Super Sent.* 2.5.2.1; cf. 2.28.4.1.
[13] *ST* 1–2.109.6.
[14] On the difficulties inherent in using a term like 'the medieval Augustinian heritage', see Erik Leland Saak, *Creating Augustine: Interpreting Augustine and Augustinianism in the Later Middle Ages* (Oxford: Oxford University Press, 2012), pp. 1–22.
[15] Saak, *Creating Augustine*, p. 3.

directly from religious experience and a theology that had been rationally structured so as to attain a 'scientific' status. Given the great authority of both Augustine and Thomas, there was little interest in pitting them against each other.[16] Rather the difference was seen as a complementary one, in which the Augustinian focus on experience needed Thomas's scientific methodology in order for theology to be a rational discipline, while Thomistic theological science needed the existential fervour of Augustine in order not to degenerate into mere rationalism. There were, however, different emphases with regard to which was the more pressing need.

These different emphases can be seen in a collection of essays published in 1930 to commemorate the fifteen-hundredth anniversary of Augustine's death. Contributors included some of the most illustrious Catholic public intellectuals of the early twentieth century, including Jacques Maritain, Maurice Blondel and Étienne Gilson. Maritain and Gilson can rather uncontroversially be described as 'Thomists', while Blondel is sometimes described as 'Augustinian', though it was only late in his life that he turned to an actual study of Augustine.[17] All three posit a fundamental harmony between Augustine and Thomas, while recognizing real differences between them and parsing those differences in distinct ways.

Maritain describes the difference between Augustine and Thomas by quoting with approval a remark by Pascal: 'The heart has its order, and so has the mind.'[18] For Maritain, Augustine's favoured philosophical framework, neo-Platonism, is 'incontestably deficient' (p. 203), but this in no way harms his theology because it is rooted not in acquired human reason but in infused divine wisdom (p. 206). One can speak only equivocally of the 'metaphysics' of Augustine, if we mean by this a rational human discourse on being (p. 209); what he in fact offers is a rich metaphysical intuition rooted in religious experience (p. 210). Augustine's thought is best conceived of as something like the raw material upon which Thomistic science operates, giving it order and the rationally compelling power of the deductive syllogism. Maritain writes,

> How foolish to oppose Thomism and Augustinianism as two systems (I mean the Augustinianism of St. Augustine himself)! The first is a system,

---

[16] An exception seems to be Lucien Laberthonnière (1860–1932), who early on identified himself as an 'Augustinian' and later in his life apparently harangued the young Étienne Gilson while riding together on a trolley concerning the evils wrought by Thomas Aquinas in Catholic thought. See Marvin O'Connell, *Critics on Trial: An Introduction to the Catholic Modernist Crisis* (Washington, DC: Catholic University of America Press, 1994), p. 367.

[17] See Oliva Blanchette, *Maurice Blondel: A Philosophical Life* (Grand Rapids, MI: Eerdmans, 2010), p. 360.

[18] Jacques Maritain, 'St. Augustine and St. Thomas Aquinas', in *St. Augustine: His Age, Life and Thought* (New York: Meridian Books, 1957), p. 199. Subsequent citations in the text.

the second is not. Thomism is the scientific state of Christian wisdom; in the case of the Fathers and St. Augustine, Christian wisdom is still a mere spring. (p. 219)

The wisdom flowing from this spring has passed entirely into Thomism (p. 218), where it has been transformed into Christian philosophy. This Christian philosophy must 'live and spiritualize itself in contact with the living faith and experiences of the Christian soul', while at the same time, it 'is rigorously independent of the subject's own dispositions, and wishes to be regulated by objective necessities and intelligible constraints' (p. 223). It is Augustine who recalls for us the former truth, and Thomas who reminds us of the latter, and in this division of labour, we find their complementarity.[19]

Gilson, perhaps thinking of philosophers like Maritain, notes the 'disfavor of which St. Augustine, *qua* philosopher, has been the butt in the minds of many Catholic thinkers'.[20] Augustinianism is, Gilson says, 'structurally quite different' (p. 291) from Thomism, particularly in its 'incompleteness' and the 'intuitive rather than systematic genius' with which Augustine Christianized Platonism (p. 292). These features leaves it open to the kinds of misunderstanding and distortions we find in Cartesianism and Ontologism. These can be overcome, however, by a return to Augustine himself (pp. 300–01) and a recognition of the role of grace in his thought. Without grace, Augustinianism is 'a strange metaphysical monster' (p. 307), for it is grace that 'turns knowledge into wisdom and moral effort into virtue' (p. 308). The very notion of a metaphysics in which grace plays an essential role already indicates Gilson's distance from Maritain. Like Maritain, Gilson sees Thomas's thought as proceeding along a path quite distinct from Augustine, but he sees this as the difference between two different philosophies, rather than between what is philosophy and what is something else. By comparison with Augustine's philosophy, Thomas's is oriented less towards the soul and more towards the cosmos – a cosmos that operates according to the laws intrinsic to created natures (p. 310). With their philosophical differences, Augustine and Thomas 'can meet again in the same conclusions, but the roads leading to them, though constantly crossing, never follow at any point the same direction' (p. 311).

---

[19] There seems to be at least a formal similarity between the relationship of Augustinian religious experience to Thomist theological science, on the one hand, and Maritain's understanding of the relationship of 'eidetic visualization' (i.e. the intuition of being) and metaphysics proper on the other hand. For the latter, see the description of Maritain's metaphysics in Helen James John, *The Thomist Spectrum* (New York: Fordham University Press, 1966), pp. 17–24.

[20] Étienne Gilson, 'The Future of Augustinian Metaphysics', in *St. Augustine: His Age, Life and Thought*, p. 291. Subsequent citations in the text.

For Maritain, there is a single philosophy, Thomism, which alone can raise theology to the status of a true science. For Gilson, there are multiple philosophies that can be employed by theologians, and Augustine and Thomas provide two of these, one more subjectively focused and the other more objective. Despite his philosophical pluralism, however, Gilson shows a clear preference for Thomism, which has in his eyes already shown its ability to incorporate the insights flowing from Augustine's focus on the human soul; it remains to be seen for Gilson whether Augustinianism can similarly incorporate the insights that flow from Thomas's cosmological focus.

Like Gilson, Blondel finds in Augustine a philosophy worthy of the name. Unlike, Gilson, however, he sees this philosophy as in no need of having to prove itself vis-à-vis Thomism. Rather, because it presumes 'a unity of thought and life', it is 'a novel and superior kind of philosophy in close relation to the aspirations and needs of many contemporary minds'.[21] It combines to a supreme decree 'a generally successful effort to achieve such intelligibility as might satisfy a mind possessed of the highest degree of acuteness and perspicacity' with 'an impetuosity which masters every detail and seems to transport the whole soul far beyond the regions where dialectic, however vivid and swift, seems a mere bloodless and desiccated assortment of bones' (p. 320). In common with Maritain and Gilson, he rejects all attempts to pit Augustine and Thomas against each other. However, he rejects Maritain's approach, in which Augustine and Thomas were seen as pursuing quite distinct ends by quite distinct means; he likewise reject Gilson's approach, in which Augustine and Thomas follow distinct paths to a common end (p. 325). Blondel, rather, seems to interpret Thomas in light of Augustine. He agrees in a sense with Maritain that there is no *separable* philosophy in Saint Augustine, but says that the same is true of Thomas himself. Both Augustine and Thomas affirm that 'there is in the nature of a spiritual being a desire to see God, an aspiration toward beatitude . . . a desire which sets our mind and will in motion toward a goal inaccessible in the order of nature' (pp. 330–31). In other words, Blondel interprets Thomas's account the mind's dynamic orientation towards knowledge of causes in light of Augustine's account of the restless heart that can find rest only in God.

In Blondel's reading of Thomas in light of Augustine, we see sketched what would become a key issue in mid-twentieth-century Catholic theology: the question of the natural desire for the supernatural vision of God and the implications of this for how one understands the relationship between nature and grace. This is not unrelated to how one conceives of the 'scientific' status of theology: is theology, as many Thomists would have it, a deductive process

---

[21] Maurice Blondel, 'The Latent Resources in St. Augustine's Thought', in *St. Augustine: His Age, Life and Thought*, p. 319. Subsequent citations in the text.

employing natural human reason to draw conclusions from revealed premises, or is it the quest of the soul, stirred by grace, to seek an understanding adequate to that experience of grace. Blondel saw the thought of Augustine as needed to 'stimulate a science of inner dynamism' that can overcome the tendency of neo-scholastic Thomism to see grace as an extrinsic gift 'subsequently imposed on a nature in full possession of itself and capable of ensuring its self-sufficiency' (pp. 340–41). Augustine's account of the restless heart is a necessary reminder that while theology may be a science, it is a science that seeks to conform thought to the exigencies of the spiritual life, and without such a reminder, Thomist science becomes mere rationalism. 'The revival of Thomism makes the revival of Augustinianism still more desirable' (p. 342).

If we think of 'Augustine' and 'Thomas' as rhetorical figures or tropes, then Maritain, Gilson and Blondel agree in letting Augustine stand for a way of thinking oriented to the human subject and the dynamic of the spiritual life and in letting Thomas for a style of thought more oriented towards a rational grasp of the order of the cosmos. 'Augustine' means existential engagement and 'Thomas' means objectivity and abstraction. For Maritain, this means that only Thomas offers a true philosophy and the possibility of a genuinely scientific theology. For Gilson, the Augustinian and Thomist approaches present two different philosophical possibilities, the latter of which has proved its usefulness for theology, and the former of which must still be developed. For Blondel, it is Augustine who has proved himself capable of uniting thought and life, and it is Thomism (if not Thomas himself) that must be transformed by contact with the philosophical insights of Augustine, so as to become capable of articulating the truth that can satisfy the heart's restless yearning for God.

It is Blondel's position that would prove to be influential among many mid-twentieth-century Catholic theologians. As Jürgen Mettepenningen says, 'Known for his *theologia affectiva*, Augustine was employed as a sort of crowbar, as it were, to help break through the monopoly of neo-scholasticism'.[22] Not least among the theologians who saw Augustine in this way was Joseph Ratzinger, who in recalling his early theological formation in the immediate aftermath of the Second World War comments that his encounter with the personalist philosophy of Martin Buber 'was for me a spiritual experience that left an essential mark, especially since I spontaneously associated such personalism with the thought of St. Augustine, who in his *Confessions* had struck me with the power of all his human passion and depth'. He continues, 'by contrast, I had difficulties penetrating the thought of Thomas Aquinas, whose crystal-clear logic seemed to me to be too closed in on itself, too impersonal and ready-made'. Ratzinger does go on to acknowledge that

---

[22] Jürgen Mettepenningen, *Nouvelle Théologie – New Theology: Inheritor of Modernism, Precursor of Vatican II* (London: T&T Clark, 2010), p. 145.

at least part of his difficulty was the 'rigid, neoscholastic' form of Thomism that he was taught,[23] and later in life he would describe Thomas's thought not as 'impersonal' but as 'precise, lucid and pertinent'.[24] We might say that the Thomas that Ratzinger comes to appreciate is not the Thomas of Thomist science, but the Thomas who is read, in the manner of Blondel, as an heir to the Augustinian project of seeking a knowing adequate to the yearnings of the restless heart. Interestingly, this is not how many modern interpreters of the post-conciliar theological scene understand the Augustinianism of Ratzinger and how it differs from Thomism.

III. Church and World: Pessimism and Optimism

Various theologians seeking to map the world of Catholic theology after the Second Vatican Council have employed 'Augustine' and 'Thomas' as tropes in ways quite different from the way they are employed by Maritain, Gilson and Blondel. Here, the relevant distinction is not between subjectivity and objectivity or between the heart and the mind but between pessimism and optimism, particularly with regard to the modern world. Thus Ratzinger's early attraction to Augustine and rejection of Thomism is seen as an incipient manifestation of a pessimistic theology.[25] Such an interpretation is given a degree of plausibility inasmuch as one accepts a particular use of 'Augustine' and 'Thomas' as rhetorical tropes for pessimism and optimism and ignores earlier uses, such as we find in Maritain, Gilson and Blondel.

To choose one example among many of such use, Dominic Doyle, in discussing the 'Augustinian' character of Pope Benedict's encyclical *Spes Salvi*, notes that he will use the terms 'Augustinian' and 'Thomist' as 'imprecise generalizations that attempt to name differing emphases in theologians who take their lead from Augustine or Thomas respectively'. He goes on to say that 'an "Augustinian" sensibility would insist on a sharp contrast between eschatological and secular hope, the deep and ineradicable nature of sin, and thus the limits – even tragic flaws – of all human projects'. A Thomist sensibility, in contrast, would follow Thomas in his defence of '"true yet imperfect virtues" that intend temporal goods, such as "the welfare of the state"'.[26]

---

[23] Joseph Ratzinger, *Milestones: Memoirs: 1927–1977* (trans. Erasmo Levia-Merikakis; San Francisco: Ignatius Press, 1998), p. 44.
[24] Benedict XVI, General Audience, 23 June 2010. Available at www.vatican.va/holy_father/benedict_xvi/audiences/2010/documents/hf_ben-xvI_aud_20100623_En.html. Accessed September 2012.
[25] See, for example, Massimo Faggioli, *Vatican II: The Battle for Meaning* (Mahwah, NJ: Paulist Press, 2012), p. 72.
[26] Dominic Doyle, '*Spes Salvi* on Eschatological and Secular Hope: A Thomistic Critique of an Augustinian Encylcical', *TS* 71 (2010), pp. 350–79, at p. 351 n. 3.

In other words, an Augustinian casts a wary eye at the modern world and its projects for human progress, seeing them as irrevocably marked by human pride, whereas a Thomist embraces, albeit not uncritically, the genuine goods that the modern world has to offer, seeing human historical progress as contributing in some way to the growth in history of God's Kingdom.

This distinction is often used, without Doyle's caveat concerning 'imprecise generalizations', to describe the way in which those who at the Second Vatican Council were united in their opposition to neo-scholasticism split in the aftermath of the council into opposed camps. Massiomo Faggioli identifies not only Ratzinger, but also Henri de Lubac, Jean Daniélou, Hans Urs von Balthasar and Louis Bouyer as 'neo-Augustinians' and Yves Congar, Marie-Dominique Chenu, Edward Schillebeeckx, Karl Rahner and Bernard Lonergan as examples of 'reinterpreted Thomism' (presumably to distinguish their views from pre-conciliar neo-Thomism).[27] Prior to the council, one sometimes finds 'Augustine' and 'Thomas' used, particularly by those who identify as 'Thomist', as tropes for pessimism and optimism – world-denial and world-affirmation –, but it is with the debate over 'Schema 13', which became the Pastoral Constitution on the Church in the modern world, *Gaudium et spes*, that divisions within the pre-conciliar 'progressives' begin to become apparent.[28] So let us look at a representative figure that Faggioli identifies with each of these two camps to see the sense in which they are 'Thomist' and 'Augustinian'.

Perhaps no one was as resolute in identifying an optimistic affirmation of the world as 'Thomist' against a purported 'Augustinian' pessimism than the Dominican Marie-Dominique Chenu. Writing prior to the council, he contrasted Augustine's view that the workings of grace in history appears to us only as incomprehensible 'haphazard events', with Thomas's 'ontological optimism' that the order of the world is graspable by the human mind.[29] In a collection of essays published a few years after the council, Chenu speaks of Thomas's recognition of the value of corporeality as the foundation of 'his optimistic vision of man and of the world'.[30] This optimistic vision is that 'it is the human and divine truth of man that his spirit should penetrate the corporeal world, including his own body, for man is the demiurge of that world and responsible for it before his Creator' (p. 134). This provides the foundation

---

[27] Faggioli, *Vatican II: The Battle for Meaning*, pp. 69, 75–6.
[28] See Joseph A. Komonchak, 'Augustine, Aquinas or the Gospel *sine glossa*? Divisions over *Gaudium et Spes*', in *Unfinished Journey: The Church 40 Years after Vatican II: Essays for John Wilkins* (ed. Austen Ivereigh; London: Tablet, 2003), pp. 102–18.
[29] Marie-Dominique Chenu, *Aquinas and His Role in Theology* (trans. Paul Philibert; Collegeville, MN: The Liturgical Press, 2002 [French original 1959]), p. 88.
[30] Marie-Dominique Chenu, *Faith and Theology* (trans. Denis Hickey; New York: MacMillan, 1968), p. 136. Subsequent citations in the text.

for engagement with the world, for secular history is the theatre in which the world's salvation is played out. Chenu describes Augustine, on the other hand, as 'a temporary victim of Manicheism' whose 'whole life was coloured by an unusually sad experience of uncontrolled passion' (p. 108). Whereas Blondel had seen Augustine's thought as close to the aspirations of modern people, Chenu argues that 'it is only by accepting this [Thomist] view of creation and in accepting this Christian meaning of man that the Christian can take his place in our new scientific and technological civilization' (p. 111). Just as Thomas embraced the new Aristotelian science of his day and put it to an evangelical purpose, so modern-day Christians should embrace the insights and aspirations of their day – even those coming from modern-day 'Pagans' – and place them in service of the Gospel.

One frequently named 'Augustinian' is Jean Daniélou, who early in his career made remarks critical of neo-scholastic Thomism and proposed the Fathers of the early Church as the way forward for theology. Further, Daniélou writes that in comparison to optimistic views of history, 'pessimistic doctrines . . . seem far more sensible' and that 'those who have seen furthest into human nature are all pessimists, like Augustine, Pascal, and Kierkegaard'.[31] He speaks with approval of Augustine's spiritual interpretation of the season of Lent as representing life in this world, 'through which we make our way under the constant attractions and repulsions of the march of time, the instability and mutability of human affairs, the irresistible flow of change'.[32] Our modern period is, Daniélou asserts, 'heathen . . . and divided, and ruinous' (p. 346). Here the charge of an Augustinian pessimism seems to be borne out. However, despite his mention of Augustine, Daniélou never identifies his own position as an 'Augustinian' one. In fact, while the author of *The City of God* would seem to necessarily play a significant role in any Western theologian's account of history, Daniélou has a greater affinity for the Greek Fathers.[33] And when he comes to discuss hope, which he sees as the true Christian attitude towards history, rather than pessimism, Daniélou invokes Thomas (*ST* 2–2.17.3) to make the point that, because of the bonds of charity, the object of hope is never simply the individual, but 'the final destiny of the world and of the whole human race' (p. 353). In the end, hope trumps both pessimism and optimism.

When we compare Chenu and Daniélou, we can see the curious asymmetry in the assigning of the labels 'Augustinian' and 'Thomist' in the post-conciliar theological world. That is, it seems to be primarily those who assign the label

---

[31] Jean Daniélou, *The Lord of History: Reflections on the Inner Meaning of History* (London: Longmans, Green, 1958), p. 342. Subsequent citations in the text.
[32] Augustine, *s.* 252 (*PL* 38:1177–8), quoted in Daniélou, *The Lord of History*, p. 266.
[33] He was also appreciative of the thought of Teilhard de Chardin, who is rarely accused of pessimism.

'Thomist' to themselves who are the ones who assign the label 'Augustinian' to others. While one can certainly find theologians who, like Daniélou, write sympathetically of Augustine's views on a range of issues, one has a bit more trouble finding those who identify *themselves* as 'Augustinian' *rather* than 'Thomist'. It is perhaps a measure of the esteem accorded to Thomas after the encyclical *Aeterni Patris* that everyone felt that they needed to be Thomist in some sense, and that the theological high ground could be seized by identifying oneself as 'Thomist', even if, as sometimes happens, a closer inspection of the actual theological views of the one claiming the Thomist mantle proved to be quite different from those of Thomas himself. Massimo Faggioli speaks of the recognition by '"progressive" neo-Thomist' of the need 'to adopt Thomas's approach rather than his conclusions'.[34] This is an interesting contrast with the view of Gilson noted earlier, in which Augustine and Thomas, while their philosophical approaches differed, were compatible inasmuch as their theological conclusions concurred. For Faggioli, Thomas's actual conclusions seem somewhat beside the point; it is his approach of openness to the world, so different from Augustinian pessimism that is to be valued today. One cannot help but suspect that in such cases Thomas is being invoked more as an ornament than as an expert.[35] It is certainly to the advantage of theologians to be able to claim the authority of Thomas for their own position, particularly is the post-conciliar context when so much seems up for grabs. It is reassuring to have the 'common doctor' endorse one's policy of openness to the modern world.

This focus on Thomas's general approach rather than his specific conclusions also helps in separating 'Augustinians' and 'Thomists' into distinct camps. As we have seen, Thomas agrees with Augustine in many of his theological positions. But if one relativizes the importance of those positions in favour of claiming kinship with his 'approach', then it becomes easier to map the theological territory of contemporary Catholicism. Thus Augustine, who in the early twentieth century served as a crowbar to break through the stranglehold of neo-scholasticism on Catholic theology, can become a metonym for reactionary pessimism.

IV. Thomas the Augustinian *redux*: *peregrini* and *viatores*

The shifting significance of Augustine makes us question how helpful it is to speak, as Faggioli does, of Augustinian or Thomist 'schools'. Both Augustine

---

[34] Faggioli, *Vatican II: The Battle for Meaning*, p. 79.
[35] The terms 'expert' and 'ornament' are taken from Carlo Leget, who gives a nuanced taxonomy of the different ways the authority of Thomas can be invoked in various realms of argumentation. See 'Authority and Plausibility: Aquinas on Suicide', in *Aquinas as Authority* (ed. Paul van Geest et al.; Leuven: Peeters, 2002), pp. 277–93, esp. pp. 286–87.

and Thomas were thinkers whose written output is vast in scope and variegated in character. Any 'school' that we might identify as Augustinian or Thomist will surely be characterized by only a small subset of the positions held by the historical figure from which it draws its name. If we are concerned that the terms 'Augustinian' and 'Thomist' are actually meaningful, then it is incumbent upon us to specify exactly what we mean by the terms. If we speak of someone's position as 'Augustinian', do we mean that he/she holds to some form of knowledge via divine illumination rather than abstraction from sense experience, or do we mean that he/she holds to a theology whose form of rationality is not some version of Aristotelian science, or do we mean that he/she sees the virtues of non-Christians as 'splendid vices' rather than real but imperfect human virtues or do we mean that he/she holds that there is a plurality of substantial forms that make up the human person rather than the rational soul being the single substantial form of the human being. All of these and more have be used at various points in history to identify an 'Augustinian' view over and against a 'Thomist' one. But it is not only dubious that these positions were all held by the historical figure Aurelius Augustinus Hipponensis, but it is also not clear that these various positions necessarily hold together in such a way as to form a school of thought.

Even if one specifies that one means by 'Augustinian' not specific theological conclusions but an attitude of pessimistic suspicion towards the world, and by 'Thomist' an attitude of optimistic openness to what the modern world has to offer, problems remain. Marie-Dominique Chenu made as good an effort as anyone to show how Thomas's metaphysics, ethics and theology all hung together in a way that allowed a joyful embrace of the world, an embrace that should characterize Christians in their approach to the world today. But in the end, his picture of Thomas remains somewhat unconvincing. Even if we prescind from specific theological positions, Thomas remained by disposition as 'otherworldly' as Augustine – indeed, perhaps more so. Augustine was not only a fierce combatant in the theological controversies of his day, but he was also involved in very mundane aspects of life in Hippo by virtue of his role as bishop, ranging from providing pastoral care to settling property disputes.[36] In the case of Thomas, there is more than simply hagiography at work in the story of the student who, admiring the city of Paris from a distance, said to him, 'what a beautiful city Paris is', to which Thomas replied, 'I would rather have the homilies of Chrysostom on the Gospel of blessed Matthew'.[37] We misread Thomas if we forget that he was a thirteenth-century mendicant friar who lived a highly ascetic lifestyle that was single-mindedly devoted to

---

[36] See F. van der Meer, *Augustine the Bishop: The Life and Work of a Father of the Church* (trans. Brian Battershaw and G. R. Lamb; London: Sheed and Ward, 1961), pp. 255–70.
[37] William of Tocco, *Ystoria sancti Thome de Aquino*, XLII.

the preaching of the Gospel for the edification of Church and the intellectual defeat of her enemies. Even his meticulous commentaries on Aristotle were ordered to that end. Moreover, it is good to remember that the Thomas who wrote that 'grace perfects and does not destroy nature'[38] also wrote, 'alacrity of will and fervor of divine love are chiefly shown when that which we do for God is repugnant to our own inclination'.[39] Thomas, no less than Augustine, recognizes the damage that sin has done to nature and the need for ascetical practices, cooperating with divine grace, to reorient our nature. Commenting on Rom. 12.2, Thomas writes,

> Just as a person with a diseased palate does not have right judgment concerning the taste of foods but sometimes recoils from what is sweet and desires what is disgusting, whereas a person with a healthy palate has right judgment concerning tastes, so too a person whose affections are corrupted by conformity to worldly things does not have right judgment concerning the good, whereas a person who has upright and sound affections, because his sense has been renewed by grace, has right judgment concerning the good.[40]

Rather than an undifferentiated, optimistic embrace of the world, Thomas offers criteria by which we can discern between the world as God's good creation and the worldliness that leaves us with a diseased palate, unable to distinguish between the sweetness of divine love and the bitterness of worldly concupiscence.

Likewise, Augustine cannot be characterized simply as a pessimist. We forget at our peril that Augustine and Thomas were alike in rejecting dualist forms of religion – for Augustine the Manichees and for Thomas the Cathars – and affirming the fundamental goodness of creation. In the final book of the *City of God*, Augustine famously catalogues at great length the miseries of this life: oppressive laws, tedious labour, lies and fraud, extremes of heat and cold, floods and earthquakes, rabid dogs and famines so severe that mothers eat their children. Such things, Augustine says, teach us 'to bewail the calamities of this life and to desire the felicity of the life to come' and remind us that, 'from this hell upon earth there is no escape, save through the grace of the Saviour Christ, our God and Lord'.[41] What is less often recalled, however, is the catalogue of the blessings in this life that follows this: our very existence and the human capacity for reproduction, the powers or reason and understanding

---

[38] Aquinas, *ST* 1.1.8.
[39] *De perfection vitae spiritualis* 12.
[40] *Super Rom.* 12.1.967.
[41] Augustine, *civ. Dei* 22.22.

and the arts and sciences that flow from them, human language and culinary arts, mathematics and astronomy, the functioning of our bodily organs and senses, the beauty and utility of our embodied existence, heavenly bodies and earthly creatures, ants and whales and the subtle variety of all the shades of green that adorn the world.[42] Even amid the devastation wrought by original sin, Augustine can discern the fundamental goodness of creation, not simply the goodness of the natural world, but also and especially the goods of human culture, human scientific ingenuity and human love. If even in our misery God bestows such gift on us, what shall be the reward of the blessed?

Without denying the real differences between Augustine and Thomas, with regard to how Christians should relate to the world, they share is a keen sense of Christians as *peregrini* or *viatores* – those who are on a journey to their heavenly *patria* or homeland. For Thomas, the wayfarer 'is threatened by many dangers both from within and without',[43] the object of her hope is veiled,[44] and yet this hope has a kind of certainty born of faith.[45] For both Augustine and Thomas, the wayfarer's life is characterized by a restless desire to know the God who is the source of his/her being, a desire to advance towards the God in whom he/she will find rest. Of course the form the pilgrim's life took in Augustine's day was quite different from the form it took in Thomas's, reflecting the quite different situation of Augustine's Church from Thomas's – the difference between a Church that still lived to a large degree alongside a Pagan culture, albeit one in the beginning of its death-throes, and a Church that had for centuries been the conserver and conveyor of the culture of antiquity. Yet there remains substantial continuity between Augustine's *peregrini* and Thomas's *viatores*.

Thomas quotes with approval Augustine's statement that the wayfarer advances towards God 'not by steps of the body but by affections of the soul', particularly the virtue of love.[46] For Augustine and Thomas, with regard to whether one embraces or rejects the world, pessimism and optimism are somewhat beside the point. What matters is the pilgrim's journey through this world, which is undertaken by means of love – love of God and love of neighbour. The wayfarer's attitude towards the world is neither simple acceptance nor rejection, but a love of neighbour for the sake of God. In this sense, there is for both Augustine and Thomas an openness to the world, but it is an openness that takes seriously the possibility that the world will hate and persecute the followers of Jesus, and that recognizes that even the good things of this world must be subordinated to the supreme good of the vision of God

---

[42] Ibid., 22.24.
[43] Aquinas, *ST* 1.113.4.
[44] Ibid., 2–2.17.2 *ad* 1.
[45] Ibid., 2–2.18.4.
[46] Ibid., 2–2.24.4, quoting Augustine, *Jo. ev. tr.* 32.

in the world to come. In this regard, Augustine and Thomas share not simply certain theological conclusions, but also a common theological approach.

V. Augustine and Thomas in the Modern Theological Tropics

How then ought we assess the use of 'Augustine' and 'Thomas' in post-conciliar Catholic theology as tropes for pessimism and optimism with regard to the modern world?

First, we ought not to think that such tropes tell us anything useful about Augustine or Thomas as historical figures. To state the obvious, neither Augustine nor Thomas had any knowledge of our modern world and were neither pessimistic nor optimistic regarding it. Perhaps less obviously, to characterize Augustine as a pessimist and Thomas as an optimist with regard to the world outside the Church in their own times ignores both the complexity of each thinker's views and the historical differences between how the Church was situated vis-à-vis the world in the fourth century and how it was situated in the thirteenth century. Thomas's *viator* is the direct descendent of Augustine's *peregrinus*, though how this pilgrim status was lived out was quite different for a thirteenth-century friar than it was for a fourth-century bishop. To distil these complexities into a simple attitude of pessimism or optimism with regard to the world outside of the Church or to human culture is to miss both the similarities and the differences between Augustine and Thomas.

Further, even prescinding from historical claims about Augustine or Thomas, the use of these tropes to map the post-conciliar theological landscape is not particularly illuminating of the situation of Catholic theology. For example, theologians who are typically grouped together as 'Augustinian' or 'Thomist' often reveal, upon closer examination, their own complexities. For example, Chenu's Thomist optimism grows, at least in part, from Blondel's Augustinian view of the relationship of theology to the experience of grace. That is, according to the way these terms were used in the 1930s, Chenu is more 'Augustinian' than 'Thomist', because he sees theology as 'a spirituality that has found rational instruments adequate to its religious experience'.[47] Similarly, one might see the Augustinian pessimism of Daniélou, which sharply distinguishes historical progress from the growth of the Kingdom of God, as observing a properly Thomist distinction between nature and grace. The differences between theologians of the depth and subtlety of Chenu and Daniélou calls for a deeper analysis than applying the labels that 'Augustinian' and 'Thomist' allows, even if, as in the case of Chenu, they sometimes themselves resort to these tropes.

---

[47] Marie-Dominique Chenu et al., *Une école de théologie: Le Saulchoir* (Théologies; Paris: Cerf, 1985), pp. 148–49.

Finally, while rhetorical tropes might help us satisfy the 'blessed rage for order' that seeks to identify the species of everything it encounters, they do not carve the theological world at the joints. We should not fool ourselves into thinking that categories like 'Augustinian' or 'Thomist' describe natural kinds, nor that they are innocent terms, particularly given the status of Thomas in Catholic theology and the persistent suspicion that there is something vaguely Protestant or Jansenist in excessive enthusiasm for Augustine. For that matter, why should we think that terms like 'optimism' and 'pessimism', or 'acceptance' and 'rejection', are adequate to characterizing the Christian's relationship to the world? How convincing is it really to think that there are only two fundamental attitudes towards the modern world among post-conciliar theologians? As Tom Robbins notes in his novel *Still Life with Woodpecker*, 'There are two kinds of people in this world: those who believe there are two kinds of people in this world and those who are smart enough to know better.'[48] If one's first move is to map the terrain in terms of Augustinian pessimism and Thomist optimism, one risks forgetting that the map is not the territory.

In Verhaghen's painting of Augustine and Thomas, a baroque cherub stands in the foreground, holding up a heart that burns with the flame of charity, the source of light by which Thomas reads the passage indicated to him by Augustine and by which he writes in his own book. The danger of using 'Augustine' and 'Thomas' as rhetorical tropes for different tendencies in modern theology is that it can lead us to overlook that, for all their differences, it is the common light of charity in which they read and write their texts that unites Augustine and Thomas in a shared theological project. If we read their texts, and write our own, by the light of that same charity, then both Augustine and Thomas can offer us a way to engage the modern world, its joys and hopes, its sorrows and fears, in a way that is neither pessimistic nor optimistic, offering neither blanket acceptance nor rejection, but rooted in the discerning faith, hope and love that are God's gifts to his people.

For Further Reading

Chenu, Marie-Dominique, *Toward Understanding St. Thomas* (trans. A.-M. Landry and D. Hughes; Chicago: Henry Regnery, 1964).

D'Arcy, Martin C. et al., *St. Augustine: His Age, Life and Thought* (New York: Meridian Books, 1957).

---

[48] One of the strengths of Joseph Komonchak's essay 'Augustine, Aquinas or the Gosple *sine glossa?*' is that in addition to the Augustinian Ratzinger and the Thomist Chenu he also discusses Giuseppe Dossetti, who seems to offer an alternative that is more radically evangelical than either 'Augustinianism' or 'Thomism'.

Dauphinais Michael, Barry David and Matthew Levering (eds), *Aquinas the Augustinian* (Washington, DC: Catholic University of America Press, 2007).
Komonchak, Joseph A., 'Augustine, Aquinas or the Gospel *sine glossa*? Divisions over *Gaudium et Spes*'. In *Unfinished Journey: The Church 40 Years after Vatican II: Essays for John Wilkins* (ed. Austen Ivereigh; London: Tablet, 2003), pp. 102–18.
Torrell, Jean-Pierre, *Saint Thomas Aquinas, Vol. 2: Spiritual Master* (trans. Robert Royal; Washington, DC: The Catholic University of America Press, 2003).

8 Augustine and Bonaventure

Joshua C. Benson

On 1 June 1285, the Franciscan archbishop of Canterbury, John Pecham (d. 1292), wrote a heated letter to the bishop of Lincoln. He had agitated the Dominicans when he renewed certain condemnations of his predecessor, the Dominican Robert Kilwardby (d. 1279), at the University of Oxford: particularly, the condemnation of the unicity of form in a human being.[1] The Dominicans, recognizing an attack on Aquinas, responded in a pamphlet filled with wit and invective against the archbishop. Pecham was not amused. He attempted to defend himself in the letter, especially his own adherence to a plurality of forms in the human person: a theory he believed had implications for the identity of Christ's body in the tomb. At one point, he declares against his Dominican detractors:

> What is the more safe and sound teaching? Is it the teaching of the sons of Saint Francis, especially Brother Alexander of blessed memory, Brother Bonaventure and others like them, who in their treatises that are free of all reproach depend upon the saints and philosophers? Or is it that novel and practically entirely antithetical teaching that embroils the whole world in a war of words, [a teaching that] destroys and weakens as far as it can whatever Augustine teaches about the eternal rules and the unchangeable light, the powers of the soul, the seminal reasons implanted in matter and any number of similar things?[2]

The archbishop's diatribe reveals two key things regarding Bonaventure's Augustinianism: as early as 1285, Bonaventure could be associated with Augustine as a mark of philosophical and theological orthodoxy; this

---

[1] See Decima L. Douie, *Archbishop Pecham* (Oxford: Clarendon Press, 1952); Gordon A. Wilson, 'The Critique of Thomas Aquinas's Unicity Theory of Forms in John Pecham's Quodlibet IV (Romanum)', *Franciscan Studies* 56 (1998), pp. 423–31; Alain Boureau, *Théologie, Science et Censure Au XIIIe Siècle. Le Cas de Jean Peckham* (Paris: les Belles Lettres, 1999); John F. Wippel, 'Thomas Aquinas and the Unity of Substantial Form', in *Philosophy and Theology in the Long Middle Ages. A Tribute to Stephen F. Brown* (ed. Kent Emery Jr., Russell L. Friedman and Andreas Speer; Leiden: Brill, 2011), pp. 117–54.

[2] Pecham, *Registrum epistolarum fratris Johannis Peckham, archiepiscopi cantuariensis* (ed. Charles Trice Martin; vol. 3; London: Longman 1882–85), p. 901.

association included fidelity to a complex of doctrines. Not without reason, historians of the twentieth century will represent these two aspects of Pecham's letter as standard elements of Bonaventure's Augustinianism. The letter also shows that describing Bonaventure's relationship to Augustine reveals as much about the author giving the account, as it reveals about Bonaventure's thought itself.

I will approach Bonaventure's relation to Augustine by first reviewing some of the ways scholars characterized his Augustinianism during the last century. This task would require an essay in itself. A brief overview is necessary since understanding Bonaventure's Augustinianism today is interwoven within the historiography concerning his thought. This will lead to a discussion of how Bonaventure describes Augustine's pre-eminence as a philosopher and theologian. I will then examine two places where Bonaventure disagrees with Augustine's authority in the *Breviloquium*. The ultimate position of this essay is that Bonaventure is an Augustinian insofar as he consistently uses Augustine as a frame of reference for his theology and he presents Augustine as the model philosopher, theologian and exegete.

I. Scholarly Assessments of Bonaventure's Augustinianism

In 1973, John Francis Quinn offered a detailed summary of how historians of philosophy viewed Bonaventure's thought during late nineteenth and twentieth century.[3] Though aspects of Quinn's summary may require revision, it is a useful starting point for this essay. Four of Quinn's intellectual historians deserve particular mention for their lasting influence: Maurice De Wulf, Pierre Mandonnet, Etienne Gilson and Ferdinand Van Steenberghen.[4] De Wulf's early work locates Bonaventure among the 'Augustinians' whom he preferred to designate as the 'pre-Thomists' and 'old Scholasticism', since their doctrines sometimes distorted Augustine's authentic views.[5] He understood Thomas Aquinas as the exemplar of medieval philosophy and Bonaventure as the best of the 'pre-Thomists'.[6] By the 1920's, De Wulf described Bonaventure's Augustinianism as 'a tendency to superimpose doctrines from Augustine on the principles of Aristotle'.[7] De Wulf ultimately maintained that the term 'Augustinian' only had meaning after 1270 as a polemical term.

Pierre Mandonnet would challenge many of De Wulf's positions, but he agreed that Bonaventure was the chief representative of the Augustinians,

---

[3] Quinn, *The Historical Constitution of St. Bonaventure's Philosophy* (Studies and Texts 23; Toronto: PIMS, 1973), pp. 17–100.
[4] For the bibliography on their works and others, see Ibid., pp. 904–11.
[5] Quinn, *The Historical Constitution*, p. 19.
[6] Ibid., p. 20.
[7] Ibid., p. 28.

who were opposed to the Aristotelian learning emerging in the thirteenth century. According to Mandonnet, a set of philosophical theses bound the Augustinians as well as common negative tendencies, such as 'no formal distinction of philosophy from theology', bolstered by their doctrine of illumination which led to 'a total wisdom which confused reason and revelation'.[8] Mandonnet held that Albert the Great and Thomas Aquinas overcame the Augustinians through a progressive integration of Aristotelian learning.[9]

By 1919, Etienne Gilson entered the debates between Mandonnet and De Wulf. He brought far more clarity to the conception of the Augustinian school and sought to appreciate Bonaventure in his own right, rather than qualify him as an 'incipient Thomist'.[10] In his 1955 *History of Christian Philosophy in the Middle Ages*, he lists the key doctrinal commonalities that came to constitute his vision of the Augustinian school.[11] First, the Augustinians share a common definition of the soul, which leads naturally to their second commonality: the doctrine of divine illumination, 'conceived as a light required for the perfect cognition of necessary truth over and above the natural light of the changeable intellect of man'.[12] A third doctrinal commonality arises from their concept of matter. 'All the scholastics', Gilson explained, 'who either maintained the seminal reasons, or refused to deprive matter of all actuality . . . can be called Augustinians.'[13] Gilson's clear presentation became a standard picture of the commonality of doctrine that many scholars of the twentieth century understood to exist among the 'Augustinians'. Gilson's work suggests a fourth factor: the Augustinians utilized Anselm's argument for God's existence in the *Proslogion*.[14] Among these four factors, the doctrine of divine illumination most distinguished the Augustinians and Aquinas for Gilson.[15] De Wulf would disagree that illumination was such a defining feature, but later twentieth-century scholarship largely followed Gilson.

In 1942, Ferdinand Van Steenberghen advanced the debates between Gilson, De Wulf and Mandonnet by drawing different distinctions. Rather than demarcate Bonaventure philosophically as Augustinian, he suggested that Bonaventure was theologically Augustinian but philosophically a

---

[8] Ibid., pp. 18–19.
[9] Ibid., p. 19.
[10] Ibid., p. 24.
[11] Étienne Gilson, *The History of Christian Philosophy in the Middle Ages* (New York: Random House, 1955), pp. 361–63. Notably, I was unable to locate a similar discussion of the characteristics of the Augustinian school in Gilson's history of Christian philosophy authored with Philotheus Boehner: *Die Geschichte der christlichen Philosophie von ihren Anfängen bis Nikolaus von Cues* (Paderborn: Verlag Ferdinand Schöningh, 1952).
[12] Gilson, *The History of Christian Philosophy*, p. 362.
[13] Ibid., p. 363.
[14] See Ibid., pp. 332–35.
[15] Quinn, *The Historical Constitution*, p. 29.

Neoplatonizing Aristotelian.[16] Van Steenberghen also disagreed with Gilson on illumination as the defining feature of Augustinianism. He noted that illumination was not a factor in the *Correctorium fratris Thomae* of the Franciscan, William de la Mare.[17] This text, composed in the 1280s, was meant to be read alongside Aquinas's *Summa* as a corrective to its 'erroneous' positions. This text clearly presents a polemical distinction between Franciscans and Dominicans, but illumination is not one of its defining features.

The figures in Quinn's survey seem involved in a common discussion. The conversation among historians after his survey is more fragmented and the picture of Bonaventure's relation to Augustine becomes more clouded. In some quarters, scholars continue to utilize 'Augustinian' as a way to characterize Bonaventure's thought and divine illumination remains one of the most persistent reasons for this characterization.[18] In another quarter, Bonaventure's approach towards proving God's existence places him in an Augustinian school.[19] Other scholars completely drop the designation 'Augustinian'. Thus, two recent surveys of medieval philosophy do not use the term 'Augustinian' to demarcate any thinkers and pay little or no attention to Augustine's influence on Bonaventure.[20] This is a departure from earlier scholars who felt compelled to treat Bonaventure at length as the best representative of the Augustinian school. In a different quarter, the whole tradition of nineteenth- and twentieth-century historiography is challenged, levelling the distinctions made by earlier scholars.[21]

Among all these approaches, illumination continues to garner the most attention. Yet the demarcation of Bonaventure as an Augustinian thanks to his doctrine of illumination has been challenged in different ways. The scholarship of Wendy Petersen-Boring argues that the doctrine of illumination is not rooted in thirteenth-century texts and figures, but in nineteenth- and

---

[16] Ibid., p. 52.

[17] See the latest edition of Van Steenberghen's 1966 study, *La Philosophie au XIIIe Siècle, Deuxième édition, mise à jour* (Louvain: Éditions Peeters, 1991), p. 231.

[18] See the study of illumination by Stephen P. Marrone, *The Light of Thy Countenance: Science and Knowledge of God in the Thirteenth Century* (2 vols; Leiden: Brill, 2001). Marrone treats Bonaventure mainly in the first volume.

[19] See Louis Mackey, *Faith Order Understanding: Natural Theology in the Augustinian Tradition* (Toronto: Pontifical Institute of Medieval Studies, 2011).

[20] See Alain De Libera, *La philosophie médiévale* (3rd edn; Paris: Presses universitaires de France, 1998), pp. 404–06. De Libera identifies Pseudo-Dionysius and Avicenna as the principal constituents of Bonaventure's philosophical synthesis (*La philosophie*, p. 405). See also John Marenbon, *Medieval Philosophy: An Historical and Philosophical Introduction* (New York: Routledge, 2007), pp. 230–32.

[21] See for instance John Inglis, *Spheres of Philosophical Inquiry and the Historiography of Medieval Philosophy* (Leiden: Brill, 1998). See also, Bonnie Kent, *Virtues of the Will. The Transformation of Ethics in the Late Thirteenth Century* (Washington, DC: The Catholic University of America Press, 1995), pp. 1–38.

twentieth-century intellectual historians. She suggests that these historians developed a doctrine of 'illumination' as a foil for showing the philosophical relevance of Aquinas's epistemology.[22] She finds that Bonaventure and Aquinas were both concerned to integrate Aristotle and Augustine in their theories of understanding but their respective integrations do not correspond well with what scholars commonly define as 'illumination' nor with the way the term has been used to distinguish Bonaventure as a backwards-looking Augustinian.[23] Lydia Schumacher has taken a different approach to the doctrine of illumination and its significance for defining Bonaventure's relationship to Augustine and Aquinas. For Schumacher, there is an Augustinian tradition and illumination figures in its constitution but Bonaventure is no longer one of its members. She reinterprets many of the factors that historians once used to define Bonaventure's Augustinianism and locates him within a distinctive Franciscan tradition. She argues that Bonaventure has misrepresented Anselm's argument in the *Proslogion* (giving rise to the objections against it), distorted Augustine's authentic teaching on illumination (giving rise to the later rejection of it) and departed from Augustine's Trinitarian teaching, all of which places him outside any proper definition of an Augustinian tradition.[24] For Schumacher, in distinction to earlier historians, it is not Bonaventure but Aquinas who is the great Augustinian of the thirteenth century.[25]

The reader should now see how difficult it is to define Bonaventure's Augustinianism. One can use 'Augustinian' to place Bonaventure against Aquinas like many nineteenth- and twentieth-century historians, or use 'Augustinian' to place Aquinas and Augustine against Bonaventure like Schumacher.[26]

---

[22] Wendy Petersen-Boring, 'St. Bonaventure's "Doctrine of Illumination": An Artifact of Modernity', in *Dreams and Visions. An Interdisciplinary Enquiry* (ed. Nancy van Deusen; Leiden: Brill, 2010), pp. 137–66.

[23] Wendy Petersen-Boring, 'Revising our Approach to "Augustinian Illumination", a Reconsideration of Bonaventure's *Quaestiones disputate de scientia Christi IV*, Aquinas's *Summa Theologiae* Ia.84, 1–8, and Henry of Ghent's *Summa Quaestionum Ordinarium*, Q. 2, art. 1,2', *Franciscan Studies* 68 (2010), pp. 39–81.

[24] See Lydia Schumacher's conclusion to her *Divine Illumination. The History and Future of Augustine's Theory of Knowledge* (Oxford: Wiley-Blackwell, 2011), pp. 234–39.

[25] Ibid., p. 237.

[26] A different view emerges from Domenico Facin, *S. Bonaventura Doctor Seraphicus Discipulorum S. Augustini Alter Princeps* (Venetiis: Typis Aemilianis, 1904). He describes Bonaventure's use of Augustine while placing him next to, but not against, Aquinas. This move was somewhat unique to the period and was occasioned by a remark in a letter of Pius X to the Franciscans, which called Bonaventure 'the other prince of the Scholastics with Aquinas'. See 'Doctoris Seraphici sapientiam', in *Pii X Pontificis Maximi Acta* (vol. 1; Rome: Ex Typographia Vaticana, 1905), pp. 235–37. The remark seemed to widen the scope of Leo XIII's *Aeterni Patris* which singled out Aquinas as *the* prince and master of the scholastics. See *Leonis XIII Pontificis Maximi Acta* (vol. 1; Rome: Ex Typographia Vaticana, 1881), pp. 255–84 (p. 272).

'Illumination' can be viewed as the focal point of this definition (Gilson), as ancillary at best (Van Steenberghen), as a chimera at worst (Petersen-Boring) or as eliminating him altogether from the tradition (Schumacher). There is no simple way to cut through these many distinctions and paths of thought. We must turn to Bonaventure and allow him to speak.

II. How Bonaventure Views Augustine

The most famous passage regarding Bonaventure's view of Augustine comes from his *Letter to an Unknown Master*, composed around 1254 to address questions of an unidentified master of arts regarding poverty, manual labour and studies.[27] Bonaventure's remarks about Augustine occur within his comments on the pursuit of studies, and particularly philosophical studies, which seem troublesome to the master since they may entail the sin of curiosity. Bonaventure proposes, however, that 'some who seem curious are actually being studious', since someone might study the opinions of heretics, not out of curiosity, but in order to refute them.[28] They study of philosophical writings will be crucial to this task since 'there are many questions of faith which cannot be settled without recourse to them'.[29] Bonaventure advises his addressee that if we defined curiosity too broadly, we might even accuse the saints of curiosity. He then states:

> After all, no one describes the nature of time and of matter better than Augustine as he probes and discusses them in his *Confessions*; no one has explained the origins of forms and the development of things better than he in his *Literal Commentary on Genesis*; no one has better treated questions on the soul and on God than he in his book *On the Trinity*; and no one has better explained the nature of the angels and the creation of the world than he in *The City of God*. To put it briefly, our masters of theology have set down little or nothing in their writings that you will not find in the books of Augustine himself.[30]

---

[27] The letter has been translated and introduced by Dominic Monti, *St. Bonaventure's Writings Concerning the Franciscan Order* (St. Bonaventure: The Franciscan Institute, 1994), pp. 39–56. See the edition in *Opera Omnia* (vol. 8; Quaracchi: Collegium S. Bonaventurae, 1898), pp. 331–36 and Ferdinand Delorme, 'Textes franciscains', *Archivo italiano per la storia della pietà* 1 (1951), pp. 212–18. For some of the historical context see David Burr, *Olivi and Franciscan Poverty* (Philadelphia: University of Pennsylvania Press, 1989), pp. 149–51.
[28] Bonaventure, 'Letter', *Opera Omnia* 8.335b; trans. Monti, p. 53.
[29] Bonaventure, *Opera Omnia* 8.335b; trans. Monti, p. 53.
[30] Ibid., 8.335b–336a; trans. Monti, p. 53.

We might be tempted to read this passage in tandem with Pecham's letter and infer the definition of an Augustinian school from Bonaventure's own mouth. Bonaventure's immediate purpose, however, is to combat the unknown master's concerns regarding study and curiosity. Bonaventure responds that study is neither out of step with the rule, nor is it prey to curiosity if performed in the proper way. Augustine shows that proper way in what must be considered the top three of Augustine's theological works in the Middle Ages: the *Confessions*, the *Literal Commentary on Genesis* and *On the Trinity*.[31] Augustine is the model theologian whose rich philosophical insights were developed at the service of his theology and not out of a vain and sinful curiosity. Franciscan intellectuals should be 'Augustinian' – that is, they should view Augustine as their exemplar. They are not thereby opposed to 'Aristotelians', but to a perverted approach to study: curiosity. Although, some of the doctrines Bonaventure lists will later divide him and like-minded thinkers from Aquinas, here these doctrines are primarily listed in their connection with Augustine's works to demonstrate his model theological use and development of philosophy.

If the above passage does not immediately demarcate an Augustinian school, it is still true that Bonaventure desired to follow Augustine's lead in philosophical questions. One of the defining characteristics of Bonaventure's Augustinianism for Gilson was his conception of matter. This was not without reason, since we have already seen that Bonaventure lauds Augustine's view of matter. A passage from Bonaventure's *Commentary on the Sentences* shows just how much reverence he held for Augustine's view. Bonaventure's understanding of matter comes into particular relief in the constitution of angels.[32] In this context, he accords Augustine an outstanding title: he is the *altissimus metaphysicus* – 'the highest metaphysician' – thanks to his understanding of matter.[33] The specific text in which Bonaventure praises Augustine is too complicated to consider here. Nevertheless, two features of the text deserve mention in connection with his praise for Augustine. First, Bonaventure's praise of the *altissimus metaphysicus* immediately relates to how the *theologian* should understand matter. In other words, at issue in the question for Bonaventure is not just a solution regarding how matter should be understood, but how the theologian should use philosophical data: Augustine, as in

---

[31] Bonaventure's letter also cites *De doctrina Christiana* in the same context – another staple of the medieval Augustine.

[32] For Bonaventure's conception of matter see Christopher Cullen, *Bonaventure* (Oxford: Oxford University Press, 2006), pp. 44–51; in more detail in his dissertation, 'The Semiotic Metaphysics of Saint Bonaventure' (PhD diss., The Catholic University of America, 2000), pp. 254–308.

[33] The remark may be found in book 2, distinction 3, part one, article one, question two of Bonaventure's commentary on the *Sentences*, in the response, *Opera Omnia* 2.98a.

the letter to the unknown master, shows the way.[34] The passage is also notable because Bonaventure cites the *De mirabilibus sacrae Scripturae* to demonstrate Augustine's model metaphysical acumen. This treatise does not belong among Augustine's authentic works. It is the work of a seventh-century Irish monk, whose first name – Augustinus – caused medieval scribes confusion and led to its acceptance into the thirteenth century as a work of Saint Augustine.[35] Though Bonaventure's Augustinian understanding of matter does not hinge on this passage, his citation of this inauthentic work shows that his Augustine was different from ours at a fundamental level: the very corpus of Augustine had not yet been settled.

These two passages show that Bonaventure's praise for Augustine's philosophical acumen concerns more than philosophical doctrines. He is concerned with how Augustine properly utilized philosophy within his theology and offers Augustine as the model philosopher for the theologian. We can now turn to classic Bonaventurean passages that describe Augustine more explicitly as a theologian.

Bonaventure's brief *De reductione artium ad theologiam* is closely associated with his Augustinianism.[36] The work has a complicated history. Bonaventure initially delivered the text as a sermon that fulfilled part of the formal academic exercises required of new masters of theology at the University of Paris in the thirteenth century.[37] The text may therefore be dated to 1254.[38] However, the current form of the text was revised at some later date in order to function apart

---

[34] Briefly, in the response to the question, Bonaventure offers various positions regarding how matter in spiritual and physical things can be reconciled. One way centres on the difference between how physicists and the metaphysician consider matter. When a theologian discusses matter, he can do so from the perspective of the natural philosopher or the metaphysician 'because he can use the methods of all the sciences, since they are subordinate to him'. The theologian should ultimately adopt the view of the metaphysician, 'since the metaphysician makes his judgment from a higher position than the lower sciences', and regarding the question of matter, 'judged better and were raised higher'. He then praises Augustine as the *altissimus metaphysicus*. See Bonaventure, *Opera Omnia* 2.97b–98a.

[35] Brief biographical information on Augustinus Hibernicus can be found in Marina Smyth, 'The Body, Death and Resurrection: Perspectives of an Early Irish Theologian', *Speculum* 83 (2008), pp. 531–71. Bonaventure may have never learned that the work did not belong to Saint Augustine, since as late as 1269, he cited the work under Augustine's name (see *Apologia Pauperum*, *Opera Omnia* 8.276).

[36] See for example Cullen, *Bonaventure*, pp. 29–30.

[37] See Joshua C. Benson, 'Identifying the Literary Genre of the *De reductione artium ad theologiam*: Bonaventure's Inaugural Lecture at Paris', *Franciscan Studies* 67 (2009), pp. 149–78 and Idem., 'Bonaventure's *De reductione artium ad theologiam* and Its Early Reception as an Inaugural Sermon', *ACPQ* 85/1 (2011), pp. 7–24. See also Idem, 'Bonaventure's Inaugural Sermon at Paris: Omnium artifex docuit me sapientia. Introduction and Text', *Collectanea Franciscana* 82/3–4 (2012), 517–62.

[38] Jay Hammond, 'Dating Bonaventure's Inception as Regent Master', *Franciscan Studies* 67 (2009), pp. 179–226.

from its original academic context. The text has at least two main ends. One is to distinguish all the branches of knowledge. Bonaventure ultimately defines six 'lights' of knowledge: sensation, the mechanical arts, rational, natural and moral philosophy and Sacred Scripture.[39] The text's second end is to utilize the senses of Scripture (allegorical, moral and anagogical) as a lens for understanding the content of all the other branches of knowledge – thereby showing how Scripture illuminates all the other lights of knowledge. Bonaventure's description of the light of Scripture is most important for our purposes.

When Bonaventure initially defines the light of Sacred Scripture, he divides it into the literal sense and the three spiritual senses. He further describes what each sense studies: allegory considers the divinity and humanity of Christ; the moral sense shows us how to live; anagogy reveals how we cling to God. He then relates:

> All of Sacred Scripture teaches these three things: the eternal generation and incarnation of Christ, the order of life, and the union of God and the soul. The first relates to faith, the second to morals, and the third to the goal of both. The study of doctors should be earnestly focused on the first, the study of preachers on the second, and the study of contemplatives on the third. Augustine chiefly teaches the first, Gregory chiefly teaches the second, but Dionysius teaches the third. Anselm follows Augustine, Bernard follows Gregory, Richard follows Dionysius. [This is because] Anselm [follows Augustine] in reasoning, Bernard [follows Gregory] in preaching, and Richard [follows Dionysius] in contemplation. Hugh, however, [teaches] all these things.[40]

The order and dynamic of the passage reveals much about Bonaventure's view of Augustine. First, of the things Scripture teaches, Augustine is explicitly related to what concerns faith, and faith is principally concerned with the eternal generation and incarnation of Christ. Following the dynamic of the passage, Trinitarian theology and Christology form the basis of all that Scripture tells us, inasmuch as they tell us of faith and faith comes first in this threefold spiritual understanding. This placement of faith in no way diminishes the importance of the moral and mystical life that follow. Yet the order is important: the moral and mystical life of the Christian would be unimaginable without the saving truth revealed in Christ, who is the Word of the Father. The explication of this faith is the concern of doctors. It follows, then,

---

[39] Bonaventure, *De reductione*, paragraph 6, *Opera Omnia* 5.321b; *On the Reduction of the Arts to Theology* (trans. Zachary Hayes; St. Bonaventure: Franciscan Institute, 1996), p. 45.
[40] Bonaventure, *Opera Omnia* 5.321b; trans. Hayes, p. 45. I have significantly modified the translation.

that Augustine is the chief doctor, and indeed, Bonaventure elsewhere praises Augustine in these terms.[41] Bonaventure then connects Augustine to Anselm, and ultimately to Hugh of Saint Victor, who is uniquely related to all the doctors and disciplines in the passage. Though we might be tempted to see the definition of an Augustinian school with these three figures, we should pause and consider the substance of the passage. Bonaventure's intention is to single out models for the study of the truths Scripture communicates, not to define an Augustinian school of theology against something else. Augustine is the model for doctors who strive to understand the faith; Anselm and Hugh follow him as more recent models. We might infer that they are such models in view of both the substance of their teaching and their methods of thought. Anselm hoped that his peers would recognize the 'Augustinian' character of his work;[42] Hugh's peers did, since they lauded him as the *Alter Augustinus* and *Lingua Augustini*.[43] Bonaventure has therefore singled out authors his own peers would recognize as standing in the tradition of Augustine, whom he views as the chief metaphysician and the chief doctor.

The *De reductione* suggests that Augustine's theological pre-eminence flows from his role as exegete. This insight comes to explicit focus in another famous passage from Bonaventure's corpus: the fourth question of his disputed questions on the knowledge of Christ. This question, which considers the role of the eternal reasons in certain knowledge, is the locus classicus for Bonaventure's doctrine of illumination and has enjoyed the attention of scholars since its discovery and publication in the late nineteenth century.[44] Bonaventure must have composed the work as a master of theology at Paris (1254–57) and scholars surmise that the disputations were part of Bonaventure's inaugural exercises as a master of theology.[45] The text is littered with the authority of Augustine. Following the format of the scholastic question, Bonaventure opens the text with a series of authorities and arguments in favour of his

---

[41] See, for instance, Bonaventure's commentary on book 4, *Sentences*, where he praises Augustine as *doctor praecipuus* (*Opera Omnia* 4.926a).

[42] See the prologue to his Monologion in *Anselm of Canterbury: The Major Works* (trans. Brian Davies and G. R. Evans; Oxford: Oxford University Press, 1998), p. 6.

[43] See Jerome Taylor, *The Didascalicon of Hugh of Saint Victor: A Medieval Guide to the Arts* (New York: Columbia University Press, 1991), p. 8, n. 22.

[44] See Fidelis a Fanna, *Ratio novae collectionis operum omnium sive editorum sive anecdotorum Seraphici Eccl. Doctoris S. Bonaventurae* (Taurini: Marietti, 1874).

[45] Disputed questions were typically the purview of masters of theology, who chose the topic for dispute. See Anthony Kenny and Jan Pinborg, 'Medieval Philosophical Literature', in *The Cambridge History of Later Medieval Philosophy* (ed. N. Kretzmann et al; Cambridge: Cambridge University Press, 1982), pp. 11–42 (pp. 21–9). In more detail: Bernardo C. Bazàn, 'Les questions disputées, principalement dans les facultés de théologie', in *Les questions disputées et les questions quodlibétiques dans les facultés de theologie, de droit et de médecine* (ed. Bazàn; Typologie Des Sources Du Moyen Âge Occidental, Fasc. 44–5; Turnhout: Brepols, 1985), pp. 15–149.

position: a staggering 34 in all. The first eight are taken from Augustine. The message seems clear: understanding the role of the eternal reasons in certain knowledge means attention to Augustine, and above all to his *De Trinitate* which is cited four times. Augustine also plays a key role in the objections to Bonaventure's position: of the 26 arguments and authorities, the *De Trinitate* is cited three times and the last four arguments are rubricated as directed explicitly against the arguments of Augustine.[46] One passage of the response deserves particular attention.

The response initially summarizes two insufficient explanations of the role of the eternal reasons in certain knowledge. The first way holds that the eternal reasons are the total and sole principle of certain knowledge. Bonaventure condemns this position as the least acceptable, since 'it allows for no knowledge of reality except in the Word. In this case there would be no difference between knowledge in this life and knowledge in heaven . . . between the knowledge of reason and the knowledge of revelation. Since all these are false, that path must not be held in any way'.[47] The second way, by contrast, holds that certain knowledge requires the *influence* of the eternal reasons, 'in such a way that the knower does not attain the eternal reasons themselves in knowledge, but only their influence'.[48] Bonaventure also takes issue with this position. He writes:

> This way of speaking is insufficient according to the words of blessed Augustine, who shows by explicit words and arguments that the mind must be regulated in certain knowledge by the unchangeable and eternal rules, not as through a habit of the mind but as through those things which are above the mind in the eternal truth. For that reason, to say that when our mind knows it does not extend itself beyond the influence of the uncreated light is to say that Augustine was deceived: for when we explain his arguments, it is not easy to pull them to that meaning. Now this would be very absurd to say about so great a Father and the most authoritative (*maxime authentico*) Doctor among all the interpreters of sacred Scripture.[49]

Whereas the first way was objectionable since it confused a fundamental distinction like reason and revelation, the second way is problematic because it distorts Augustine's authority. Bonaventure clearly views the problem of the eternal reasons' role in certain knowledge as a theoretical problem and a problem of properly interpreting Augustine. Bonaventure will not

---

[46] See Bonaventure, *Opera Omnia* 5.21a and 22b.
[47] Bonaventure, *Opera Omnia* 5.23a; *Disputed Questions on the Knowledge of Christ* (trans. Zachary Hayes; St. Bonaventure: The Franciscan Institute, 1992), pp. 132–33.
[48] Bonaventure, *Opera Omnia* 5.23a; trans. Hayes, p. 132.
[49] Bonaventure, *Opera Omnia* 5.23a; trans. Hayes, p. 133. I have modified the translation.

allow any distortion of Augustine's thought (as he sees it), on what must be such a fundamental question. We need look no further for evidence that Bonaventure understood himself as a follower of Augustine (at least on this score), whatever later scholars may make of how he followed him. We must also note the precise way he invokes Augustine's authority. He does not appeal to Augustine's philosophical superiority, or his metaphysical acumen: he appeals to Augustine's status as Father and Doctor and to his maximal authority – his maximal authenticity – as an interpreter of Scripture, which we might presume is what makes him so great a Doctor. Perhaps Bonaventure is chiding his audience: could someone who so credibly interprets the truth God has revealed, be mistaken about how we come to know certain truth at all? Augustine's authority must be respected in this question of philosophical and theological import, not simply for his philosophical acumen but for his sure exegetical powers. Having seen how Bonaventure praises Augustine's authority, we can appreciate it all the more by examining two ways in which he disagrees with it.

III. Augustine's Contested Authority in the *Breviloquium*

Bonaventure cites Augustine over 3,050 times throughout his corpus, far outweighing his citations of any other authority besides Scripture itself.[50] The *Breviloquium*, Bonaventure's brief synthesis of theology, also gives precedence to Augustine's authority, referencing it over 100 times and mentioning him by name 14 times. For such a brief text (about 90 pages in the Quaracchi edition), this is already a surprising amount of references. Additionally, the style of the *Breviloquium* does not lend itself to the accumulation of authoritative citations, since the work does not employ the scholastic device of the *quaestio*, which naturally leads to amassing citations. The *Breviloquium* is comprised of chapters, in which a particular Christian belief is first stated and then reasons for the belief are given. In nearly every chapter, Bonaventure's reasons stem, not from an authority, but from a statement about God himself. In this way, he believes he can show that 'the truth of Sacred Scripture' is totally rooted in God.[51] This atypical method should impact how we view the *Breviloquium*'s use of Augustine's authority: since the style of the text does not lend itself to utilizing authorities, their instances become more important.

---

[50] See Jacques-Guy Bougerol, 'The Church Fathers and *Auctoritates* in Scholastic Theology to Bonaventure', in *The Reception of the Church Fathers in the West: From the Carolingians to the Maurists* (ed. Irena Backus; vol. 1; Leiden: Brill, 1997), pp. 289–335 (pp. 305–10).

[51] See the Prologue to Bonaventure's Breviloquium, *Opera Omnia* 5.208b; *Breviloquium* (trans. Dominic Monti; St. Bonaventure: The Franciscan Institute, 2005), p. 23.

The *Breviloquium* is thus a unique synthesis of medieval theology. Scholars agree that Bonaventure composed the work in 1257, the same year he left the University of Paris to become the Minister General of the Franciscan Order – a position he held until 1274, the final year of his life.[52] The *Breviloquium* consists of a prologue and seven parts. The seven parts treat in order: Trinity, creation, sin, incarnation of the Word, grace of the Holy Spirit, sacraments and final judgement. The text is more intricately composed than this bare listing of its parts suggests.[53] Bonaventure reveals something of the work's purpose towards the end of the prologue:

> This teaching [the total content of the faith in its seven parts] has been transmitted, both in the writings of the saints and in those of the doctors, in such a diffuse manner that those who come to learn about Sacred Scripture are not able to read or hear about it for a long time. In fact, today's theologians (*novi theologi*) often dread Sacred Scripture itself, feeling it to be as confusing, disordered and uncharted as some impenetrable forest. That is why my colleagues have asked me, from my own modest knowledge to draw up some concise summary of the truth of theology.[54]

The *Breviloquium* is a systematic theology at the service of understanding Sacred Scripture; or perhaps better, it is an exposition of the rule of faith meant to serve the exposition of God's Word. Augustine therefore plays a substantial role in the work, since he was Bonaventure's pre-eminent exegete. Two places where Bonaventure disagrees with Augustine's authority, however, may reveal more about his relationship to Augustine than the many instances where he simply agrees with him.

In part two of the *Breviloquium*, Bonaventure considers creation, and in the second chapter, he considers how the universe of things came into being, tracing the days of creation. In conclusion, he notes that God could have accomplished the works of the six days simultaneously, but 'preferred to accomplish them over a succession of times'.[55] This is fitting for three reasons: the sequence of days allows for the clear manifestation of God's power, wisdom and benevolence; it allows for a correspondence between the days

---

[52] See the chronology in the latest work of Bougerol, *Introduction*, pp. 3–10.
[53] See my forthcoming essay 'The Christology of the Breviloquium' in a companion to Bonaventure's thought from Brill. The contribution of the essay lies in its Christological interpretation of the *Breviloquium*'s structure.
[54] Bonaventure, *Opera Omnia* 5.208a; trans. Monti, p. 22 (modified). I depart from the majority of scholars who understand the words *novi theologi* to mean beginning theologians – as in new students of theology. I take *novi* here to be related to the meaning it often has for medieval writers – 'recent' – and perhaps as pejorative in tone.
[55] Bonaventure, *Opera Omnia* 5.220a; trans. Monti, p. 65.

and activities; and it allows the prefigurement of all future ages, for the seven days 'contain seminally, as it were, the division of all times to come'.[56] On the other hand, Bonaventure relates, one could hold that all things were made at once from the perspective of the angels. 'Nevertheless', he concludes, 'the first manner of speaking is more in keeping with Scripture and the authorities of the saints, *both those before and after Saint Augustine*.'[57]

Bonaventure has here isolated Augustine's authority as a distinct and less desirable path of interpretation. Significantly, his understanding of Augustine is animated by his reading of Peter Lombard's *Sentences*. In book 2, distinction 12, the Lombard suggests that Augustine seems to have held the simultaneity of creation but other Fathers held to the need for the succession of the six days – a view more in accord with Genesis.[58] Bonaventure clearly follows the Lombard's lead. In fact, throughout the *Breviloquium*, Bonaventure often tracks with the Lombard's reading of Augustine, even drawing his citations of Augustine directly from the *Sentences*. Like most medieval theologians, Bonaventure read Augustine through the lens of the tradition in which he received him. Using the Lombard's Augustine in the *Breviloquium* would have also made good pedagogical sense, since the *Sentences* formed a core part of the curriculum at the University of Paris. Bonaventure could therefore show his readers how to approach the *Sentences* and, obliquely, how to approach Augustine's authority within them.

Bonaventure's treatment of this same issue within his commentary on the *Sentences* adds a further layer of nuance to his position in the *Breviloquium*. In the response to the second question of his commentary on book 2, distinction 12, Bonaventure underscores that Augustine's position on the simultaneity of creation follows a more philosophical path, while other saints held to a more theological one.[59] He explains that Augustine's philosophical path is more consonant with reason, given that it would seem that the supreme power would create all things at once. Further, Augustine was able to confirm his interpretation with Scripture and explained how the days of creation should not be understood as material, but spiritual days. Augustine's position, Bonaventure relates, 'was entirely reasonable

---

[56] Ibid., 5.220; trans. Monti, p. 65.
[57] Ibid., 220b; trans. Monti, p. 66, emphasis mine.
[58] See Peter Lombard, *Sententiae in IV Libris Distinctae*, tom. 1, part two (ed. Ignatius Brady; Grottaferata: Collegium S. Bonaventurae, 1971), p. 385; *The Sentences Book 2: On Creation* (trans. Giulio Silano; vol. 2; Toronto: Pontifical Institute of Medieval Studies, 2008), p. 50.
[59] He writes, 'Regarding this question, some saints followed a more theological path, drawing their argument toward the faith. But some, among whom the principal one was Augustine, followed a more philosophical path. This path presents what seems more consistent with reason. Therefore, he drew the understanding of Scripture towards the confirmation and attestation of reason' (Bonaventure, *Opera Omnia* 2.296b).

and very subtle'.[60] Nevertheless, Bonaventure confidently asserts that the theological path of the other saints, which holds to the necessity of the six days, is more safe and closer to the text of Genesis.[61] He admits that this position is apparently less consonant with reason than Augustine's, but it can still be reasonable. He then suggests how reason can come to a deeper understanding of the truth of the six days. 'Reason', he writes 'may not perceive the congruity of this position [i.e. the necessity of the six days], so long as it relies upon its own way of thinking. Yet, it does perceive <its congruity> so long as it is captivated by the light of faith. For there is a fourfold reason for this successive formation and distinction: a literal, moral, allegorical and anagogical reason.'[62] Reason, seeking understanding, will come to a fuller grasp of the world and hence the rationale for the six days by utilizing Scripture and the hermeneutic of the four senses. As Bonaventure details the allegorical and anagogical readings of Genesis, he returns to Augustine: allegorically, Augustine typifies how to read the days of Genesis in relationship to the ages of history; anagogically, he explains how the days refer to angelic knowledge, which he carefully notes, is Augustine's literal reading of the text.[63]

While we might initially see confusion in Bonaventure's use of Augustine here, we can see that his procedure is consistent with how he views Augustine. As we saw above, Augustine is the model philosopher for Bonaventure, outstripping the acumen of the man normally accorded that title: Aristotle. Here, he uses this conviction to qualify Augustine's unique position regarding the simultaneous production of created things. Bonaventure never suggests that Augustine's position is wrong. Rather, he offers that Augustine's particular approach here does not follow the biblical narrative as closely as other doctors. Nevertheless, as the pre-eminent exegete, Augustine still shapes the allegorical and anagogical reading of the text, the bookends of the spiritual senses. We should further observe that Bonaventure identified Augustine's authority with allegory in the *De reductione*, and so it should come as little surprise that he fills out this understanding of the days of creation.

Combining the two approaches of the *Breviloquium* and the *Sentences*, we can see that Bonaventure has very carefully departed from Augustine's authority in one way, but preserved it in another. Rather than simply suggest that Augustine is incorrect, he works to demonstrate the uniqueness of his position and its philosophical quality. He never disparages the value of this

---

[60] *Opera Omnia* 2.296b.
[61] Bonaventure understands the position of the other saints in this precise way: 'Therefore, they presented that all physical things are simultaneously created in matter, but are distinguished in form through the six days and not all at once' (*Opera Omnia* 2.296b).
[62] *Opera Omnia* 2.297a.
[63] See *Opera Omnia* 2.297a–b.

position in either the *Sentences* or the *Breviloquium*; but he does isolate it. At the same time, he uses Augustine to further articulate how faith grants further understanding to reason by means of the spiritual senses. Despite his own disagreement with Augustine, he still arrives at an Augustinian way to view creation through the spiritual senses.

Another passage of the *Breviloquium* provides a further instance of how Bonaventure will qualify Augustine's authority. This passage comes from part three of the *Breviloquium* (on sin), which seems to have the most references to Augustine, along with part five on grace. Part three begins with a consideration of evil in general; chapters 2 through 4 theologically examine the narrative of the fall; chapters 5 through 7 consider original sin; the last four chapters examine four other classes of sin. In chapter 5, Bonaventure discusses how original sin damages the human person.[64] Thanks to our lack of original justice, Bonaventure explains, 'our souls incur a four-fold penalty: weakness, ignorance, malice, and concupiscence . . . These spiritual punishments are matched in the body by all kinds of pain, imperfection, labor, sickness and affliction. To these are finally added the penalty of death and the return to dust . . . the deprivation of the vision of God and the loss of heavenly glory.'[65] Bonaventure then notes that the loss of the vision of God is a punishment for adults and unbaptized children. He emphasizes, following the Lombard's reading of Augustine's *Enchiridion*, that unbaptized children will receive the 'mildest form of punishment', which will entail the lack of the vision of God without any further sensory punishment.[66] Bonaventure returns to the issue of unbaptized children at the end of the chapter. He stresses that they will not receive sensory punishment in hell, though they will lack the vision of God. He then states that 'we ought to believe that blessed Augustine was aware of this, even though on the surface his words seem to state otherwise, because he was reacting so strongly against the errors of the Pelagians, who conceded them some blessedness. To lead them back to the middle, he turned back extravagantly (*abundantius declinavit*) towards the extreme.'[67]

This passage further reveals the complexities of Bonaventure's reading of Augustine. He believes Augustine held that unbaptized children receive the 'mildest form of punishment'. Yet, at the close of the chapter, he seems concerned that Augustine's position is stronger. In fact, Bonaventure does think that Augustine held a stronger position, specifically that unbaptized children receive sensory punishment in hell. We must here turn briefly to Bonaventure's commentary on the second book of *Sentences*, distinction thirty-three,

---

[64] *Opera Omnia* 5.234a; trans. Monti, p. 109.
[65] Bonaventure, *Opera Omnia* 5.234a–b; trans. Monti pp. 109–10.
[66] Ibid., 5.234b; trans. Monti, p. 110. See Peter Lombard's *Sentences*, book 2, distinction 33, chapter 2, pp. 518–19; trans. Silano, pp. 164–66.
[67] Bonaventure, *Opera Omnia* 235a; trans. Monti, pp. 111–12 (modified).

question one, where he discusses the fate of unbaptized children. His first two authorities put the matter starkly: unbaptized children will lack the vision of God and be punished by hell fire. Bonaventure takes both authorities from *De fide ad Petrum*, which he and other medieval theologians understood as the work of Augustine. The Lombard often cites the text under Augustine's name, but it belongs to Fulgentius of Ruspe. In his response to the question, Bonaventure shows how certain theologians combine the harsh citations from *De fide ad Petrum* with the citation from the *Enchiridion* regarding 'the mildest form of punishment'. They therefore read 'mildest' to mean 'in reference to the punishment of others, not absolutely'.[68] Thus, these children receive a milder punishment than some, but still receive the punishment of hell fire. They hold that this takes nothing away from divine mercy but places greater emphasis on divine justice.[69] Bonaventure believes, however, that there is a milder position, 'which agrees better with the piety of faith and the judgment of reason': these children lack the vision of God but are not punished further in their body.[70]

He then responds to the objections and must therefore interpret the authorities from *De fide ad Petrum* which he ascribes to Augustine. His response provides a better backcloth against which to understand his meaning at the end of the passage in the *Breviloquium*: wanting to pull the Pelagians away from their error, Augustine pushed to the other extreme. He writes:

> With those words, Augustine did not intend to say that children are tortured in their senses. Rather, he intends to point out their punishment as it relates to the lack of the vision of God and to the unpleasantness of the place. He expresses this very extravagantly, saying a lot and wanting less of it to be meaningful (*plus dicens et minus volens intelligi*). He did not speak this way without reason. He did this in order to uproot that heresy which stated that children receive no punishment. Now, just as the Philosopher [i.e. Aristotle] teaches, it is a teaching in morals that whoever wants to arrive at the middle from one of the extremes should practically turn back to the other extreme. Thus saint Augustine asserted without qualification that they were damned eternally with other sinners. [He did this] in order to uproot the heresy which states that children are free of all punishment and to lead [them] back to the middle: to the punishment of lacking the vision of God. He explained that as his own meaning in the *Enchiridion*, where he said their punishment is the mildest, just as the Master states in the text [i.e. the *Sentences*].[71]

---

[68] Ibid., 2.793b.
[69] See *Opera Omnia* 2.793b–794a.
[70] Ibid., 2.794a.
[71] Ibid., 2.794a–b.

Here as in the *Breviloquium*, Bonaventure qualifies Augustine's authority by showing that his comments were historically contingent. Augustine needed to move the Pelagians away from their error and attempted to snap them out of their position by offering them the other extreme. This is simply good rhetorical practice within the discipline of morals: it is the very advice of Aristotle from the *Nicomachean Ethics*.[72] Confronted with a position of Augustine he will not hold, and unaware that the authorities he offered were not from Augustine, Bonaventure still sought to understand Augustine's position. In this way, he preserved Augustine's authority by examining it more deeply and attempting to understand its rhetoric. He never simply dismissed Augustine's authority, but always sought to understand and preserve it.

IV. Conclusion

Is Bonaventure an 'Augustinian'? Historians have continued to battle over the term. It seems clear that Bonaventure must be an 'Augustinian' if that means an attempt to remain faithful to Augustine even in disagreement, continually mining his authority for theology and revering him as the model philosopher, theologian and exegete. Bonaventure is not an 'Augustinian' if this means he must reproduce Augustine's thought without qualification, he cannot utilize other resources to understand him, or must have an exacting knowledge of his corpus. I have not discussed the question of Bonaventure's relation to Augustine in Trinitarian thought, because I believe it requires an essay in its own right. Suffice it to say that Bonaventure is not Augustinian in key elements of his Trinitarian theology, but nonetheless invokes him throughout his different treatments of the Triune God.[73] When approaching Bonaventure's Augustinianism, we must be clear about what 'Augustinian' means, and be equally clear about Bonaventure's avowed commitments. We may conclude with a final encomium from Bonaventure's pen.

Bonaventure's famous sermon, 'Christ the one teacher of all', praises Augustine in a similar way to his *Disputed Questions on Christ's Knowledge*. The doctrinal parallels between the sermon and questions have even prompted

---

[72] The citation comes from Aristotle, *Nicomachean Ethics* 2.9 (1109b, 24). The Latin translation of the *Ethics* by Robert Grosseteste may have shaped Bonaventure's language in both the *Sentences* and the *Breviloquium*. See *Ethica Nicomachea. Translatio Roberti Grosseteste Lincolniensis sive 'Liber Ethicorum'* (Aristoteles Latinus XXVI 1–3, Fasciculus Tertius; ed. Renatus Gauthier; Leiden: Brill, 1972), p. 178.

[73] On Bonaventure's departure from Augustine, see the recent work of Russel Fridemann, *Medieval Trinitarian Thought from Aquinas to Ockham* (Cambridge: Cambridge University Press, 2010), pp. 15–30. To complicate matters, one could examine Bonaventure's presentation of the Trinity in the *Breviloquium* which utilizes elements from Augustine and Richard of Saint Victor (*Opera Omnia* 5.210–218; trans. Monti, pp. 29–57).

some scholars to argue that the sermon and the disputations were given at the same time.[74] Bonaventure's praise of Augustine comes in the middle of the sermon as he is summarizing his solution to the problem of certain knowledge. He writes:

> Plato was rightly criticized by Aristotle since he turned all certain knowledge towards the intelligible or ideal world; not because Plato improperly said that there are eternal reasons and ideas, since the greatest doctor, Augustine, praises him for this. Rather, it was because, having no use for the sensible world, he wanted to reduce all certain knowledge to those ideas. Although by maintaining this position he seemed to stabilize the path of wisdom which proceeds according to the eternal reasons, he destroyed the path of science which proceeds according to created reasons. On the other hand, Aristotle stabilized the path of science, but to the neglect of the higher one. For that reason, it seems that among the philosophers the word of wisdom may be given to Plato, but the word of science to Aristotle. For the former looked chiefly to higher realities, while the latter looked towards the lower. But through the Holy Spirit, both words, of wisdom and science, were given excellently enough to Augustine as the preeminent exegete of the whole of Scripture, just as it appears from his writings. Yet in a more excellent way both words were in Paul and Moses . . . However, both were most excellently in the Lord Jesus Christ, who was the principal law-giver and perfectly had at the same time the knowledge we have in this life and the knowledge the blessed have in the next (*et simul perfectus viator et comprehensor*). For that reason, he alone is the principle master and doctor.[75]

Bonaventure here anticipates in words the very brushstrokes of Raphael's Academy. Yet, Bonaventure's medieval academy is different from that of the Renaissance. Augustine stands between and above Plato and Aristotle, to whom the Holy Spirit gave the light of both philosophers. We can see the immense contrast: what we *might accord* to these two Pagan philosophers – wisdom and science – the Spirit *did grant* to Augustine. The sign of this gift?

---

[74] See Jacques-Guy Bougerol, *Introduction to the Works of Saint Bonaventure* (trans. José de Vinck; Patterson: St. Anthony Guild Press, 1964), p. 122; but compare to his comments in the edition of the sermon in *Sermons de Diversis* [sic] (vol. 1; Paris: Les Editions Franciscaines, 1993), pp. 402–20. John F. Quinn held that this sermon and these disputations were given as part of Bonaventure's inaugural exercises: 'Chronology of St. Bonaventure (1217–1257)', *Franciscan Studies* 32 (1972): pp. 168–86 (pp. 180–81).

[75] Bonaventure, *Sermons De Diversis* [sic] (ed. Jacques Guy Bougerol; vol. 1; Paris: Editions Franciscaines, 1993), pp. 415–16. The sermon has never been translated from Bougerol's edition, but a translation from the Quaracchi edition may be found in: *Bonaventure. Mystic of God's Word* (ed. Timothy Johnson; Hyde Park: New City Press, 1999), pp. 152–66.

Bonaventure returns us to the *maximus doctor*'s exegetical powers – not to his philosophical gifts. Yet, what was *given to* Augustine, is *in* Paul and Moses. Higher in Bonaventure's academy stand the great doctors of the Old and New law. Over them all must rise the sun that gives them light: Christ, the law giver, the perfect man of knowledge, the one and only master and doctor. Augustine could not be placed in greater company, and though his role is less than the scriptural figures and more than the classical ones, he stands alone. He is not surrounded, as in the *De reductione*, with Gregory and Dionysius; Anselm, Bernard, Richard and Hugh. He is the greatest Doctor. He is not the principal one. Bonaventure's one master must remain the one who is the way, the truth and the life. So it is, that while ever keeping Augustine's authority in sight, he will develop, supplement, alter and even disagree with his authority, for his authority must ever remain at the service of Truth.

For Further Reading

Bonaventure, *St. Bonaventure's Writings Concerning the Franciscan Order* (trans. Dominic Monti; St. Bonaventure: The Franciscan Institute, 1994).
— *Breviloquium* (trans. Dominic Monti; St. Bonaventure: The Franciscan Institute, 2005).
Bougerol, Jacques-Guy, 'The Church Fathers and *Auctoritates* in Scholastic Theology to Bonaventure'. In *The Reception of the Church Fathers in the West: From the Carolingians to the Maurists*; ed. Irena Backus, vol. 1; Leiden: Brill, 1997), pp. 289–335.
Cullen, Christopher, *Bonaventure* (Oxford: Oxford University Press, 2006).
Mackey, Louis, *Faith Order Understanding: Natural Theology in the Augustinian Tradition* (Toronto: Pontifical Institute of Medieval Studies, 2011).
Quinn, John Francis, *The Historical Constitution of St. Bonaventure's Philosophy* (Studies and Texts 23; Toronto: PIMS, 1973).

9 Augustine and Luther

Phillip Cary

Like most Christian theologians in the West, Martin Luther is an Augustinian. Even when he departs from Augustine, it is by developing themes that arose in the deeply Augustinian theology of the Middle Ages. The two most important points of departure can be described as a more inward conception of sin and a more outward conception of grace (I). This chapter will locate these points of departure in the development of Luther's doctrine of justification (II) and show how they resulted in a distinctive Reformation theology, which deals with medieval Catholic anxieties in a way that needs to be distinguished from most later forms of Protestantism (III).

I. Two Points of Contrast

First, Luther makes sin more inward than Augustine by highlighting the issue of motivation. In Augustine's deeply teleological view, love is a desire for the good, and what matters most is what goods we desire and in what order. Sin is found in the will whenever we do not love God first and foremost, then secondarily our neighbours and ourselves and lastly external goods, using them so as to arrive together with our neighbours at the enjoyment of God as the supreme Good. Augustine did not scrutinize our motives for loving God, since it never occurred to him that there could be something wrong with desiring to have the best of all goods. Medieval theologians, however, raised the possibility that we could love God selfishly, and therefore unjustly and immorally, in a way that violated rather than obeyed the Law of God. Luther makes much of this possibility, even giving it a memorable new name, the 'curvedness' (*curvitas*) of the self that is curved in on itself (*incurvatus in se*).[1] He contends that this is the actual state of even the most saintly human will after Adam, with the result that every human act is in fact sin. Hence his doctrine of justification entails that every righteous person is actually a sinner at the same time – in a famous, contentious formula: *simul iustus et peccator*.[2]

---

[1] An especially prominent theme in the Romans lectures, LW 25:291–2, 313, 345.
[2] Literally, 'at the same time a righteous man and a sinner'. (Readers without Latin must continually bear in mind, when studying the medieval and Reformation doctrine of justification, that 'righteous' and 'just' translate one and the same word, as do 'righteousness'

Second, Luther makes grace more outward than Augustine by making it more sacramental. Whereas Augustine's doctrine of justification has us praying for the grace to become righteous, Luther has us finding grace and righteousness in the Gospel, which is an external word that has a sacramental kind of efficacy, in that it gives what it signifies. The Gospel of Jesus Christ gives us nothing less than Christ himself, with all that he is and all that he has, including his righteousness, grace, holiness and goodness. In a lapidary formulation, Luther puts it this way: 'The promises of God give what the commandments of God demand.'[3] Here the commandments and promises are Law and Gospel, respectively. Both are forms of the word of God but they must be distinguished, because the Law is God requiring us to do something while the Gospel is God giving us something – and there is no more important distinction to grasp, by Luther's reckoning.[4]

The distinction between *Law and Gospel* is in effect Luther's revision of Augustine's reading of the Pauline contrast between *Law and grace*, as we can see by contrasting Luther's formulation with its Augustinian predecessor, a prayer for grace: 'Give what you command, and command what you will'.[5] Faced with the Law's demand for a righteousness that is beyond our power to acquire, Augustine seeks grace by prayer, a human word addressed to God, whereas Luther finds grace in the Gospel, a divine word addressed to human beings.

This word is sacramental because the Gospel, as Luther understands it, is an external word that gives what it signifies – just as in medieval scholasticism a sacrament is an external sign that not only signifies the inner help of grace (as Augustine says) but also confers it (which Augustine does not

---

and 'justice'.) Perhaps the most famous occurrence of this formula is in the 1535 Galatians lectures, *LW* 26:232, but it is first elaborated in the Romans lectures in 1515–16, *LW* 25: 258–60. Also, it is worth noting that Luther has many other ways of making exactly the same point, for example, in the Galatians lectures, quite simply, 'I am a sinner, I am not a sinner' (*LW* 26:168), and in his Commentary on Psalm 51, most fundamentally: 'Though I am a sinner in myself, I am not a sinner in Christ' (*LW* 12:311).

[3] Luther, *The Freedom of a Christian* (1520), *LW* 31:349.

[4] For the importance of the distinction, see the 1535 Galatians commentary (*LW* 26:115–6 and 313) and the Table Talk (*LW* 54:106, 127). For the content of the distinction, see Luther's Preface to the New Testament (*LW* 35:357–62) and Preface to Romans (*LW* 35:365–9), 'Brief Instruction on What to Look for and Expect in the Gospels' (*LW* 35:117–24), and most succinctly, the second page of 'How Christians Should Regard Moses' (*LW* 35:162) as well as the Galatians commentary (*LW* 26:208–9). The idea of distinguishing Law and Gospel is present already in the first Psalms lectures (*LW* 11:161–2), but the content of the distinction is different in the early period, before Luther has the concept of Gospel as efficacious promise.

[5] Augustine, *conf.* 10.29.40. The prayer, 'Give what you command', which Augustine often repeats, was particularly offensive to Pelagius according to *persev.* 20.53. (All translations from Augustine are mine. Translations from Luther are mine when *WA* is cited).

say).[6] In this regard, Luther belongs with scholastic theology rather than with Augustine, as he explicitly defines the power of the Gospel in terms of sacramental efficacy: 'All the words and stories of the Gospel are a kind of sacrament, that is sacred signs, through which God brings about, in those who believe, whatever the story tells of.'[7] Thus Lutheran piety, like medieval piety but unlike Augustine and much Protestant piety, involves a kind of outward turn, clinging to word and sacrament as efficacious means of grace.

In Luther's mature theology, the external power of the Gospel is the divine remedy for the inward perversity of sin. But in the course of his theological development, these two departures from Augustine, concerning grace and sin, do not take place at the same time. Early in his career, Luther has the conception of sin as ineradicable selfishness without anything like what he later calls the Gospel of Jesus Christ to remedy it. Of course he has the term 'Gospel' from the Bible itself – along with, surprisingly, other key terminology of his later theology, including *iustitia Dei*, *sola fide* and *sola gratia* ('the righteousness of God', 'faith alone' and 'grace alone') as well as the concept of imputation and the formula *simul iustus et peccator*. But in the absence of the mature Law/Gospel distinction, these terms do not say quite the same thing as when they are used in the familiar Lutheran way, later in his career. In his early works, Luther fills out the content of the Augustinian prayer for grace with penitential works of humiliation, confession of sin, self-accusation, self-hatred and ultimately the desire to be damned. 'Justification by faith alone', in this early stage of Luther's thought, means that we must never believe we are justified but must continually seek justification by agreeing with the Word of a God who accuses, judges and condemns us. Luther's initial use of Augustine takes shape in an ultimately very un-Augustinian way within this early project of condemnation and self-hatred.

II. Luther's Early Doctrine of Justification

a. The Counterfactual Test

In the four years before he posted his 95 theses on indulgences on 31 October 1517, Luther was a monk lecturing on the Bible at the University

---

[6] In the very first paragraph of the *Sentences*, Lombard describes the 'Gospel sacraments' (*evangelica sacramenta*) as signs which 'not only signify but confer that which inwardly helps' (*non solum significant, sed conferunt quod intus adjuvet*), *Sententiae* 1.1.1. That sacraments signify grace is an idea to be found in Augustine, but that they also confer it is a medieval addition to Augustinian thought – or so I argue in *Outward Signs: The Powerlessness of External Things in Augustine's Thought* (New York: Oxford University Press, 2008), chapters 6–8.

[7] *Omnia verba, omnes historiae Euangelicae sunt sacramenta quaedam, hoc est sacra signa, per quae in credentibus deus efficit, quidquid illae historiae designant* (from a sermon on Christmas day, 1519 [WA 9:440]). I know of no published English translation of this text.

of Wittenberg.[8] We have his notes for the courses he taught in these years, including one on Paul's letter to the Romans in 1515–16, which constitutes his most extended and coherent theological work in this period. (His earlier course, the lectures on the Psalms in 1513–15, was exploratory, often daringly original, but not yet quite coherent.[9]) In the Romans lectures, he returns again and again to Augustine's anti-Pelagian treatise *On the Spirit and the Letter*, one of the fundamental texts of the Western Church's doctrine of grace.[10] Augustine's text helps him explain the nature of true righteousness as well as why – in stark contrast to his later theology – we must seek it all our lives without ever believing we have received it.

True righteousness, Augustine teaches, is found in the will, not in outward works. It must come to us by the Spirit, not the letter, which is to say by the inner help of divine grace rather than by human efforts to keep the Law. To explain why, Augustine offers a deft analysis of the human will after Adam, the will of sinners who hear the commandment of God but don't like what they hear, because there is something they love more than God and his righteousness. They want to be righteous in order to avoid being punished, not because they actually love righteousness for its own sake. So Augustine proposes a kind of counterfactual test: if there were no Law of God and therefore no punishment for disobedience, would you still do what the Law commands? If the answer is no, then there is a difference between the apparent righteousness of the good works you do before human beings (*coram hominibus*) and the inward disobedience of your will, which is what really counts before God (*coram Deo*). As Augustine explains, in a passage Luther quotes:

> Even those who did what the Law commanded, without help from the Spirit of grace, did it from fear of punishment and not from love of righteousness, and hence there was not in the will before God what appeared in the works before human beings [and conversely, what did not appear in the works, was nonetheless before God in the will], and they were held guilty of

---

[8] Of the massive amount of writing that has been devoted to Luther's life in this period, perhaps the two best introductions are Roland Bainton's lively *Here I Stand: A Life of Martin Luther* (Nashville: Abingdon, 1950) and the first volume of Martin Brecht's magisterial biography *Martin Luther: His Road to Reformation, 1483–1521* (trans. James Shaaf; Philadelphia: Fortress, 1985).

[9] The best thematic study of these early writings in English remains that of Jared Wicks, *Man Yearning for Grace: Luther's Early Spiritual Teaching* (Washington and Cleveland: Corpus Books, 1968).

[10] Augustine's *De spiritu et littera* is the very first text Luther cites in his scholia on Romans as he explains the purpose of the whole letter, WA 56:157 (= LW 25:135).

committing what God knew they would rather have done, if it could have been done with impunity.[11]

This counterfactual test means that God judges us not outwardly by our works but inwardly by our will, as determined by what we would do if there were no Law and punishment to restrain us. What the commandment requires in the will is not fear but love, for 'if the commandment is done from fear of punishment and not from love of righteousness, it is done slavishly, not freely, and thus it is not done at all'.[12] Only the grace of the Holy Spirit can provide the inner gift of delight which causes the will to obey in the freedom of love rather than the servitude of fear.[13] From this Luther regularly draws the conclusion that without grace, the Law can only make us slaves who inwardly hate what we're doing, hate the Law itself and hate the God who gave it.[14]

b. The Righteousness of God
For Luther, Augustine's counterfactual test explains why all the good works in the world can't make us righteous, contrary to Aristotle's notion that we acquire the virtue of righteousness or justice by repeatedly doing what is righteous or just.[15] Luther frequently contrasts Augustine with Aristotle and the scholastic theologians on this point: whereas Aristotle and his followers teach that we become righteous by doing good works, Augustine follows Paul in teaching that we must first become righteous by faith before we can hope to do works that are any good. Thus the Augustinian teaching Luther most treasured was about the righteousness of God (*iustitia Dei*), which he says,

---

[11] Augustine, *spir. et litt.* 8.13, as quoted in Luther's Romans lectures, WA 56:200 (= LW 25:184). Translations from Luther's Romans lectures are mine, based on the Weimar edition. The bracketed insertion is Luther's addition. Earlier Luther gives a paraphrase of the same passage, WA 56:191 (= LW 25:174).
[12] Augustine, *spir. et litt.* 14.26.
[13] Ibid., 3.5.
[14] See, for example, the Preface to Romans in Luther's German Bible: 'If the law were not there, you would prefer to act otherwise. The conclusion is that from the bottom of your heart you hate the law' (LW 35:367), and the 1535 Galatians commentary: 'this righteousness of works is nothing but to love sin, to hate righteousness, to despise God and his Law', because those who obey out of fear 'would prefer that there were no Law, no punishment, no hell, and finally no God' (LW 26:336–7).
[15] Luther's criticisms of Aristotle typically centre on this point: 'the righteousness of God is not acquired by means of acts frequently repeated, as Aristotle taught' (*Heidelberg Disputation*, LW 31:55; cf. Aristotle, *Nicomachean Ethics* 2:4,1105b10). Luther, who began his career in the university giving required lectures on Aristotle's ethics, was quite familiar with passages like *Nicomachean Ethics* 2.1,1103b1 ('We become just by doing just actions'), which present what looks very much like a doctrine of justification by good works. However, it makes a difference that Luther's reading of Aristotle follows the voluntarism of the Franciscan theological tradition, as Dieter argues (Theodor Dieter, *Der junge Luther und Aristoteles* [Berlin and New York: Walter de Gruyter, 2001], pp. 214–27).

quoting Augustine, 'is called the righteousness of God because by imparting it (*impertiendo*) he makes people righteous'.[16] Augustine's lesson here is that God's justice does not mean that he punishes people, but that he justifies them, making them partakers in his justice or righteousness. Luther adds that it is called the righteousness *of God* 'to distinguish it from the righteousness of human beings (*iustitia hominum*), which is brought about by works – just as Aristotle plainly establishes in book 3 of the *Ethics*, according to which righteousness follows and is brought about by actions, whereas according to God it precedes works and works are brought about by it'.[17]

Throughout his career, Luther's doctrine of justification centres on this Augustinian conception of the righteousness of God, by which we become inwardly righteous and thus capable of doing good works out of love rather than fear. For the inner person and will must be good, by the grace of God, before the outward actions or works can be truly good. Using Christ's metaphor of tree and fruit (Mt. 7.18), Luther describes this as a reversal of Aristotle's misguided ethics: 'The tree is not brought about by the fruit, but the fruit by the tree. So virtue is not brought about by works and actions, as Aristotle teaches, but actions are brought about by virtues as Christ teaches.'[18] This tree-fruit contrast becomes a recurrent motif in Luther, as a way of expressing the priority of person to work, inner to outer, the passive righteousness imparted to us by faith to the active righteousness by which we do our own good works.

At this juncture, it is opportune to mention two points at which my presentation here differs from long-standing trends in Luther scholarship. First of all, twentieth-century Luther scholarship put a great deal of energy into tracing Luther's early readings of Augustine in order to fix a date for when he discovered this Augustinian concept of the righteousness of God.[19]

---

[16] WA 56:172 (= LW 25:151), commenting on Rom. 1.17 and quoting Augustine's *spir. et litt.* 11.18. Luther goes on to note that the same point had been made also in *spir. et litt.* 9.15.

[17] WA 56:172 (= LW 25:152). Luther is undoubtedly thinking of *Nicomachean Ethics* 3.5, where Aristotle explains why virtue and vice are up to us.

[18] WA 56:364 (= LW 25:354). Here Luther is most likely thinking of *Nicomachean Ethics* 2.4, where Aristotle argues against the view that 'if we do what is just or temperate, we must already be just or temperate' (1105a.21) and for the view that 'A person comes to be just from doing just actions' (1105b10).

[19] For a sampling of the scholarship on this issue, see the collections edited by Bernhard Lohse, *Der Durchbruch der reformatorischen Erkenntnis bei Luther* (Darmstadt: Wissenschaftliche Buchhandlung, 1968) and *Der Durchbruch: Neuere Untersuchungen* (Stuttgart: F. Steiner, 1988). The classic studies of Luther's early reading of Augustine with this issue in mind are Erich Vogelsang, *Die Anfänge Luthers Christologie nach der ersten Psalmenvorlesung, insbesondere in ihren exegetischen und systematischen Zusammenhänge mit Augustine und der Scholastik dargestellt* (Berlin and Leipzig: de Gruyter, 1929) and Adolf Hamel, *Der junge Luther und Augustine: Ihre Beziehungen in der Rechfertigungslehre nach Luthers ersten Vorlesung 1509–1518 untersucht* (reprint edn; Hildesheim and New York: Georg Olms, 1980 [originally 1934–35]). For a sophisticated examination of Luther's early understanding of

Where my presentation differs from most of this scholarship is in avoiding the assumption that the advent of this particular concept should be equated with a 'Reformation breakthrough', as though it alone were sufficient to make Luther a Protestant. On the contrary, I will be arguing that Luther is not quite Lutheran until he has a concept of Gospel as efficacious word of grace, which comes quite some time after his acquaintance with the Augustinian concept of the righteousness of God. Second, I will shortly argue that for Luther the righteousness of God is not simply imputed to us, as in the many purely forensic doctrines of justification to be found in later Protestantism. Rather, it is infused in us, makes a deep inner change in our hearts and grows in an ongoing process of justification. Imputation plays a role, but it is secondary and only fully intelligible in light of Luther's Augustinian understanding of justification as a lifelong process. The resulting account of justification coheres with recent Finnish Luther scholarship, which sees union with Christ as the ground of justification.[20]

c. Praying for Grace

Always, for Luther, the righteousness of God is given to us by grace, not achieved by works of the Law. Hence it becomes ours only by faith, which in the Romans lectures means we obtain it by praying. This again is an Augustinian lesson. Luther quotes Augustine explaining that God 'commands some things which we cannot do, so that we may know what we must ask him for. Precisely this is *faith, which acquires by prayer what the Law requires*'.[21] Here faith does not cling to a divine word of promise but utters its own word of prayer which, as we have already seen, can be summed up in the words 'Give what you command'. Augustine develops this point in a memorable passage in *On the Spirit and the Letter*, which Luther quotes twice in the Romans lectures: 'What the law of works requires by threatening, the law of faith acquires by believing . . . By the law of works God says, "Do what I command". By the law of faith what is said to God [that is, by humble prayer] is, "Give what you command".'[22]

Augustine in general, see Leif Grane, *Modus Loquendi Theologicus: Luthers Kampf um die Erneuerung der Theologie (1515–1518)* (Leiden: Brill, 1975).

[20] See Carl E. Braaten and Robert W. Jenson (eds), *Union with Christ: The New Finnish Interpretation of Luther* (Grand Rapids: Eerdmans, 1998), for an introduction to this Finnish scholarship, in a collection of papers presented by its major practitioners.

[21] Augustine, *gr. et lib. arb.* 16.32, as quoted in WA 56:356. (All italics, for English words, are mine.) LW 25:345 mistranslates here, missing the difference between the verbs. A very similar formulation, which likewise plays on the verbal contrast between the Law which requires (*imperat*) and faith which acquires (*impetrat*), is found in Augustine's *ench.* 117, and echoed closely in Luther's 1518 Heidelberg Disputation, Thesis 26 (LW 31:56).

[22] Augustine, *spir. et litt.* 13.22, as quoted in WA 56:256–7 (= LW 25:243). The bracketed insertion is Luther's; cf. the second quotation in WA 56:264 (= LW 25:251).

The contrast between Luther's early version of Augustinianism and what we now know as Lutheran theology opens up when Luther proceeds to teach that this prayer is never quite answered: 'We all pray, "Give what you command", and yet we do not receive. *We all believe . . . and yet we are not all justified.*'[23] Here, despite his previous insistence that the righteousness of God 'is revealed in the Gospel alone . . . through faith alone (*per solam fidem*), by which the Word of God is believed',[24] it turns out that faith alone is not enough to obtain the righteousness of God. Luther goes on to explain why: the new will that obeys the Law 'sweetly, in joy and love and fullness of will' is ours only by grace, but it is not given without extensive self-cultivation, *agricultura suiipsius*.[25] Faith is therefore only the beginning of a long process of working to obtain justification by prayer, which is never completed in this life: 'Therefore we must always be praying and working (*orandum et operandum*) that grace and the Spirit may grow . . . For *God has not justified us*, that is, he has not perfected or completed the righteous or their righteousness. But he has made a beginning, in order to perfect it.'[26]

d. Working for Justification

The process of justification in the Romans lectures consists in a lifelong work of praying for grace. This is not the works of the Law, but it is explicitly and emphatically *work*. After quoting Augustine again on the difference between the law of works (which says, 'Do what I command') and the law of faith (which replies, 'Give what you command'), Luther develops an extensive contrast between two kinds of people corresponding to these two laws: 'the people of the Law' trust in the righteousness they think they have, whereas for the 'the people of faith', things are different:

> All of life until death is spent always begging, seeking, asking to be justified by the groans of their heart, *the voice of their works, the works of their bodies*, never standing still, never apprehending, with none of their works putting an end to obtaining righteousness but waiting for it as something always still outside of them, while they still live and are always in their sins.[27]

The work of praying and seeking justification never ends in this life, precisely because it does not consist of works of the Law but works of grace and

---

[23] WA 56:257 (= LW 25:244).
[24] WA 56:171–2 (= LW 25:151).
[25] WA 56:257 (= LW 25:244).
[26] WA 56:258 (= LW 25:245). LW here mistranslates *absoluit* ('completed') as 'declared', and adds the word 'yet' to Luther's flat statement that God has not justified us, *non enim iustificavit nos*.
[27] WA 56:264 (= LW 25:251–2). One variant reading of Luther's manuscript has 'the voice of their mouth' rather than 'the voice of their works' (reading *oris* for *operis*).

faith: 'Hence when the apostle says that "we are justified without the works of the Law" (Rom. 3.28) he is not talking about *the works which are done to seek justification*. For these are *not works of the Law but of grace and faith*, since one who works at them does not trust himself to have been justified by them, but desires to be justified.'[28]

In stark contrast therefore to Luther's later teaching, the Romans lectures persistently warn us that we must never believe we are actually justified: 'we can never know whether we are justified, whether we believe.'[29] There is no certainty that we have the righteousness of God, for we must never presume that we are in fact 'free and cheerful about the works of the Law, seeking only to please God and do his will, not working from fear of punishment or love of ourselves'.[30] At this point Luther deploys Augustine against Augustine, using the Augustinian counterfactual test to expose the presumption of believing that God ever answers the Augustinian prayer to 'give what you command':

> For who does good and avoids evil by that will which, even if there were no commandment or prohibition, he would still do and avoid them? I believe that if we scrutinized our heart rightly, none would find himself to be such unless he were absolutely perfect, but rather *if it were allowed he would avoid many good things and do many evil things*. This is what it is to be in your sins before God, whom we are bound to serve freely by that will of which I was speaking [i.e. 'free and cheerful about the works of the Law' etc.] ... But who knows or can know, even if it seems to him that he is doing good and avoiding evil by that will, whether it is really so, since God alone will judge this?[31]

Therefore in Luther's Romans lectures, the formulas 'grace alone'[32] and 'faith alone' do not altogether exclude works. On the contrary, they imply works

---

[28] WA 56:264 (= LW 25:252).
[29] WA 56:252 (= LW 25:239). Here I take issue with Karl Holl's influential contention that Luther teaches certainty of justification in the Romans lectures. Holl argues that for Luther in this text faith must take the promise of grace to heart just as seriously as the divine word of judgement (Karl Holl, Gesammelte Aufsätze zur Kirchengeschichte. Vol. 1: Luther [6th edn; Tübingen: J.C.B. Mohr, 1932 (1st edn, 1921)], pp. 133–34). But in fact the two words do not have equal force. The word of judgement tells us who we presently are *in re*, whereas the promise tells us what we shall be in the future, *in spe*, if we follow the doctor's orders. But because doctor's orders are such bitter medicine, any present peace or comfort the promise affords is necessarily hidden under its opposite, which is to say fear, tribulation and condemnation. It is a peace we must believe in but not experience (*LW* 56:412).
[30] WA 56:235 (= LW 25:220).
[31] WA 56:236 (= LW 25:221). Bracketed insertion is mine.
[32] The formula appears in WA 56:255 (= LW 25:242): *sola gratia justificat*.

of grace and faith, which are penitential versions of the Augustinian prayer for grace, involving humble confession of sin, self-accusation, contrition and self-hatred. This work is never completed in this life, for the ongoing process of justification requires us to remain continually aware of our sins and praying for grace, 'always in fear' because of the imperfection of our justification and the bottomless iniquity of our will, which we can never scrutinize closely enough.[33]

e. Sinners in Process

For the early Luther, faith in God's promise does not mean we have what is promised. It is like a sick man believing the doctor's promise that he will be healed if he follows the doctor's orders. 'He is sick in actual fact (*in rei veritate*) but healthy by the certain promise of the doctor whom he believes, who already counts (*reputat*) him as healthy because he is certain he will heal him, for he has begun healing him and does not impute (*imputavit*) to him a sickness unto death.'[34] Justification here means God imputes righteousness to those who have faith, like a doctor who pronounces his patient healthy even though he is still in fact sick, because the patient believes the doctor's promise of healing and the promise is sure to be fulfilled. But the patient must not believe he is healed yet, because the essential prescription for his healing is precisely that he be humble enough to keep confessing his sickness.[35] Therefore for sinners who believe, righteousness is hidden under its opposite: God regards them as righteous, but they can arrive at righteousness only by confessing and believing they are sinners. The doctor promises them health in the future, but what they know in the present is only their own disease. They are each 'perfectly healthy in hope (*in spe*), but in fact (*in re*) a sinner', and thus each is *simul peccator et iustus*, 'a sinner and a righteous man at the same time, a sinner in actual fact (*re vera*) but righteous by the imputation (*ex reputatione*) and sure promise of God'.[36]

Luther's *simul* thus does not exclude the notion that justification is a process but is based on it. He explains the process in both Aristotelian and Augustinian terms. In Aristotelian terms which Luther explicitly endorses (for 'on these matters Aristotle philosophizes, and well'), justification is a process in which we are *semper in motu*, always moving from a present state of sin to a future state of righteousness.[37] As he had explained earlier in his Psalms lectures,

---

[33] 'Always in fear': LW 25:268, 278, 497 (= WA 56:281, 291, 503); bottomless iniquity: LW 25:221,313 (= WA 56:235,325).
[34] WA 56:271 (= LW 25:260).
[35] Cf. WA 56:217 (= LW 25:202–3).
[36] WA 56:272 (= LW 25:260).
[37] WA 56:441–2 (= LW 25:434). For this positive use of Aristotle's theory of change or motion, as well as its idiosyncratic features, see the very helpful discussion in Dieter, *Der junge Luther und Aristoteles*, pp. 302–45.

'according to philosophy a motion is an imperfect act, always in part acquired and in part to be acquired, always in the midst of opposites, and standing at the same time (*simul*) at the starting point and at the goal'.[38] It is like saying: so long as you are still in the process of healing, you are still sick. Luther's use of the Aristotelian theory of motion here may owe its inspiration to a passage in which Augustine explains how, for as long as we live on earth, the virtue of charity is never present 'to the fullest extent, which cannot be increased; but as long as it can be increased, that which is less than it should be actually comes from vice . . . And because of this vice, no matter how much we progress, we must always pray, "forgive us our debts".'[39] After quoting this passage Luther draws the conclusion, 'doing good works, we sin – unless God through Christ covers this imperfection and does not impute it to us (*non imputaret*)'.[40]

In Augustinian terms, we are 'sinners in fact but righteous in hope'.[41] The key terms of this contrast come from Augustine's explanation of how we can be saved in baptism (as the apostle says, 'saved . . . by the washing of regeneration', in Tit. 3.5), even though not everyone who is baptized is saved in the end. Augustine turns to Rom. 8.24 ('by hope you are saved') and distinguishes between being saved in hope (*in spe*) and being saved in fact (*in re*).[42] The former takes place in baptism, when we receive the hope of salvation by being made members of Christ, but the latter takes place only when we persevere in faith to the end and receive eternal life.

Of course, something must make up for the fact that our present, imperfect righteousness is actually sin. At this point Luther calls on a specifically Augustinian notion of imputation. In the treatise *On the Perfection of Human Righteousness*, for example, Augustine observes that in this life we are saved only in hope because 'there is full righteousness only when there is full health'.[43] He proceeds to teach that God does not impute sin to those who pray in faith for forgiveness.[44] This explains why Scripture can speak of believers as walking unblemished (*immaculati*) in the way of righteousness. A sin that doesn't count, in effect makes no blemish:

> It's not absurd to say someone is walking without blemish who is not yet perfect, but running toward that perfection blamelessly, lacking damnable crimes and not neglecting to cleanse even venial sins by alms. For our walk,

---

[38] Luther, the first Psalms lectures, on Ps. 119(118).121 (*LW* 11:494).
[39] Augustine, *ep.* 167:4.15, as quoted in *WA* 56:289 (= *LW* 25:276). Luther identifies this as Epistle 29, but that is not the numbering in modern editions.
[40] *WA* 56:289 (= *LW* 25:276).
[41] *WA* 56:269 (= *LW* 25:258).
[42] For example, Augustine, *pecc. mer.* 1.18.23, *c. ep. Pel.* 3.3.5.
[43] *Perf. just.* 3.8.
[44] Ibid., 6.15, commenting on Ps. 32(31).2, *Beatus vir cui non imputabit Dominus peccatum*.

which is to say our journey toward perfection, is cleansed by clean prayer . . . so that, as long as what is not imputed is not blamed (*non reprehenditur quod non imputatur*), our path to perfection may be taken without blame, which is to say without blemish.[45]

What medieval Aristotelians describe as a process or movement (*motus*), Augustine describes as a *via* or *iter*, a way or journey. But however you describe it, the implication is that so long as our justification is not completed, there remains some degree of imperfection in our righteousness, which implies some kind of moral deficit which God must either condemn or else not count against us. Imputation, for both Augustine and Luther, is God not counting this remaining sin against us.

f. When Good Is Evil

Where Luther goes beyond Augustine most strikingly is in his account of this remnant of sin, which is not just a weakness or an evil tendency, but a heart that sins in everything it does. Picking up on an analysis of moral imperfection developed by Bernard of Clairvaux, Luther argues that even when we love God, it is for our own sake (*amor Dei propter se*) rather than for God's sake (*amor Dei propter Deum*).[46] This enables him to add a startling new twist to Augustine's teaching that sin means seeking to enjoy (*frui*) temporal goods, which we ought instead merely to use (*uti*) in order to come to enjoyment of God as the eternal Good. In a strikingly un-Augustinian conception, Luther insists that even in seeking the best and most spiritual goods, we *use* God.[47] That is because we are always *incurvatus in se*, 'curved in on ourselves', bending every good thing, even God himself, back to our own use, seeking only ourselves in all things.[48] This radical selfishness means that all good things become bad for us; they are 'evilly good' (*male bona*).[49]

The result is a severe undermining of the teleological assumptions that Augustine shares with the ethics of ancient philosophy. Luther rejects 'the good deduced from philosophy', because 'even though all things are very

---

[45] *Perf. just.* 9.20 (end). Augustine has just finished quoting a number of passages where people are described as *immaculati*, including *Beati immaculati in via, qui ambulant in lege Domini* (Ps. 119[118].1).

[46] WA 56:390 (= LW 25:380–1); cf. Bernard of Clairvaux, *On Loving God* 9.26.

[47] WA 56:304 (= LW 25:291); cf. likewise WA 56:325 (= LW 25:313). Luther describes this way of loving God as concupiscence (WA 56:307, translated 'selfish desire' in LW 25:295) or *amor concupiscentia* (WA 56:390, translated 'covetous love' in LW 25:380). Augustine's *uti/frui* ethics, developed at length in the first book of *De doctrina Christiana*, became a fundamental organizing principle of medieval theology after Peter Lombard, *Sententiae* 1.1.2, to which Luther refers in WA 56:305 (= LW 25:292).

[48] In addition to the references in the previous note, see WA 56:356 (= LW 25:345).

[49] WA 56:355 (= LW 25:344).

good [Gen. 1.31], *for us* there are no good things . . . *for us* everything is evil'.[50] So in place of desire for the good, we must cultivate desire for our own evil, which is how we must aim to achieve perfect righteousness, culminating in the heartfelt desire to suffer the ultimate evil:

> Thus we need to flee good things and take on evil things. Not by words alone or in pretense of heart, but in full feeling we must confess and *wish ourselves to be destroyed and damned*. We need to act toward ourselves like someone who hates someone else. He doesn't just pretend to hate him, but seriously desires to destroy and kill and damn the person he hates. So if we also in a true and heartfelt way destroy and persecute ourselves, and offer ourselves to hell for God's sake and his righteousness, then we have truly made satisfaction to his justice, and he will have mercy and deliver us.[51]

Justification by faith alone here means we are justified by hating ourselves thoroughly enough, so as to anticipate and agree with God's eternally hating us. This is not the sort of thing Augustine ever had in mind. It runs entirely counter to Augustine's insistence that the will for happiness is the foundation of all ethics and philosophy.[52] Luther therefore must turn Augustine's prayer for grace inside out, making it a desire for damnation rather than happiness, in order to incorporate it into his fierce late medieval programme of penitential works, consisting of self-accusation, self-condemnation and self-hatred, and culminating in the effort to be sincere and earnest in desiring to be damned.

g. Faith in a Word of Accusation

For the young Luther, the good people are the ones who will evil, in the sense of desiring what is bad for themselves. This is how to conform to the will of God, 'who hates, damns and chooses evil for all sinners, that is, for all of us'.[53] Faith wills what God wills by agreeing with his word, which is always against us, for 'the word of God, if it comes, comes against what we feel and wish

---

[50] WA 56:392 (= LW 25:383).
[51] WA 56:393 (= LW 25:384); cf. similarly in WA 56:419 (= LW 25:411) the notion of making satisfaction by ceding all good things, including God, and 'going into nothingness, death and damnation . . . which is done by faith'.
[52] As we learn in Augustine, *Trin.* 13.4.7, 'Surely we all want to be happy' is in the exordium of Cicero's *Hortensius*, the book that turned Augustine's thoughts towards philosophy and God according to *conf.* 3.4.7–8. The saying recurs throughout Augustine's works, especially when he inquires into the foundations of ethics, for example, *b. vita* 2.10; *c. Acad.* 1.2.5; *lib. arb.* 1.12.25 and 2.10.28; *mor.* 1.3.4; *conf.* 10.20.29; *civ. Dei* 10.1 (cf. 19.1, 'the only purpose for philosophizing is to attain happiness'). This account of the human telos is absolutely non-negotiable for Augustine.
[53] WA 56:392 (= LW 25:382).

(*contra sensum et votum nostrum*)'.[54] For Luther, faith always means clinging to the Word of God, but at this stage in his career, the word to which faith must cling is one that accuses and condemns us: 'by faith alone we are to believe we are sinners ... standing under the judgment of God and believing His words by which He says we are unrighteous ... Faith is content with only the words of God ... so it is necessary that we thoroughly accuse, judge, condemn and confess ourselves to be evil, that God may be justified in us.'[55] Thus the Romans lectures present a doctrine of justification by faith alone based on what Luther will later call Law,[56] not Gospel. That is why justification requires that we hate ourselves and seek to be damned.

This does not mean Luther has no inkling of a Law/Gospel contrast in the Romans lectures, but rather that he does not yet conceive of the Gospel as a word that has the power to bestow the good thing that it signifies. The Gospel 'teaches where and whence we are to have grace and charity, which is to say, Jesus Christ, whom *the Law promised* and the Gospel exhibits. The Law commands us to have charity and Jesus Christ, but the Gospel offers and exhibits them both.'[57] The promise here means the promise of Christ's coming – which is why it is associated not with the Gospel but with the Law, that is, the Old Testament and its prophecies. The Gospel offers us Christ, but as always in the Romans lectures, this means a good thing hidden under its opposite, justification hidden under condemnation, salvation hidden under humiliation and grace hidden in the cross.[58] In this version of the theology of the cross, it is our responsibility to participate in Christ's humiliation by desiring to be humiliated rather than saved, for 'to love is to hate, damn, and choose evil for oneself'.[59] Thus even the Word of Christ is a word that comes against us, like an enemy who accuses us and demands our agreement: 'Christ called his Word our adversary in Matthew 5, "Be in agreement with your adversary".'[60]

---

[54] WA 56:425 (= LW 25:415). See similarly LW:439 (= WA 56:446).

[55] WA 56:231 (= LW 25:215).

[56] Cf. for instance the 1535 Galatians lectures: 'When a man is taught this way by the Law ... he justifies God in His Word and confesses that he deserves death and eternal damnation' (LW 26:126). This could serve as a summary of the doctrine of justification developed in Luther's comments on Rom. 3.4–7, WA 56:212–233 (= LW 25:197–218).

[57] WA 56:337 (= LW 25:326).

[58] The exception that proves the rule: in WA 56:424–5 (= LW 25:416), commenting on Paul's reference to the 'Gospel of peace' in Rom. 10.15, Luther says that the Gospel gives peace to troubled consciences – but it is not a peace that is visible or experienced (it is *sine exeperientia*). Here Bayer's work provides a necessary corrective to Demmer's contention that there is already in the Romans lectures a distinctively Lutheran contrast between Law and Gospel, going beyond anything in Augustine (Dorothea Demmer, *Luther interpres: Der theologische Neuansatz in seiner Römerbriefexegese unter besonderer Berücksichtigung Augustins* [Witten: Luther Verlag, 1968], pp. 237–42).

[59] WA 56:392 (= LW 25:382).

[60] WA 56:446–7 (= LW 25:439); the reference is to Mt. 5.25.

III. Luther between Catholicism and Protestantism

a. The Gospel as Sacramental Promise

In the Romans lectures, the promise of justification is for the future, like a doctor promising health to a sick patient, so long as she follows the doctor's orders. But it turns out the doctor has ordered some very bitter medicine: a lifetime of praying for and seeking grace by way of self-accusation, self-condemnation and self-hatred. Luther's early doctrine of justification is thus driven by a kind of hopeful spiritual masochism: if we sincerely agree with God's word of accusation and condemnation, then he will justify us. One wonders how Luther thought this way of praying for grace could ever result in the kind of will that passes Augustine's counterfactual test, freely doing the works of the Law out of love and delight rather than fear and coercion. It seems much more like a recipe for what Luther later calls torture of conscience, an unending vicious circle of self-accusation producing fear of punishment, which must be confessed as sin, producing further self-accusation, producing yet more fear, and so on.[61] No wonder he looked back on this time and agreed with the judgement of the priest who told him that underneath his continual confessions of sin, he was actually angry at God.[62]

Once Luther has dug himself into this hole, Augustine's doctrine of grace does not have the wherewithal to pull him out. Luther cannot presume to believe in his own justification if the Word of God is against him. What he needs is a word that is actually *for* him, a word which not only promises a future righteousness but also bestows righteousness and grace in the present, and which does so in no uncertain terms, so that he is required to believe that he actually possesses what is promised. What he needs, in short, is the kind of word that he later calls the Gospel.[63] He cannot find such a thing in Augustine, for reasons that were pointed out at the time by his colleague Andreas Karlstadt in a commentary on Augustine's treatise *On the Spirit and the Letter*. For Augustine, the grace of the Spirit is an inner gift, whereas external words belong in the category of letter, not Spirit – and 'the letter kills, but

---

[61] I make this argument briefly, from a non-specialist, pastoral perspective, in 'Where to Flee for Grace: The Augustinian Context of Luther's Doctrine of the Gospel', *Lutheran Forum* 30/2 (May 1996), pp. 17–20.

[62] From the Table Talk, *LW* 54:15; cf. his famous retrospective remarks in *LW* 34:337.

[63] For the notion of Gospel as sacramental promise, see Cary, 'Why Luther Is Not Quite Protestant: The Logic of Faith in a Sacramental Promise', *Pro Ecclesia* 14/4 (2005), pp. 447–86. For Luther's distinctive conception of faith as sacramental, see Jared Wicks, '*Fides sacramenti – fides specialis*: Luther's Development in 1518', in *Luther's Reform: Studies in Conversion and the Church* (ed. Jared Wicks; Mainz: von Zabern, 1992), pp. 117–42. For the development of Luther's sacramental thinking in the crucial period around 1518, see Wolfgang Schwab, *Entwicklung und Gestalt der Sakramententheologie bei Martin Luther* (Frankfurt: P. Lang, 1977).

the Spirit gives life' (2 Cor. 3.6). There is no such thing as an efficacious external word of grace, because 'external things cannot save'.[64]

Luther came to think otherwise, in large part because the indulgence controversy ignited by his 95 theses forced him to think more deeply about penance as a sacrament (which is the context of the theology of indulgences) rather as a work of prayer. The first time he writes about an efficacious external word of grace is when he points to Christ's institution of the sacrament of penance in Mt. 16.19 as a promise that grounds the words of absolution, 'I absolve you of your sins in the name of the Father, the Son and the Holy Spirit'.[65] He comes to think of this as a sacramental word that confers the grace it signifies, requiring penitents to believe they have actually received forgiveness, so that it is not presumptuous to believe oneself justified by God but presumptuous to deny or doubt it. In short, he comes to think of it as the Gospel, an external word that justifies those who believe it. From this point on, Luther's teaching about the Word of God begins to sound a note of comfort, joy and certainty that was missing from the Romans lectures. The concept of an efficacious promise of Christ soon becomes the heart of Luther's sacramental theology in his major 1520 treatise on *The Babylonian Captivity of the Church*, where penance retains its sacramental efficacy even though it is no longer counted as a sacrament distinct from baptism.[66] In the same year, the notion of the Word of God as efficacious promise becomes central to his doctrine of justification in the famous

---

[64] *Quae foris sunt non salvant*. In *Karlstadt und Augustin. Der Kommentar des Andreas Bodenstein von Karlstadt zu Augustins Schrift* De Spiritu et Littera (ed. Ernst Kähler; Halle: Max Niemeyer, 1952) p. 84, note k. For an attempt at a properly nuanced account confirming Karlstadt's view of Augustine on this point, see Cary, *Outward Signs*, especially chapters 6–8.

[65] One can see this concept under development in 1518 as Luther reconceives sacramental absolution as an efficacious word in his defence of the 95 theses, especially in his explanations of theses 7 and 38 (LW 31:98–107 and 191–6). The key point appears in his letter to Cardinal Cajetan after the 1518 Augsburg interview, where he defends these theses, making the notion of justification by faith alone a prominent point of contention for the first time (LW 31:271). According to Bayer, the first time Luther's new concept of efficacious promise appears fully developed is in a set of disputation theses from 1518, *Pro veritate inquirenda et timoratis conscientiis consolandis* (WA 1:630–3). The theses are not available in English, but many of them appear *verbatim* in the little 1519 treatise on *The Sacrament of Penance* (LW 35:3–22), for which Luther evidently used the theses as an outline. The notion that absolution has sacramental efficacy for those who believe remains important in the Lutheran confessional writings composed by Melanchthon, including the *Augsburg Confession*, article 12 (Theodore G. Tappert, *The Book of Concord: The Confessions of the Evangelical Lutheran Church* [Philadelphia: Fortress Press, 1959], p. 34) and the *Apology of the Augsburg Confession*, article 13.4 (Tappert, *The Book of Concord*, p. 211), a document in which absolution is called 'the true voice of the Gospel' (art. 12.39, Tappert, *The Book of Concord*, p. 187).

[66] Over the course of the treatise, Luther actually changes his mind about whether to count penance as a distinct sacrament or a part of baptism (cf. LW 36:18 and 124). In any case, it has a sacramental efficacy due to the power of Christ's promise in Mt. 16.19.

little treatise on *The Freedom of a Christian*, one of the founding documents of Protestant theology.[67]

b. Christ and Justification

Luther's mature doctrine of justification centres on his distinctive notion of the Gospel of Jesus Christ, which integrates the concept of an efficacious promise with two Christological concepts that have an Augustinian pedigree. The first is union with Christ, which results in an exchange of properties, so that our sin and death become Christ's, while his righteousness and life become ours.[68] For Augustine, this is grounded in the communion of souls bound together by love in the body of Christ united to its head.[69] For Luther, it is grounded in faith rather than love, for what is received simply by believing in the Gospel of Christ is nothing less than Christ himself. Yet this faith is hardly unloving. The promise it believes functions as a kind of wedding vow, so that true faith 'with arms outstretched joyfully embraces the Son of God given for it and says, "He is my beloved and I am his"'.[70] By believing the Gospel we take hold of Christ himself, being united with him like a bride with her bridegroom, and thereby receive all that he is and all that he has, including his righteousness, goodness and grace. This blessed exchange, based on union with Christ, is at the heart of Luther's mature doctrine of justification.[71]

Second, the notion that Christ is ours by faith is reinforced by Luther's appropriation of Augustine's contrast between sacrament and example, with the added medieval conviction that a sacrament is an efficacious external means of grace. Hence the sermon in which Luther identifies the Gospel as a sacrament begins by explaining that in the narrative of the Gospel, Christ is not merely an example for our good works, like any other saint or good man, but a sacrament from which we seek all the good things we see in the story.[72]

---

[67] *LW* 31:348–9.

[68] This Christological concept is found in many places in the Augustinian tradition, beginning in Augustine's own thoughts about the *totus Christus*, the union of Christ with Christians in the 'whole Christ', head and members sharing in one body. The marital imagery is a later development. See David Steinmetz, *Luther and Staupitz* (Durham, NC: Duke University Press, 1980), p. 29.

[69] For love as the source of inner unity in Augustine's ecclesiology, see Cary, 'United Inwardly by Love: Augustine's Social Ontology', in *Augustine and Politics* (ed. K. Paffenroth et al.; Lanham, MD: Lexington Books, 2005), pp. 3–33, as well as *Outward Signs*, pp. 185–86.

[70] Luther, Thesis 22 from the 1535 *Theses on Faith and Law*, *LW* 34:110.

[71] Two key examples of this marital imagery for union with Christ, together with the consequence that his righteousness belongs to the believer, are found in the 1519 sermon 'On Two Kinds of Righteousness' (*LW* 31:297–8) and the 1520 treatise on *The Freedom of a Christian* (*LW* 31:351–2).

[72] *WA* 9:439. Augustine's notion of the life of Christ as both sacrament and example (*Trin.* 4.3.6) is familiar to Luther at the time of the Romans lectures (*LW* 25:309–10), where it is already interpreted in medieval terms, as having a sacramental efficacy (*LW* 25:284).

This is a precursor to the more familiar language of Luther's later explanations of the nature of the Gospel, where he admonishes Christians to receive Christ as a gift (in the Gospel), not merely an example (in the Law).[73]

c. Justification as Process

When the concept of an efficacious promise of grace drops into the centre of Luther's early doctrine of justification, it turns things inside out, so that the righteousness of God no longer come to us hidden under accusation and condemnation, but proclaimed as good news. Instead of seeking it endlessly in prayer, one finds it simply by believing the Gospel. Yet much of the Augustinian structure of Luther's doctrine remains in his mature writings, including his conception of justification as a process, begun in faith and not perfected until death. (To understand what follows, readers without Latin will need to bear in mind that *perfectus* – 'perfect' or 'perfected' – is a process term, denoting the completion of a process.) This Augustinian notion of justification as process sets Luther apart from later Protestantism.

For example, in Luther's most elaborate treatment of doctrine of justification, based on his lectures on Galatians in the 1530s, true Christian righteousness is described as consisting of two parts, faith and imputation.[74] Faith is a 'formal' righteousness, in the Aristotelian sense of real and substantial.[75] The scholastics identified our formal righteousness with charity or sanctifying grace (*gratia gratum faciens*), but Luther here identifies it with faith or Christ, because Christ is present in faith as its true inner form. This righteousness transforms a person inwardly, in heart and will, so as to become, in Christ's words, the good tree that can bear good fruit – in other words, a doer who can do good deeds.[76] But because our faith is always weak, having only '*begun* to take hold of Christ', God for Christ's sake 'reckons this *imperfect* faith as perfect righteousness'.[77] As in Luther's earlier works, the imputation by which God reckons us perfectly righteous makes up for the imperfection of the righteousness we receive by faith. Thus, in a striking version of the *simul*, Luther proceeds to speak of justification in process terms, saying 'we are justified, and nonetheless not yet justified', because 'we have indeed *begun* to be justified by faith . . . but are not yet *perfectly* righteous', that is, not yet

---

[73] For example, 'Brief Instruction on What to Look for and Expect in the Gospels' (*LW* 35:119) and the 1535 Galatians lectures (*LW* 27:34).
[74] The 1535 Galatians lectures, *LW* 26:229.
[75] Ibid., *LW* 26:129–30. This is a passage of central importance for the Finnish interpreters of Luther; cf. Tuomo Mannermaa, *Christ Present in Faith: Luther's View of Justification* (ed. K. Stjerna; Minneapolis: Fortress, 2005).
[76] Luther, the 1535 Galatians lectures, *LW* 26:255–7.
[77] Ibid., *LW* 26:129–30.

possessing a perfected *formal* righteousness, so that the familiar Augustinian language is still appropriate: 'our righteousness is not yet in fact (*in re*) but still in hope (*in spe*).'[78]

This is substantially the same account of the process of justification that Luther introduced in a famous 1519 sermon 'On Two Kinds of Righteousness', in which the righteousness of Christ, by which we are justified, 'is not infused all at the same time, but begins, progresses and is perfected in the end at death'.[79] Luther says explicitly that this righteousness is 'infused from without',[80] using the Augustinian theological term for the kind of grace that God pours into the soul in order to make a real change in us. Luther famously calls this an 'alien righteousness', but this is not because it remains outside us – as if it were merely imputed to us – but because it is the righteousness of another (*alieni*), that is, of Christ, just as original sin comes to us as the sin of another, that is, of Adam.[81] Luther also says quite explicitly that this alien righteousness is something we *possess*. For in faith we are united with Christ himself, with the result that just as 'a bridegroom possesses all that is his bride's and she all that is his',[82] so also 'Christ's righteousness becomes our righteousness and all that he has becomes ours'.[83]

Thus Luther locates the progress of believers towards the fullness of righteousness and holiness in the process of justification, not in what the later Protestant tradition calls sanctification. The righteousness by which we are justified is a righteousness in us that progresses towards a future perfection. There is another kind of righteousness, consisting of our good works, which Luther calls 'proper' righteousness because it is our own (*propria*) rather than Christ's. But these good works – which are the focus of later Protestant doctrines of sanctification – do not in Luther's account make us truly good persons. Quite the opposite: they are merely the outward effects, 'the fruit and consequence' of the alien righteousness working inwardly in our hearts.[84] To identify our spiritual progress with growth in this 'proper' righteousness would be to get things backwards, like saying that good fruit makes a good tree grow rather than the other way round.

---

[78] The 1535 Galatians lectures, translated from WA 40/2:24 (= LW 27:21).

[79] WA 2:146 (= LW 31:299): *Non enim tota simul infunditur, sed incipit, proficit et perficitur tandem in fine per mortem.*

[80] WA 2:145 (= LW 31:297). Most English translations, including LW, obscure the scholastic language Luther uses here by translating *ab extra infusa* as 'instilled from without', avoiding the notion of infused grace which Luther deliberately invokes here.

[81] WA 2:145 (= LW 31:297). The point is more fully developed in an earlier, untranslated sermon 'On Three Kinds of Righteousness', WA 2:44.

[82] WA 2:145 (= LW 31:297).

[83] WA 2:146 (= LW 31:298).

[84] WA 2:147 (= LW 31:300).

d. Baptism and Conversion

It is important to add that for Luther, the righteousness of Christ is not something we receive only once. It is given to us many times, 'in baptism and any time of true repentance'.[85] Therefore, as in scholastic theology, justification takes place whenever we truly repent,[86] which the mature Luther takes to mean whenever we return in faith to the sacramental promise of baptism, the unique ground of all subsequent repentance, grace and righteousness.[87] Hence Luther should not be read as supporting later Protestant notions of conversion, in which justification is equated with salvation and takes place in a once-in-a-lifetime event of accepting Christ. On the contrary, in Luther as well as in the early Lutheran confessional documents, 'conversion' is a repeated event that takes place whenever we repent and turn to Christ.[88]

By the same token, book 8 of Augustine's *Confessions* should not be read as if it were a Protestant conversion narrative, describing the moment of salvation when Augustine first became a Christian. This way of thinking about conversion had not been invented yet. For Augustine, as for Luther and all the Catholics in between, one becomes a Christian in baptism, 'the washing of regeneration' (Tit. 3.5) through which one is born again in Christ.[89]

A crucial point on which Luther does belong with Protestantism rather than Catholicism concerns the concupiscence or sin that remains after baptism. After the Romans lectures, Luther continues to follow Augustine in teaching that God does not impute this sin to baptized Christians who do not consent to it.[90] But he has trouble with the passage where Augustine says that this is

---

[85] WA 2:145 (= LW 297).

[86] For example, for Aquinas, the justification of the ungodly happens whenever sin is remitted, which typically takes place in the sacrament of penance, which should be repeated more than once in life (*ST* I-II, 113.1; cf. III, 85.6 ad3).

[87] The theme of penance as 'return to baptism' appears in the 1519 treatise on baptism (*LW* 35:38), is elaborated in the *The Babylonian Captivity of the Church* (*LW* 36:58–9), remains important in his later sacramental thinking in treatises like the *Confession Concerning the Lord's Supper* (*LW* 37:370) and is incorporated into the Lutheran tradition through documents like Luther's *Large Catechism* (in Tappert, *The Book of Concord*, p. 445–46).

[88] *Augsburg Confession*, art. 12, Latin version (Tappert, *The Book of Concord*, p. 34) and *Apology of the Augsburg Confession*, art. 12.1 (Tappert, *The Book of Concord*, p. 182). Both documents are composed by Melanchthon, and thus indicate not something unique to Luther but a common understanding at this early stage in the Lutheran tradition.

[89] Augustine is quite explicit that he already believed in Christ before the narrative of book 8 (cf. *conf.* 7.5.7 [end] and 7.7.11), and he opens the book with a story meant to show that belief without baptism does not make one a Christian (*conf.* 8.2.4). For a reading of *conf.* 8 which takes these facts into account and does not make Augustine look like a Protestant getting saved, see Cary, *Outward Signs*, pp. 168–77.

[90] Augustine, *nupt. et conc.* 1.25.28 (quoted, e.g., in Romans lectures 25:261 and in his reply to the papal bull, *LW* 31:28). For a study of the Augustinian notions of non-imputation and consent in relation to the *simul*, see Rudolf Hermann, *Luthers These 'Gerecht und Sünder zugleich'* (reprint edn; Darmstadt: Wissenschaftliche Buchgesellschaft, 1960, [originally 1930]).

not *really* sin because 'concupiscence itself is not now sin', even though 'in a manner of speaking it is *called* sin'.[91] In his polemical writings, Luther will cite other passages of Augustine that suggest we always remain sinners in reality, or else he will interpret this passage as if all it meant was that concupiscence after baptism is counted as only a venial, not a mortal sin.[92] Luther's point is that concupiscence in the baptized is not only real sin, but in substance mortal sin, and the only reason it does not cause our damnation is because God does not impute it to us. This point supports Luther's doctrine that all sin is mortal and that every good work is in itself sin, which becomes a central bone of contention in his response to the papal bull in 1520.[93]

e. Luther in Catholic Context

Luther's severe concept of sin and its effects on human nature continued to generate contention in Rome long after the 1520s. It helped produce the kind of exaggerated Augustinianism that received papal condemnation in the teachings of Baius (Michael de Bay) in 1567.[94] Often it is rejected by Catholic critics as overly pessimistic. But I think this is a misapprehension, which fails to grasp why Luther's 'pessimism' was received as such good news by so many of those who first heard him – all of whom were Catholics. The notion that we are always mortal sinners freed them from a gnawing and destructive anxiety; it meant there is simply no point in worrying whether one's righteousness is good enough to merit eternal life. It's a foregone conclusion that it isn't. There is no hope left for any of us sinners except Jesus Christ alone. And that is very good news.

When followed up thus by the preaching of the Gospel of Christ, Luther's radical doctrine of sin solved a problem that many ordinary, late medieval Catholics shared with the extraordinary, masochistic monk lecturing on the letter to the Romans. It is a problem that Augustine's doctrine of grace and justification was not well equipped to solve. For all medieval Catholics, justification was an Augustinian process in which, so long as we remain in this mortal life, we are always still *in via*, on the road towards a goal we have not yet reached. What this doctrine could not quite take account of is the serious

---

[91] Augustine, *nupt. et conc.* 1.23.25 (quoted in the Romans lectures, LW 25:342).
[92] Luther makes both argumentative moves in *Against Latomus*, LW 32:204 and 238, although when push comes to shove, he is also willing to say, in the former passage, 'I do not entirely believe Augustine'.
[93] Already in the Romans lectures, Luther argues that sins are venial only by God's imputation (LW 25:268, 278; cf. also the 1518 Heidelberg Disputation, LW 31:45–6). Against the papal bull he defends the theses that 'A righteous man sins in all his good works' (Thesis 31 in LW 32:83–6) and that all sins are mortal unless God does not impute them to us (Theses 32 and 35, LW 32:86–7 and 91). He defends the former thesis at great length in his most important treatise on sin and grace, *Against Latomus* (LW 32:137–260).
[94] DS, par. 1001–80.

terror experienced by a soul that is aware of the imperfection of its righteousness and contemplating the prospect of coming before the judgement throne of God.[95]

The prospect of hell and the last judgement was not central to Augustine's theological imagination.[96] It came to the forefront of the medieval imagination, however, because of vivid preaching in the late Middle Ages about hell as well as purgatory – which was not usually depicted as a place like Dante's purgatory, full of hope and even music, with benevolent angels literally around every corner, but rather as a place of demon torturers and screams of agony, which was no better than hell except that it did not last forever. It is no wonder people were willing to pay for indulgences to shorten their time in such a place.

What such an imagination meant for ordinary Catholics is depicted in a typical scene, found in woodcuts reproduced in books like Roland Bainton's Luther biography and Eamon Duffy's study of late medieval piety. The woodcuts represent a man on his deathbed, surrounded by devils who are whispering in his ear the names of his sins, trying to deprive him of all hope of salvation.[97] This is a picture of what late medieval Catholics such as Luther meant by the experience of 'conscience', a consciousness of sin that resulted in vivid fear of judgement rather than the depressed state of feeling we now call 'guilt'. The demons used conscience to torture and terrorize poor sinners, driving them to the ultimate sin of despair. In the midst of such assaults and temptations, an imperfect righteousness was scant encouragement.

Dying well required something more deeply Christian than that, and a good medieval pastor could provide it with a gesture made familiar by the story of Julian of Norwich, the fourteenth-century visionary and theologian. As she was sinking fast in what everyone thought would be her final illness, her parish priest held up a crucifix in front of her eyes, so that all she could see was Jesus.[98] The sort of thing a good priest said on such an occasion is given in a late medieval treatise on the art of dying (*ars moriendi*) reported by Duffy: 'Put all thy trust in his passion and in his death, and think only of

---

[95] Calvin urges those who would appreciate the importance of the doctrine of justification to try vividly imagining themselves before the judgement seat of God (*Institutes* 3.12.1); cf. similarly Luther, *Against Latomus* (LW 32:19).

[96] Contrast how powerfully Augustine portrays the misery of his soul in this life far from God in the *Confessions* (e.g., *conf.* 4.10.15; 5.2.2; 7.7.11; 10.28.39) with how little he evokes the fear of hell, except when describing his mother's anxieties on his behalf (5.9.16). It's not as if he doesn't believe in hell and divine judgement, but this belief is not the source of his own anxieties.

[97] Bainton, *Here I Stand*, p. 21; Eamon Duffy, *The Stripping of the Altars: Traditional Religionin England 1400–1580* (New Haven: Yale University Press, 1992), plate 117.

[98] Julian of Norwich, *Revelations of Divine Love* (longer text) (trans. Clifton Wolters; New York: Penguin, 1966), chapter 3.

it and nothing else. Wrap thyself in his death . . . and have the cross before thee, and say: ". . . Lord, father in heaven, the death of our lord Jesus Christ, Thy Son, which is here imaged, I set between Thee and my evil deeds, and the merit of Jesus Christ I offer in place of what I should have merited but have not".[99]

Luther's sacramental Gospel serves the same purpose as this medieval admonition and the gesture it accompanies. It bids us despair of our own good works, dispense with worries about our insufficient merits and put all our trust in Christ alone. Luther's theology of justification by faith alone is, in effect, an extension of this eleventh-hour sermon to cover the whole of Christian life. It is a theology that will seem outdated, quaint or fanatical whenever the thought of divine judgement is far from us, but it will continue to offer good news for all who suffer the same uncertainty and fear as these medieval Catholics.

For Further Reading

Althaus, Paul, *The Theology of Martin Luther* (trans. R. Schultz; Philadelphia: Fortress, 1966).
Bainton, Roland, *Here I Stand: A Life of Martin Luther* (Nashville: Abingdon, 1950).
Braaten, Carl E. and Robert W. Jenson (eds), *Union with Christ: The New Finnish Interpretation of Luther* (Grand Rapids: Eerdmans, 1998).
Brecht, Martin, *Martin Luther: His Road to Reformation, 1483–1521* (trans. James Shaaf; Philadelphia: Fortress, 1985).
Mannermaa, Tuomo, *Christ Present in Faith: Luther's View of Justification* (ed. K. Stjerna; Minneapolis: Fortress, 2005).
Wicks, Jared, *'Fides sacramenti – fides specialis*: Luther's Development in 1518'. In *Luther's Reform: Studies in Conversion and the Church* (ed. J. Wicks; Mainz: von Zabern, 1992), pp. 117–42.

---

[99] Duffy, *The Stripping of the Altars*, pp. 314–15. I have translated from the Middle English. For an introduction to Luther's relation to the tradition of *ars moriendi*, see Jared Wicks, 'Applied Theology at the Deathbed: Luther and the Late-Medieval Tradition of the *Ars moriendi*', *Gregorianum* 79 (1998), pp. 345–68.

10 Augustine and Calvin

Anthony N. S. Lane

I. Introduction

In August 1536, the young and relatively unknown John Calvin[1] wrote a *Prefatory Address to King Francis* for the brief first edition of his *Institutio christianae religionis*,[2] in which already we can see his interest in the Church Fathers in general and Augustine in particular. He complains that evangelical teaching is called 'new' and 'of recent birth',[3] but rejects the charge:

> First, by calling it 'new' they do great wrong to God, whose Sacred Word does not deserve to be accused of novelty. Indeed, I do not at all doubt that it is new to them, since to them both Christ himself and his gospel are new. But they who know that this preaching of Paul is ancient, that 'Jesus Christ died for our sins and rose again for our justification', will find nothing new among us.[4]

This essentially amounts to an appeal from tradition to Scripture, to the claim that evangelical doctrine is ancient because scriptural. 'Now, if our interpretation be measured by this rule of faith, victory is in our hands.'[5] While formally sufficient for one professing the final authority of Scripture, this defence is vulnerable to the following charge of Cardinal Sadolet:

> The point in dispute is, Whether [it is] more expedient for your salvation, and whether you think you will do what is more pleasing to God, by

---

[1] I have previously tackled this topic in 'Calvin', in *Augustin-Handbuch* (ed. V. H. Drecoll; Tübingen: Mohr Siebeck, 2006), pp. 622–27 and in 'Calvin, John (1509–64)', in *Oxford Guide to the Historical Reception of Augustine* (ed. Karla Pollmann et al.; Oxford: Oxford University Press, 2013 [forthcoming]). Some degree of overlap is inevitable. I have also touched upon the topic in a number of other writings on Calvin, which are cited below, especially in *John Calvin: Student of the Church Fathers* (Edinburgh: T&T Clark, 1999).
[2] See Lane, *John Calvin: Student*, pp. 33–4.
[3] John Calvin, *Institutes of the Christian Religion* (trans. F. L. Battles; Grand Rapids: H. H. Meeter Center for Calvin Studies/Eerdmans, 2nd edn, 1986), p. 5, which is a translation of the 1536 *Institutio* (hereafter: Battles); *Johannis Calvini Opera Selecta* (ed. P. Barth et al.; Munich: Chr. Kaiser, 1st–3rd edns, 1926–68) (hereafter: *OS*) 1:25.
[4] Battles, p. 5; *OS* 1:25.
[5] Battles, p. 3; *OS* 1:24.

> believing and following what the Catholic Church throughout the whole world, now for more than fifteen hundred years, or (if we require clear and certain recorded notice of the facts) for more than thirteen hundred years, approves with general consent; or innovations introduced within these twenty-five years, by crafty, or, as they think themselves, acute men; but men certainly who are not themselves the Catholic Church?[6]

Such a charge could not lightly be brushed aside, especially in an age for which, unlike ours, authority lay with antiquity rather than modernity. Calvin meets it with his appeal to the Fathers. While this was not formally necessary since the Fathers can all err and Scripture alone is normative, it was practically and apologetically essential in that a theology contrary to the unanimous interpretation of the Christian Church since apostolic times would seriously lack credibility. Furthermore, the Reformers were not Anabaptists who saw themselves as founding a new church. They believed that they were reforming the old church and that they therefore stood in continuity with the church of the early Fathers and even, to a lesser extent, with the church of the Middle Ages. This claim needed to be substantiated.

Calvin's opponents appealed to the Fathers against him 'as if in them they had supporters of their own impiety'. Calvin rejected their claim. 'If the contest were to be determined by patristic authority, the tide of victory would turn to our side.'[7] Calvin's counterclaim reduces to two essential points: the Fathers do not support the heresies of Rome, which are contrary to the teaching of the early church; the teaching of Calvin and the Reformers is very close to that of the sounder teachers in the early church, especially Augustine. This apologetic use of the Fathers was to continue throughout Calvin's career.[8]

Calvin does not deny that the Fathers made mistakes. That was to be expected. But the Roman Catholics seize only on these errors, ignoring the good teaching of the Fathers.

> Now, these fathers have written many wise and excellent things. Still, what commonly happens to men has befallen them too, in some instances. For

---

[6] *Selected Works of John Calvin. Tracts* (ed. H. Beveridge; Calvin Translation Society edn; Grand Rapids: Baker, 1983 reprint) (hereafter *CTS*) 1:14; *OS* 1:450 from his 1539 letter to the Genevans. These words were of course written some four years later than Calvin's *Prefatory Address*, but they have been quoted here because they express most succinctly the charge that Calvin then had to face. For Calvin's response to these words of Sadolet see his *Iacobi Sadoleti epistola. Ioannis Calvini responsio* (*Calvin: Theological Treatises* [ed. J. K. S. Reid; Library of Christian Classics 22; London: SCM and Philadelphia: Westminster Press, 1954] [hereafter: *LCC* 22], pp. 231–33; *OS* 1:466–7).

[7] Battles, p. 6; *OS* 1:27. Later editions add an extra phrase (*OS* 3:17, n. f).

[8] In Lane, *John Calvin: Student*, I repeatedly call his use of the Fathers 'polemical'. I am grateful to Irena Backus for helping me to see that 'apologetic' more accurately expresses what I wished to say.

these so-called pious children of theirs, with all their sharpness of wit and judgment and spirit, worship only the faults and errors of the fathers. The good things that these fathers have written they either do not notice, or misrepresent or pervert. You might say that their only care is to gather dung amid gold.[9]

We are not under any obligation to follow the Fathers when they go astray. Their writings are given to us to serve us, not to lord it over us. It is Christ alone whom we obey.[10] It is God's Word that we are bound to, not to that of human beings. Also, it is not only the Reformers who reject parts of the teaching of the Fathers. The Roman Catholics 'transgress them so wilfully as often as it suits them'.[11] Calvin then gives a list of patristic passages which contradict Roman teaching.[12]

> Why, if the fathers were now brought back to life, and heard such brawling art as these persons call speculative theology, there is nothing they would less suppose than that these folks were disputing about God! But my discourse would overflow if I chose to review how wantonly they reject the yoke of the fathers, whose obedient children they wish to seem.[13]

Roman teaching is contrary to the teaching of the Fathers. On the other hand, Calvin's teaching is supported by the Fathers, especially Augustine. 'We do not despise the fathers; in fact, if it were to our present purpose, I could with no trouble at all prove that the greater part of what we are saying today meets their approval.'[14]

II. Calvin's Use of the Fathers

Calvin made considerable use of the early Church Fathers.[15] R. J. Mooi, in his pioneering study, identified over three thousand explicit citations of the Fathers in Calvin's writings, a narrow majority of which come from Augustine.[16] Luchesius Smits, in his magisterial study of Calvin's use of

---

[9] Battles, p. 6; OS 1:27.
[10] Ibid.
[11] Battles, p. 7; OS 1:27.
[12] Battles, pp. 7–8; OS 1:27–9.
[13] Battles, p. 8; OS 1:29. There are minor textual variations in later editions (OS 3:22, n. c and d).
[14] Battles, p. 6; OS 1:27.
[15] I have tackled this topic at length in Lane, *John Calvin: Student*.
[16] There were 1,708 out of 3,405 (using the table in R. J. Mooi, *Het Kerk- en Dogmahistorisch Element in de Werken van Johannes Calvijn* [Wageningen: Veenman, 1965] [hereafter: KDE], pp. 396–97). A further 28 come from pseudo-Augustine. Mooi's tables include medieval as well as patristic authors; my statistics here and below consider only patristic material.

Augustine, identified many more passages,[17] for two reasons. First, there is no single correct way of counting the number of citations,[18] so comparing Mooi's figures with Smits would be highly misleading, while comparing Mooi's figures for different works of Calvin or for different Fathers does provide a fair comparison. Second, Smits, unlike Mooi, lists suspected allusions in addition to places where Calvin explicitly cites Augustine.[19]

Throughout his career, Calvin's primary (but not exclusive) motive for citing the Fathers was apologetic, as in the *Prefatory Address*. In his controversial writings, citations of the Fathers usually take the form of appeal to an authority. When he was arguing for his own teaching or against the teaching of his opponents, he was glad to be able to call upon the Fathers as witnesses to support him. Calvin was not primarily documenting his work (as with modern footnotes), nor declaring influences, but calling witnesses.[20] This apologetic appeal to authorities accounts for most, but not all, of Calvin's use of the Fathers in general and of Augustine in particular. He also, less frequently, criticizes them – especially where a patristic view has been cited against him and he is unable to interpret the Father satisfactorily.

In addition to the apologetic and dogmatic use of the Fathers, Calvin also cites them extensively in his exegesis, and this will be considered further below. He also sometimes cites them for literary reasons, because they have stated something elegantly, which shows that he appreciated their writings for their own value, not just as an apologetic resource.

As we turn to Augustine in particular, we will consider first Calvin's use of Augustine, focusing especially on three of Calvin's works, and ask how representative was his picture of Augustine. We will then examine his method in citing Augustine, including the question of which edition(s) he used.

The reader should be warned that the index of authors and sources in *Calvin: Institutes of the Christian Religion* (ed. J. T. McNeill and F. L. Battles; Library of Christian Classics vols 20–1; London: SCM and Philadelphia: Westminster Press, 1960), pp. 1592–1634, is to the footnotes of that work rather than to Calvin's own text. Treating it as the latter can seriously mislead, and has done so for some scholars.

[17] L. Smits, *Saint Augustin dans l'oeuvre de Jean Calvin* (2 vols; Assen: van Gorcum, 1956 and 1958) (hereafter: *SAOJC*), vol. 2.

[18] For example, where there is a series of quotations and paraphrases of different passages from the same work.

[19] By a citation is meant a quotation of, a paraphrase of, or a clear reference to an author. This must be explicit mention, but it may be indirect – so mention of *De civitate Dei* is a citation of Augustine. An allusion, by contrast, is not explicit. Studying allusions is highly subjective as it depends on the extent of the scholar's knowledge, not to mention the scope of their imagination! Quotations form a subset of citations, in that one can cite an author without actually quoting them. In the sixteenth century, the borders between quotation and paraphrase are blurred as loose quotation was acceptable and quotation marks were not used.

[20] See the first two theses in Lane, *John Calvin: Student*, pp. 1–3.

We will proceed to a brief comparison of their teaching, assessing the validity of Calvin's claims to Augustine's support before tackling the elusive issue of whether or not Augustine influenced Calvin. Finally, we shall consider the scope for future research.

III. Calvin's Use of Augustine

Calvin cited Augustine in every one of his significant works. We will consider in turn the *Institutio* (which has the greatest number of citations), his controversial treatises and his biblical commentaries.

a. Augustine in the *Institutio*

A substantial proportion of Calvin's Augustine citations are found in the *Institutio*. This work grew from the modest size of the first, 1536, edition into a substantial volume divided into four books in the definitive 1559 edition.[21] Throughout the successive editions, Calvin built up his dossier of Augustine citations, from 24 + 3 in 1536, to 131 + 6 in 1539, to 297 + 7 in 1543, to 389 + 9 in 1559 (the second figure referring to pseudo-Augustine).[22] Furthermore, Augustine's *share* of the patristic material rose steadily from 39 per cent in 1536, to around 54 per cent from 1539 to 1543, to 60 per cent in 1559.[23]

These are not evenly distributed. Thus the figures for the four books of the 1559 *Institutio* are 43, 112, 100 and 134, respectively. Again, they are not evenly distributed within books. In book 1, the chapter on the Trinity, unsurprisingly, evokes the most citations. In book 2, they are concentrated heavily in the chapters on sin and grace (77) and apart from the two chapters on the law (22) are very sparse indeed. A similar picture is found in book 3, where the bulk is found in three chapters on faith and repentance (33) and in the chapters on predestination (33). Otherwise they are spread thinly between the different chapters. It is noteworthy that there is no single Augustine citation in the five chapters on the Christian life. These chapters are less controversial, so there is no need to appeal to authorities and they contain just a single patristic citation, of Cyprian. In the eight chapters on justification citations of

---

[21] Some have mistakenly argued that it is the French translation made the following year by Calvin himself that is the definitive edition (being later) and that it can be used to correct the Latin. This is to misunderstand the role of Calvin's French translations, which was to be accessible to a lay readership. Where the two versions diverge, this is normally because Calvin has simplified the meaning. See the words of Calvin's 1560 Dutch translator in R. Peter, J.-F. Gilmont, *Bibliotheca Calviniana. Les oeuvres de Jean Calvin publiées au XVI siècle* (vol. 2; Geneva: Droz, 1991–2000), p. 758.

[22] For details, see the tables in *KDE*, pp. 366–70, 372–73, 379, 384–91.

[23] These figures increase slightly (especially in 1536 and 1539) if pseudo-Augustine is included.

both Augustine in particular (22) and the other Fathers (19, including 9 from Bernard) are relatively few, not because Calvin was not deeply concerned about the topic but because he recognized that Augustine's support in that area was limited. In book 4 again, the citations are unevenly distributed. The bulk of them (80) are found in the six chapters on the sacraments, though few (only four) in the two chapters on baptism. A lesser concentration is found in the two chapters on church discipline and vows (21). Looking at the *Institutio* as a whole, about a half of the citations are found in the chapters on sin and grace, predestination and the sacraments.

b. Augustine in Calvin's Treatises

After the *Institutio*, the next biggest concentration of citations is found in Calvin's controversial treatises, which is not surprising given that Calvin's use of the Fathers in general, and of Augustine in particular, is primarily (but not exclusively) apologetic. In fact, the six works with the most citations after the *Institutio* are all controversial treatises. These are, in descending order of the number of citations (given in brackets):[24]

- *Defensio sanae et orthodoxae doctrinae de servitute et liberatione humani arbitrii adversus calumnias Alberti Pighii Campensis* (1543) [hereafter: *DSOD*] (232 + 5)
- *Ultima admonitio ad Ioachimum Westphalum* (1557) (about 140)[25]
- *De aeterna praedestinatione* (1552) (96)
- *Acta Synodi Tridentinae. Cum antidoto* (1547) (49)
- *Dilucida explicatio doctrinae ad discutiendas Heshusii nebulas* (1561) (35)
- *Articuli a facultate Parisiensi determinata. Cum antidoto* (1544) (33)[26]

Thus it is controversial works on sin and grace, on predestination and on the Eucharist that especially bring out appeal to Augustine, following the pattern of the *Institutio*.

Pride of place goes to *DSOD*, which contains far more patristic material than any other work of Calvin's, apart from his *Institutio*.[27] This work is a response to books 1–6 of Pighius's *De libero arbitrio*. In these books, Pighius had attacked chapter 2 of Calvin's 1539 *Institutio*, on 'the knowledge of man

---

[24] See the tables in *KDE*, pp. 365–97.
[25] 'About' because *KDE*, p. 382, combines this with Calvin's two other works against Westphal.
[26] For the sake of consistency, I have followed Mooi in placing this work after the previous one. On Smits's reckoning their places should be reversed (*SAOJC* 2:85–7, 116–7).
[27] See on this Lane, 'Anthropology: Calvin between Luther and Erasmus', in *Calvin – Saint or Sinner?* (ed. H. J. Selderhuis; Tübingen: Mohr Siebeck, 2010), pp. 185–205 (especially pp. 195–99). In editing *DSOD* for J. Calvin, *Opera omnia denuo recognita et adnotatione*

and free choice'. This chapter is rich in citations of Augustine, containing almost 40 per cent of the total number found in that edition. Pighius devoted considerable space to refuting Calvin's claim that apart from Augustine the early Fathers are so confused, vacillating and contradictory on the subject of free choice that almost nothing can with certainty be ascertained from their writings.[28] Pighius sought to refute the claim both that the early Fathers were inconsistent and that Augustine supported Calvin. He also claims Augustine for himself, but not without reservations.[29] He admits that Augustine teaches that God's efficacious grace is not offered to all and that we cannot obtain it by our own efforts but God bestows it on those whom he pleases – yet confesses that he finds this teaching difficult and perplexing.[30]

Pighius had claimed the support of the Fathers for his own doctrine of free choice (which was not completely orthodox by Roman Catholic standards).[31] Calvin sought, so far as possible, to neutralize Pighius's appeal to the other Fathers and to claim Augustine for his own view. According to Mooi, three quarters of the patristic citations in DSOD are from Augustine.[32] Pighius had accused Calvin of quoting Augustine out of context and without understanding him,[33] and of quoting mutilated passages contrary to Augustine's meaning.[34]

Calvin was stung by this charge and devoted the third of his six books to Augustine, taking care that it would not be open to such accusations. About a third of the text of book 3 consists of quotations from Augustine, and Calvin quotes lengthy passages with reference to their context. He concludes this book with extended quotations from some of Augustine's last works and ends by stressing that these are not mutilated, maimed statements.[35] He also

---

critica instructa notisque illustrata (Geneva: Droz, 1992) (hereafter: *COR*) IV/3, I checked all of Calvin's Augustine citations very carefully. A very few times I disagreed with the source identified in *SAOJC* 2:68–83 and a number of times I disagreed as to the precise extent of a citation. I was impressed by how accurate Smits's work was, bearing in mind especially that he sought to trace the Augustine citations from *all* of Calvin's works while I had the luxury of concentrating on just one work. See *COR* IV/3:10, 62.

[28] *Institutio* [hereafter, *Inst.*] 2.2.9 (1539), referring back to an earlier statement in *Inst.* 2.2.4 (1539). Pighius repeatedly returns to one or other of these statements (e.g. *De libero arbitrio* 10b, 24b, 28a, 32b, 35b, 36b).

[29] Especially in *De libero arbitrio* 45b.

[30] Ibid., 102b, with reference to Augustine, *correct*. 8.17 especially.

[31] According to the Council of Trent and the theology faculties of Louvain and Douai (*COR* IV/3:14–5).

[32] 232 out of 304 (*KDE*, p. 374).

[33] Pighius, *De libero arbitrio* 37a–b.

[34] Ibid., 64a–b.

[35] *COR* IV/3:200–8. I do not agree that in this work Calvin's relies as little on the Fathers in general, and Augustine in particular, as is stated by Irena Backus, 'Calvin and the Church Fathers', in *Calvin Handbook* (ed. H. J. Selderhuis; Grand Rapids: Eerdmans, 2009), pp. 125–37 (p. 135).

accuses Pighius in turn of twisting Augustine and, in one place, of inserting his own phrase into a quotation.[36] Calvin quotes at length from (unsurprisingly) Augustine's anti-Pelagian works especially. Pighius, by contrast, had made extensive use of some of Augustine's earlier writings, such as *De libero arbitrio*, where Augustine's approach to free choice was closer to his own, and Calvin made extensive use of *Retractationes* to undermine Pighius's appeal to them.[37] In *DSOD*, unlike Pighius's *De libero arbitrio*, there are as many citations of Augustine outside of book 3 as in it. There are substantial number of citations in (listed in order of quantity) books 4, 5, 6 and 2.

Both Pighius and Calvin pile up endless quotations from Augustine, but occasionally the dispute becomes more interesting. At the end of book 6, there is an extended discussion of *corrept.* 12.33. Calvin had argued that the gift of being not able to sin (*non posse peccare*) described in *corrept.* 12.33 applies to believers here and now,[38] to which Pighius responded that it applies only after the Resurrection.[39] In *DSOD*, at the end of book 6, there is an extended discussion of this passage, where Calvin argues that the passage applies both to the future and to the present,[40] a concession that he fails to make in any edition of the *Institutio*.[41] Clearly there is a future reference in Augustine's words but recent scholarship supports the idea that there is also some reference to the present.[42]

c. Augustine in Calvin's Commentaries

After the *Institutio* and the six controversial treatises, the work with the next highest number of Augustine citations (about 30)[43] is the John commentary (1553).[44] The most significant Old Testament commentaries are those on Psalms (1557) and Genesis (1554), with some 20 and 17 citations respectively.

Almost a quarter of Calvin's patristic citations are to be found in his commentaries on Scripture. These contain two main types of citations. Some are dogmatic, where the use of the Fathers is likely to be apologetic and much of this material is drawn from Calvin's earlier works. Others are exegetical and here Calvin cites others more often to disagree with them. Where exegesis is

---

[36] *COR* IV/3:192–3.
[37] Lane, *John Calvin: Student*, pp. 151–57, 174–76; *COR* IV/3:161–70.
[38] 1539 *Inst.* 2.3.13.
[39] Pighius, *De libero arbitrio* 100a–106a.
[40] *COR* IV/3:324–9.
[41] For more on this controversy, see Lane, *John Calvin: Student*, p. 185.
[42] D. F. Wright, '*Non posse peccare* in this life? St. Augustine, *De correptione et gratia* 12:33', *Studia Patristica* 38 (Leuven: Peeters, 2001), pp. 348–53.
[43] 'About' because *KDE*, p. 393, combines this with other New Testament commentaries.
[44] On the authority accorded to Augustine in Calvin's exegetical works, see G. Besse, 'Saint Augustin dans les oeuvres exégétiques de Jean Calvin', *Revue des Études augustiniennes* 6 (1960), pp. 161–72.

concerned, Calvin is less interested in citing authorities (as in his *Institutio* and controversial treatises) and more interested in dialogue partners. He treats them much as a modern commentator would treat distinguished predecessors. Citation, even in disagreement, is a mark of respect.[45] This probably explains the frequency of the references to Augustine's exegesis, most of which are critical. Augustine was so worthy of respect that it was necessary to explain why one was departing from his interpretation.

Calvin's almost unqualified respect for Augustine's authority in dogmatic matters was not paralleled in the exegetical realm. Here it is Chrysostom who was Calvin's hero, at least for the New Testament. Augustine's exegesis is severely criticized. While in the area of dogmatics, he surpasses all others, in his exegesis he was excessively subtle, passing over the plain sense of Scripture and indulging in vain speculations.[46] He was too free with the letter of Scripture, indulging in allegory, of which Calvin did not approve. But Calvin could on occasions praise Augustine's exegesis and he often followed him. He described Augustine as a *fidus interpres* of Scripture,[47] although this statement comes in a doctrinal context. In exegesis as in theology Calvin always remained courteous when disagreeing with Augustine.

Calvin's 1554 Genesis commentary illustrates his use of the Fathers, and of Augustine especially, in his exegesis. He cites many different authors and works, but a careful study of these yields a much smaller number that he appears actually to have used while preparing the commentary. Some ten works account for the great majority of Calvin's citations and these include two by Augustine: his *De Genesi ad litteram* (for chapters 1–3) and his *Quaestiones in Genesim* (for the rest). The latter is cited five times – three times disapprovingly.[48]

There are 17 citations of Augustine, which become 22 when one allows for multiple references to more than one passage. Six of these are to passages which Calvin had already cited (either in the *Institutio* or in a previous commentary) and so need reflect no new reading of Augustine. Four are already found in Luther's commentary, which Calvin was using. Between four and six originate in *De civitate Dei* but this is a work that Calvin repeatedly cited and there is no reason to suppose that he read the work for this commentary, rather than rely upon remembered earlier reading. A number are too general

---

[45] See Theses 3 and 4 in Lane, *John Calvin: Student*, pp. 3–4.
[46] *Ioannis Calvini Opera Quae Supersunt Omnia* (ed. G. Baum, E. Cunitz and E. Reuss; Braunschweig and Berlin: Schwetschke, 1863–1900) (hereafter: *CO*) 9:835; W. I. P. Hazlett, 'Calvin's Latin Preface to His Proposed French Edition of Chrysostom's Homilies: Translation and Commentary', in *Humanism and Reform: The Church in Europe, England and Scotland, 1400–1643* (ed. J. Kirk; Oxford: Basil Blackwell, 1991), pp. 129–50.
[47] John Calvin, *Inst.* 3.2.35.
[48] Lane, *John Calvin: Student*, pp. 218–20, 232–34, 246–47.

to be tied to any one passage of Augustine. The upshot is that there are five citations of *Quaestiones in Genesim* (on 6.14, 21.8, 22.12, 25.1, 35.10) for three of which no alternative source has been found. *De Genesi ad litteram* is quoted once (on 2.9), but the quotation had already appeared in the 1550 *Institutio*. It is also a possible source of another citation (on 3.6). It is possible that Calvin read this for his Genesis lectures (1550–52), and that this reading caused him to add a quotation to the 1550 edition of his *Institutio*, as well as twice citing it in a work of 1552. He also once refers to *De Genesi adversus Manicheos* to which he had referred in the 1539 *Institutio*. Thus to account for his Augustine citations, one need only suppose that he read *Quaestiones in Genesim* and probably *De Genesi ad litteram*. He may have refreshed his memory of specific passages from *De civitate Dei* and *De Genesi adversus Manicheos*.

d. Which Works Does Calvin Cite?

Calvin constantly cited Augustine, but did he cite the whole Augustine or only a selection of his corpus? Which were Calvin's favourite Augustinian works?[49] Most cited are the letters and sermons, in that order, which is not surprising, given their bulk. Next are *In Ioannis evangelium tractatus*, *Enarrationes Psalmos* and *De civitate Dei*, all being major works. All but one of the next five are anti-Pelagian (or anti-semi-Pelagian) works, reflecting Calvin's theological interest: *De correptione et gratia*, *Contra duas epistulas Pelagianorum*, *De gratia et libero arbitrio*, *Enchiridion* and *De praedestinatione sanctorum*. For all of these works, Calvin cites widely from a range of passages.

There are many other works which are cited relatively infrequently. Calvin made little use of Augustine's philosophical writings. He was firmly opposed to speculation in theology, in sharp contrast to Augustine. He was not fond of Augustine's anti-Manichaean writings, mainly because of their teaching on free will, teaching which Augustine himself needed to 'reinterpret' in *Retractationes*. He also paid little attention to Augustine's works on moral theology, doubtless because he found Augustine's asceticism uncongenial.

There are 18 works from which Smits detects no citation by Calvin: *Adnotationes in Iob*, *De beata vita*, *Contra sermonem Arianorum*, *De dialectica*, *De disciplina Christiana*, *De fide rerum invisibilium*, *De immortalitate animae*, *Adversus Iudaeos*, *Locutionum in Heptateuchum*, *De magistro*, *De musica*, *De natura boni*, *Psalmus contra partem Donati*, *Quaestiones in Matthaeum*, *De octo quaestionibus ex Veteri Testamento*, *De rhetorica*, *Speculum*, *De utilitate jejunii* and *De sancta virginitate*. There are no great surprises here. The authenticity of some of these has been questioned (*De dialectica*, *De disciplina Christiana*, *Quaestiones in Matthaeum* and *De octo quaestionibus ex Veteri Testamento*). In addition, there

---

[49] Here I am relying on the lists in *SAOJC* 2:155–257. Mooi gives tables for authors, not for works.

are two further works from which Smits detects allusions in Calvin, but where Calvin doesn't actually name Augustine: *De anima et eius origine* and *Conlatio cum Maximino*. Finally, there are 14 works which Smits sees as possible sources for explicit citations of Augustine but which Calvin never names and for which there is no hard evidence that he had this particular work in mind: *De adulterinis conjugiis*, *Contra sermonem Arianorum*, *De bono viduitatis*, *De continentia*, *De divinatione daemonum*, *Gesta cum Emerito*, *De fide et operibus*, *Contra Fortunatum*, *De patientia*, *Contra Secundinum*, *Sermo ad Caesariensis ecclesiae plebem*, *De symbolo ad catechumenos*, *De excidio urbis Romae* and *De unico baptismo*. Again, the authenticity of some of these has been questioned and Erasmus rejected *De bono viduitatis*, *De continentia* and *De patientia*.

Calvin's citations do not represent the full range of Augustine's writings, but they do represent a wide range and those neglected are mostly peripheral and primarily from the younger Augustine. They include no major works. Also, the fact that Calvin did not unequivocally cite a work does not prove that he was not familiar with it.

What about the considerable bulk of pseudonymous works attributed to Augustine?[50] Mooi finds 28 references to pseudo-Augustine, compared to 1,708 from the genuine Augustine.[51] Calvin cites seven pseudo-Augustinian works and three sermons: *De dogmatibus ecclesiasticis*, *De fide ad Petrum diaconum*, *De fide sanctae trinitatis* (= *Sermo 38 de tempore*), *De praedestinatione et gratia*, *De spiritu et anima*, *De vera et falsa poenitentia*, *Hypognosticon*, and *Sermones 107 & 236 de tempore* and *Sermo 215 de sanctis*. These fall into two groups. First there are those which Calvin recognized to be spurious which he chided his opponents for fraudulently using – as with Pighius and *De dogmatibus ecclesiasticis* and *Hypognosticon*.[52] Pighius had also cited pseudo-Augustine, s. 236, an unfortunate choice as it was in fact the *Confession of Faith to Pope Innocent* submitted by none other than *Pelagius*! Calvin mostly followed Erasmus's judgement with these works, though he gave his own independent reasons for rejecting *De dogmatibus ecclesiasticis*;[53] he recognized the inauthenticity of s. 236 without knowing the source of Pighius' quotation,[54] though he did not realize just how incriminating was Pighius' appeal to this sermon.

The second group are those which Calvin cites without recognizing them to be spurious. Calvin's first theological work was first written in the early 1530s and then published in 1542 and again in 1545 as *Psychopannychia*. In this, he twice mentions *De spiritu et anima*, without any indication that it was

---

[50] For this and the following two paragraphs, see *SAOJC* 1:183–96; 2:261–8 – where other works are listed that Calvin never names.
[51] *KDE*, p. 396.
[52] *COR* IV/3:178, 197–8.
[53] Lane, *John Calvin: Student*, p. 160.
[54] *COR* IV/3:199–200.

not by Augustine. He also three times, between 1539 and 1543 refers (without quoting) to *De fide sanctae trinitatis* (= *Sermo 38 de tempore*) without suggesting that it was in any way spurious. He four times cites *De praedestinatione et gratia*, in the 1539 and 1559 *Institutio*, and in his 1552 work on predestination. In 1561, he cited pseudo-Augustine, s. 107, and in 1563 pseudo-Augustine, s. 215, without realizing that both were inauthentic. These works were all accepted as authentic in the Erasmus edition, with the one exception of *De spiritu et anima*.

Thus the only time he accepts as authentic a work rejected by Erasmus is in his earliest theological work and it is possible that at that stage he did not yet have access to the Erasmus edition. After this initial blemish, his record improved, either because of his greater care or because of his better library. Calvin also refrained from citing *De bono viduitatis*, *De continentia* and *De patientia*, works now considered genuine but which Erasmus considered spurious. Thus Calvin was concerned to confine himself to the authentic works, relying heavily on Erasmus for guidance, but capable of making his own independent judgements. He (correctly) accepted *De diversis quaestionibus* as genuine, despite the fact that Erasmus had rejected it. Thus Calvin was concerned not to confuse pseudo-Augustine with the genuine article, exercised care and his own critical acumen to that end and chided his opponents for their appeal to pseudo-Augustine. After *Psychopannychia*, he took every possible care to avoid confusing pseudo-Augustine with Augustine, at times this being to his polemical advantage.

IV. Calvin's Method in Using Augustine

a. Authority of Augustine

Calvin did not lightly depart from the teaching of the Fathers and believed that it largely supported his own. This was especially true of Augustine, to whose support he made sweeping claims: 'In this matter [God's chastisement of his people], Augustine is plainly on our side';[55] 'If I wanted to weave a whole volume from Augustine [on predestination], I could readily show my readers that I need no other language than his';[56] 'Further, Augustine is so much at one with me [on predestination] that, if I wished to write a confession of my faith, it would abundantly satisfy me to quote wholesale from his writings';[57] 'I shall not heap up – even out of Augustine – everything that

---

[55] John Calvin, *Inst.* 3.4.33. Quotations from the *Institutio* are taken from *Calvin: Institutes of the Christian Religion* (ed. McNeill) and Battles.
[56] John Calvin, *Inst.* 3.22.8.
[57] *Concerning the Eternal Predestination of God* (trans. J. K. S. Reid; London: James Clarke, 1961), p. 63; (COR III/1:30).

pertains to the matter [of the Eucharist]; but I shall be content to show by a few testimonies that he is wholly and incontrovertibly on our side.'[58] In *DSOD*, Calvin repeatedly claimed that Augustine was wholly on his side.[59]

Calvin clearly believed that, on a wide range of issues, he was simply restoring the teaching of Augustine. Augustine was fallible and subordinate to Scripture, but Calvin was nonetheless reluctant to *admit* that he was departing from him. Occasionally, however, he did criticize Augustine, as for his sanctioning of intercession for the dead. Augustine acceded to his mother's request, being led astray by his natural affection and following custom without testing it by the norm of Scripture.[60] More significantly, on justification, Calvin did not find Augustine's view, or at any rate his manner of stating it, entirely acceptable. Augustine clearly taught that we are righteous by grace alone, but referred this to the grace of regeneration, neglecting the imputed righteousness of Christ.[61] On other occasions, Calvin opposed Augustine's teaching without naming him. For example, he rejects the idea that babies dying without baptism are unsaved. While Augustine was not the only one to teach this, it is he that Calvin has just named.[62] When he did openly dissent from Augustine, he always remained respectful, a favour not granted to all of the Fathers.

Calvin held Augustine in such high regard that his judgement was sufficient to counterbalance all the other Fathers. Why did Calvin give such authority to Augustine? One reason is the close affinity between his teaching and Calvin's. Calvin's teaching was to a considerable extent, if not to the extent that he actually claimed, a revival of Augustinianism. Furthermore, Calvin was not alone in ascribing such authority to Augustine. Augustine was accepted in the sixteenth-century (as the medieval) Western Church as the Father *par excellence*.[63]

The significance of Augustine can be seen from Calvin's controversy with Pighius. Why did Calvin and Pighius bother with the teaching of Augustine? As a Protestant who held to the final authority of Scripture, why did Calvin need to bicker over the interpretation of Basil or Augustine? At one level, he did not need to. Calvin is perfectly frank in stating that if the Fathers' teaching

---

[58] John Calvin, *Inst.* 4.17.28.
[59] *COR* IV/3:171, 188, 196, 200, 209, 262. He claims Augustine as *prorsus nostrum* (*COR* IV/3:171, 200) and *prorsus nobiscum* (*COR* IV/3:188).
[60] Augustine, *conf.* 9.11.27; 9.13.37; John Calvin, *Inst.* 3.5.10.
[61] *Inst.* 3.11.15.
[62] *Inst.* 4.15.20.
[63] To illustrate this, of the material on justification in 23 patristic anthologies up to 1,565, nearly two thirds of the passages are attributed to Augustine (2,745 out of 4,360), with about one in seven of these being apocryphal: A. N. S. Lane, 'Justification in Sixteenth-Century Patristic Anthologies', in *Auctoritas Patrum. Contributions on the Reception of the Church Fathers in the 15th and 16th Century* (ed. L. Grane, A. Schindler and M. Wriedt; Mainz: Philipp von Zabern, 1993), pp. 69–95, especially 85, 95.

is contrary to Scripture, it is invalid. Even the consensus of the Fathers does not count if it is contrary to Scripture.[64] But this battle was being fought at different levels. For Calvin, all must be tested by Scripture. For Pighius, the pronouncements of the pope are the final norm. As they are arguing from different premises, there is little chance of a meeting of minds. But there is a secondary battle under way. What is historic Christianity? Pighius claims that his view is in accord with the universal consensus of the Catholic Church over the centuries. While Calvin theoretically could have conceded this claim, to have done so would have gravely undermined the plausibility of his case.[65]

b. Calvin's Scholarly Standards
The level of Calvin's scholarship was high by the standards of his day. He did not confine himself merely to commenting on the Fathers or to giving brief quotations, as did many of his fellow Reformers. His quotations are long and plentiful and reflect a deep knowledge of the Fathers, especially Augustine.[66] He was not, however, always concerned to quote with verbal accuracy. Sometimes this may be because he is citing from memory or abbreviating long passages, but sometimes this is simply because he does not regard such accuracy as important, which would be unacceptable today but was not frowned upon in Calvin's time. It is rare for his inaccuracies in quotation to be theologically motivated. He usually, but not always, gives his source in Augustine and the accuracy of such references is generally very high, by contrast with many of his contemporaries.

In his response to Pighius (*DSOD*), Calvin's quotations of Augustine (and other writers) are often very loose. He omits words, adds words, changes words, changes tenses, changes word order, et cetera. He also on occasions paraphrases, using similar words, or just summarizes the meaning of passages in his own words. Such a method of working was not unusual in the sixteenth century, where scholarly standards were different from today's. The reasons for Calvin's looseness in citation are simple – lack of resources and pressure of time. He wrote the whole work in a couple of months.[67] For some of his sources he was relying upon his memory of earlier reading, either because he did not have the volume to hand or because he did not have time to consult it. With the major works of Augustine that he was expounding, it is likely that having seen what Pighius had to say, he read through the work and then wrote his response from memory of that (recent) reading. At times,

---

[64] For example, *COR* IV/3:150.
[65] For more on this, see Lane, *John Calvin: Student*, pp. 35–40.
[66] I agree with Backus, 'Calvin and the Church Fathers' (p. 136), that Calvin was not a patristic scholar, but not that he lacked interest in such scholarship nor that his firsthand knowledge of that Fathers was 'apparently superficial' (p. 126), especially where Augustine is concerned.
[67] Lane, *John Calvin: Student*, pp. 152–53.

he would have had the work open and have taken longer quotations from it, but again without bothering about total accuracy. Pighius, by contrast, quotes longer passages than Calvin and generally much more accurately, though not with total accuracy. Why was this? As Calvin notes in his preface, his Roman Catholic adversaries had considerably more time, leisure and peace to prepare their attacks.[68] In addition, while Calvin laments his lack of books while writing the 1539 *Institutio*,[69] Pighius had an extensive personal library, an inventory of which was made after his death.[70]

When it comes to interpretation, Calvin followed the humanist principles of his day. His aim was to be faithful to the intention of the author, and he criticized his opponents for failing to do this. Smits lists six principles of interpretation followed by Calvin. Four are internal: the importance of individual words is stressed as is the need to give them the meaning that they had when first used, not later meanings; the literary genre must be taken into account; passages must be interpreted in their contexts; light can be shed on obscure passages by other clearer passages by the same writer. Two are external: the person of the author must be remembered, such as the fact that Augustine later revised some of his earlier views; each writing must be set in the context of the age in which it was written.[71]

While these may have been Calvin's principles of interpretation, it by no means follows that he was always faithful to them. At least two factors worked against him. First, Calvin nearly always wrote under great pressure of time. This led him to take shortcuts and at times to violate his own better principles. Second, he was not a detached historical critic seeking to give an impartial account of Augustine's teaching. He used the best tools of humanist scholarship, but for an apologetic end. He was an advocate arguing a case. Humanist scholarship of a high standard is used, but in a carefully controlled way as a means to an end.

c. Edition(s) Used by Calvin

Which edition of Augustine did Calvin use?[72] One cannot assume that he used the same edition throughout his career as he did not always own the books

---

[68] *COR* IV/3:70. Pighius wrote the prefatory material for the 1542 Cologne edition of his *Controversies* in that city on 5 January 1542 and the prefatory material for his *De libero arbitrio* on 13 August in the same city. The intervening seven months were probably mainly devoted to writing the latter work.

[69] *COR* IV/3:226.

[70] M. E. Kronenberg, 'Albertus Pighius, Proost van S. Jan te Utrecht, zijn Geschriften en zijn Bibliotheek', *Het Boek* 28 (1944–46), pp. 125–58.

[71] *SAOJC* 1:249–52.

[72] On the issues involved, see Thesis 11 in Lane, *John Calvin: Student*, pp. 11–3; for a justification of this paragraph, see Lane, *John Calvin: Student*, pp. 157–62.

that he used, he was sometimes forced by poverty to sell some of his books and, of course, he also acquired more volumes over the years. An important clue is found in *DSOD*, written shortly after his (permanent) return to Geneva after a spell in Strassburg.[73] Here he twice refers to the gap between two citations ('five lines earlier' and 'over the page'), which helps to point to the edition used. Careful comparison of the available editions indicates that Calvin was using either the 1531/32 or the 1541 Paris reprints of Erasmus's 1528/29 edition.[74] If these were his own volumes, he is likely to have continued to use them for the rest of his life.

V. Calvin's Claim to Augustine

Calvin repeatedly claimed Augustine's support. How justified was this? B. B. Warfield boldly claimed that 'the system of doctrine taught by Calvin is . . . from the theological point of view a great revival of Augustinianism'.[75] He was aware, however, that this is only one side of the picture. Elsewhere he more even-handedly stated: 'The Reformation, inwardly considered, was just the ultimate triumph of Augustine's doctrine of grace over Augustine's doctrine of the church'.[76] We need to examine the truth of these claims, comparing the two theologians on a variety of topics.

a. Speculation
Calvin was scrupulously opposed to speculation beyond what is revealed, a stance that put him at odds with Augustine.[77] This can be nicely illustrated from the issue of what God was doing before the creation of the world. Calvin approvingly quotes the quip that God had been building hell for the curious. Augustine mentions this, but in order to reject it. He explains that there was no time before creation because God created time along with the universe.[78]

b. Original Sin
In *DSOD*, Calvin claims Augustine's full support for his doctrine of original sin. But while Calvin follows Augustine closely, there is a significant difference. For Augustine, all human beings sinned 'in Adam' and thus share

---

[73] The spelling of Strassburg is to remind the readers that this was then a German city.
[74] This is contrary to the claim of *SAOJC* 1:196–205.
[75] B. B. Warfield, *Calvin and Augustine* (Philadelphia: Presbyterian and Reformed, 1956), p. 22.
[76] Ibid., p. 322.
[77] E. P. Meijering, *Calvin wider die Neugierde. Ein Beitrag zum Vergleich zwischen reformatorischem und patristischem Denken* (Nieuwkoop: de Graaf, 1980) makes much of this difference. It cannot be assumed that Calvin always consistently followed this policy.
[78] John Calvin, *Inst.* 1.14.1; Augustine, *conf.* 11.12.14–13.15.

the responsibility for his sin. Concupiscence or lust is God's punishment on humanity for this sin.[79] For Calvin, by contrast, it was Adam alone who sinned but all people bear the consequences of that sin. The newborn are guilty not because they sinned 'in Adam' but because they have a depraved nature, inherited from Adam.[80]

c. Grace and Free Choice

On the relation between God's grace and human choice,[81] Calvin claimed, especially in *DSOD*, that Augustine was wholly on his side.[82] That this is largely true is recognized today by many Roman Catholic scholars.[83] There are however, some differences. Augustine, while clearly teaching the bondage of the will and the sovereignty of grace, took care to preserve human free will and responsibility; Calvin, by contrast, was much more polemical in his assertion of human impotence. This led Calvin, unlike Augustine, to reject the term *liberum arbitrium*. Pighius seized on this, assuming that because Augustine and the Fathers affirmed free choice and Calvin rejects it, Calvin is opposed to the Fathers. Calvin responded by saying that he accepted free choice as Augustine defined it, but thought that the term was best dropped because of possible misunderstanding.[84] Again, Calvin disliked the idea of cooperation

---

[79] For example, *c. ep. Pel.* 1.15.31; 1.17.35; 4.4.6–7.
[80] John Calvin, *Comm. Rom.* 5.12; *Inst.* 2.1.5–7.
[81] See A. N. S. Lane, 'Bondage and Liberation in Calvin's Treatise against Pighius', in *Calvin Studies IX* (ed. J. H. Leith and R. A. Johnson; Davidson, NC: Davidson College and Davidson College Presbyterian Church, n.d.), pp. 16–45. Also, H. Barnikol, 'Die Lehre Calvins vom unfreien Willen und ihr Verhältnis zur Lehre der übrigen Reformatoren und Augustins', *Theologische Arbeiten aus dem Wissenschaftlichen Prediger-Verein der Rheinprovinz NF* 22 (1926), pp. 49–193, especially pp. 130–49.
[82] See n. 59, above.
[83] The influential essay by the Benedictine Odilo Rottmanner in the nineteenth century (*Der Augustinismus* [Munich: J. J. Lentner, 1892]) marked a new willingness by Roman Catholics to acknowledge those aspects of Augustine's teaching on grace and predestination that were appealed to by the Reformers. More recently, H. J. McSorley, *Luther: Right or Wrong?* (New York: Newman and Minneapolis: Augsburg, 1969), pp. 353–55, 367–69, argued that the Reformers (especially Luther) were basically justified in their claim to represent the Augustinian tradition of the church on this issue. As early as the 1920s, a Dominican writer concluded that while Thomas accepted and Calvin rejected free will, there is no contradiction because they meant different things by the term (C. Friethoff, *De predestinatie-leer van Thomas en Calvijn* [Zwolle: Fa. J. M. W. Waanders, 1925], which was translated into German: *Die Prädestinationslehre bei Thomas von Aquin und Calvin* [Freiburg: St. Paulus, 1926]). Also 'Die Prädestinationslehre bei Thomas von Aquin und Calvin', *Divus Thomas* 4 (1926), pp. 71–91, 195–206, 280–302, 445–66. This conclusion is found on p. 461 in the last of these versions. Friethoff does not deny that there are other points where Calvin does contradict Thomas. The interpretation of J. P. Burns, *The Development of Augustine's Doctrine of Operative Grace* (Paris: Études Augustiniennes, 1980) supports these scholars.
[84] John Calvin, *Inst.* 2.2.8; *COR* IV/3:137–9, 208–9.

with grace, but admitted that it was true in the sense that Augustine used it. What Augustine had carefully safeguarded, Calvin grudgingly conceded.[85]

d. Predestination

Some of Calvin's boldest claims to Augustine relate to predestination.[86] When it comes to the positive decree of election, these claims would be widely accepted. When it comes to reprobation, the condition of those who are not elected for salvation, there is a significant contrast. Augustine saw God's role in reprobation as primarily the passive one of permission.[87] Calvin rejected this, affirming that God positively ordained both the Fall and the damnation of the lost. Adam fell voluntarily, of his own will, by misusing his free choice.[88] Yet at the same time he fell because God did not merely permit it but positively ordained it.[89]

e. Justification

As has been noted above, Calvin's teaching on justification differed from Augustine's, but he did not claim otherwise.[90]

f. Eucharist

Calvin claimed Augustine's support on the Eucharist, but the latter's teaching is notoriously ambiguous and has plausibly been claimed in support of a variety of different views.[91]

---

[85] For these points, see Lane, 'Bondage and Liberation in Calvin's Treatise against Pighius'. There are also a few places in *DSOD* where Calvin's interpretation is open to question, as indicated in the notes to *COR* IV/3, for example, p. 172, n. 116; p. 183, n. 188.

[86] See n. 56–7, above.

[87] See, for example, E. TeSelle, *Augustine the Theologian* (London: Burns & Oates, 1970), p. 319.

[88] John Calvin, *Inst.* 1.15.8.

[89] *Inst.* 3.23.7–8. Calvin seeks to blur his difference from Augustine by citing him for support.

[90] G. Bavaud, 'La doctrine de la justification d'après saint Augustin et la Réforme', *Revue des Études augustiniennes* 5 (1959), pp. 21–32, draws out the differences. G. de Ru, *De Rechtvaardiging bij Augustinus, vergeleken met de leer der iustificatio bij Luther en Calvijn* (Wageningen: H. Veenman, 1966), chapters 6–7, compares Augustine and Calvin, drawing out similarities. F. W. Snell, *The Place of Augustine in Calvin's Concept of Righteousness* (New York: Union Theological Seminary ThD thesis, 1968) explores Augustine's relation to and possible influence upon Calvin.

[91] J. Beckmann, *Vom Sakrament bei Calvin, Die Sakramentslehre Calvins in ihren Beziehungen zu Augustin* (Tübingen: J. C. B. Mohr [Paul Siebeck], 1926) examines Calvin's use of Augustine, arguing that his interpretation was faithful and claiming that he was probably dependent upon Augustine. J. Fitzer, 'The Augustinian Roots of Calvin's Eucharistic Thought', *Augustinian Studies* 7 (1976), pp. 69–98, argues that Calvin's teaching is substantially the same as Augustine's. W. F. Dankbaar, *De Sacramentsleer van Calvijn* (Amsterdam: H. J. Paris, 1941) devotes chapter 5 specifically to Calvin's relation to Augustine.

VI. Augustine's Influence upon Calvin

How much was Calvin influenced by Augustine? Augustine's indirect influence upon him was incalculable, since Calvin was a zealous inheritor of the tradition of Augustinian theology. But how much of this influence was direct, how much came from his own reading of Augustine? There are striking parallels in thought between Calvin and Augustine, with whom he was undoubtedly intimately acquainted, but it is hard to prove that Calvin reached his Augustinian positions through the direct influence of Augustine rather than through the Augustinianism of others.[92] Where Calvin cites Augustine in support of his teaching, he is calling him as a witness, rather than stating where he first derived his teaching.

Smits claimed that Augustine played a significant role in Calvin's transition from humanism to reform and that this to some extent accounts for his later respect for Augustine.[93] In his 1539 *Institutio*, Calvin states that it was Augustine who first opened the way for him to understand the Tenth Commandment.[94] To equate understanding that commandment with conversion is, however, a big jump. Smits also claims this role more specifically for Augustine's *De spiritu et littera*, since in his 1532 commentary of Seneca's *De clementia*, Calvin already cited a passage on that topic.[95] Also, in the 1539 *Institutio*, Calvin cites *De spiritu et littera* to the effect that in this life we can never perfectly love God.[96] This all falls far short of proving Augustine's role in Calvin's *conversion* and Smits's proposal has not been well received.

Augustine's influence can be discerned in Calvin's teaching on the destruction of the will.[97] If conversion is a new creation, does it involve the destruction of the will? In the 1539 *Institutio*, Calvin at times appears to teach this, inspired by the language of Ezekiel (11.19; 36.26). God destroys our depraved will and substitutes a good will from himself. The heart of stone is replaced by a heart of flesh so that 'whatever is of our own will is effaced. What takes its place is wholly from God'.[98] In short, the beginning of regeneration is 'to wipe out what is ours'. However, Calvin immediately adds the qualification from Augustine that 'grace does not destroy the will but rather restores it'. The will is said to be made new inasmuch as it receives a new nature.[99]

---

[92] See the comments of A. Lang in 'Recent German Books on Calvin', *Evangelical Quarterly* 6 (1934), pp. 73–6, on Barnikol, 'Die Lehre Calvins' and on Beckmann, *Vom Sakrament bei Calvin*. See also Theses 8 and 9 in Lane, *John Calvin: Student*, pp. 8–10.
[93] *SAOJC* 1:22–4.
[94] John Calvin, *Inst.* 2.8.50.
[95] *CO* 5:136, where he loosely quotes Augustine's *spir. et litt.* 4.6.
[96] John Calvin, *Inst.* 2.7.5.
[97] For this, see Lane, 'Bondage and Liberation in Calvin's Treatise against Pighius', pp. 37–40; Lane, *John Calvin: Student*, p. 187–89.
[98] John Calvin, *Inst.* 2.3.6–8.
[99] *Inst.* 2.5.15.

Pighius, in his *De libero arbitrio*, accused Calvin of teaching that grace destroys the will, that conversion involves the destruction of the substance or faculty of the will and its replacement by another.[100] Calvin retorted by accusing Pighius of wilfully misunderstanding him, and goes on to explain his teaching more fully and clearly than in 1539. He qualifies language of the destruction of the will by quoting Augustine especially. For example, in conversion 'it is certain that it is we who will when we will, but it is he who causes us to will the good. It is certain that it is we who act when we act, but it is he who, by giving the will fully effective powers, causes us to act.'[101] In the light of Augustine's teaching, 'it is not that we ourselves do nothing or that we without any movement of our will are driven to act by pressure from him, but that we act while being acted upon by him'.[102] Christ does not draw us violently or unwillingly, says Augustine, and we therefore follow him of our own accord, albeit of a will which he has made.[103] Pighius accused Calvin of reducing human beings to stones by denying their ability to act well. Calvin denied this pointing out that Augustine spoke positively about the human role in order to safeguard the fact that 'God is working in a human being, and not in a stone, since he has a will born and prepared for willing'.[104]

The fuller teaching of *DSOD* leaves its mark on the 1559 *Institutio*. The statement that 'whatever is of our own will is effaced' is qualified, 'I say that the will is effaced; not in so far as it is will, for in man's conversion what belongs to his primal nature remains entire. I also say that it is created anew; not meaning that the will now begins to exist, but that it is changed from an evil to a good will' (2.3.6).

Augustine is quoted with approval to the effect that when God acts upon us we also act. 'He indicates that man's action is not taken away by the movement of the Holy Spirit, because the will, which is directed to aspire to good, is of nature' (2.5.14). The Augustinian qualification to the destruction of the will that is found in 1539 is further reinforced, 'But even if there is something good in the will, it comes from the pure prompting of the Spirit. Yet because we are by nature endowed with will, we are with good reason said to do those things the praise for which God rightly claims for himself' (2.5.15).

---

[100] Pighius, *De libero arbitrio* folio 89a–b.
[101] John Calvin, *The Bondage and Liberation of the Will: A Defense of the Orthodox Doctrine of Human Choice against Pighius* (ed. A. N. S. Lane; trans. G. I. Davies; Grand Rapids: Baker Book House & Carlisle: Paternoster, 1996) [hereafter: *BLW*], p. 142; COR IV/3:216.
[102] *BLW*, p. 152; COR IV/3:227.
[103] *BLW*, p. 232; COR IV/3:315. Calvin is here summarizing Augustine rather than citing a specific passage.
[104] *BLW*, p. 115; COR IV/3:186. See also COR IV/3:190, 261, all referring to Augustine, *pecc. mer.* 2.5.6.

In the 1539 *Institutio,* Calvin came dangerously close to teaching the destruction of the will. Pighius's challenge on this point, so vehemently rejected by Calvin, did cause him to qualify his teaching, first in *DSOD* and later in the 1559 *Institutio.* The reason why Calvin allows himself to be moved in this direction is that the debate concerned the teaching of Augustine, for whom he had such a high regard.[105]

VII. Areas for Further Research

Calvin's relation to Augustine is a vast topic and there is much that remains unexplored. There are three aspects to it, which we have explored in this article: his use of Augustine, Augustine's influence upon him and comparison of their teaching. The first two, like the two natures of Christ in the Chalcedonian Definition, must be distinguished but not separated. Some have fallen into the 'Nestorian' error of claiming that one or more of the Fathers influenced Calvin without taking due account of how the Reformer cites (or does not cite) that Father.[106] Others have fallen into the opposite 'Eutychian' error of confusing citation of a Father with declaration of having been influenced by him.[107]

Calvin's theological indebtedness to Augustine has been fairly well explored.[108] Less well explored is his exegetical indebtedness to Augustine. This is not quite the same as studying his use of Augustine in his commentaries. Here Calvin engages both with Augustine's theology and his exegesis and it is the latter that is of interest here. Here again, there are two dangers in approaching this task. The first is to suppose that Calvin is engaging Augustine only when he actually names him. The opposite error is to assume that he is engaging with him simply because Calvin refers to a view held by Augustine – even though many others may have said the same.[109]

---

[105] See Lane, *John Calvin: Student,* pp. 187–89. We have already noted above that, on the matter of grace and free choice, Augustine's authority led him to make grudging concessions.

[106] For more on this, see Thesis 9 in Lane, *John Calvin: Student,* pp. 9–10, and, for some examples, pp. 67–86.

[107] For more on this, see Theses 7–8 in Lane, *John Calvin: Student,* pp. 7–9, and, for some examples, pp. 16–25, 87–95.

[108] A thorough comparison of their doctrines of the church is overdue. S. H. Russell, *A Study in Augustine and Calvin of the Church Regarded as the Number of the Elect and as the Body of the Faithful* (Oxford: Oxford University DPhil thesis, 1958) compares their teaching on predestination, baptism and eschatology as well as ecclesiology. See also In-Sub Ahn, 'Calvin's View of Augustine and the Donatist Church', in *Calvinus sacrarum literarum interpres* (ed. H. J. Selderhuis; Göttingen: Vandenhoeck & Ruprecht, 2008), pp. 271–84.

[109] For an attempt to avoid both dangers for Calvin's Genesis commentary, see Lane, *John Calvin: Student,* chapter 9. See also Thesis 4 in Lane, *John Calvin: Student,* p. 4.

With Calvin's exegetical engagement with Augustine, as with other areas, what is needed is not more generalizing overviews but detailed studies focusing, for example, on specific commentaries of Calvin.

For Further Reading[110]

Lane, A. N. S., *John Calvin: Student of the Church Fathers* (Edinburgh: T&T Clark, 1999).
Lange van Ravenswaay, J. M. J., *Augustinus totus noster. Das Augustinverständnis bei Johannes Calvin* (Göttingen: Vandenhoeck & Ruprecht, 1990).
Mooi, R. J., *Het Kerk- en Dogmahistorisch Element in de Werken van Johannes Calvijn* (Wageningen: H. Veenman, 1962).
Pollmann, K. et al. (eds), *Oxford Guide to the Historical Reception of Augustine* (Oxford: Oxford University Press, 2013 [forthcoming]).
Selderhuis, H. J. (ed.), *Calvin Handbook* (Grand Rapids: Eerdmans, 2009).
Smits, L., *Saint Augustin dans l'oeuvre de Jean Calvin* (2 vols; Assen: van Gorcum, 1956–58).

---

[110] For a complete list of material to 1999, see Lane, *John Calvin: Student*, chapter 10.

11 Augustine and Henri de Lubac

C. C. Pecknold and Jacob Wood

> *Tu excitas [homo], ut laudare te delectet, quia fecisti nos ad te et inquietum est cor nostrum, donec requiescat in te* ['You stir man to take pleasure in praising you, because you have made us for yourself, and our heart is restless until it rests in you']
>
> (Augustine, *conf.* 1.1)

Henri de Lubac is often called an 'Augustinian Thomist'. Commentators rarely, however, use the description with enough precision to tell us what this might mean. Inevitably, the description is intended to tell us not so much about de Lubac's relationship to Saint Augustine as it is intended to tell us that de Lubac offers an alternative to the so-called neo-scholastic interpretation of Saint Thomas. 'Augustinian Thomism' is thus shorthand for his famous critique of the neo-scholastic commentarial tradition which he made most famous through his landmark study *Surnaturel*. The purpose of this essay is not to re-examine Henri de Lubac's trenchant and much-disputed criticism of those 'bifurcated' approaches to Saint Thomas – approaches that he thought were modern distortions of Thomistic distinctions – good treatments of de Lubac's work are widely available. Rather, the purpose of this essay is to locate Henri de Lubac not in some imagined 'Augustinian Thomism' – some novel reading of Thomas the Augustinian – but to locate his arguments in an actual tradition of 'Augustinian Thomism' that precedes him.

The description 'Augustinian Thomist' is too vague to be genuinely helpful. Saint Thomas himself cited Saint Augustine more than any other Church Father, and Bl. Duns Scotus developed an influential theological tradition that has often been called an 'Augustinian Thomism'. One could sensibly argue that there are actually two 'Augustinian Thomist' traditions – both proceeding from the thirteenth-century mendicant orders. At this point, we might as well stop using the description, and simply ask whether we follow Augustine, Thomas or Scotus on a particular point. As a Jesuit, Henri de Lubac belongs to an early modern tradition that frequently sought to learn from both the Dominicans and the Franciscans, and as a result, a Jesuit theologian like

Suarez would combine theses from Thomas and Scotus alike. So perhaps we might see Henri de Lubac as one more Jesuit synthesis of these two scholastic traditions. Contemporary critics of de Lubac, such as Lawrence Feingold, are attracted to this notion – and find a number of texts to support it – but such criticisms leave Henri de Lubac looking incoherent. Neither fully Thomist, nor fully Scotist, it seems that he is neither hot nor cold. Another possibility has so far eluded our discussion of de Lubac as an Augustinian Thomist. Henri de Lubac participates in a revival of the school of Giles of Rome (*Aegidius Romanus*), whose interpretations of Thomas Aquinas became standard in the *Ordo Eremitarum Sancti Augustini* – also known as the Augustinian Order. The Aegidian tradition within the Augustinian Order waned in the early modern period, eclipsed by circumstances, but that this tradition was revived in the nineteenth century and early twentieth century. We argue that Henri de Lubac's work is best understood in the light of this neo-Aegidian 'Augustinian Thomist' revival, and that the subsequent debates about his work should be re-examined in light of recontextualizing his work in this neglected tradition.

I. Augustine, the Schools and Henri de Lubac

In opening his famous *Confessions* with the equally famous line 'our hearts are restless until they find their rest in you', Augustine set in motion a permanent theme of Christian theology concerning our 'natural desire' for God. There is an ambiguity in the famous quote which heads this essay. We can readily acknowledge that our 'restless hearts' indicate a natural desire for God. But what is the nature of that desire? The quote begins with reference to God 'exciting' the human person to praise God – consistent with Saint Augustine's consistent stress on the priority of divine agency. But then he provides a reason for God so exciting us to praise him, namely that this is the purpose of our existence – we have been made for God, we have been made to return to God as our final good. If God excites us to praise, does that mean we do not do this naturally? If our hearts our restless, is our desire for God not innate? There is an ambiguity in Augustine that medieval commentators will begin to unfold. When they look to Augustine, they will look to his accounts of creation, to his theology of history and to his treatment of nature and grace in his disputes with the Pelagians.

In his treatment of creation, Augustine attends to the concept of *rationes causales* or *rationes seminales*, terms which articulate capacities or powers (potencies) in creation. Though the 'seminal' language may make us think of an immanent capacity in creation, Augustine does not seem to understand these potencies as internal principles of necessity at all. Rather these potencies within the order of creation can resonate only by God 'stirring us'. In the human person, such a *pondus* (weight) of our nature is like a depth that can be sounded only by God (*Dei voluntas rerum necessitas est*) (*Gen. litt.* 6.14.25–17.29).

This *pondus* of our nature, of course, derives from the fact that we are created in the image of God. The image or imprint of God upon our nature indicates our capacity to be made deiform. This is what makes the heart restless. But what exactly is this *pondus*? Since Augustine teaches *creatio ex nihilo*, there is never any hint of emanation in this idea. It cannot be some divine spark waiting to escape, in Manichean fashion, from the body and return to the One. It can only be an image, an analogy, a mirror, a *capacitas Dei* within the soul.

As well, in the *City of God*, Augustine speaks about our desire to be happy, and our desire for peace. Book 10, for example, begins with an acknowledgement that all people desire to be happy. Similarly, all men desire peace – an argument which so famously culminates in book 19. These are natural desires – to know, to be happy, to be at peace –, they can be observed in human nature, and one can see these desires tending in many different directions. But Augustine argues that they can only have their proper terminus in God. Again, we are left with a certain ambiguity. That such natural desires go in multiple directions demonstrates that there does not seem to be a necessary end for these desires – even though there is clearly a most fitting end for them in God. Augustine himself does not supply us with particularly careful distinctions between such terms.

The dispute with the Pelagians is quite crucial for the reception of Augustine on such questions. Augustine will never allow that internal principles, powers or capacities of our nature could attain a goal which transcends human nature. We have a natural desire for God because God has made us for himself, and we can only delight in praising God because God has made us to do so. That is, for Augustine, while we have a natural desire for God, which he usually marks as a restless for 'more' of whatever term of perfection we seek (happiness, peace, beauty), but only God can supply us with Himself. At times he allows the notion that we have an innate desire for God, even a natural desire for the vision of God, who alone can make us happy; but at other times, and more often, he insists that the most fitting terminus for our natural desires simply exceed our nature and could only be 'excited' by God from without. It is in the examination of these tensions and ambiguities in Saint Augustine that the medieval schools seek to develop their teaching on the natural desire for God.

a. Augustine and Thomas

Generally speaking, most Western theologians agreed that Augustine was the single most important patristic authority in any theological question, including those about nature and grace, and the natural desire for God. As Saint Isidore once quipped, 'If Augustine is on your side; that is all you need!

(*Si Augustinus adest, sufficit tibi*)'.[1] Yet the medieval discussion of Augustine's teaching typically produced a diverse set of distinctions to explain Augustine's complex teaching.

The diversity of theological schools, all claiming Augustine, was partly due to the dialectical method of the emerging schools and the reintroduction of Aristotle into Western theology in the thirteenth century encouraged a new set of questions and distinctions concerning Augustine's restless heart. How should Aristotelian categories be appropriated into a largely Augustinian theological tradition? This thirteenth-century question remains the question at the heart of the contemporary debate about Henri de Lubac and his relation to Augustine and Thomas Aquinas.

Obviously, the most significant of the scholastics to push first beyond the limits of Augustine's own speculations was Thomas Aquinas (1225–74). Aquinas provides the pre-eminent example of attempts to interpret Augustine in light of new, more refined categories. Aquinas quotes the aforementioned passage from Augustine's *Confessions* six times.[2] When he quotes it in spiritual works, he repeats what he then took to be Augustine's argument: Created goods always leave us something to be desired; but God is that greater than which nothing can be desired; therefore our heart's desire is fulfilled in God. But in his dialectical works, for example, the *Disputed Questions on Truth* and the *Summa Theologiae*, Aquinas begins to distinguish, against his objectors, between a twofold movement of the human heart: one according to its own powers from creation, and one added to it by grace.[3] One can readily hear the debt to Augustine's own concern about the gratuity of grace against his Pelagian interlocutor here. The question Aquinas asks is *whether or to what extent that natural motion towards God has a resting place of its own apart from the beatific vision*. At times, Aquinas seems to suggest, with Aristotle, that it is reasonable or even necessary to posit a naturally achievable end to our heart's natural motion,[4] while in other places he seems to suggest, with Augustine, that our natural motion towards God has its final end in the beatific vision alone.[5] In this way, we can see that Thomas stands as a direct heir of Augustine,

---

[1] Isidore of Seville, PL 83.1109A.
[2] See the excellent essay in this volume by Frederick C. Bauerschmidt, 'Augustine and Thomas Aquinas'.
[3] It may be speculated that this development in Thomas's thought, at least in the *Summa*, is due to his late discovery of Aristotle's works on luck as well as Augustine's anti-Pelagian works, which encourages, along with the Aristotelian categories, a stronger distinction between the natural capacities of nature, and the supernatural power of God's sanctifying grace (see Bauerschmidt above).
[4] Aquinas, *De veritate* q. 14 a. 2 co.
[5] *ST*, Ia-IIae, q. 3, a. 8.

asking the same questions, refining his answers, but also retaining some of the ambiguities still to be unfolded in time.

To understand Henri de Lubac's relationship to Augustine and Thomas, then, we need not look as much to Augustine and Thomas as we must look to the subsequent traditions which had to deal with them both if we want 'Augustinian Thomism' to have any meaningful content. First, we need to understand four different medieval and early modern approaches to the encounter of Augustinianism with Aristotelianism – all associated with religious orders (including de Lubac's own order) – Augustinian, Franciscan, Dominican and Jesuit.

b. The Augustinian or Aegidian School

Giles of Rome (1246–1318), from the Order of the Hermits of Saint Augustine, was among the first to develop Aquinas's thought on our desire for God.[6] Owing to his religious order's particular devotion to Augustine, and the influence of Aquinas himself, Giles also sought to put Aristotelian philosophy at the service of what he understood to be Augustine's theological affirmations. In his *Treatise on God's Influence upon the Blessed*,[7] Giles reflects on Augustine's passage concerning the heart's restless desire to know God. What is the end of that desire? Evoking the famous *quinque viae* of Aquinas's approach to natural knowledge of God's existence,[8] Giles offers five ways of demonstrating that *the desire of any intellectual creature can only rest in the immediate vision of God.* In summary, Giles argues that nothing in motion is at rest, and thus all intellectual creatures must be ordered towards and tend towards God as their final cause. In this way, Giles resists the Aristotelian attempt to secure a natural end for our desire to know. He resolves the ambiguity in Augustine by arguing that there is one end for our natural desire: the vision of God.[9]

Maintaining that the vision of God is the resting place of our natural desire left Giles open to the Aristotelian criticism that truly natural desires are owed their end, and thus God was in some way constrained to give creatures the end they desire. Giles responded to this criticism by making a distinction between two kinds of constraint. It is true that the vision of God remains, *absolutely speaking* (*simpliciter*), gratuitous, because it is above the power of our

---

[6] A member of the Order of the Hermits of Saint Augustine, Giles had been a student of Aquinas's from 1269–72, during the latter's second regency at Paris. See David Gutiérrez, *The Augustinians in the Middle Ages, 1256–1356* (History of the Order of St. Augustine v. 1, pt. 1; Villanova, PA: Augustinian Historical Institute, 1984), p. 138.

[7] The best published edition of this work remains Aegidius Romanus, *Tractatus de divina influentia in beatos* (Rome: Antonius Bladus, 1555).

[8] Aquinas's *quinque viae* are five proofs for the existence of God given in *ST*, Ia, q. 2, a. 3, corp.

[9] *De divina influentia in beatos* 1.

nature to achieve it.[10] But that does not mean that we cannot say that God is constrained *to a certain extent* (*secundum quid*). After all, it would be unthinkable for a benevolent God, who, the Scriptures tell us, wills the salvation of all,[11] to create humanity in a state of 'pure nature (*in puris naturalibus*)' without any possibility of achieving a resting place for his heart's desire.[12] In this way, Giles is able to understand Augustine, in the light of Thomas, to be teaching that it is not necessary that God grant human creatures this end, but it is fitting. We argue that this is precisely the kind of 'Augustinian Thomism' that describes the position of Henri de Lubac.

When Giles was adopted as the official teacher of the Augustinian Order in 1287, his position on the unicity of our heart's resting place, together with the understanding that God grants this not by a strict necessity, but by the necessity of fitness, was understood *as the authentic interpretation of Aquinas* within the Augustinian Order.[13] Their school, called 'Aegidian' after Giles's Latin name, *Aegidius Romanus*, flourished for the most part alongside other scholastic schools until the eighteenth century. But, in 1794, in response to certain more radical Augustinians – such as those two figures who predominate the argument of *Surnaturel*, Michael de Bay and Cornelius Jansen – the school's protection of the gratuity of grace was branded by Pope Pius VI as 'suspicious'.[14] Giles's delicate balance between absolute and limited constraint in God had slowly been lost in the Aegidian tradition, and, as a result, they compromised the gratuity of grace, which led to censure and suspicion, which led to the near abandonment of the Augustinian School for nearly a century. At the end of the nineteenth century, however, a tentative revival of this Aegidian school was hatched – a revival that directly benefits Henri de Lubac.

In 1896, a lay theologian at the Dominican college in Rome (the 'Angelicum'), Gioacchino Sestili (1862–1939), defended the Augustinian 'Aegidian' position in his doctoral dissertation, appropriately titled, 'On the Natural Capacity

---

[10] Giles of Rome, *Ordinatio* I, d. 42, q. 2, no. 2, ad 4. The best published edition of this work remains Aegidius Romanus, *Primus Sententiarum* (Venice: n.p., 1521).

[11] 1 Tim. 2.4.

[12] Giles of Rome, *Ordinatio* II, d. 31, q. 1, a. 1, corp. The best published edition of this work remains Aegidius Romanus, *In secundum librum sententiarum quaestiones* (2 vols; Venice: n.p., 1581).

[13] This decree remained in effect until 1885. The only changes were that, from 1539–51, and again from 1581–1885, Aquinas himself was to be followed in matters that Giles did not treat explicitly, while in between that time, Aquinas was replaced with Thomas of Strasbourg; David Gutiérrez, *The Augustinians from the Protestant Reformation to the Peace of Westphalia, 1518–1648* (Villanova, PA: Augustinian Historical Institute, 1979).

[14] Pius VI, *Auctorem fidei* 19; DS 2619. It is important to see Henri de Lubac's own response to Michael de Bay and Cornelius Jansen as putting distance between the Aegidian tradition and the radical Augustinianism of Baius and Jansen.

and Appetite of the Intellectual Soul to See the Divine Essence'.[15] Like Giles, Sestili presented his dissertation as an explication of Thomas Aquinas, yet he delicately criticized certain 'more recent theologians', along with the Thomistic commentator Cajetan (whose opinions we will discuss below), who had departed from the idea that man has a natural desire for the vision of God, which is 'natural with respect to desire, but supernatural with respect to achievement'.[16] Thus far he stands in substantial agreement with Giles. But, when discussing the gratuity of that supernatural gift, Sestili is severely critical of Giles's suggestion that God is constrained to grant his creatures grace, even in a limited sense. For Sestili, to say that God is not absolutely bound to give his creatures grace, but that it is unthinkable for him not to do so, runs the risk of compromising God's simplicity by dividing among the divine attributes of justice and mercy too sharply. Instead, Sestili safeguards the gratuity of grace by suggesting, against Giles, that God is not constrained to grant us grace *in any respect whatsoever*.[17]

By the 1920s, Sestili's Augustinianism caught on within de Lubac's own order, the Society of Jesus. Specifically, Guy de Broglie, S. J. (1889–1983), devoted several articles to supporting his neo-Aegidian position on the natural desire for God.[18] Unlike the work of Sestili, which had, for the most part, confined comments on the history of theology to the past, and referenced only in a veiled manner his contemporaries, *de Broglie engaged directly in polemics with contemporary Thomists, seeking to show that the neo-Aegidian school was the best, most authentic way of understanding Augustine and Aquinas*. The polemics of these debates with Thomists set the terms of the debate that Henri de Lubac's work would revive a generation later.

According to de Broglie, fear of more radical Augustinians had pushed neo-scholasticism away from a more authentic understanding of our natural desire for God.[19] Highlighting elements of Augustinianism even within the

---

[15] Gioacchino Sestili, *In Summam theologicam S. Thomae Aquinatis* Ia. Pe., Q. XII, A. I: *De naturali intelligentis animae capacitate atque appetitu intuendi divinam essentiam: theologica disquisitio* (Rome: A. et Salvatoris Festa, 1896).

[16] Ibid., p. 27.

[17] Ibid., p. 174. Although our hearts would not find an absolute resting place if God left us without grace in a state of pure nature, because the vision of God would be outside our reach, still we could at least enjoy a certain relative resting place in contemplating whatever natural reason can know about God.

[18] Guy de Broglie, 'De la place du surnaturel dans la philosophie de saint Thomas', *Recherches de Science Réligieuse* 14 (1924), pp. 193–246, 481–96; Idem., 'Sur la place du surnaturel dans la philosophie de saint Thomas: Lettre à M. l'abbé Blanche', *Recherches de Science Réligieuse* 15 (1925), pp. 5–53; Idem., 'Autour de la notion thomiste de la béatitude', *Archives de philosophie* 3/2 (1925), pp. 55–96; Idem., 'De ultimo fine humanae vitae asserta quaedam', *Gregorianum* 9 (1928), pp. 628–30.

[19] De Broglie, 'De la place du surnaturel dans la philosophie de saint Thomas', p. 203.

other scholastic schools, de Broglie argues, with Sestili, that the unbridled use of the Aristotelian axiom 'nature cannot be vain', had led scholastics to place an unnecessary restriction of our natural desire by suggesting that it must be naturally, not supernaturally fulfillable.[20] Yet still, like Sestili, when pressed about the gratuity of grace, de Broglie embraced pure nature as had Sestili, impugning the Aegidian School's method of preserving the gratuity of grace as a 'useless imagination (*inanis imaginatio*)'.[21] In the early twentieth century, therefore, while affinities for the Aegidian School grew, there remained nevertheless a certain reticence about the feasibility of its central thesis about our desire for the vision of God. Many of de Lubac's key criticisms we can see developing in this neo-Aegidian tradition, which is now dialectically unfolding under Sestili, and through de Broglie, it is influencing the Jesuits who will train de Lubac. This is the school that, we argue, gives definition to the 'Augustinian Thomism' that rightly describes de Lubac. However, the influence of those two original mendicant schools, Franciscan and Dominican, still need to be taken into account for their influence upon the Jesuit Cardinal. For it is by incorporating distinctions from both these schools into his basically neo-Aegidian framework that de Lubac is able to make a new contribution (the Jesuit tendency to combine points from both Dominican and Franciscan schools).

c. The Franciscan School

From within the Franciscan Order, John Duns Scotus (c. 1266–1308) developed scholastic thinking on the natural desire for God in a manner similar to that of Giles of Rome.[22] Like Giles, Scotus insists on the unity of man's final end in the beatific vision. But Scotus introduces arguments that are at once more technical than those of Giles, and unlike those of Giles, do not seek to follow Aquinas. In particular, Scotus introduces a new set of terms for understanding Augustine's restless heart and our desire to see God. Scotus argues that there are two kinds of desires: *natural* and *elicited*.[23] Natural desires are synonymous with the inclination of anything towards its highest perfection – they do not presuppose any conscious activity on the part of the one desiring, and they are found in rational and irrational creatures. Elicited desires, on the other hand, presuppose knowledge of the thing desired. According to Scotus, Aquinas

---

[20] Ibid., p. 223.
[21] De Broglie, 'De ultimo fine humanae vitae asserta quaedam', p. 630.
[22] For a brief introduction to Scotus's life and thought, see Richard Cross, *Duns Scotus on God* (Burlington, VT: Ashgate, 2005), pp. 1–14.
[23] On the distinction between natural and elicited appetites, see Scotus, 'Ordinatio IV, d. 49, q. 10, n. 2ff', in *Opera Omnia* (vol. 10; Louvain: Lawrence Durand, 1539; reprint: Hildesheim: G. Olms, 1968).

teaches that we have a natural desire for beatitude in *general*, but must elicit a desire for beatitude in *particular* for the vision of God.[24] To Scotus, however, this would make man a metaphysical anomaly. So Scotus argues that man, like any other creature, must have a *natural* desire for the highest possible perfection of his nature. Since, moreover, the highest possible perfection of man is the vision of God, it must be the case that man necessarily and continuously desires the vision of God *in particular*.

Scotus was thus faced with the same Aristotelian question as Giles had been: if we have a natural desire for the vision of God, how can we say that God is not absolutely constrained to grant it to us? For Scotus, Giles's solution would have been insufficient, because any constraint on the divine will to grant us grace would make it less gratuitous. Instead, Scotus makes a distinction in us, not in God. His distinction is between *two natural potencies in the will*: one, which is naturally *fulfillable*, tends towards the highest level of natural human happiness that God is bound to allow us to have, and one, which is naturally *receivable*, is open to the vision of God, which God is by no means bound to give us.[25] In both cases, man has a natural motion towards the goal of his desires, but in the case of our natural desire for the vision of God, this motion is more like a *pondus naturae* (literally, a 'weight of nature').[26] A *pondus naturae* implies no right or title to be in one place rather than another; it simply describes the natural tendency of a thing to move in one direction rather than another. For Scotus, God remains free, in spite of our *pondus*, to grant people the vision of God as and when he chooses. The only thing that limits God is his own free choice to do this ordinarily in response to his gift of grace and not to the endowments of nature.[27]

Scotus's distinction in our natural desire for God sought to safeguard the gratuity of grace by denying a rigorous proportion between natural desires and natural powers. This solution became characteristic of the Franciscan School that followed Scotus, and which remained prominent for several centuries. In the early twentieth century, it was made contemporary by the work of Jorge Laporta, OSB. Recognizing the controversy that was beginning to stir over the work of Sestili and de Broglie, Laporta employed a Scotistic approach to Aquinas in order to try to resolve it. Relying on the witness of the sixteenth-century Dominican, Domingo de Soto, O. P., Laporta argued not only

---

[24] Ibid., n. 4.
[25] Ibid., n. 13.
[26] *Pondus naturae* was a technical term assigned by scholastics, in the ignorance of gravity, to the force, which they supposed to move heavy objects downwards and light objects upwards.
[27] Richard Cross, *Duns Scotus* (New York: Oxford University Press, 1999), p. 10; cf. Alister McGrath, *Iustitia Dei: A History of Christian Doctrine of Justification* (New York: Cambridge University Press, 1998), pp. 178–79.

that, for Aquinas, man has a natural desire for the vision of God, which should be conceived as a *pondus naturae*, but also that a long chain of commentators on his work had been mistaken in supposing that Aquinas thought anything different.[28] Needless to say, Laporta's charge elicited vigorous responses in the twentieth century from Aquinas's confreres in the Dominican Order, even as Scotus's original work had done several centuries beforehand. But these responses were concerned only secondarily with the historical relationship between Aquinas and Scotus. Much rather, they alleged that Scotus, and Laporta after him, had fundamentally compromised the gratuity of grace by admitting on our part a natural motion towards a supernatural end. As we shall see below, Henri de Lubac utilized aspects of this tradition in his own neo-Aegidian formulation.

d. The Dominican School

A tradition of Dominican opposition to the Scotist formulation slowly built over the two hundred years after Scotus, until the dispute between these schools came to a head in the work of the Dominican theologian Tomasso de Vio Gaitanus (1469–1534), commonly known as 'Cajetan' – one of Henri de Lubac's targets in *Surnaturel*. Cajetan had been at the University of Padua around the turn of the sixteenth century, when the Aristotelian-Augustinianism of theologians like Aquinas was being called into question by neoclassical Aristotelians as well as rising groups of neo-Platonist humanists, like Pico della Mirandola. While having much in common with the neoclassical Aristotelians in Padua, Cajetan perceived the neo-Platonist humanists as the legitimate successors of John Duns Scotus, whose insistence on a natural desire for a supernatural end Cajetan thought to be inconsistent and dangerous.[29] It was inconsistent, Cajetan argued, because Scotus does not offer a sufficient reason why the fulfilment of a naturally receivable potency is not also due human nature. As M. W. F. Stone notes, it is dangerous, moreover, because by admitting in human nature *any unconditional natural motion whatsoever* towards the beatific vision, even a *pondus naturae*, it constrains God to grant that vision to man according to the Aristotelian principle that 'nature does nothing in vane'.[30]

In response, and understanding Aquinas's position as Scotus had understood it, Cajetan affirms with Aquinas a natural desire for beatitude *in general*,

---

[28] Jorge Laporta, 'Les notions d'appétit naturel et de puissance obédientielle chez saint Thomas d'Aquin', *Ephemerides theologicae Lovanienses* 5 (1928), pp. 257–77.

[29] M. W. F. Stone, 'Michael Baius and the Debate on Pure Nature', in *Moral Philosophy on the Threshold of Modernity* (ed. Jill Kraye and Risto Saarinen; European Science Foundation; Dordrecht: Kluwer Academic, 2005), p. 78.

[30] Ibid.

not *in particular*, and only an elicited desire for beatitude in particular. But, since elicited desires for something follow upon our knowledge of the thing, as Scotus had noted, and since we can have both natural knowledge of God by reason, as well as revealed knowledge of him by faith, Cajetan postulates that man in fact has a *twofold elicited desire for God*. One is an elicited desire to know God as fully as he may be known in general by our natural powers – through knowledge abstracted from our sense experience of corporeal creatures; this is the act that fulfils our natural desire (we can know by the light of reason that God exists). The other is an elicited desire to see God; this is the act that fulfils a desire caused in us not only by an encounter with the effects of grace, but also by grace itself working in us to elevate the objects of our natural powers – it is synonymous with the theological virtue of hope.[31] For Cajetan, apart from grace and the virtue of hope, there is *no unconditional movement of the soul towards the vision of God*, only a conditional sigh, a 'velleity' in scholastic terminology, that we might have such a vision *if it were possible*. Anything more would compromise the gratuity of grace by constraining God to grant it as the fulfilment of our natural desire. To avoid that consequence, and to safeguard the affirmation of a naturally achievable resting place for our natural desires, Cajetan insisted on the possibility and reasonableness of a state of pure nature. By affirming the reasonableness of such a state, Cajetan and his successors argued, a theologian could implicitly affirm everything necessary to protect the gratuity of grace.

Cajetan's position, though not de jure the official position of the Dominican Order, became over the coming centuries the de facto position of a 'Dominican School' (often called simply 'Thomist', or 'neo-Thomist'), which, in contrast to the Aegidians and Franciscans, affirmed the possibility both of a natural and a supernatural beatitude, consisting in the natural and supernatural knowledge of God respectively. In the early twentieth century, together with the Suarezian position among the Jesuits, which will be discussed below, the Cajetanian position among the Dominicans became one of the default positions taught in Catholic seminaries.[32] For this reason, although Sestili, de Broglie and Laporta, all appealed to Thomas Aquinas in their explanation of Augustine's restless heart, they met with a large number of Cajetanian critics. The most significant of these came from Réginald Garrigou-Lagrange, who seized on the notion of 'proportion' in his critique of the other two schools. To suggest that we have an unconditional natural motion towards the vision of God is to suggest, he argues, that we are somehow proportioned to it; but if we are proportioned to

---

[31] Although this was not always Cajetan's position, we may take his commentary on Ia-IIae, q. 3, a. 8 as corrective of his argument in Ia, q. 12, a. 1.

[32] This was on account of Leo XIII making Thomas Aquinas's thought the norm in Catholic priestly formation by the encyclical *Aeterni Patris* in 1879.

it, then it is neither divine nor gratuitous.[33] Garrigou-Lagrange's critique was to become all the more prominent because he not only taught at the Dominican college in Rome and thus formed all the Dominicans with whom de Lubac would later interact, but in 1955 he was also made a consultor to the Holy Office (today the Congregation for the Doctrine of the Faith), and thus became partly responsible for determining the acceptable bounds of Catholic theological discourse. The polemics between the neo-Aegidians and neo-Thomists of the previous generation had not been forgotten.

f. Francisco Suárez and the Jesuits
Finally, the school in which de Lubac received his intellectual formation, that of the Jesuits, *sought to strike a balance between the Franciscans and the Dominicans*. When the Society of Jesus was founded in 1540 to preach against the Protestant heresies, the Jesuits were grafted on to the already prevailing theological disputations among the existing schools. Their chief contribution to the debates on our desire for God was made by Francisco Suárez (1548–1617). In his *Treatise on the Final End and Happiness of Man*,[34] Suárez takes as a given, following Cajetan, that we must begin any consideration of our heart's desire by distinguishing between a natural and supernatural satisfaction of it.[35] Asking, however, about the nature of our desire for those respective beatitudes, Suarez proceeds not by affirming, with Cajetan, a natural desire for beatitude in general, and a twofold elicited desire for God in particular, but rather by affirming, with Scotus, a natural desire for God in particular prior to any conscious act of the will (an 'innate' desire, in his terminology).[36] The affirmation of an innate desire for God, however, left Suárez liable to the same criticism which Cajetan had levied against Scotus – by positing any natural motion towards the vision of God, the vision of God becomes due man according to Aristotelian principles. Suárez avoids this criticism in an innovative way – he restricts, unlike Scotus, *all* innate desires by the limits of our natural powers.[37] Thus, Suárez affirms, with Scotus and against Cajetan, the existence of an innate desire for natural beatitude in specific, and suggests, with Cajetan and against Scotus, that any desire beyond it would have to be proportioned

---

[33] Réginald Garrigou-Lagrange, 'L'appétit naturel et la puissance obédientielle', *Revue Thomiste* 33 (1928), pp. 474–78. See also Idem., 'La possibilité de la vision béatifique peut-elle se démontrer?' *Revue Thomiste* 38 (1933), pp. 669–88; and 'An supernaturalia possint naturaliter cognosci?' *Angelicum* 13 (1936), pp. 241–48.
[34] Suárez, 'De ultimo fine hominis ac beatitudo', in *Opera Omnia* 4 (Paris: Vivès, 1856), pp. 1–156.
[35] Ibid., disp. 4, par. 3, no. 2.
[36] Ibid., disp. 4, par. 3, no. 3. Cf. Lawrence Feingold, *The Natural Desire to See God According to St. Thomas Aquinas and His Interpreters* (Faith and Reason: Studies in Catholic Theology and Philosophy; Ave Maria, FL: Sapientia Press, 2nd edn, 2010), p. 222.
[37] Ibid.

to the knowledge which gave rise to it: elicited desires based on naturally achievable knowledge lead to natural beatitude; elicited desires based on the theological virtue of faith lead to supernatural beatitude.[38]

Although the doctrine of Suárez become de jure the official doctrine of the Jesuit Order, there was some variation over the course of the centuries as to how rigorously this rule was to be applied. The Jesuit scholasticate in which Henri de Lubac himself was formed was just such an example. In metaphysics, de Lubac studied with Pedro Descoqs, S. J., an ardent defender of a strict Suarezianism in philosophy. However, Descoqs became involved in the late 1930s in a controversy over our natural desire for God with none other than his neo-Aegidian confrere, Guy de Broglie, S. J. While de Broglie alleged that Descoqs's Suarezianism limited natural desires unnecessarily to what can be naturally achieved, and thereby upset an authentically 'Augustinian' (Aegidian) approach to our heart's restlessness,[39] Descoqs charged that de Broglie's neo-Aegidian 'Augustinianism' compromised the gratuity of our heart's resting place by placing it within the reach of nature.[40] In theology however, de Lubac studied with Joseph Huby, S. J., a public defender of the renascent Aegidianism, who, de Lubac tells us, was a main source of inspiration for his own work on the subject. By the time de Lubac came to study with him, Huby had been banned from teaching theology on account of his previous support for this strand of Augustinianism. But he remained on the theological faculty as a teacher of Sacred Scripture, and, as history has shown us, continued to influence the next generation of Jesuits just as powerfully.

II. Henri de Lubac and the Modern Debate Concerning the Supernatural

Henri de Lubac argued that our supernatural destiny is expressed in our natural desire for God. He writes, 'my finality, which is expressed by this desire, is

---

[38] Suárez's recourse to the distinction between a twofold elicited desire introduced Cajetan's protection for the gratuity of grace into the thought of the other schools, while at the same time preserving some of their concern for the particular satisfaction of our natural desire for beatitude in God. It is not surprising, then, that in addition to being made the official position of the Jesuit Order, and consequently of the Jesuit School, the thought of Suárez had a wide appeal among the schools in the centuries that followed. But nor is it surprising that it would be from among this school, rather than the Dominican School, that one such as de Lubac would later arise to advocate a purification of scholasticism from Cajetanian influences. For undergirding the Cajetanian distinctions in elicited desires lay all the while Gile's and Scotus's natural desire for a supernatural end.

[39] Guy de Broglie, 'Le mystere de notre élévation surnaturelle. Réponse au R.P. Descoqs', *Nouvelle revue théologiques* 65 (1938), p. 1163.

[40] Pedro Descoqs, 'Autour du mystère de notre élévation surnaturelle', *Nouvelle revue théologiques* 66 (1939), pp. 418–19.

inscribed upon my very being as it has been put into this universe by God . . . No other finality now seems possible for men than that which is now really inscribed in the depths of my nature.'[41] In his eyes, the neo-Thomists had misconstrued our supernatural destiny as something 'added on' to our natural beatitude.[42] The principal critic was Father Reginald Garrigou-Lagrange, who coined the critical phrase *nouvelle théologie* in 1946, and who spearheaded a vigorous resistance which influenced even the pope. Many thought this critical response culminated in the 'lightning bolt' *Humani Generis*, the papal encyclical which denounced those who would 'destroy the gratuity of the supernatural order, since God, they say, cannot create intellectual beings without ordering and calling them to the beatific vision'. As Balthasar notes, de Lubac was branded as the scapegoat for this denunciation. For 'the next ten years became a *via crucis* for him . . . it was a silent ostracism that drove the sensitive man into complete isolation'.[43]

After a decade of silence, however, the clouds surrounding de Lubac's work slowly lifted. 'The course was finally turned when John XXIII nominated him (together with Fr. Congar) as *consultor* for the preparatory theological commission of the Council.'[44] His influence upon many of the council fathers was considerable, and can be discerned in many of the documents. For example, in one of Vatican II's pastoral constitutions, *Gaudium et Spes* – 'the ultimate vocation of man is in fact one, and divine'[45] – many observers saw an explicit affirmation of de Lubac's commitment to the unicity of ends over and against the neo-Thomistic account of dual ends. The extraordinary reversal of Henri de Lubac's fortunes has caused endless fascination, not least because his own reversal of fortune seems bound up with the importance of determining the significance of the Second Vatican Council.

In reviewing the main scholastic opinions on our heart's restlessness, and their influence upon Henri de Lubac, it should be clear that none of our schools can lay exclusive claim to Saint Augustine. Yet one thing should be clear: Henri de Lubac's position bears greatest affinity to the neo-Aegidian school which is sometimes referred to unhelpfully as 'Augustinian'. Moreover, standing in this renascent Aegidian tradition *as a Jesuit*, necessarily placed him in another tradition that habitually sought to strike a balance between Franciscans and

---

[41] Henri de Lubac, *The Mystery of the Supernatural* (trans. Rosemary Sheed; New York, NY: Crossroad Herder, 1998), p. 55.
[42] Henri de Lubac, 'The Mystery of the Supernatural', in *Theology in History* (San Francisco: Ignatius, 1996) pp. 296–97; cf. Augustine, *conf.* 3.6.11: 'But you were more inward than my most inward part and higher than the highest element within me.'
[43] Hans Urs von Balthasar, *The Theology of Henri de Lubac: An Overview* (San Francisco: Ignatius, 1991), pp. 17–18.
[44] Ibid.
[45] Ibid., p. 22.

Dominicans. A brief examination of Henri de Lubac's *Surnaturel*, and the debate which has followed its publication to this day, is now possible in light of our main thesis.

a. Surnatural

Henri de Lubac's first major contribution to the theological tradition on our natural desire for God occurred in 1946 with the publication of *Surnaturel: Études historiques*.[46] While this work contains a detailed theological engagement with the opinions of his contemporaries on the natural of our heart's restlessness, it is first and foremost, as the very title suggests that, a work of history. This emphasis reveals the extent to which, by the 1940s, the question of the historical development of the theology on the natural desire for God had become as important a question to theologians as the doctrine itself. In order to discuss the work more effectively, therefore, it is helpful to separate these two aspects, so as to be able to show more accurately how de Lubac relates to the other forms of Augustinianism that we have discussed.

On the side of history, de Lubac follows directly in the line of Sestili, developing, deepening and extending his historical narrative of theological development on the nature desire for God, while enriching it with his renowned and copious citations of both popular and obscure theological figures, and his proposal of the far-reaching consequences of Cajetanianism. Looking towards the past, if Sestili had attributed the advent of the doctrine of pure nature to Cajetan, de Lubac goes even further than both of these, arguing that it was, in fact, Denys the Carthusian (1402–71), who had first applied the principle of proportionality between natural desires and natural powers so rigorously, and that Cajetan had likely read Denys's work at the University of Padua. Thenceforth, de Lubac argued, the doctrine of pure nature, alien to scholastics of the thirteenth and fourteenth centuries, like Aquinas and Scotus, had become ubiquitous. Moreover, looking towards the present (and here de Lubac levies an even more serious charge), the hypothesis of pure nature, emphasized by scholastic theologians as a necessary precaution against Baianism and Jansenism, had, in fact, provided secularism with an idea of a happiness achievable by his own powers apart from the beatific vision. And this idea, so de Lubac argues, is to a large extent responsible for the advance of secularism and the decline of the spiritual life in contemporary society.

On the side of theology, de Lubac argues that the Augustinian School affirmed a fundamental truth about our restless hearts, which he argues was common to all the great scholastics before Cajetan – namely that we have a 'natural desire for a supernatural end'. By maintaining this affirmation, they did not compromise the gratuity of grace, as many feared. They simply

---

[46] Henri de Lubac, *Surnaturel: Études historiques* (Paris: Aubier, 1946).

established it elsewhere, by distinguishing between God's power, absolutely speaking (*de potentia absoluta*), to withhold grace from a creature made for the vision of God, and the complete unreasonableness that, according to his providentially ordered power (*de potentia ordinata*), he would ever deny any creature the sole means of achieving its natural end. While de Lubac's Augustinian predecessors, Sestili and de Broglie, had both been critical of this particular defence of the gratuity of grace within the Aegidian School, de Lubac responded that, by assenting to the possibility of a 'natural beatitude', they had in fact betrayed the school's fundamental thesis.

De Lubac's work thus stands simultaneously in two traditions. On the one hand, it stands within a historical tradition, tracing back to Sestili of attempting to give an historical apology for the Augustinian thesis that we have a natural desire for a supernatural end, and of attempting to describe the developments in theology that led to the denial of this thesis by Cajetanians and Suarezians. In this respect, de Lubac's work represents and remains the most comprehensive effort devoted to that task to date. On the other hand, it also stands within a centuries-old tradition, tracing back to Giles of Rome, of rejecting the reasonableness of a state of pure nature, and of protecting the gratuity of grace by distinguishing between God's justice and his providence. In this respect, de Lubac parts company with his early twentieth-century predecessors and accuses them of having failed to go far enough towards purifying contemporary theology from the corruptions of Cajetanianism.

b. The Debate over the Supernatural

Assessing the reception of Henri de Lubac's *Surnaturel* has proven complicated to scholars since its publication. Chief among the complicating factors is the magisterial *Humani Generis* which condemned a range of theological 'novelties' that had 'borne their deadly fruit' in modern theology, including a condemnation of those theologians who would 'destroy the gratuity of the supernatural order, since God, they say, cannot create intellectual beings without ordering and calling them to the beatific vision'.[47] When this was promulgated in 1950, his critics inferred that this condemnation implicated precisely the position advocated by de Lubac. However, de Lubac himself always insisted that this condemnation did not touch his position at all. In effect, he denies that *Humani Generis* has described his position. Why? Either de Lubac is insincere, which a charitable reading must exclude, or he misunderstands, and is simply incorrect. But is it possible that he is, in fact, correct in thinking that *Humani Generis* does not implicate him precisely because he does not believe the Aegidian position destroys the gratuity of grace? As long as he is careful not to make the mistake of the 'radical Augustinians' which

---

[47] *Humani Generis* 26.

once derailed the Aegidian tradition, he is simply convinced that the tradition is secure, that it can be revived, and that the condemnation cannot apply.

De Lubac does, however, slowly modify his positions because of the scrutiny. For example, in revising *Surnaturel*, de Lubac does explicitly admit the usefulness of the theory of pure nature which he originally denied more vehemently (as all good Aegidians had before him). The problem, he insists, and not without the support of Giles of Rome, as cited above, is not its use as a hypothesis, but its illegitimate transfer to the actual state of human nature. He specifically affirms the limited theoretical usefulness of the neo-Thomistic concept of 'pure nature' as a tool to help theologians 'avoid any conception of "nature" which did not preserve the gratuitousness of the supernatural'.[48] De Lubac agrees with Aquinas that 'man may be considered in his nature independently of his relationship with God'.[49] These admissions have confused contemporary critics, leading to charges of incoherence in his thought from both Augustinian and Thomistic directions. Some of these confusions may be alleviated, however, if the neo-Aegidian context of his work is taken into account.

c. The Shape of Contemporary Debate

Radical Augustinian and neo-Thomistic responses to Henri de Lubac have continued to the present day. Interestingly, polar opposite ways of receiving de Lubac see his theology as inconsistent at crucial junctures. This common recognition of inconsistency in de Lubac, however, continues to challenge our understanding of him. But is Henri de Lubac inconsistent as an Aegidian? We think not, but whatever judgements are made about de Lubac (critical, appreciative or some admixture of the two), we must take into account the way in which he belongs to an established tradition in the Catholic Church. In the space that remains, we examine both the neo-Thomist and radical Augustinian reception of de Lubac in contemporary debate, as well as look to the work of Nicholas Healy and Pope Benedict XVI provide a middle way of reading de Lubac as a man of the Church.

Few have done more to reinvigorate these debates, and from opposite sides, than have John Milbank and Lawrence Feingold. And in contrast to these polar responses, more centrist responses, such as those by Nicholas Healy, have given us a healthy spectrum of theological opinion with which to judge the debate as a whole. While none of these positions take into account the neo-Aegidian context, we think that the shape of the spectrum largely reflects the relation of the schools originating in medieval Christendom.

---

[48] De Lubac, *The Mystery of the Supernatural*, p. 73.
[49] Henri de Lubac, *Augustinianism and Modern Theology* (New York, NY: Crossroad Herder, 2000), p. 190.

1. John Milbank

At the heart of Milbank's reading of Henri de Lubac in *The Suspended Middle* is a wholehearted embrace of Balthasar's own assessment that 'De Lubac soon realized that his position moved into a suspended middle in which he could not practice any philosophy without its transcendence into theology, but also any theology without its essential inner structure of philosophy'.[50] In Milbank's account, Henri de Lubac was untying the very knots of autonomy that modernity had hoisted upon the categories of nature and grace. Put differently, Milbank sees de Lubac not as post-metaphysical, but as offering a properly Christian account of metaphysics against neo-Thomist accounts of a metaphysics of substance, or a 'purely natural' foundation upon which theology might be set. While any disavowal of 'natural law' would constitute a misreading of de Lubac, Milbank is certainly correct that de Lubac wanted to exclude a Cajetanian or purely Aristotelian understanding of nature that would allow for a perfectly adequate anthropology, ethics, politics, philosophy, et cetera.

Yet when Milbank insists that de Lubac should have more consistently embraced the 'suspended' nature of his thought, is he not cutting de Lubac off from the very traditions that nourished his thinking – returning him to the era of Aegidian decline rather than ascent? Milbank's approach has the advantage of maximizing de Lubac's own way of describing the nature-grace relation as 'paradoxical'. De Lubac never tires of telling us that human nature is the one nature in the universe that cannot attain the supernatural finality which inscribed upon its very being. As Milbank writes, 'The natural desire cannot be frustrated, yet it cannot be of itself fulfilled. Human nature in its self-exceeding seems in justice to require a gift – yet the gift of grace remains beyond all justice and all requirement.'[51] There is no nature *as such*. In Milbank's view, this paradoxical understanding of our natural desire is the only one which can maintain distinctions within deeper unity. Only this paradox can save us from what he sees as the Cajetanian and Jansenist polarities that either err on one side or another of a hard distinction – one which places us wholly on the side of the integrity of nature or solely on the side of the depravity of nature.[52] Only this paradox preserves the real gratuity of grace as gift. But are the distinctions maintained? 'Grace, like the act of creation, presupposes *nothing* – not even creation.'[53] Milbank writes that 'the subtle

---

[50] John Milbank, *The Suspended Middle* (Grand Rapids, MI: William B. Eerdmans, 2005), p. 11, citing von Balthasar, *The Theology of Henri de Lubac*, p. 15. The language of the suspended middle, however, is borrowed from Erich Przywara, for whom the term is central for understanding the *analogia entis*. See Erich Przywara, *Analogia Entis* (trans. John Betz; Grand Rapids: Eerdmans, forthcoming 2013).

[51] Milbank, *The Suspended Middle*, p. 30.

[52] Ibid., p. 46. We would argue that he, as well as de Lubac, misunderstand Cajetan here.

[53] Milbank, *The Suspended Middle*, p. 45.

heart of de Lubac's theology' consists in becoming the reception of the light of grace, to the extent that 'there is no longer any additional "natural" recipient of the reception'.[54] What could this mean? Perhaps it means simply what Augustine says to his Pelagian opponents, namely that God gives the gift of grace quite apart from our natures. It can never be owed to us as Pelagius once thought. But it seems that Milbank believes de Lubac means more than this basic Augustinian view of the gratuity of grace (and the priority of divine agency). Milbank reads de Lubac as inclining to the view that Christian illumination gives us a new nature ('born from above') in a way which depends on no created capacities whatsoever, for even the 'natural desire' is created 'out of nothing'. In Milbank's view, grace can be gratuitous for de Lubac *only if grace does not presuppose nature.*

What Milbank appreciates most is the way de Lubac's theology points consistently towards a 'supernatural nature' – indeed, the emphasis upon deification as the end of our natural desire in de Lubac comes not only from the Greek Fathers, but also through the medieval schools. Milbank does not do proper justice to nature *as such*, and this might be owing to de Lubac's own confusion around the metaphysical categories he uses. But it is precisely at this point that de Lubac and Milbank alike are less indebted to Augustine than they are to the theology of Origen, Pseudo-Dionysius and Maximus the Confessor. Milbank rightly sees the basis for a 'Eucharistic ontology' in de Lubac that owes more to the East than to the Western tradition. Yet we should recall Augustine's famous words in a sermon for the newly baptized preparing to receive the Eucharist in which he counsels the recipients of grace to 'become what you are'. Henri de Lubac himself drew heavily upon the writings of Saint Paschasius Radbertus, as well as Saint Augustine and Saint Thomas, in a way which would incline to a mystical ontology in which our 'substance' would be transformed just as the natural substance of the bread and wine are transformed into the supernatural substance of Christ's body and blood.

On this analogy we can, perhaps, better understand what Milbank means when he says, 'Grace, like the act of creation, presupposes *nothing* – not even creation'.[55] Grace does not presuppose nature for Milbank because, on this Eucharistic analogy, the bread and wine cease to exist by their own substance. In the mystical transformation of substance (transubstantiation), the bread and wine only retain the appearance (or accidents) of their natures, but their existence is rooted solely in the supernatural nature of Christ's body and blood. If the bread and wine cease to exist by their own nature, but now exist only by virtue of single divine-human substance of Christ, then why not the same

---

[54] Ibid., p. 46.
[55] Ibid., p. 45.

for us? 'Become what you are.' When seen in light of the Eucharistic ontology that Milbank envisions, it is easy to see why he reads Henri de Lubac the way that he does. De Lubac clearly spent his life seeking to reconnect Catholic theological anthropology to the *corpus mysticum*, so Milbank presents a creative development of him precisely by making these connections explicit and sufficiently complex to demand our attention.

Even given the plausible support that can be found in Henri de Lubac for such a theological anthropology, worries remain about the annihilation of nature qua nature in his theological anthropology. Set aside the question of whether he destroys the gratuity of grace, does his Lubacian Eucharistic ontology destroy nature? The patristic Augustinian tradition stressed the medicinal aspect of grace (the healing of our nature), and the Thomistic tradition (largely following the Greek Fathers) stressed the elevating aspect of grace (raising our natures to deiformity). But both the medicinal and the elevating metaphors for grace do seem to presuppose nature qua nature. Yet this is precisely what Milbank thinks de Lubac's Christian metaphysics excludes if he is correct that for de Lubac 'grace does not presuppose nature'. Perhaps what Milbank means is that de Lubac sides with Origen, for whom grace elevates, but sets this in a more radically non-foundationalist key wherein elevation reveals not a nature which precedes, but reveals that our natures have always been suspended over the *nihil* out of which they were made. In this way, we can see how Milbank understands de Lubac's theology as a pointed response to contemporary nihilism and atheist materialism – but it presents problems for how we understand de Lubac. It confirms the worry that de Lubac is weak on metaphysics (nature) and makes everything grace. We do not mean to settle the question of whether Milbank provides a legitimate or a distorted development of Henri de Lubac's theology, though we incline to the view that he develops his 'Eucharistic ontology' legitimately, though not his account of nature, which as David Braine has shown, is not so much metaphysically wrong as it is terminologically confused.[56]

2. Lawrence Feingold

In *The Natural Desire to See God According to St. Thomas Aquinas and His Interpreters*, Lawrence Feingold offers a post-Lubacian apology for the Suarezianism of the early twentieth-century Jesuits, and a critical evaluation of de Lubac's 'neo-Augustinian' anthropology. Where Milbank maximalizes de Lubac's account of grace in such a way as to overwhelm nature itself, Feingold maximalizes de Lubac's account of nature in such a way as to overwhelm the gratuity of grace itself. Feingold writes of de Lubac's view, 'the

---

[56] David Braine, 'The Debate between Henri de Lubac and His Critics', in *Nova et Vetera* (English) 6/3 (2008), pp. 543–90.

great difficulty with the notion of an innate, absolute desire to see God lies in showing how grace and the beatific vision would not be *due* to a nature endowed with such a desire'.[57] For Feingold, like Garrigou-Lagrange, natures are defined by ends, and so to say that nature has a supernatural end is to contradict any distinction between natural and supernatural ends. As Feingold puts it, 'A nature with a divine end can only be the divine nature'.[58]

De Lubac's thought, according to Feingold, arrives at its difficulty from a misconception of the way in which finality determines nature. De Lubac had used the principle of finality (natures determined by their ends) to defend the Augustinian commitment to the unicity of man's final end, going even so far as to suggest that human nature, considered apart from grace, would be radically different than human nature in its present, historical state. Feingold argues that de Lubac overlooked the fact that the principle of finality only applies to ends which are naturally attainable; this principle does not apply to those ends which raise the creature by the agency of another, such as the beatific vision.[59] The latter, supernatural end is accidental to a given creature, and can only be obtained by the acquisition of an accidental form (such as the scholastics supposed 'created grace' to be), which orders it towards that further end.[60] To admit the existence of a creature intrinsically ordered to the beatific vision, and not simply to the natural desire for God, would require that such a creature be, by nature, divine.[61]

As a consequence of de Lubac's alleged misconception of the relationship between nature and finality, Feingold suggests that de Lubac misconstrues the gratuity of grace. Supposing that a natural desire for the beatific vision does not create an exigency for it on the part of the creature, de Lubac thought it sufficient for safeguarding the gratuity of the beatific vision that man desire it as a gift.[62] But a subjective desire that something be given as a gift does nothing to alter the existence of an underlying metaphysical *exigency* on the creature's part for the fulfilment of its natural desires.[63] De Lubac had thought that no such exigency could possibly exist, because he supposed it would make God dependent on his creatures.[64] But, argues Feingold, he had simply misunderstood the cause of the exigency in the first place, which is the fulfilment of God's providence in the creature, not any debt on God's part towards it.[65]

---

[57] Feingold, *The Natural Desire to See God*, p. xxxii.
[58] Ibid., p. 322.
[59] Ibid., p. 320.
[60] Ibid., p. 321.
[61] Ibid., pp. 321–22.
[62] Ibid., p. 386.
[63] Ibid., p. 382.
[64] Ibid., p. 378.
[65] Ibid., pp. 378–79.

At the heart of Feingold's critique is the rejection of the use of the distinction between God's absolute and his ordered power which he thinks is operative in de Lubac's account.[66] When human nature is considered in light of such a distinction, Feingold notes, it 'entails an unresolved tension or contradiction', between our natural and supernatural finality.[67] For, if human nature has the beatific vision as its only end, Feingold argues, it is difficult not also to affirm that it is 'intrinsically ordered' to its end without grace.[68]

In order to remain consistent, Feingold argues that de Lubac would have to make one of two alterations to his thought. One possibility would be to abandon the use of the distinction between God's absolute and ordered power altogether. This possibility would lead to the conclusion that a human nature not called to the beatific vision would simply not be human (since such a call is constitutive of human nature as such) – a solution at once more philosophically consistent and laden with 'insuperable theological problems'.[69] The other possibility would be to admit as 'natural' only that which is implied by human nature considered absolutely.[70] But this would be to abandon de Lubac's commitment to the unicity of man's final end and to conclude, with Suarez, that the vision of God is accidental to human nature considered *as such*[71]; it would also require the hypothesis of the possibility of a state of pure nature.[72]

Rather, it is only the infusion of sanctifying grace which inscribes in human nature a supernatural end. In this way, Feingold rejects Lubac's view that our nature is ordered to the beatific vision of God *in particular* prior to grace. In order to safeguard the gratuity of grace, de Lubac argues that the human creature is the only being in the universe who cannot achieve such intrinsic ends. But what de Lubac is happy to call paradox, Feingold thinks is self-contradictory.

> It appears therefore that de Lubac's position entails an unresolved tension or contradiction, and that he must logically choose between (1) his repeated affirmation that our nature itself is intrinsically determined by having received a supernatural finality (also referred to as an 'essential finality'), prior to the reception of grace, and (2) his clear avowal – following St. Thomas – that our nature itself is *not intrinsically ordered* to a supernatural end without sanctifying grace.[73]

---

[66] Ibid., pp. 318–19.
[67] Ibid., pp. 319, 330.
[68] Ibid., p. 319.
[69] Ibid., p. 336.
[70] Ibid., p. 337.
[71] Ibid., p. 338.
[72] Ibid., p. 392.
[73] Ibid., p. 524.

However, it seems to us that if Henri de Lubac is read within the Aegidian tradition it might be admitted that (1) we are not intrinsically ordered to the beatific vision without sanctifying grace, and (2) all of humanity is nevertheless called to the beatific vision *in general* prior to grace. This solution would, however, require a revision of the several places in de Lubac's work where he seems to insist on an 'essential finality' that is wedded more to a Scotistic notion of the distinction in our will between fulfilment and reception. Such a correction would have the advantage of making de Lubac a *more consistent* Aegidian by restraining his misappropriation of a Scotistic distinction.

3. Nicholas Healy

Henri de Lubac has not been without his more moderate defenders. Nicholas Healy has responded to the revival of neo-Thomist criticism stemming from Lawrence Feingold's work in a different way from Milbank.[74] For Healy, the neo-Thomist criticisms stem from a misunderstanding of what Lubac means by 'the natural desire for the supernatural'. For in this phrase, de Lubac preserves the distinction between the gift of created human nature and the second gift of sanctifying grace, 'provided that one acknowledges that the desire is truly natural and the ultimate end is truly supernatural'.[75]

Healy argues that the premise which undergirds the arguments of de Lubac's critics 'is that the final end of nature must be proportionate to nature' (p. 543). If the Aristotelian definition of the final end of nature as necessarily proportional holds, then de Lubac clearly has made a mistake – just as the critics claim. But if the premise, that the end must be proportionate to a nature, is refused, then de Lubac's position is not contradictory even if it is paradoxical. Healy invokes Thomas Aquinas (but not Augustine) at critical junctures of his argument in support of de Lubac's view that the *human nature alone has a final end which is not proportionate to its nature*.[76] In seeking rapprochement with neo-Thomist critics, Healy concludes that de Lubac holds to *a twofold end*: one penultimate end proportionate to our natural capabilities, and one final end which is supernatural.[77]

Straightforwardly putting the matter of the relative integrity of nature at the centre, Healy explains that 'de Lubac's teaching, rightly understood, actually requires the affirmation of such a relative perfection or consistency

---

[74] Nicholas J. Healy, 'Henri de Lubac on Nature and Grace: A Note on Some Recent Contributions to the Debate', *Communio* 35 (Winter 2008), pp. 535–64.

[75] Ibid., p. 550. Healy's argument here has the advantage of working from the plain sense of Henri de Lubac's own argument in *Surnaturel*.

[76] Healy cites Aquinas *ST* I-II, q.5, a.5; q. 91, a.4 ad 3; q. 109, a.4 ad 2; Aquinas, *Disputed Questions on Truth*, q. 8, a.3 ad 12; q. 24 a.10 ad 1; *On Evil*, q. 5, a.1; *The Divisions and Methods*, q. 6, a.4.

[77] Healy, 'Henri de Lubac on Nature and Grace', p. 562.

[of the natural order]. In this sense, Lubacians have good grounds for making common cause with Neo-Thomists in defense of a robust concept of nature.'[78] Likewise, he seems to suggest that critics who worry about 'innate desire' in de Lubac should pay attention to what this means to de Lubac. It does not mean some univocal bond to the being of God inscribed into our nature, as in some Platonic emanationism, but always has the character of 'receptivity'. Healy suggests that if the natural desire is nothing but receptivity, then this is simply a different way of speaking about natural desire as an 'obediential potency' as neo-Thomists do. The difficulty with Healy's position is that he is rightly striking out against understanding de Lubac's position in terms of Scotus (univocal Platonic emanationism) but wrongly imagines 'receptivity' as equivalent to 'obediential potency'.

When Healy points out that for de Lubac, 'God places in created intellectual nature a natural basis for his call' to the supernatural end, he does not seem to recognize that this is precisely the point of contention for critics.[79] The neo-Thomist point about obediential potency is that our receptivity to obedience or supernatural elevation is *not innate* in us, but is *elicited* as a potency that can only be actualized with God's help. Healy has established real, substantial agreement about the need for God to be first mover in the soul (*initium fidei*), but he has not yet dealt with the problem of rooting our supernatural end in nature rather than in a potency. Saint Thomas understands this, though his distinction is between a natural passive potency in us, and an obediential potency that can only be made active by divine agency. But by utilizing the language of 'receptivity', Henri de Lubac implicitly employs the Scotist distinction. In Scotus, there are only natural potencies – those which are naturally fulfillable, and those which are naturally receivable (see above). These natural potencies are in the will as a 'weight of nature' (*pondus*), that is, as innate. More than anything, we are arguing that de Lubac is not so much an inconsistent Thomist, or an inconsistent Scotist, but he is a remarkably consistent neo-Aegidian who would be made more consistent still if he had restrained his use of Scotistic categories at this point, since they do not fit within his own synthesis.

Examining defences of de Lubac against his neo-Thomist critics provides us with another crucial insight into the debate over nature and grace. If Healy is right about de Lubac, we have a minor debate about the fitness of our distinctions. If Milbank is right about de Lubac, then de Lubac is indeed implicated by *Humani Generis* and a portion of his thought stands condemned. As a faithful son of the Catholic Church, indeed, as a Cardinal of the Catholic Church, it is difficult to imagine that de Lubac would agree with the whole of Milbank's

---

[78] Ibid.
[79] Ibid.

interpretation of him in *The Suspended Middle*. As well, if Milbank is right, then every neo-Thomist fear about de Lubac is proved correct. If Healy's more moderate reading is correct, then this should ameliorate neo-Thomist fears, even if it does not end an argument about the most apt distinctions for understanding the relationship between nature and elevating grace. Where Milbank confirms neo-Thomist critique, Healy qualifies and clarifies in the same ways that de Lubac himself did in the years subsequent to the controversy. Though Milbank's own theology is fascinating and rich, and deserves separate assessment, it is Healy who leads Catholic readers towards a better set of disagreements about the kind of distinctions theologians make between God and creation.

III. Conclusion

Future research on Henri de Lubac needs to appreciate these strands of the contemporary debate, but also needs to reconsider de Lubac as part of a quiet, neglected but nevertheless real renascence of the Aegidian tradition. It is tempting to say that the real target of de Lubac's anxieties was not external (in the Dominican tradition) but internal (in the Jesuit tradition). In attacking the Suarezian tendencies in the Society of Jesus (e.g. Descoqs), Henri de Lubac was correctly reacting against a radical 'grace extrinsicism' that does indeed entail a bifurcation of the relationship between nature and grace. De Lubac is right that Thomas Aquinas himself is not the origin of this problem, but he is mostly wrong to think that this problem touches the Dominican tradition.

For example, as Christine Wood has persuasively shown, Garrigou-Lagrange does not understand human nature as 'closed-off' from transcendent being, but has 'an infinite capacity for being, truth, and goodness in the orders of knowledge and love'.[80] Wood argues that the 'closed-off' interpretation (which we have now learned to call 'exclusive humanism') is not legitimate for Cajetan or Garrigou-Lagrange she argues, but it *is* legitimate for Suarez and Descoqs – and Henri de Lubac was right to critique it. His only fault was in projecting Jesuit problems on Dominican targets. Balthasar notes that de Lubac 'expressly stressed that his true opponents were not the Roman authorities but a group of integralist professors both in and outside the Society of Jesus'.[81] But we think Wood is correct that it is really the Suarezian elements within the Society of Jesus that always remained his core target, and that this primarily entailed a correction internal to the Jesuits. Since the problem with

---

[80] Christine E. Wood, 'The Metaphysics and Intellective Psychology in the Natural Desire for Seeing God: Henri de Lubac and Neo-Scholasticism' (unpublished PhD diss., Marquette University; March 2011), p. 85.

[81] von Balthasar, *Theology of Henri de Lubac*, p. 19.

Suarez was the way in which he fused Thomistic theses and Scotistic distinctions to produce a dualistic 'bifurcated philosophy', it is the height of irony that the contemporary debate has now come full circle to accuse Henri de Lubac of precisely the same Thomistic-Scotistic fusion in the overcoming of dualism.

Perhaps such speculation may help explain why Henri de Lubac's work has so often been associated with a critique of Scotism and *also* why his thought has been thought to employ problematically Scotistic distinctions. It further may help to explain why Dominicans so strongly resisted his critique since it implied that they were not, in fact, true Dominicans, but that they were secretly Scotists! What it does not explain is why Henri de Lubac never explicitly embraced his view as neo-Aegidian. It is entirely possible that while he knew that Sestili, de Broglie and Huby were key inspirations, he understood this more as a development within his own Jesuit society, rather than as a rebirth of Aegidianism.[82]

The 'openness to transcendent being' that Garrigou-Lagrange could affirm as a *capacitas Dei*, Henri de Lubac affirmed as well. It was a thesis that Giles of Rome had once affirmed, following Saint Thomas, following Saint Augustine. Our hearts are restless because of a lack. Yet as Augustine notes, it is God who excites us to praise him. Our nature can desire many things of its own accord, and we might understand those things in the highest possible perfection, and we might call those highest perfections 'God'. And we will be right to do so. But these natural desires will be faint perceptions of the desire for the specific vision of the Triune God, whose love infuses human intellect and will with sanctifying grace at the instant of our baptism. It is the reception of this sanctifying grace, and our actual participation in it, that Henri de Lubac would affirm as an Augustinian Thomist. Thus, perhaps Augustine and de Lubac converge less on the specific distinctions between nature and grace than they do in their stress upon the medicinal grace of the Eucharist. This is the way Joseph Cardinal Ratzinger followed Augustine too, and learned from both old and new fathers, to speak about the 'call to communion'. Perhaps we can see, in the teachings of Pope Benedict XVI, the elevation of so many of Henri de Lubac's most fruitful theological contributions. It is one of the benefits of the Catholic faith that everything true can eventually be carried up into the whole. This fact should give us confidence that there is still so much more to say about Henri

---

[82] Our thesis concerning Henri de Lubac's 'Augustinianism' does not touch upon the popular thesis that de Lubac is primarily indebted to Maurice Blondel. It is certainly true that Blondel's work deeply impressed Henri de Lubac, but we wonder if this is finally very helpful in placing Henri de Lubac in an Augustinian tradition. For an account of the influence of Blondel, see Aidan Nichols, 'Henri de Lubac: Panorama and Proposal', *New Blackfriars* 93/1043 (January 2012), pp. 3–33.

de Lubac as an 'Augustinian Thomist' who can only be rightly understood a theologian who was also a pilgrim, on his way to the City of God.

For Further Reading

Braine, David, 'The Debate between Henri de Lubac and His Critics', *Nova et Vetera* 6 (2008), pp. 543–90.
Feingold, Lawrence, *The Natural Desire to See God According to St. Thomas Aquinas and His Interpreters* (2nd edn; Naples, FL: Sapientia Press, 2010).
Healy, Nicholas, 'Henri de Lubac on Nature and Grace: A Note on Some Recent Contributions to the Debate', *Communio* 35 (2008), pp. 535–64.
Hütter, Reinhard, 'Aquinas on the Natural Desire for the Vision of God: A Relecture of Summa Contra Gentiles III, c. 25 après Henri de Lubac', *The Thomist* 73 (2009), pp. 523–91.
— 'Desiderium Naturale Visionis Dei – Est autem duplex hominis beatitudo sive felicitas: Some Observations about Lawrence Feingold's and John Milbank's Recent Interventions in the Debate over the Natural Desire to See God', *Nova et Vetera* (English) 5/1 (2007), pp. 81–131.
Mansini, Guy, 'The Abiding Significance of De Lubac's *Surnaturel*', *The Thomist* 73 (2009), pp. 593–619.
Milbank, John, *The Suspended Middle: Henri de Lubac and the Debate Concerning the Supernatural* (Grand Rapids, MI: Eerdmans, 2005).

12 Augustine and John Zizioulas

Will Cohen

I. Introduction

Augustine's harshest critics, if they are Orthodox, often point to what they regard as his errors as evidence that the Eastern and Western Christian traditions are so fundamentally at odds that there is no hope for reuniting the two through ecumenical engagement – Augustine's thought is simply too deeply embedded in the tradition of the Catholic West.[1] Metropolitan John Zizioulas, however, tirelessly works and hopes to find principled grounds for Catholic-Orthodox unity as a member and, since 2006, co-chair of the Joint International Commission for Theological Dialogue between the Roman Catholic Church and the Orthodox Church. The fact that his writing is as heavily laced as it is with negative references to Augustine is therefore more curious in his case. It is also significant given his stature: Zizioulas is widely recognized as one of the most creative and influential theologians of recent times.[2]

Of the criticisms Zizioulas levels against Augustine, by far the most prevalent concerns Augustine's Trinitarian theology; a second, also important area of Zizioulas's criticism has to do with Augustine's anthropology, his exploration of the interior consciousness or psychology of the individual person. Before turning to Zizioulas's understanding of Augustine on the

---

[1] Yannaras expresses a view easily found among Orthodox theologians today: 'The first *heretical differentiation* which not merely survives historically, but has transformed radically the course of human history is one which denies the fundamental presupposition of orthodoxy, the apophaticism of truth . . . Augustine is surely the first great stage in the theoretical foundation of the rejection of apophaticism' (C. Yannaras, *Elements of Faith: An Introduction to Orthodox Theology* [trans. K. Schram; Edinburgh: T&T Clark, 1991], pp. 154–55; emphasis added).

[2] Zizioulas has been described as 'the most brilliant and creative theologian in the Orthodox Church today' by Metropolitan Kallistos (Ware) of Diokleia and as 'one of the outstanding theologians of our time' by Cardinal Walter Kasper, former president of the Vatican's Pontifical Council for Promoting Christian Unity. Zizioulas's book *Communion and Otherness* (T&T Clark, 2006) was its publisher's best-selling title at both the 2006 and 2007 annual meetings of the American Academy of Religion.

223

Trinity, it should be noted that not everything that Zizioulas has written about Augustine has been critical. In *Eucharist, Bishop, Church* (1965), putting forward his understanding of Christ as an eschatological, corporate personality, Zizioulas alludes to *'the whole Christ* in Augustine's apt phrase'.[3] The idea of the *totus Christus* would seem to be an important point of reference for Zizioulas, one that might be expected to lead him to make significant use of Augustine's thought as it relates especially to Eucharistic ecclesiology; but in fact throughout his oeuvre, Zizioulas develops the latter independently of Augustine. Zizioulas refers positively to Augustine again in his discussion of the need for a synthesis of the more historical (Western) and the more eschatological (Eastern) understandings of the church's continuity with the apostles. Here Zizioulas lays particular emphasis on the role of the Holy Spirit in the life of communion where the divine and human levels intersect. He does not yet refer to Augustine in the following passage in which there are typically Zizioulan themes on the difference between individuality and personhood:

> The event of Christ must be regarded as *constituted* pneumatologically. I stress the word 'constituted' because my intention is to say that Christ is not Christ unless He is an existence in the Spirit, which means an *eschatological existence*. Such a pneumatological constitution of Christology implies, from the viewpoint of ontology, the understanding of Christ not in terms of individuality which affirms itself by distancing itself from other individualities, but in terms of personhood which implies a particularity established in and through *communion*.[4]

The reference to Augustine comes in the ensuing footnote where Zizioulas explains why there can be no properly understood ontology (no 'being as communion', one may say) without a robust pneumatology. 'It is noteworthy that it is the function of the Holy Spirit to open up being so that it may become relational. Without Pneumatology, ontology becomes substantialistic and individualistic. The Spirit was understood as "communion" both by the Greek (e.g., St. Basil) and the Latin (e.g., St. Augustine) Fathers – especially by the latter.'[5]

Augustine wrote much indeed about the Holy Spirit as the bond or gift of love between the Father and the Son, as well as about the Holy Spirit

---

[3] Zizioulas, *Eucharist, Bishop, Church: The Unity of the Church in the Divine Eucharist and the Bishop during the First Three Centuries* (trans. Elizabeth Theokritoff; Brookline, MA: Holy Cross Orthodox Press, 2001), p. 15.
[4] Zizioulas, *Being As Communion* (Crestwood, NY: St. Vladimir's Seminary Press, 1985), p. 182.
[5] Ibid., p. 182, n. 37.

as the *caritas* in which the life of Christians flourishes in the church. This relational quality of the Holy Spirit as understood by Augustine is certainly what Zizioulas had in mind in writing what he did in the passage above. Here again, a promising affinity seems to emerge between Augustine's thought and Zizioulas's central theological concerns; but it too remains undeveloped. In fact, as will be seen in section III below, Zizioulas will repeatedly associate Augustine *with* the problems of a 'substantialistic and individualistic' ontology and cast him as the theological opponent of an ontology that is properly relational, pneumatological and personal – just the reverse of how Zizioulas represents Augustine in the passage just quoted.

II. Zizioulas on Augustine and the Trinity

Zizioulas's criticism of Augustine's Trinitarian theology is epitomized in the following charge: 'There can be no doubt that Augustine makes otherness secondary to unity in God's being. God *is* one and *relates* as three. There is an ontological priority of substance over against personal relations in God in Augustine's Trinitarian theology.'[6] This statement appears in an essay of 2006; much the same observation may be found in a work of Zizioulas published some 20 years earlier: 'The subsequent developments of trinitarian theology [subsequent to the Cappadocians], especially in the West with Augustine and the scholastics, have led us [to Zizioulas's regret] to see the term *ousia*, not *hypostasis*, as the expression of the ultimate character and the causal principle (ἀρχή) in God's being.'[7] And again in his *Lectures in Christian Dogmatics*, Zizioulas observes: 'The Cappadocians believed it is crucial to begin with the person of the Father, and thus with the persons of the Trinity. Augustine however makes the "substance" of God prior, and regards the persons as relations within the substance of God.'[8]

During the period of Zizioulas's theological formation in the mid-twentieth century, this interpretation of Augustine in contrast to the Cappadocians in their way of approaching the doctrine of God reigned supreme. Were it not that it would have reached Zizioulas from all sides – from Lossky, Yannaras, Rahner, Kelly, Wolfson, to name several authors whom Zizioulas either cites

---

[6] Zizioulas, *Communion and Otherness*, p. 33. The same point is made in Zizioulas's earlier work *Being As Communion*, p. 40, where he critically characterizes ancient Greek ontology for holding the view that 'God first *is* God (His substance or nature, His being), and then exists as Trinity, that is, as persons. This interpretation in fact prevailed in Western theology . . .'

[7] Zizioulas, *Being As Communion*, p. 88.

[8] Zizioulas, *Lectures in Christian Dogmatics* (London: T&T Clark, 2008), p. 66.

directly or can be sure to have read⁹ – it is unlikely that in his own writing he would present it as often as he does with such simplicity and so little examination of the actual texts of Augustine. In the background of the scholars whose views would have shaped Zizioulas's thinking on the subject stands the work of the Catholic historian of doctrine Théodore de Régnon, whose publication of 1892, *Études de théologie positive sur la sainté Trinité*, advances, precisely, the thesis that in treatments of the doctrine of the Trinity, the Cappadocians began with the diversity of the divine persons and Augustine and the scholastics with the unity of the divine nature.¹⁰ It is a thesis that, interestingly, seems not to have characterized interpretations either of Augustine or the Cappadocians in earlier centuries.¹¹ Zizioulas cites de Régnon once, and only in a very recent essay.¹² Remarkably, given how many scholars today regard what has come to

---

⁹ Cf. Zizioulas, *Communion and Otherness*, p. 33, n. 59, citing J. N. D. Kelly, *Early Christian Doctrines* (New York: Harper & Row, 2nd edn, 1977), p. 272: '"[I]n contrast to the tradition which made the Father its starting-point, he [Augustine] begins with the divine nature Itself",' and in the same footnote, citing H. A. Wolfson, *The Philosophy of the Church Fathers* (Cambridge: Harvard University Press, 1956), p. 326, 'Augustine "identifies the substratum (of the Trinity) not with the Father but with something underlying both the Father and the Son"' – to which Zizioulas adds the clarification, as to the underlying something, 'i.e., divine substance'. Cf. also Zizioulas, *Being As Communion*, p. 88: 'By contrast [with Augustine and the scholastics], the Cappadocians' position – characteristic of all the Greek Fathers – lay, as Karl Rahner observes, in that the final assertion of ontology in God has to be attached not to the unique *ousia* of God but to the Father, that is, to a *hypostasis* or *person*' (citing K. Rahner, *The Trinity* [London: Herder & Herder, 1970], especially pp. 58–61).

¹⁰ The scholar who has done most to demonstrate and critically examine the scope of De Régnon's influence is Michel René Barnes; see his articles, 'De Régnon Reconsidered', *AugStud* 26/2 (1995), pp. 51–79 and 'Augustine in Contemporary Trinitarian Theology', *TS* 56 (1995), pp. 237–50. One of the more interesting things to be brought to light in Barnes's study of the reception of de Régnon is that in the original French edition of Vladimir Lossky's *Éssai sur la théologie mystique de l'église d'orient* (Paris: Aubier, 1944), 12 of the 43 footnotes in the chapter dealing with Greek Trinitarian theology refer to de Régnon, while in the 1957 English translation of the French original, 'all the citations to de Régnon are missing except two direct quotations, and his name does not appear in the book's index of authors cited. What, in the original, were Lossky's footnote references to passages in de Régnon's *Études*, become, in the English translation, footnote references to the Cappadocian texts originally discussed by de Régnon' (Barnes, 'De Régnon Reconsidered', p. 58).

¹¹ When in medieval times Augustine was found by Byzantines to have supported the *filioque*, his Trinitarian theology was not questioned; it was either thought that the *filioque* passages must have been later interpolations, or suggested that as with Noah and his sons, the nakedness of one of the Fathers should not be exposed. The dependence of Gregory Palamas on the Trinitarian theology of Augustine has been widely noted, and most persuasively shown by Reinhard Flogaus, 'Palamas and Barlaam Revisited: A Reassessment of East and West in the Hesychast Controversy of 14th Century Byzantium', *StVTQ* 42/1 (1998), pp. 1–32, especially at pp. 16 and 20; see also Jacques Lison, '*L'esprit comme amour selon Grégoire Palamas: une influence augustinienne?*' *StudPat* 32 (1997), pp. 325–31.

¹² Zizioulas, *Communion and Otherness*, p. 34.

be known as de Régnon's paradigm as a grossly oversimplified and misleading characterization of both Augustine and the Cappadocians, Zizioulas's own purpose in citing de Régnon is still, simply, to highlight what he presents as '[t]he fact, well-known as an observation of historians, that the West always started with the one God and then moved to the Trinity, whereas the East followed the opposite course'.[13]

However obvious the thesis may have been to the twentieth-century scholars on whom Zizioulas seems to rely, within the actual pages of Augustine's *De Trinitate*, one is hard-pressed to find support for it. Indeed strong evidence appears that directly contradicts the claim that Augustine makes the substance prior to the persons. This counterevidence is perhaps most clear where Augustine discusses genus and species as offering a possible analogy for the relationship between the divine essence and the divine persons. Might the essence be viewed as the genus, and the hypostasis as a species of it – much as 'animal' is the genus of which 'horse' is a species? Augustine rejects the analogy. Among other reasons, we speak of three horses (species) as *three* animals (genus), whereas in regard to the Trinity we speak of three persons as *one* essence. 'So the Father and the Son and the Holy Spirit', Augustine insists, 'are not three species of one being.'[14] He goes on:

> But perhaps it is like our saying that three men of the same sex, the same physique and the same character are one nature – they are three men but one nature . . . There is at least this similarity here, that the ancients who spoke Latin before they had these terms, that is being or substance . . . used to talk about nature instead. So now we are not talking anymore in terms of genus and species, but rather in terms of what you could call the same common material. For example, if three statues were made of the same gold we would say three statues, one gold; and here we would not be using statue as a specific and gold as a generic term, nor even gold as a specific term and statue as an individual one.[15]

Augustine next clarifies how the analogy of statues made of gold differs from the earlier analogy of horses as a species belonging to the genus animal. 'When I define animal, since horse is a species of this genus, every horse will be an animal. But not every statue is gold. So although with three golden statues we rightly say three statues, one gold, we do not say it in such a way that we understand gold to be the genus and statues the species.'[16] It is in

---

[13] Ibid.
[14] Augustine, *Trin.* 7.3.11.
[15] Ibid.
[16] Ibid.

the continuation of the passage that the gap between Augustine himself, and Zizioulas's portrayal of him as someone who 'makes the "substance" of God prior' and sees 'the persons as relations within the substance', becomes most strikingly plain.

> Well now, it is not in this way either that we talk about the trinity as being three persons or substances, one being and one God, as though they were three things consisting of one material, even if whatever that material might be it were wholly used up in these three; for there is nothing else, of course, of this being besides this triad. And yet we do talk of three persons of the same being, or three persons one being; but we do not talk about three persons out of the same being, as though what being is were one thing and what person is another, as we can talk about three statues out of the same gold.[17]

Augustine unequivocally rejects the notion of being as any sort of substance prior to the persons of Father, Son and Holy Spirit. He resolutely refuses to say *what* the persons are *as persons*, as though personhood were something one could then identify which make the three *three of* whatever they are.[18] Interestingly, it is Zizioulas who ventures to pour into the empty linguistic container of *person* as used in Trinitarian reflection something in the way of content, while Augustine apophatically insists on leaving it empty.

The consistent commitment to the monarchy of the Father is a feature of Augustine's Trinitarian theology that has been widely recognized by Orthodox scholars as well as those of Western Christian traditions.[19] Zizioulas himself seems to stop just short of stating outright that Augustine taught, exactly, that either the Son or the Holy Spirit has his origin from anyone or anything other than the Father. Yet Zizioulas so often and so closely *associates* Augustine with such an idea that it becomes difficult to avoid the impression that he attributes it to Augustine. For example, shortly after accusing Augustine of giving priority to substance over persons, Zizioulas, without naming Augustine again but with no other theologian having been named in the interim, pivots slightly to observe: 'The decisive point in Cappadocian theology concerning our subject

---

[17] Ibid.

[18] 'So the only reason, it seems, why we do not call these three together one person, as we call them one being and one God, but say three persons while we never say three Gods or three beings, is that we want to keep at least one word for signifying what we mean by trinity, so that we are not simply reduced to silence when we are asked three what, after we have confessed that there are three' (Augustine, *Trin.* 7.11).

[19] For a recent careful treatment by an Orthodox author of Augustine's attention to the monarchy of the Father, see A. Edward Siecienski, *The Filioque: History of a Doctrinal Controversy* (Oxford: Oxford University Press, 2010), especially pp. 61–2.

is the association of divine *monarchia* in its ontological sense with the person of the Father *and not with divine substance.*'[20] In context of the earlier remarks about Augustine, the implication is that Augustine does, somehow, identify the ἀρχή with the substance/essence rather than with the Father.[21] However, once again such a conclusion is virtually impossible to maintain in the face of numerous passages from *De Trinitate*, such as the following:

> By saying then, Whom I will send you from the Father (Jn. 15.26), the Lord showed that the Spirit is both the Father's and the Son's. Elsewhere too, when he said, whom the Father will send, he added, in my name (Jn. 14.26). He did not however say, 'whom the Father will send from me' as he had said whom I will send from the Father (Jn. 15.26), and thereby he indicated that the source of all godhead, or if you prefer it, of all deity, is the Father. So the Spirit who proceeds from the Father and the Son is traced back, on both counts, to him of whom the Son is born.[22]

It is true that Augustine holds together with his commitment to the monarchy of the Father the view that the one true God is to be identified not strictly as the Father but as the three persons of the Trinity in their unity. He interprets 1 Tim. 6.14[23] differently from how Zizioulas would surely say it ought to be understood. 'In these words neither Father nor Son nor Holy Spirit is specifically named', Augustine writes, 'but the blessed and only mighty one, King of kings and Lord of lords, which is the one and only true God, the three.'[24] To so interpret the passage, which after all does name the Son when it names Jesus Christ, is really a stretch – it seems utterly clear that the King of kings is the Father – but all that Augustine is intent on stressing here in his battle against the Arians is, of course, the way that the persons of the Trinity all share each other's nature, so that, for example, the epistle's phrase 'who alone has immortality' (on which the Arians naturally seized) cannot be restricted to the Father. And this hardly compromises the uniqueness of the Father as origin and principle cause. Zizioulas seems to assume that to call the Trinity the one

---

[20] Zizioulas, *Communion and Otherness*, p. 34; original emphasis.
[21] Elsewhere Zizioulas writes, similarly, that the theology of Augustine (and Aquinas) 'had no difficulty in maintaining the filioque precisely because it identified the being, the ontological principle, of God with His substance rather than with the person of the Father' (*Being As Communion*, p. 41, n. 3).
[22] Augustine, *Trin.* 4.5.29.
[23] 'That you keep the commandment untarnished and irreproachable until the coming of our Lord Jesus Christ, whom in his own proper times he has manifested who is the blessed and only mighty one, King of kings and Lord of lords, who alone has immortality and dwells in light inaccessible, whom no man has ever seen or can see, to whom is honor and glory for ever and ever.'
[24] Augustine, *Trin.* 1.2.10.

God must be incompatible with holding that the Son and the Spirit are from the Father. Yet Augustine's manner of referring to the three as the one God is not as unusual among the Fathers as Zizioulas's reflections would lead us to believe. Consider the following passage from Maximus the Confessor:

> The Word then leads [the soul] to the knowledge of theology made manifest after its journey through all things, granting it an understanding equal to the angels as far as this is possible for it. He will teach it with such wisdom that it will comprehend *the one God, one nature and three persons*, a tri-personal unity of essence, and a consubstantial trinity of persons, trinity in unity and unity in trinity, not one and another, nor one beside another, nor one through another, nor one in another, nor one from another, but the same in itself, according to itself, with itself, by itself.[25]

The Cappadocians themselves invoked the *ousia* more than they invoked the Father to speak about divine unity. This has been noted by Nigel Rostock in his comments on a passage from Basil relevant to our discussion; it may be noticed at once, for example, that Basil is *less* hesitant than Augustine to liken the relationship between genus and species to the inner-Trinitarian relationship between essence and hypostasis.

> The distinction between οὐσία and ὑπόστασις is the same as that between the general and the particular; as, for instance, between the animal and the particular man. Wherefore, in the case of the Godhead, we confess one essence or substance so as not to give a variant definition of existence, but we confess a particular hypostasis, in order that our conception of Father, Son and Holy Spirit may be without confusion and clear. If we have no distinct perception of the separate characteristics, namely, fatherhood, sonship, and sanctification, but form our conception of God from the general idea of existence, we cannot possibly give a sound account of our faith. We must, therefore, confess the faith *by adding the particular to the common*. The Godhead is common; the Fatherhood particular. We must

---

[25] Maximus the Confessor, *Mystagogia* 23, as quoted (for a very different purpose) by Andrew Louth, 'Love and the Trinity: Saint Augustine and the Greek Fathers', *AugStud* 33/1 (2002), pp. 1–16 (p. 12). For another English translation not markedly different from Louth's, see the same passage in *Maximus Confessor: Selected Writings* (trans. George C. Berthold; Mahwah, NY: Paulist, 1985), p. 205, and also the *Commentary on the Our Father*, par. 4, pp. 110–11, for related material in another text of Maximus. Scholarly opinion on the possible influence of Augustine on Maximus remains open; cf. Brian E. Daley, 'Making a Human Will Divine: Augustine and Maximus on Christ and Human Salvation', in *Orthodox Readings of Augustine* (ed. A. Papanikolaou and G. Demacopoulos; Crestwood, NY: St. Vladimir's Seminary Press, 2008), pp. 101–26.

therefore combine the two and say, 'I believe in God the Father'. The like course must be pursued in the confession of the Son; we must combine the particular with the common and say, 'I believe in God the Son', so in the case of the Holy Spirit we must make our utterance conform to the appellation and say 'in God the Holy Spirit'. Hence it results that there is a satisfactory preservation of the unity by the confession of the one Godhead, while in the distinction of the individual properties regarded in each there is the confession of the peculiar properties of the Persons.[26]

One can easily imagine the response of Zizioulas had this passage been by Augustine's hand rather than Basil's. For starters, the divine unity is clearly associated with the essence, the 'Godhead'. Worse, the phrase emphasized by my added italics gives priority to that which is common while representing that which is particular as a mere add-on. A further contravention of Zizioulas's understanding of what is normative in Trinitarian theology may be seen in the sense given to the phrase 'God the Father'. Note what Zizioulas has said about this: he asks whether in regard to the creedal statement 'I believe in God the Father almighty', it is correct for 'the clause to be read as "I believe in God who is Father almighty", or as "I believe in God the Father, who is almighty"?'[27] Zizioulas argues that the West interpreted the phrase in the first sense and the East in the second. 'Augustine', he complains, 'proceeded to a disjunction between God and Father, making of divine substance a notion (*divinitas*) logically prior to that of the Father, and assigning to it the role of expressing divine unity. The "one God" became thus identical with the "one substance" . . .'[28] In this way, the West solved the problem of Arianism but too glibly, Zizioulas says, while in the East the biblical identification of God with the Father was too strong for this. 'The East, therefore, did not adopt the easy way of dissociating the "one God" from "God the Father", and preferred to face the Arian challenge in a way that was faithful to the biblical equation of God with the Father.'[29] But in the quotation given above from Basil, things do not line up so neatly as Zizioulas suggests. Basil associates 'God' with what is general and 'Father' with what is particular, so that he turns out to be quite as capable as Augustine of making a 'disjunction between God and Father' and of 'assigning to [divine substance] the role of expressing divine unity'.

---

[26] Basil, *ep.* 236.6, quoted in part by N. Rostock, 'Two Different Gods or Two Types of Unity? A Critical Response to Zizioulas' Presentation of "The Father as Cause" with Reference to the Cappadocian Fathers and Augustine', *New Blackfriars* 91 (May 2010), pp. 321–34 (p. 329); emphasis mine.
[27] Zizioulas, *Communion and Otherness*, p. 113.
[28] Ibid., p. 118.
[29] Ibid.

This could not be more evident than in the step Basil takes in urging a confession of 'God the Father', 'God the Son' and 'God the Holy Spirit'.[30]

The indications given so far of a considerably more complex picture than Zizioulas has drawn of Eastern and Western patristic approaches to Trinitarian theology will not be sufficient in themselves, perhaps, to produce unanimous agreement with the conclusion of the contemporary Orthodox theologian David Bentley Hart that 'in the case of Augustine there can be no doubt that, in its basic shape, his account of the order of intra-trinitarian relations is all but indistinguishable from that of the Cappadocians'[31]; nor will they be likely to set beyond all dispute Hart's kindred assertion that 'as for the accusation that Augustine's "filioquism" logically entails a belief on his part in some sort of divine essence prior to the trinitarian relations, or more original than the Father, neither in *De Trinitate* (*On the Trinity*) nor in any other of his works can one find a single sentence to justify it'.[32] They should be enough, however, to make clear that Zizioulas has done much to sharpen distinctions between Augustine and the Cappadocians, and has taken advantage of few opportunities to bring out affinities and resonances.

Of such missed opportunities in Zizioulas's analysis of Augustine's Trinitarian theology, a last example may be mentioned. Zizioulas devotes significant energy to making the case that if otherness is to be understood as constitutive of ontology, then person must be seen as primary, rather than essence. What Zizioulas repeatedly calls 'substantialist' approaches to Trinitarian theology are to be rejected in favour of what he calls 'personalist' approaches.[33] However, in a section in which he offers a defence of the Cappadocians against their critics, Zizioulas comes at the question from a quite different angle. Here he seeks to respond to those who criticize the Cappadocian idea of 'the Father as cause'. Zizioulas believes that the ground of the criticism lies in a mistaken understanding that '[b]eing and personhood are juxtaposed as two parallel or different ideas, as if the notion of person did not connote being'.[34] In fact, he argues, for the Cappadocians '[t]he three persons of the Trinity denote God's being just as much as the term "substance". In speaking of the divine persons we speak of God's very being.'[35]

---

[30] In this same connection, one may also note that the Greek Fathers from Athanasius to Gregory Nazianzen were not speaking of merely an impersonal divine 'essence', yet neither obviously were they referring to the Father, when they said that God became man so that man might become God.

[31] D. B. Hart, 'The Hidden and the Manifest: Metaphysics after Nicaea', in *Orthodox Readings of Augustine*, pp. 191–226 (p. 195).

[32] Ibid., p. 196.

[33] Cf. Zizioulas, *Communion and Otherness*, p. 124.

[34] Ibid., p. 125.

[35] Ibid.

The question then arises whether the same correlation may not be made in reverse. In other words, if the notion of divine person connotes divine being as Zizioulas says that it does for the Cappadocians, is it not also true that the notion of divine being connotes – at least, can and should connote – divine person? Zizioulas's perception that too often it has not done so is obviously no real basis for suggesting that it somehow never does and never has. In regard to Augustine in particular, the criticism frequently voiced by Zizioulas that there is an impersonal quality to the divine essence runs up against many clear statements in Augustine that insist, in so many words, that it is always and only an enhypostasized essence that is at issue when it comes to *divinitas*. In the first of the following two brief passages which the Augustine scholar Lewis Ayres enlists to make the point that '[f]or Augustine . . . there is nothing in God other than the three persons', it may be noticed how remarkably consonant Augustine's words are with those of Maximus quoted earlier.[36] 'Hold with unshakable faith that the Father and the Son and the Holy Spirit are a Trinity and that there is, nonetheless, one God, not that the divinity is common to these as if it were a fourth, but that it is itself the ineffably inseparable Trinity . . .'[37] And: 'It remains, then, that we should believe the Trinity is of one substance, in the sense that the essence is nothing other than the Trinity itself.'[38] In this Trinitarian theology, otherness certainly *is* wholly constitutive of ontology. The reason is that for Augustine *ousia* is always personal – it is always enhypostasized. Zizioulas himself in another context makes the point well when he writes, 'Only when nature is hypostatic or personal, as is the case with God, does it exist truly and eternally'.[39] Here again we find Zizioulas affirming that the divine essence – which he so often views negatively as an impersonal reality when discussing Augustine's theology – is indeed personal, after all. This would seem to crack open the door for a more favourable Zizioulan interpretation of Augustine than one finds in Zizioulas.

---

[36] See above, p. 230. It may be noted that Zizioulas goes to some lengths to make the case, quite rightly, that in the work of Maximus (as with the other Greek Fathers) 'nature or substance coincides fully with personhood in God's existence, no conflict between the two being conceivable', so that when *Maximus* 'speaks of being "according to nature" (κατα φύσιν)', *he* means it in the good way of 'nature *personalized*' (Zizioulas, *Communion and Otherness*, pp. 64–5). Though it would be possible to go to similar lengths to make the same case with regard to Augustine, Zizioulas does not do so.

[37] Augustine, *ep.* 120.2.12, quoted by Ayres, 'Augustine's Pneumatology and the Metaphysics of Spirit', in *Orthodox Readings of Augustine*, pp. 127–52 (p. 136).

[38] Augustine, *ep.* 120.2.12, quoted by Ayres, 'Augustine's Pneumatology', p. 136.

[39] Zizioulas, *Communion and Otherness*, p. 168. Cf. also *Being As Communion*, pp. 41–2, where Zizioulas lays out an understanding of the relationship between divine substance or being and divine person that differs little if at all from the perspective of Augustine. For example, 'Outside the Trinity there is no God, that is, no divine substance . . .'

III. Zizioulas on Augustine and Christian Anthropology

According to Zizioulas, Augustine did much to lay the groundwork for whatever tendencies there have been in subsequent Western culture towards a solipsistic preoccupation with the self. Augustine was the one, more than any other patristic writer, to open theology up to the realm of inwardness and individual psychology. A person's identity, rather than being rooted in communion and otherness, is – in Zizioulas' gloss on Augustine – self-contained and self-enclosed. As Zizioulas puts it,

> [T]he self continues to dominate western philosophy as logically prior to the Other. To a decisive degree, the matter is cultural, in that it would appear to be absurd to think otherwise . . . A decisive role in the formation of this culture must be attributed historically to the emergence of *consciousness* as a dominant factor in western anthropology. The contribution of St Augustine to this development can hardly be exaggerated.[40]

Zizioulas adds in a footnote: 'As far as we know, Augustine was the first among the early Christian writers to write Confessions, in which man's relationship to God passes through his consciousness or even self-consciousness.'[41] He continues this line of thought by observing, 'This introspectiveness is characteristic of the Augustinian tradition, which has never really been abandoned by the western mind and which has affected even modern Orthodox "spirituality", as if self-consciousness and self-examination were the way to salvation.' Zizioulas concludes, 'In fact, this introspectiveness is essentially nothing other than a confirmation of our fallen existence, of the domination of selfhood'.[42] In these and other similar observations on the subject, Zizioulas clearly associates introspection with self-centeredness and atomistic individualism.

For Augustine himself, of course, the inward realm of the self does not stand in opposition to or isolation from the realm of communion, of one's relationships either with God or with others. Indeed for Augustine, there is no depth or extent of inwardness that could possibly separate a person from God since, as Augustine famously wrote in his *Confessions*, themselves *addressed to* God, 'You were more inward than the most inward place of my heart' (3.6.11). The self in this conception is the place of recollection and integration and encounter with the transcendent God, while exteriority implies a movement away from such integration and towards dissipation into superficiality, the restless attempt to escape whatever is uncomfortably true about oneself. Augustine

---

[40] Zizioulas, *Communion and Otherness*, p. 46.
[41] Ibid., p. 46, n. 93.
[42] Ibid., p. 46.

certainly does not suggest, however, that all that is interior is consonant with, let alone to be identified as, the one true God, which would amount to a conflation of the self and divinity. Phillip Cary makes this point where he writes that whereas for Plotinus 'there is a part of us that is never separated from the divine Mind', and therefore when 'we turn [inward] to it, we are *ipso facto* turning to God', for Augustine 'there is no such divine part of soul. Hence we can turn to the highest and best part of our self and still find nothing but our own solitary self'.[43] As Augustine writes, 'Just as you [God] are not any corporeal image, nor any of the emotions that belong to a living person, such as we experience when we are joyful or sad, when we desire or fear something, when we remember or forget or anything similar, so too you are not the mind itself.'[44] Yet as Cary points out, in spite of Augustine's insistence that Christ is *other* than the soul, 'he still locates Christ *within* the soul rather than outside it, and this means the soul must have enough "room" within itself to hold what is higher and greater than itself. One can look inside the self to find what is not self.'[45] Here is a theology of interiority that is simultaneously a theology of otherness. Zizioulas's critique of Augustinian introspection misses this point.

Indeed, Zizioulas fails to take seriously the claim of Augustine that his exploration of his own interior landscape is a relational, communal act. 'What point is there in other people hearing my confessions?' Augustine asks, and gives the initial outline of an answer when he observes, 'It is cheering to good people to hear about the past evil deeds of those who are now freed from them'.[46] The purpose is not to focus on one's sin but on the movement away from it; it is to give others hope by means of a first-hand testimony of the power of Christ to free a human being from sin.[47] Zizioulas argues that in Western thought since Augustine, 'The emergence of consciousness and subjectivity as fundamental anthropological categories has led to a confusion between ontology and psychology in our ordinary way of thinking',[48] and he laments the 'substituting [of] psychology for ontology ...'[49] Viewed, however, from the perspective of an authentically Augustinian theology in which, as Carey describes it, the 'inward turn' entails 'two distinct movements, first "in" then "up"',[50] it becomes more difficult to set the psychological and the ontological in opposition to each other

---

[43] P. Cary, *Augustine's Invention of the Inner Self* (Oxford: Oxford University Press, 2000), p. 114.
[44] Augustine, *conf*. 10.24.35.
[45] Cary, *Augustine's Invention of the Inner Self*, p. 114.
[46] Augustine, *conf*. 10.3.3 and 10.4.
[47] 'When the confession of my past evil deeds is read and listened to – those evil deeds which you have forgiven and covered over to make me glad in yourself, transforming my soul by faith and your sacrament – that recital arouses the hearer's heart, forbidding it to slump into despair and say, "I can't"' (Augustine, *conf*. 10.3.4).
[48] Zizioulas, *Communion and Otherness*, p. 46.
[49] Ibid., p. 63.
[50] Cary, *Augustine's Invention of the Inner Self*, p. 105.

as Zizioulas does. Instead, it emerges that Augustine's project actually entails an integration of psychology into ontology. It is an effort at taking seriously enough the attentive presence of God to every human particularity that there is seen to be *good ontological reason* for allowing all one's interior life to be cast into the light of that divine presence. When theology devolves into navel-gazing, the mere movement 'in' without the movement 'up', then, without doubt, it has lost its ability to elevate – it is rendered solipsistic rather than ecstatic. But a theology too quick to denigrate the psychological runs the opposite, Apollinarian risk: there is then a movement upward that has not first gone far enough inward and hence does not carry with it the whole of the person whose rich, interior life we ought not to understand as being somehow vacated by his integration into the corporate personality of the risen Christ. Augustine's Christian embodiment of the Socratic exhortation to 'know thyself' is surely nothing if not an attempt to come to know himself ontologically as created and loved by God, but not just according to an overall set of ontological 'facts' of sin, death, nature, et cetera, that are the same for all people but in the deeply particular way in which these facts are fleshed out in one individual's life. It thereby functions also as a means for others to resonate with these facts in such a way that may lead them to be encouraged to bring to light what is most weak and vulnerable in themselves – and to do so in great hope and trust as creatures loved by God.

What alone makes this act of de-privatization an act of *ecstasis* and not of exhibitionism is the reality of *caritas* which makes it possible in the first place. To be fully present to ourselves and to one another is not possible except in the milieu of God's Spirit of love. Otherwise, because of sin, it is bound to be an inferno of self- and mutual condemnation. For the postlapsarian human being, there is no ontology of mutual indwelling that does not pass through psychology; there is no communion without confession; there is no otherness without inwardness.

The two dimensions are brought together consummately in a passage in Augustine's *Confessions* in which he addresses the question of the value of putting before his readers not only his past evil deeds but also his present struggles:

> So then, when I confess not what I have been but what I am now, this is the fruit to be reaped from my confessions: I confess not only before you in secret exultation tinged with fear and secret sorrow infused with hope, but also in the ears of believing men and women, the companions of my joy and sharers in my mortality, my fellow-citizens still on pilgrimage with me, those who have gone before and those who will follow, and all who bear me company in my life. They are your servants and my brethren, but you have willed them to be your children and my masters, and you have

ordered me to serve them if I wish to live with you and share your life. This command of yours would mean little to me if it were only spoken, and not first carried out in deed as well. So I do likewise, and I do it in deeds and in words; I do it under your outstretched wings and would do it in grave peril, were it not that under those wings my soul is surrendered to you and to you my weakness known. I am a little child, but my Father lives for ever and in him I have a guardian suited to me. He who begot me is also he who keeps me safe; you yourself are all the good I have, you are almighty and you are with me before ever I am with you.[51]

If it is true that the risen, eschatological Christ is a corporate personality as Zizioulas suggests, then it must be recognized that Augustine's act of making public his innermost heart is an eschatological act, one which draws him into deeper communion both with the God who is 'with him' and with 'all who bear him company' in his journey, not only his contemporaries but those who have gone before and those who will follow as well. Insofar as it entails and models the freedom to be oneself in all one's weakness, before the one merciful God by whom all are judged, this self-disclosure is not grandstanding but a form of service. 'To such people, then, the people you command me to serve, I will disclose myself not as I have been but as I am now, as I am still, though I do not judge myself. In this way, then, let me be heard.'[52]

V. Conclusion

One is led to wonder what rich theological fruit might have resulted – might still result – from a serious engagement of Augustine's pneumatology by Zizioulas.[53] Although he does briefly acknowledge, as was seen, the profoundly relational dimension of Augustine's understanding of the Holy Spirit,[54] Zizioulas also seems to cut short any further consideration of the implications of this understanding by the sweeping remark, 'But the importance of Pneumatology for ontology has never been a decisive one in Western thought'.[55]

---

[51] Augustine, *conf.* 10.4.6.
[52] Ibid.
[53] For important examples of recent theological interest in Augustine's pneumatology, see A. Kotsko, 'Gift and Communio: The Holy Spirit in Augustine's *De Trinitate*', *SJT* 64/1 (2011), pp. 1–12; J. Ratzinger, 'The Holy Spirit as Communio: Concerning the Relationship of Pneumatology and Spirituality in Augustine', *Communio* 25/2 (1998), pp. 324–39; and R. Wilken, 'Is Pentecost a Peer of Easter: Scripture, Liturgy, and the Proprium of the Holy Spirit', in *Trinity, Time and Church: A Response to the Theology of Robert W. Jenson* (ed. Colin E. Gunton; Grand Rapids: Eerdmans, 2000), pp. 158–77.
[54] See above, pp. 224–25.
[55] Zizioulas, *Being As Communion*, p. 182, n. 37.

One of Zizioulas's own most valuable contributions – and correctives, perhaps, of a now generally recognized Western neglect – has been his focus on the eschatological element in Christian existence: 'the eschatological dimension of the presence and activity of the Spirit deeply affects the identity of the other: it is on the basis not of someone's past or present that we should identify and accept him or her, but on the basis of their future.'[56] Although applied to individual identities in the passage where Zizioulas writes this, the same observation might be applied to ecclesial identities as well. In this perspective, Zizioulas's remark that the underemphasis on pneumatology has been 'decisive' within Western thought on the question of being would seem to fall into the trap of identifying the other (in this case, the Christian West) on the basis of a past and present that are considered closed, already 'decided'. Instead, that tradition might be more properly and eschatologically considered as open, open not so much to making an about-face or to becoming something it never has been, but to developing the resources within itself that would show it to have had, all along and at times unbeknownst to itself, a pneumatological ontology after all, just needing to be brought out. In effect and as a whole, Zizioulas's theological contribution would seem to have had just this effect of attuning Western theologians to these resources and of helping to whet their appetite for a synthesis, along the lines he calls for, between the historical and the eschatological. What is to be especially noted here is that *their* avenue for arriving at such a synthesis has not gone through the Cappadocians, or at least not so exclusively as Zizioulas's own, but very often through Augustine himself (as complementary to the Cappadocians), and with impressive results. It is as though they have taken Zizioulas's constructive theology seriously indeed but his treatment of Augustine not so very much so.

Since much if not all of what Zizioulas denounces in the work of Augustine as Zizioulas (haphazardly and wrongly) interprets it is, indeed, deserving of denunciation, we may be sure that Augustine himself would be glad for the censure of such theological faults and errors once they have been unfairly attributed to him:

> Undoubtedly, though, it is required of me by the gentle authority of Christ's law, which is charity, that when people think I meant something false in my books which in fact I did not and this falsehood is disliked by one and welcomed by another, I should prefer to be censured by the censurer of falsehood than to receive its praiser's praises. The first, though he is wrong to blame me, since I did not in fact mean what he thinks I did, is right to blame the error . . .[57]

---

[56] Ibid., p. 6.
[57] Augustine, *Trin.* 1.1.6.

For Further Reading

Ayres, L., *Augustine and the Trinity* (Cambridge and New York: Cambridge University Press, 2010).

Bradshaw, D., *Aristotle East and West: Metaphysics and the Division of Christendom* (Cambridge and New York: Cambridge University Press, 2004).

Cary, P., *Augustine's Invention of the Inner Self: The Legacy of a Christian Platonist* (Oxford and New York: Oxford University Press, 2000).

Demacopoulos, G. and Papanikolaou, A. (eds), *Orthodox Readings of Augustine* (Crestwood, New York: St. Vladimir's Seminary Press, 2008).

McPartlan, P., *The Eucharist Makes the Church: Henri de Lubac and John Zizioulas in Dialogue* (Edinburgh: T&T Clark, 1993; reprinted, Fairfax, Virginia: Eastern Christian Publications, 2006).

Rose, Father Seraphim, *The Place of Blessed Augustine in the Orthodox Church* (Platina, CA: St. Herman of Alaska Brotherhood, 1996).

Contributors

Frederick Christian Bauerschmidt is Associate Professor of Theology at Loyola University Maryland, Baltimore, MD.

Joshua C. Benson is Assistant Professor of Historical and Systematic Theology at The Catholic University of America, Washington, DC.

Phillip Cary is Professor of Philosophy at Eastern University, St. David's, PA.

Will Cohen is Assistant Professor of Theology at The University of Scranton, Scranton, PA.

Luigi Gioia, OSB, is a monk in the Benedictine Community of Monte Oliveto in Siena, Italy, and teaches theology at The Pontifical University of Sant'Anselmo in Rome, Italy.

Michael Hanby is Assistant Professor of Biotechnology and Culture at The John Paul II Institute for Marriage and Family at The Catholic University of America, Washington, DC.

Anthony N. S. Lane is Professor of Historical Theology at The London School of Theology, London, UK.

Morwenna Ludlow is Senior Lecturer in Patristics at The University of Exeter, Exeter, UK.

C. C. Pecknold is Assistant Professor of Historical and Systematic Theology at The Catholic University of America, Washington, DC.

Ronnie Rombs is Associate Professor of Theology at The University of Dallas, Dallas, TX.

Michael Root is Professor of Historical and Systematic Theology at The Catholic University of America, Washington, DC.

Tarmo Toom is Associate Professor of Latin Patristics at The Catholic University of America, Washington, DC.

Jacob Wood is a PhD candidate in Systematic Theology at The Catholic University of America.

Bibliography

For the works of Augustine, their chronology and translations into contemporary languages, see (alphabetically):

Alici, Luigi, Antonio Pieretti and Allan D. Fitzgerald (ed.), *Agostino: dizionario enciclopedico* (Roma: Città Nuova, 2007), pp. 43–67; Augustine's letters on pp. 68–74; and Augustine's sermons on pp. 75–101.

Drecoll, Volker H. (ed.), *Augustin Handbuch* (Tübingen: Mohr Siebeck, 2007), pp. 253–61.

Fitzgerald, Allan D. (ed.), *Augustine through the Ages: An Encyclopedia* (Grand Rapids: Eerdmans, 1999), pp. xxxv–xlii (xliii–il); Augustine's letters on pp. 299–305; and Augustine's sermons on pp. 774–89.

Harmless, William (ed.), *Augustine in His Own Words* (Washington, DC: The Catholic University Press, 2010), pp. xxvii–xlii.

Keller, Adalbert, *Translationes Patristicae Graecae et Latinae* (vol. 1; Stuttgart: Anton Hiersemann, 1997–2004), pp. 89–151.

Lancel, Serge, *Augustine* (trans. Antonia Nevill; London: SCM Press, 2002), pp. 533–36.

Mayer, Cornelius P. (ed.), *Augustinus-Lexikon* (Basel: Schwabe), vol. 1 (1986–94), pp. xxvi–xli; vol. 2 (1996–2002), pp. xi–xxx and Augustine's letters on pp. 1028–36; vol. 3 (2004–10), pp. xi–xxxii.

Vessey, Mark and Shelley Reid (eds), *A Companion to Augustine* (Malden: Wiley-Blackwell, 2012), pp. xxiv–xxxv.

Consult also the following websites at:

- www.augustinus.de/bwo/dcms/sites/bistum/extern/zfa/augustinus/werke/index.html
- www.augustinus.it/links/inglese/index.htm
- http://downloads.kirchenserver.net/26/2506/1/91703576406220546331.pdf
- http://findingaugustine.org
- www.augnet.org/default.asp?ipageid=1095

Secondary Sources

For a comprehensive bibliography see *Augustinus Literaturdatenbank* (*Corpus Augustinianum Giessense* [CAG 2]) by Zentrum für Augustinus-Forschung (University of Würzburg) at www.augustinus.konkordanz.de

Bibliography

Adams, Marilyn McCord, 'The Problem of Hell: A Problem of Evil for Christians'. In *God and the Problem of Evil* (ed. William L. Rowe; Oxford: Blackwell, 2001), pp. 282–309.

Ahn, In-Sub, 'Calvin's View of Augustine and the Donatist Church'. In *Calvinus sacrarum literarum interpres* (ed. H. J. Selderhuis; Göttingen: Vandenhoeck & Ruprecht, 2008), pp. 271–84.

Alexander, David C., *Augustine's Early Theology of the Church: Emergence and Implications 386–391* (Patristic Studies 9; New York: Peter Lang, 2008).

Alfaric, Prosper, *L'évolution intellectuelle de saint Augustin* (vol. 1; Du Manichéisme au Néoplatonisme; Paris: Nourry, 1918).

Alici, Luigi, Remao Piccolomini and Antonio Pieretti (eds), *Ripensare Agostino: Interiorità e intenzionalità* (SEAug 41; Rome: Institutum Patristicum Augustinianum, 1993).

Allen, Pauline and Edward Morgan, 'Augustine on Poverty'. In *Preaching Poverty in Late Antiquity: Perceptions and Realities* (ed. Pauline Allen, Bronwen Neil and Wendy Mayer; Arbeiten zur Kirchen- und Theologiegeschichte 28; Leipzig: Evangelische Verlagsanstalt, 2009), pp. 119–70.

Althaus, Paul, *The Theology of Martin Luther* (trans. R. Schultz; Philadelphia: Fortress, 1966).

Anatolios, Khaled, 'Divine Semiotics and the Way to the Triune God in Augustine's De Trinitate'. In *God in Early Christian Thought: Essays in Memory of Lloyd G. Patterson* (ed. Andrew McGowan and Lloyd G. Patterson; Supplements to Vigiliae Christianae 94; Leiden: Brill, 2009), pp.163–93.

Anselm, *Anselm of Canterbury: The Major Works* (trans. Brian Davies and G. R. Evans; Oxford: Oxford University Press, 1998).

Arnold, Duane W. H. and Pamela Bright (eds), *De doctrina christiana: A Classic of Western Culture* (Notre Dame: University of Notre Dame Press, 1995).

Ayres, Lewis, *Augustine and the Trinity* (Cambridge: Cambridge University Press, 2010).

— 'Augustine on the Spirit as the Soul of the Body, or Fragments of a Trinitarian Ecclesiology', *AugStud* 41/1 (2010), pp. 165–82.

— 'Into the Poem of the Universe: *Exempla*, Conversion, and Church in Augustine's *Confessiones*', *ZAC* 13/2 (2009), pp. 263–81.

— 'Augustine's Pneumatology and the Metaphysics of Spirit'. In *Orthodox Readings of Augustine* (ed. A. Papanikolaou and G. Demacopoulos; Crestwood, NY: St. Vladimir's Seminary Press, 2008), pp. 127–52.

— 'The Soul and the Reading of Scripture: A Note on Henri De Lubac', *SJT* 61 (2008), pp. 173–90.

— 'Giving Wings to Nicaea: Reading Augustine's Earliest Trinitarian Theology', *AugStud* 38/1 (2007), pp. 21–40.

— 'Augustine on the Rule of Faith: Rhetoric, Christology, and the Foundation of Christian Thinking', *AugStud* 36 (2005), pp. 33–49.

— 'Remember That You Are Catholic (*serm.* 52.2): Augustine on the Unity of the Triune God', *JECS* 8 (2000), pp. 39–82.

— 'Augustine on God as Love and Love as God', *Pro Ecclesia* 5 (1996), pp. 470–87.

— 'Between Athens and Jerusalem: Prolegomena to Anthropology in Augustine's *De Trinitate*', *Modern Theology* 8 (1992), pp. 53–73.

Azkoul, Michael, *The Influence of Augustine of Hippo on the Orthodox Church* (Lewiston: Mellen, 1990).

Bibliography

Babcock, William S. (ed.), *The Ethics of St. Augustine* (Atlanta: Scholars Press, 1991).
— 'Augustine and Tyconius: A Study in the Latin Appropriation of Paul', *SP* 17 (1982), pp. 1209–15.
— 'Augustine's Interpretation of Romans (A.D. 394–396)', *AugStud* 10 (1979), pp. 55–74.
Backus, Irena D. (ed.), 'Calvin and the Church Fathers'. In *Calvin Handbook* (ed. H. J. Selderhuis; Grand Rapids: Eerdmans, 2009), pp. 125–37.
— *The Reception of the Church Fathers in the West: From the Carolingians to the Maurists* (2 vols; Leiden: Brill, 1997).
Bainton, Roland, *Here I Stand: A Life of Martin Luther* (Nashville: Abingdon, 1950).
von Balthasar, Hans Urs, *The Theology of Henri de Lubac: An Overview* (San Francisco: Ignatius, 1991), pp. 17–18.
Barnes, Michel R., 'Augustine's Last Pneumatology', *AugStud* 39/2 (2008), pp. 223–34.
— '*De Trinitate* VI and VII: Augustine and the Limits of Nicene Orthodoxy', *AugStud* 38/1 (2007), pp. 189–202.
— 'The Visible Christ and the Invisible Trinity: Mt 5.8 in Augustine's Trinitarian Theology of 400', *Modern Theology* 19 (2003), pp. 329–55.
— 'Exegesis and Polemic in Augustine's *De Trinitate* I', *AugStud* 30 (1999), pp. 43–59.
— 'Re-Reading Augustine's Theology of the Trinity'. In *The Trinity: An Interdisciplinary Symposium on the Trinity* (ed. Stephen T. Davis, Daniel Kendall and Gerald O'Collins; Oxford: Clarendon Press, 1999), pp. 329–55.
— 'Augustine in Contemporary Trinitarian Theology', *TS* 56 (1995), pp. 237–50.
— 'De Régnon Reconsidered', *AugStud* 26/2 (1995), pp. 51–79.
— 'The Arians of Book V and the Genre of *De Trinitate*', *JTS* 44 (1993), pp. 185–95.
Barnikol, H., 'Die Lehre Calvins vom unfreien Willen und ihr Verhältnis zur Lehre der übrigen Reformatoren und Augustins', *Theologische Arbeiten aus dem Wissenschaftlichen Prediger-Verein der Rheinprovinz* NF 22 (1926), pp. 49–193.
Bavaud, G., 'La doctrine de la justification d'après saint Augustin et la Réforme', *Revue des Études augustiniennes* 5 (1959), pp. 21–32.
Van Bavel, Tarsicius J. *The Longing of the Heart: Augustine's Doctrine on Prayer* (Leuven: Peeters, 2009).
— (ed.), *Saint Augustine* (Brussels: Mercatorfonds, 2007).
— *Augustine's View on Women* (Villanova: Augustinian Press, 1990).
— 'The Creator and the Integrity of Creation in the Fathers of the Church, Especially in Saint Augustine', *AugStud* 21 (1990), pp. 1–33.
Bazàn, Bernardo C., 'Les questions disputées, principalement dans les facultés de théologie'. In *Les questions disputées et les questions quodlibétiques dans les facultés de theologie, de droit et de médecine* (ed. Bazàn; Typologie Des Sources Du Moyen Âge Occidental, Fasc. 44–5; Turnhout: Brepols, 1985), pp. 15–149.
Beatrice, Pier F. *Transmission of Sin: Augustine and the Pre-Augustinian Sources* (Oxford: Oxford University Press, 2012).
— '*Quosdam Platonicorum Libros*: The Platonic Readings of Augustine in Milan', *VC* 43 (1989), pp. 248–81.
Beckmann, J., *Vom Sakrament bei Calvin, Die Sakramentslehre Calvins in ihren Beziehungen zu Augustin* (Tübingen: J. C. B. Mohr [Paul Siebeck], 1926).

BeDuhn, Jason D., *Augustine's Manichaean Dilemma. Vol. 1: Conversion and Apostasy, 373–388 C.E.* (Philadelphia: University of Pennsylvania Press, 2010).
— 'Augustine Accused: Megalius, Manichaeism, and the Inception of the *Confessions*', *JECS* 17 (2009), pp. 85–124.
— 'Augustine, Manichaeism, and the Logic of Persecution', *Archiv für Religiongeschichte* 7 (2005), pp. 71–84.
Benedict XVI, Pope, *The Fathers of the Church: From Clement of Rome to Augustine of Hippo* (ed. J. Lienhard; Grand Rapids: Eerdmans, 2009).
Benson, Joshua C., 'Bonaventure's De reductione artium ad theologiam and Its Early Reception as an Inaugural Sermon', *ACPQ* 85/1 (2011), pp. 7–24.
— 'Identifying the Literary Genre of the De reductione artium ad theologiam: Bonaventure's Inaugural Lecture at Paris', *Franciscan Studies* 67 (2009), pp. 149–78.
Van den Berg, Jacob A. and Johannes Van Oort (eds), *In Search of Truth: Augustine, Manichaeism and Other Gnosticism: Studies for Johannes van Oort at Sixty* (Nag Hammadi and Manichean Studies 74; Leiden: Brill, 2011).
Bergvall, Åke, *Augustinian Perspectives in the Renaissance* (Uppsala: Uppsala University, 2001).
Besse, G., 'Saint Augustin dans les oeuvres exégétiques de Jean Calvin', *Revue des Études augustiniennes* 6 (1960), pp. 161–72.
Beumer, Johannes, 'Augustinismus und Thomismus in der theologischen Prinzipienlehre des Aegidius Romanus', *Scholastik* 32 (1957), pp. 542–60.
Bieringer, Reimund, 'Biblical Revelation and Exegetical Interpretation According to *Dei Verbum* 12'. In *Vatican II and Its Legacy* (ed. M. Lamberigts and L. Kent; Bibliotheca Ephemeridium Theologicarum Lovaniensium 166; Leuven: Leuven University Press, 2002), pp. 25–58.
Blanchette, Oliva, *Maurice Blondel: A Philosophical Life* (Grand Rapids, MI: Eerdmans, 2010).
Blans, Bert, 'Lyotard and Augustine's *Confessions*', *Augustiniana* 53 (2003), pp. 31–51.
Blondel, Maurice, 'The Latent Resources in St. Augustine's Thought'. In *St. Augustine: His Age, Life and Thought* (New York: Meridian Books, 1957).
Bochet, Isabelle, 'The Role of Scripture in Augustine's Controversy with Porphyry', *AugStud* 41 (2010), pp. 7–52.
— 'Le statut de l'image dans la pensée augustinienne', *Archives de Philosophie* 72 (2009), pp. 249–69.
— *Le firmament de l'Écriture. L'herméneutique augustinienne* (Paris: Études augustiniennes, 2004).
— *Saint Augustin et le désir de Dieu* (Paris: Études augustiniennes, 1982).
Boerma, Willem, 'Augustinus over vrijheid', *Bijdragen* 70 (2009), pp. 28–44.
Boeve, Lieven, Mathijs Lamberigts and Maarten Wisse (eds), *Augustine and Postmodern Thought: A New Alliance against Modernity?* (Leuven: Peeters, 2009).
Bogaert, Pierre-Maurice, '*Les bibles d'Augustin*'. In *Saint Augustin et la Bible. Actes du colloque de l'université Paul Verlaine-Metz (7–8 avril 2005)* (ed. G. Nauroy and M.-A. Vannier; Recherches en literature et spiritualité 15; Bern: Peter Lang, 2008), pp. 17–36.
Bonaventure, *Sermons De Diversis* [sic] (ed. Jacques Guy Bougerol; vol. 1; Paris: Editions Franciscaines, 1993), pp. 415–16.

Bonner, Gerald, *Freedom and Necessity: St. Augustine's Teaching on Divine Power and Human Freedom* (Washington, DC: The Catholic University of America Press, 2007).
— *St. Augustine of Hippo: Life and Controversies* (Norwich: Canterbury, 3rd edn, 2002).
— *Church and Faith in the Patristic Tradition: Augustine, Pelagianism, and Early Christian Northumbria* (Collected Studies Series, Variorum reprints, Brookfield, VT: Variorum, 1996).
— 'Augustine and Pelagianism', *AugStud* 24 (1993), pp. 27–47.
— 'Pelagianism and Augustine', *AugStud* 23 (1992), pp. 33–51.
— *God's Decree and Man's Destiny: Studies in the Thought of Augustine of Hippo* (Collected Studies Series, Variorum reprints, London: Variorum, 1987).
— *Augustine and Modern Research on Pelagianism* (Villanova: Augustinian Institute, 1972).
Bougerol, Jacques-Guy, 'The Church Fathers and *Auctoritates* in Scholastic Theology to Bonaventure'. In *The Reception of the Church Fathers in the West: From the Carolingians to the Maurists* (ed. Irena Backus; vol. 1; Leiden: Brill, 1997), pp. 289–335.
— *Introduction to the Works of Saint Bonaventure* (trans. José de Vinck; Patterson: St. Anthony Guild Press, 1964).
Bouton-Touboulic, Anne-Isabele, 'Augustin et le corps de la voix', *Cahiers Philosophiques* 122 (2010), pp. 43–56.
— 'Autorité et Tradition. La traduction latine de la Bible selon Saint Jérôme et Saint Augustin', *Augustinianum* 24 (2005), pp. 185–229.
— 'Origines des hommes, origines de l'homme chez saint Augustin', *Vita Latina* 172 (2005), pp. 41–51.
— *L'ordre caché: la notion d'ordre chez Saint Augustin* (Paris: Institut d'études augustiniennes, 2004).
Braaten, Carl E. and Robert W. Jenson (eds), *Union with Christ: The New Finnish Interpretation of Luther* (Grand Rapids: Eerdmans, 1998).
Brachtendorf, Johannes, 'The Human Condition as a Unifying Theme of the *Confessions*', *StudPat* 49 (2010), pp. 241–52.
— *Augustins 'Confessiones'* (Darmstadt: Wissenschaftliche Buchgesellschaft, 2005).
— *Die Struktur des menschlichen Geistes nach Augustinus. Selbstreflexion und Erkenntnis Gottes in 'De trinitate'* (Hamburg: F. Meiner, 2000).
— (ed.) *Gott und sein Bild. Augustins De trinitate in Spiegel gegenwärtiger Forschung* (Paderborn: Schöningh, 2000).
Braine, David, 'The Debate between Henri de Lubac and His Critics', in *Nova et Vetera* (English) 6/3 (2008), pp. 543–90.
Brecht, Martin, *Martin Luther: His Road to Reformation, 1483–1521* (trans. James Shaaf; Philadelphia: Fortress, 1985).
Brennecke, Hans C., 'Augustin und der "Arianismus"'. In *Die christlich-philosophischen Diskurse der Spätantike: Texte, Personen, Institutionen: Akten der Tagung vom 22.-25. Februar 2006 am Zentrum für Antike und Moderne der Albert-Ludwigs-Universität Freiburg* (Philosophie der Antike 28; Stuttgart: Steiner, 2008), pp. 175–88.
Breyfogle, Todd, 'Is There Room for Political Philosophy in Postmodern Critical Augustinianism?' In *Deconstructing Radical Orthodoxy: Postmodern Theology,*

Rhetoric and Truth (ed. Wayne Hankey and Douglas Hedley; Aldershot: Ashgate, 2005), pp. 31–47.

Bright, Pamela, 'Augustine and the Ethics of Reading the Bible'. In *The Reception and Interpretation of the Bible in Late Antiquity: Proceedings of the Montréal Colloquium in Honour of Charles Kannengiesser*, 11–13 October 2006 (ed. Lorenzo DiTommaso, Charles Kannengiesser and Lucian Turcescu; Bible in Ancient Christianity 6; Leiden: Brill, 2008), pp. 55–64.

— 'St. Augustine'. In *Christian Theologies of the Scripture: A Comparative Introduction* (ed. J. S. Holcomb; New York: New York University Press, 2006), pp. 39–59.

— (ed. and trans.), *Augustine and the Bible* (The Bible through the Ages 2; Notre Dame: University of Notre Dame Press, 1986).

Brown, Brian, John Doody and Kim Paffenroth (eds), *Augustine and World Religions* (Lanham: Lexington, 2008).

Brown, Peter, 'Augustine and a Crisis of Wealth in Late Antiquity', *AugStud* 36 (2005), pp. 6–29.

— *Augustine of Hippo* (Berkeley: University of California Press, 2nd edn, 2002).

— *Religion and Society in the Age of Saint Augustine* (London: Faber & Faber, 1972).

Bruning, Bernard, Mathijs Lamberigts and Jozef van Houtem (eds), *Collectanea Augustiniana: Mélanges T. J. Van Bavel* (Bibliotheca Ephemeridum theologicarum Lovaniensium 92; Leuven: Leuven University Press, 1990).

De Broglie, Guy, 'Le mystere de notre élévation surnaturelle. Réponse au R.P. Descoqs', *Nouvelle revue théologiques* 65 (1938).

— 'De ultimo fine humanae vitae asserta quaedam', *Gregorianum* 9 (1928), pp. 628–30.

— 'Autour de la notion thomiste de la béatitude', *Archives de philosophie* 3/2 (1925), pp. 55–96.

— 'Sur la place du surnaturel dans la philosophie de saint Thomas: Lettre à M. l'abbé Blanche', *Recherches de Science Réligieuse* 15 (1925), pp. 5–53.

— 'De la place du surnaturel dans la philosophie de saint Thomas', *Recherches de Science Réligieuse* 14 (1924).

Bubacz, Bruce, *St. Augustine's Theory of Knowledge: A Contemporary Analysis* (Texts and Studies in Religion 11; New York: Edwin Mellen, 1981).

Buenacasa, Pérez, 'Augustine on Donatism: Converting a Schism into a Heresy', *StudPat* 49 (2010), pp. 79–84.

Bultmann, Rudolf, *New Testament and Mythology and Other Basic Writings* (ed. and trans. Schubert Ogden; London: SCM, 1984).

Burnell, Peter, 'Justice and War in and before Augustine', *StudPat* 49 (2010), pp. 107–10.

— *The Augustinian Person* (Washington, DC: The Catholic University of America Press, 2005).

Burns, J. Patout, 'Baptism as Dying and Raising with Christ in the Teaching of Augustine', *JECS* 20/3 (2012), pp. 407–38.

— 'How Christ Saves: Augustine's Multiple Explanations'. In *Tradition and the Rule of Faith in the Early Church: Essays in Honor of Joseph T. Lienhard, S.J.* (ed. Alexander Hwang and Ronnie Rombs; Washington, DC: The Catholic University of America Press, 2010), pp. 193–210.

— '2000 St. Augustine Lecture', *AugStud* 32/1 (2001), pp. 1–23.

— 'The Atmosphere of Election: Augustinianism as Common Sense', *JECS* 2/3 (1994), pp. 325–39.
— 'Augustine on the Origin and Progress of Evil', *The Journal of Religious Ethics* 16/1 (1988), pp. 9–27.
— *The Development of Augustine's Doctrine of Operative Grace* (Paris: Études augustiniennes, 1980).
— 'Augustine's Role in the Imperial Action against Pelagius', *JTS* 30 (1979), pp. 67–83.
Burnyeat, Miles F. 'Wittgenstein and Augustine's *De magistro*' (Proceedings of the Aristotelian Society, supp. vol. 61; Cambridge: The Aristotelian Society, 1987), pp. 1–24.
Burr, David, *Olivi and Franciscan Poverty* (Philadelphia: University of Pennsylvania Press, 1989), pp. 149–51.
Burrus, Virginia, 'Carnal Excess: Flesh at the Limits of Imagination', *JECS* 17/2 (2009), pp. 247–65.
Burrus, Virginia, Mark D. Jordan and Karmen MacKendrick (eds), *Seducing Augustine: Bodies, Desires, Confessions* (New York: Fordham University Press, 2010).
Burton, Philip, *Language in the Confessions of Augustine* (Oxford: Oxford University Press, 2007).
Byers, Sarah C., *Perception, Sensibility, and Moral Motivation in Augustine* (Cambridge: Cambridge University Press, 2013).
— 'The Meaning of *voluntas* in Augustine', *AugStud* 37 (2006), pp. 171–89.
Bynum, Caroline Walker, *The Resurrection of the Body in Western Christianity 200–1336* (New York: Columbia University Press, 1995).
Cain, Andrew, 'The Bible and Aristotle in the Controversy between Augustine and Julian of Aeclanum'. In *Interpreting the Bible and Aristotle in Late Antiquity* (ed. Josef Lössl and John W. Watt; Aldershot: Ashgate, 2012), pp. 111–20.
Calcano, Antonio, 'Hanna Arendt and Augustine of Hippo: On the Pleasure of and Desire of Evil', *Laval Théologique et Philosophique* 66 (2010), pp. 371–85.
Calvin, John, *Institutes of the Christian Religion* (trans. F. L. Battles; Grand Rapids: H. H. Meeter Center for Calvin Studies/Eerdmans, 2nd edn, 1986).
Cameron, Michael, *Christ Meets Me Everywhere: Augustine's Early Figurative Exegesis* (New York: Oxford University Press, 2012).
Canning, Raymond, *The Unity of Love for God and Neighbour in St. Augustine* (Leuven: Augustinian Historical Institute, 1993).
Caputo, John D. and Michael J. Scanlon (eds), *Augustine and Postmodernism: Confessions and Circumfession* (Indiana Series in the Philosophy of Religion; Bloomington: Indiana University Press, 2005).
Caron, Maxence (ed.), *Saint Augustin* (Paris: Cerf, 2009).
Cary, Phillip, 'Love and Tears: Augustine's Project of Loving without Losing'. In *Confessions of Love: The Ambiguities of Greek Eros and Latin Caritas* (ed. Craig J. N. De Paulo, Bernhardt Blumenthal and Catherine Conroy de Paulo; New York: Peter Lang, 2011), pp. 39–54.
— *Inner Grace: Augustine in the Traditions of Plato and Paul* (New York: Oxford University Press, 2008).
— *Outward Signs: The Powerlessness of External Things in Augustine's Thought* (New York: Oxford University Press, 2008).

— 'United Inwardly by Love: Augustine's Social Ontology'. In *Augustine and Politics* (ed. K. Paffenroth, John Doody and Kevin L. Hughes; Lanham, MD: Lexington Books, 2005), pp. 3–33.

— 'Why Luther Is Not Quite Protestant: The Logic of Faith in a Sacramental Promise', *Pro Ecclesia* 14/4 (2005), pp. 447–86.

— *Augustine's Invention of the Inner Self: The Legacy of a Christian Platonist* (Oxford: Oxford University Press, 2000).

— 'Where to Flee for Grace: The Augustinian Context of Luther's Doctrine of the Gospel', *Lutheran Forum* 30/2 (May 1996), pp. 17–20.

Cary, Phillip, John Doody and Kim Paffenroth (eds), *Augustine and Philosophy* (Lanham: Lexington, 2010).

Catapano, Giovanni, *Agostino* (Roma: Carocci, 2010).

Cavadini, John C., 'The Anatomy of Wonder: An Augustinian Taxonomy', *AugStud* 42/2 (2011), pp. 153–72.

— 'Feeling Right: Augustine on the Passions and Sexual Desire', *AugStud* 36 (2005), pp. 195–217.

— 'The Structure and Intention of Augustine's *De Trinitate*', *AugStud* 23 (1992), pp. l03–23.

Chadwick, H. *Augustine* (Past Masters; Oxford: Oxford University Press, 1986).

— 'New Letters of St. Augustine', *JTS* 34 (1983), pp. 425–52.

Chappell, Timothy D. J., *Aristotle and Augustine on Freedom: Two Theories of Freedom, Voluntary Action, and Akrasia* (New York: St. Martin's, 1995).

Chenu, Marie-Dominique, *Faith and Theology* (trans. Denis Hickey; New York: MacMillan, 1968).

— *Aquinas and His Role in Theology* (trans. Paul Philibert; Collegeville, MN: The Liturgical Press, 2002 [French original 1959]).

Chenu, Marie-Dominique and Giuseppe Alberigo, *Une école de théologie: Le Saulchoir* (Théologies; Paris: Cerf, 1985), pp. 148–49.

Chin, M. Catherine, *Grammar and Christianity in the Late Roman World* (Philadelphia: Pennsylvania University Press, 2008).

Clark, Gillian, 'Augustine's Varro and Pagan Monotheism'. In *Monotheism between Pagans and Christians in Late Antiquity* (ed. Stephen Mitchell and Peter van Nuffelen; Leuven: Peeters, 2010), pp. 181–201.

— 'Augustine's Porphyry'. In *Studies in Porphyry* (ed. George E. Karamanolis and Anne D. R. Sheppard; London: Institute of Classical Studies, 2007), pp. 127–40.

— 'City of God(s): Virgil and Augustine', *Proceedings of the Virgil Society* 24 (2004), pp. 83–94.

Clark, Mary T., *Augustine* (Washington, DC: Georgetown University Press, 1994).

Congar, Yves, *Die Lehre von der Kirche: Von Augustinus bis zum Abendländischen Schisma* (Handbuch der Dogmengeschichte, III,3c; Freiburg: Herder, 1971).

— *Divided Christendom: A Catholic Study of the Problem of Reunion* (London: Geoffrey Bles, 1939).

Conybeare, Catherine, *The Irrational Augustine* (Oxford: Oxford University Press, 2006).

Cornwall, Susannah, *Sex and Uncertainty in the Body of Christ: Intersex Conditions and Christian Theology* (Oakville, CT: Equinox, 2010).

Corrigan, Kevin, 'The Soul-Body Relation in and before Augustine', *StudPat* 43 (2006), pp. 59–80.
Couenhoven, Jesse, 'Augustine's Rejection of the Free-Will Defense: An Overview of the Late Augustine's Theodicy', *Religious Studies* 43/3 (2007), pp. 279–98.
— 'Augustine's Doctrine of Original Sin', *AugStud* 36/2 (2005), pp. 359–96.
Courcelle, Pierre, *Recherches sur les Confessions de saint Augustin* (Paris: E. de Boccard, 1968).
— *Les confessions de Saint Augustin dans la tradition littéraire: antécédents et postérité* (Paris: Études augustiniennes, 1963).
Courcelle, Pierre and Jeanne, *Iconographie de saint Augustin* (4 vols; Paris: Études augustiniennes, 1965–80).
Coyle, J. Kevin, 'Saint Augustine's Manichaean Legacy', *AugStud* 34 (2003), pp. 1–22.
Cross, Richard, *Duns Scotus on God* (Burlington, VT: Ashgate, 2005), pp. 1–14.
— *Duns Scotus* (New York: Oxford University Press, 1999).
Cullen, Christopher, *Bonaventure* (Oxford: Oxford University Press, 2006), pp. 44–51.
— 'The Semiotic Metaphysics of Saint Bonaventure' (PhD diss., The Catholic University of America, 2000), pp. 254–308.
Curley, Augustine J., *Augustine's Critique of Scepticism: A Study of Contra Academicos* (New York: Peter Lang, 1996).
Daley, Brian E., 'Making a Human Will Divine: Augustine and Maximus on Christ and Human Salvation'. In *Orthodox Readings of Augustine* (ed. A. Papanikolaou and G. Demacopoulos; Crestwood, NY: St. Vladimir's Seminary Press, 2008), pp. 101–26.
— *The Hope of the Early Church* (Peabody: Hendrickson, 2003; Cambridge: Cambridge University Press, 1st edn, 1991).
— 'A Humble Mediator: The Distinctive Elements in St. Augustine's Christology', *Word and Spirit* 9 (1987), pp. 100–17.
Daly, Christopher, John Doody and Kim Paffenroth (eds), *Augustine and History* (Lanham: Lexington, 2008).
Daniélou, Jean, *The Lord of History: Reflections on the Inner Meaning of History* (London: Longmans, Green, 1958).
Dankbaar, Willem Frederik, *De Sacramentsleer van Calvijn* (Amsterdam: H. J. Paris, 1941).
Dassmann, Ernst, *Augustinus, Heiliger und Kirchenlehrer* (Stuttgart: Kohlhammer, 1993).
Dauphinais, Michael, Barry David and Matthew Levering (eds), *Aquinas the Augustinian* (Washington, DC: The Catholic University of America Press, 2007).
Davies, Joshua C., 'Augustine on Original Cognition', *AugStud* 40/2 (2009), pp. 251–76.
Delaroche, Bruno, *Saint Augustin. Lecteur et interprète de saint Paul dans le 'De peccatorum meritis et remissione' (hiver 411–412)* (Paris: Études augustiniennes, 1996).
Delius, Hans-Ulrich, *Augustin als Quelle Luthers. Eine Materialsammlung* (Berlin: Evangelische Verlagsanstalt, 1984).
Delorme, Ferdinand, 'Textes franciscains', *Archivo italiano per la storia della pietà* 1 (1951), pp. 212–18.
Demacopoulos, George E. and Aristotle Papanikolaou (eds), *Orthodox Readings of Augustine* (Crestwood, NY: St. Vladimir's Seminary Press, 2008).

Demmer, Dorothea, *Luther interpres: Der theologische Neuansatz in seiner Römerbriefexegese unter besonderer Berücksichtigung Augustins* (Witten: Luther-Verlag, 1968).

De Roy, Olivier, *L'Intelligence de la Foi en la Trinité selon Saint Augustin. Genèse de sa Théologie Trinitaire jusqu'en* (Paris: Études augustiniennes, 1966).

Descoqs, Pedro, 'Autour du mystère de notre élévation surnaturelle', *Nouvelle revue théologiques* 66 (1939), pp. 418–19.

Dieter, Theodor, *Der junge Luther und Aristoteles* (Berlin and New York: Walter de Gruyter, 2001).

Dittrich, Constance (ed.), *Augustinus, ein Lehrer des Abendlandes Einführung und Dokumente* (Wiesbaden: Harrassowitz, 2009).

Dixon, Sandra L., *Augustine: The Scattered and Gathered Self* (St. Louis: Chalice, 1999).

Djuth, Marianne, 'Collation and Conversion: Seeking Wisdom in Augustine's Confessions', *AugStud* 41/2 (2010), pp. 435–51.

— 'Augustine versus Julian of Eclanum on the love of Wisdom', *Augustiniana* 58 (2008), pp. 141–50.

— 'Augustine, Monica, and the Love of Wisdom', *AugStud* 39/2 (2008), pp. 237–52.

— 'Philosophy in a Time of Exile: *Vera Philosophia* and the Incarnation', *AugStud* 38/1 (2007), pp. 281–300.

— 'Saint Augustine and the Fall of the Soul', *International Philosophical Quarterly* 47/4 (2007), pp. 489–91.

— 'Augustine on Necessity', *AugStud* 31/2 (2000), pp. 195–210.

— 'Anselm's Augustinianism and "initium bonae voluntatis"'. In *Les philosophies morales et politiques au Moyen Âge : actes du IXe Congrès international de philosophie médiévale, Ottawa, 17–22 août 1992* (ed. B. Carlos Bazán, Eduardo Andújar and Leonard G Sbrocchi; vol. 2; New York: Legas, 1995), pp. 844–60.

Dobell, Brian, *Augustine's Intellectual Conversion: The Journey from Platonism to Christianity* (Cambridge: Cambridge University Press, 2009).

Dodaro, Robert, *Christ and the Just Society in the Thought of Augustine* (Cambridge: Cambridge University Press, 2004).

Dodaro, Robert and George Lawless (eds), *Augustine and His Critics: Essays in Honor of Gerald Bonner* (London: Routledge, 2000).

Dolbeau, François, *Augustin et la prédication en Afrique: Recherches sur divers sermons authentiques, apocryphes ou anonymes* (Paris: Institut d'études augustiniennes, 2005).

Doody, John, Kevin L. Hughes and Kim Paffenroth (eds), *Augustine and Politics* (Lanham: Lexington, 2005).

Dorival, Gilles, 'L'apport des Pères de l'Église à la question de la clôture du canon de l'Ancien Testament'. In *The Biblical Canons* (ed. J.-M. Auwers and H. J. De Jonge; Bibliotheca Ephemeridum Theologicarum Lovaniensium 163; Leuven: Leuven University Press, 2003), pp. 81–110.

Doueihi, Milad, *Augustine and Spinoza* (trans. Jane M. Todd; Cambridge: Harvard University Press, 2010).

Douie, Decima L., *Archbishop Pecham* (Oxford: Clarendon Press, 1952).

Doyle, Daniel E., *The Bishop as Disciplinarian in the Letters of Augustine* (New York: Peter Lang, 2002).

Doyle, Dominic, '*Spes Salvi* on Eschatological and Secular Hope: A Thomistic Critique of an Augustinian Encylcical', *TS* 71 (2010), pp. 350–79.

Drecoll, Volker H., 'Der stand der Augustinforschung', *Theologische Literaturzeitung* 134/7–8 (2009), pp. 876–900.

— *Die Entstehung der Gnadenlehre Augustins* (Beiträge zur Historischen Theologie 109; Tübingen: Mohn Siebeck, 1999).

Drobner, Hubertus R., *Augustinus von Hippo, Sermones as populum: Überlieferung und Bestand, Bibliographie, Indices* (Supplements to Vigiliae Christianae; Leiden: Brill, 2000).

Dubreucq, Eric, *Le coeur et l'écriture chez saint Augustin : Enquête sur le rapport à soi dans les 'Confessions'* (Villeneuve-d'Ascq: Presses universitaires du Septentrion, 2003).

Duffy, Eamon, *The Stripping of the Altars: Traditional Religionin England 1400–1580* (New Haven: Yale University Press, 1992).

Dulles, Avery, 'Scripture: Recent Protestant and Catholic Views', *Theology Today* 37/7 (1980), pp. 7–26.

Dunham, Scott A., *The Trinity and Creation in Augustine: An Ecological Analysis* (Albany: SUNY Press, 2008).

Dunn, Geoffrey D., 'Poverty as Social Issue in Augustine's Homilies', *StudPat* 49 (2010), pp. 175–80.

Dyson, Robert W., *The Pilgrim City: Social and Political Ideas in the Writings of St Augustine of Hippo* (Woodbridge: Boydell Press, 2001).

Ebbeler, Jennifer, *Disciplining Christians: Correction and Community in Augustine's Letters* (New York: Oxford University Press, 2012).

Eckermann, Willigis, Adolar Zumkeller and Achim Kümmel (eds), *Traditio Augustiniana: Studien über Augustinus und seine Rezeption: Festgabe für Willigis Eckermann OSA zum 60. Geburtstag* (Würzburg: Augustinus-Verlag, 1994).

Edwards, Mark J., 'The Figure of Love in Augustine and in Proclus the Neoplatonist', *The Downside Review* 127 (2009), pp. 97–214.

Eguiarte, Enrique A., *Los salmos son mi gozo: la espiritualidad agustiniana en las 'Enarrationes in Psalmos'* (Espiritualidad agustiniana 5; Madrid: Agustuniana, 2011).

Emery, Gilles, *The Trinitarian Theology of Saint Thomas Aquinas* (trans. Francesca Aran Murphy; Oxford: Oxford University Press, 2007), pp. 58–9.

Eno, Robert B., *Saint Augustine and the Saints* (Villanova: Villanova University Press, 1989).

Enos, Leo R. and Roger C. Thompson (eds), *The Rhetoric of St. Augustine of Hippo* (Studies in Rhetoric and Religion 7; Waco: Baylor University Press, 2008).

Evans, Gillian R., *The Church and the Churches: Toward an Ecumenical Ecclesiology* (Cambridge: Cambridge University Press, 1994).

— *Augustine on Evil* (Cambridge: Cambridge University Press, 1982).

Facin, Domenico, *S. Bonaventura Doctor Seraphicus Discipulorum S. Augustini Alter Princeps* (Venetiis: Typis Aemilianis, 1904).

Faggioli, Massimo, *Vatican II: The Battle for Meaning* (Mahwah, NJ: Paulist Press, 2012).

Fanna, Fidelis a, *Ratio novae collectionis operum omnium sive editorum sive anecdotorum Seraphici Eccl. Doctoris S. Bonaventurae* (Taurini: Marietti, 1874).

Fattal, Michel, *Plotin chez Augustin; suivi de, Plotin face aux gnostiques* (Ouverture philosophique; Paris: L'Harmattan, 2006).
Feingold, Lawrence, *The Natural Desire to See God According to St. Thomas Aquinas and His Interpreters* (Faith and Reason: Studies in Catholic Theology and Philosophy; Ave Maria, FL: Sapientia Press, 2nd edn, 2010).
Ferguson, Everett, *Baptism in the Early Church: History, Theology, and Liturgy in the First Five Centuries* (Grand Rapids, MI: Eerdmans, 2009), pp. 380–99.
Fiedrowicz, Michael, *Psalmus vox totius Christi. Studien zu Augustins 'Enarrationes in Psalmos'* (Freiburg im Breisgau: Herder 1997).
Finan, Tom, 'St. Augustine on the *"mira profunditas"* of Scripture: Texts and Contexts'. In *Scriptural Interpretation in the Fathers: Letter and Spirit* (ed. T. Finan and V. Twomey; Dublin: Four Courts, 1995), pp. 163–99.
Fiorentino, Francesco, 'Gregorio da Rimini a confronto con Agostino d'Ippona', *Augustinianum* 57 (2007), pp. 183–232.
Fischer, Norbert (ed.), *Augustinus: Spuren und Spiegelungen seines Denkens* (2 vols; Hamburg: Meiner, 2009).
— *Augustins Philosophie der Endlichkeit. Zur systematischen Entfaltung seines Denkens aus der Geschichte der Chorismos-Problematik* (Mainzer Philosophische Forschungen 28; Bonn: Bouvier, 1987).
Fischer, Norbert and Cornelius P. Mayer (eds), *Die Confessiones des Augustinus von Hippo: Einführung und Interpretationen zu den dreizehn Büchern* (Freiburg: Herder, 1998).
Fitzer, Joseph, 'The Augustinian Roots of Calvin's Eucharistic Thought', *Augustinian Studies* 7 (1976), pp. 69–98.
Fitzgerald, Allan D., 'When Augustine Was Priest', *AugStud* 40/1 (2009), pp. 37–48.
— 'Tracing the Passage from a Doctrinal to an Historical Approach to the Study of Augustine', *REtAug* 50/2 (2004), pp. 295–310.
Flasch, Kurt, *Logik des Schreckens: Augustinus von Hippo, De diversis quaestionibus ad Simplicianum I 2* (Excerpta classica 8; Mainz: Dieterich, 1990).
Flasch, Kurt and Dominique de Courcelles (eds), *Augustinus in der Neuzeit: Colloque de la Herzog August Bibliothek de Wolfenbüttel, 14–17 octobre 1996* (Turnhout: Brepols, 1998).
Van Fleteren, Frederick, 'Interpretation, Assimilation, Appropriation: Recent Commentators on Augustine and His Tradition'. In *Tradition and the Rule of Faith in the Early Church: Essays in Honor of Joseph T. Lienhard, S.J.* (ed. Alexander Hwang and Ronnie Rombs; Washington, DC: The Catholic University of America Press, 2010), pp. 270–85.
— (ed.), *Martin Heidegger's Interpretations of Saint Augustine: Sein und Zeit und Ewigkeit* (Collectanea Augustiniana; Lewiston: Edwin Mellen, 2005).
— 'Authority and Reason, Faith and Understanding in the Thought of St. Augustine', *AugStud* 4 (1973), pp. 33–71.
Van Fleteren, F. and Joseph C. Schnaubelt (eds), *Augustine: Biblical Exegete* (Collectanea Augustiniana; Bern: Peter Lang, 2001).
— *Augustine in Iconography: History and Legend* (Collectanea Augustiniana 4; New York: Peter Lang, 1999).
— *Augustine: Second Founder of the Faith* (Collectanea Augustiniana 1; New York: Peter Lang, 1990).

Van Fleteren, F., Joseph C. Schnaubelt and Joseph Reino (eds), *Augustine: Mystic and Mystagogue* (Collectanea Augustiniana 3; New York: Peter Lang, 1994).

Flogaus, Reinhard, 'Palamas and Barlaam Revisited: A Reassessment of East and West in the Hesychast Controversy of 14th Century Byzantium', *StVTQ* 42/1 (1998), pp. 1–32.

Foley, Michael P. 'The Liturgical Structure of Augustine's *Confessions*', *StudPat* 43 (2006), pp. 95–100.

Fontanier, Jean-Michel, *Le Beauté selon Saint Augustin* (Rennes: Presses Universitaires de Rennes, 1998).

Fortin, Ernest L., *Political Idealism and Christianity in the Thought of St. Augustine* (Saint Augustine Lecture Series; Villanova: Villanova University Press, 1972).

Förster, Guntram, Andreas E. J. Grote and Christof Müller (eds), *Spiritus et littera. Beiträge zur Augustinus-Forschung. Festschrift zum 80. Geburtstag von Cornelius Petrus Mayer OSA* (Würzburg: Augustinus bei Echter, 2009).

Fredriksen, Paula, 'Augustine on Jesus the Jew', *AugStud* 42/1 (2011), pp. 1–20.

— *Augustine and the Jews: A Christian Defense of Jews and Judaism* (New York: Doubleday, 2008).

— 'Beyond the Body/Soul Dichotomy: Augustine on Paul against the Manichees and the Pelagians', *RechAug* 23 (1988), pp. 87–114.

— 'Paul and Augustine: Conversion Narratives, Orthodox Traditions, and the Retrospective Self', *JTS* 37 (1986), pp. 3–34.

Fridemann, Russel, *Medieval Trinitarian Thought from Aquinas to Ockham* (Cambridge: Cambridge University Press, 2010), pp. 15–30.

Friethoff, Caspar, *De predestinatie-leer van Thomas en Calvijn* (Zwolle: Fa. J. M. W. Waanders, 1925).

Froehlich, Karl, '"Take Up and Read": Basics of Augustine's Biblical Interpretation', *Interpretation* 58/1 (2004), pp. 5–16.

Fuhrer, Therese, 'Augustine on the Power and Weakness of Words', *Papers of the Langford Latin Seminar* 13 (2008), pp. 365–83.

— *Augustinus* (Darmstadt: Wissenschaftliche Buchgesellschaft, 2004).

— *Augustin, Contra Academicos, Bücher 2 und 3, Einleitung und Kommentar* (Patristische Texte und Studien 46; Berlin: Walter de Gruyter, 1997).

Fürst, Alfons, *Augustins Briefwechsel mit Hieronymus* (Jahrbuch für Antike und Christentum 29; Münster: Aschendorff, 1999).

Fux, Pierre-Yves, Jean-Michel Roessli and Otto Wermelinger (eds), *Augustinus Afer: Saint Augustin, africanité et universalité: actes du colloque international, Alger-Annaba, 1–7 avril 2001* (2 vols; Fribourg: Editions universitaires Fribourg, 2003).

Gallagher, Edmond L., *Hebrew Scripture in Patristic Biblical Theory: Canon, Language, Text* (Supplements to Vigiliae Christianae 114; Leiden: Brill, 2012).

Gallagher, Kenneth T., 'Wittgenstein, Augustine, and Language', *The New Scholasticism* 56/4 (1982), pp. 462–70.

Garrigou-Lagrange, Réginald, 'An supernaturalia possint naturaliter cognosci?' *Angelicum* 13 (1936), pp. 241–48.

— 'La Possibilité De La Vision Béatifique Peut-elle Se Démontrer?' *Revue Thomiste* 38 (1933), pp. 669–88.

— 'L'appétit Naturel Et La Puissance Obédientielle', *Revue Thomiste* 33 (1928), pp. 474–78.

Gasparro, Sfameni, *Agostino. Tra etica e religion* (Collana Letteratura cristiana antica 4; Brescia: Morcelliana, 1999).
Gasti Fabio and Marino Neri (eds), *Agostino a scuola: letteratura e didattica. Atti della Giornata di studio di Pavia, 13 novembre 2008* (Testi e studi di cultura classica 43; Pisa: ETS, 2009).
Gaul, Brett, 'Augustine on the Virtues of the Pagans', *AugStud* 40/2 (2009), pp. 233–49.
Geerlings, Wilhelm, *Augustinus. Leben und Werk: eine bibliographische Einführung* (Freiburg, Paderborn: Schöningh, 2002).
— *Christus exemplum. Studien zur Christologie und Christusverkündigung Augustins* (Tübinger Theologische Studien 13; Mainz: Matthias Grünewald, 1978).
Van Geest, Paul, *The Incomprehensibility of God: Augustine as a Negative Theologian* (Late Antique History and Religion; ed. H. Amirav; Leuven: Peters, 2011).
Gerber, Chad T., *The Spirit of Augustine's Early Theology: Contextualizing Augustine's Pneumatology* (Studies in Philosophy and Theology in Late Antiquity; Aldershot: Ashgate, 2012).
Gill, Meredith J., *Augustine in the Italian Renaissance: Art and Philosophy from Petrarch to Michelangelo* (Cambridge: Cambridge University Press, 2005).
Gilson, Étienne, *The Christian Philosophy of Saint Augustine* (trans. L. E. M. Lynch; London: Victor Gollancz, 1961).
— 'The Future of Augustinian Metaphysics'. In *St. Augustine: His Age, Life and Thought* (New York: Meridian Books, 1957).
— *The History of Christian Philosophy in the Middle Ages* (New York: Random House, 1955), pp. 361–63.
— *Introduction à l'étude de saint Augustin* (Paris: Vrin 1943), pp. 286–98.
Gioia, Luigi, *The Theological Epistemology of Augustine's* De Trinitate (Oxford: Oxford University Press, 2008).
— 'La connaissance du Dieu Trinité: par delà les embarras de l'analogie et de l'anagogie'. In *Les sources du renouveau de la théologie trinitaire au XXe siècle* (ed. Emmanuel Durand and Vincent Holzer; Paris: Cerf, 2008), pp. 97–139.
— 'The Structure of Augustine's *Inquisitio* in the *De Trinitate*: A Theological Issue', *StudPat* 43 (2006), pp. 101–06.
Gorman, Michael M., *The Manuscript Traditions of the Works of St. Augustine* (Firenze: Edizioni del Galluzzo, 2001).
Grabowski, Stanislaus J., *The Church: An Introduction to the Theology of St. Augustine* (St. Louis: Herder, 1957).
Grane, Leif, *Modus Loquendi Theologicus: Luthers Kampf um die Erneuerung der Theologie (1515–1518)* (Leiden: Brill, 1975).
Green, John D., *'Augustinianism': Studies in the Process of Spiritual Transvaluation* (Studies in Spirituality Supplement 14; Leuven: Peeters, 2007).
Gregory, Eric, 'Augustinians and the New Liberalism', *AugStud* 41/1 (2010), pp. 315–32.
— *Politics and the Order of Love: An Augustinian Ethic of Democratic Citizenship* (Chicago: University of Chicago Press, 2008).
Griffiths, Paul J., *Lying: An Augustinian Theology of Duplicity* (Grand Rapids: Brazos, 2004).

Grondin, Jean, 'Gadamer and Augustine: On the Origin of the Hermeneutical Claim to Universality'. In *Hermeneutics and Truth* (ed. B. Raymond Wachterhauser; Evanston: Northwestern University Press, 1994), pp. 137–47.

Grosseteste, Robert, *Ethica Nicomachea. Translatio Roberti Grosseteste Lincolniensis sive 'Liber Ethicorum'* (Aristoteles Latinus XXVI 1–3, Fasciculus Tertius; ed. Renatus Gauthier; Leiden: Brill, 1972).

Grossi, Vittorino, 'La ricezione agostiniana della predestinazione. Difficoltà antiche e moderne', *Augustinianum* 49/1 (2009), pp. 191–221.

— 'Agostino d'Ippona e il concilio di Trento'. In *Il Concilio di Trento nella prospettiva del terzo millennio: atti del convegno tenuto a Trento il 25–28 settembre 1995* (ed. Iginio Rogger and Giuseppe Alberigo; Brescia: Morcelliana, 1997), pp. 313–41.

— 'Agustín, teólogo de la antropología cristiana. Nota sobre su somatología'. In *El Diálogo fe-cultura en la antigüedad cristiana* (ed. Domingo Ramos-Lissón, Marcelo Merino and Alberto Viciano; Navarra: Servicio de Publicaciones de la Universidad de Navarra, 1996), pp. 97–126.

Gutiérrez, David, *The Augustinians in the Middle Ages, 1256–1356* (History of the Order of St. Augustine v. 1, pt. 1; Villanova, PA: Augustinian Historical Institute, 1984).

— *The Augustinians from the Protestant Reformation to the Peace of Westphalia, 1518–1648* (Villanova, PA: Augustinian Historical Institute, 1979).

Gunton, Colin, 'Salvation'. In *The Cambridge Companion to Karl Barth* (ed. John Webster; Cambridge: Cambridge University Press, 2000), pp. 143–58.

— 'Augustine, the Trinity and the Theological Crisis of the West'. In *The Promise of Trinitarian Theology* (Edinburgh: T&T Clark, 1991), pp. 30–55.

Hamel, Adolf, *Der junge Luther und Augustine: Ihre Beziehungen in der Rechfertigungslehre nach Luthers ersten Vorlesung 1509–1518 untersucht* (reprint edn; Hildesheim and New York: Georg Olms, 1980 [Originally 1934–35]).

Hammond, Jay, 'Dating Bonaventure's Inception as Regent Master', *Franciscan Studies* 67 (2009), pp. 179–226.

Hanby, Michael, *Augustine and Modernity* (Routledge Radical Orthodoxy; London: Routledge, 2003).

Hankey, Wayne, 'Philosophical Religion and the Neoplatonic Turn to the Subject'. In *Deconstructing Radical Orthodoxy: Postmodern Theology, Rhetoric and Truth* (ed. Wayne Hankey and Douglas Hedley; Aldershot: Ashgate, 2005) pp. 17–30.

— 'Self-Knowledge and God as Other in Augustine: Problems for a Postmodern Retrieval', *Bochumer Philosophisches Jahrbuch für Antike und Mittalter* 4 (1999), pp. 83–127.

— 'Stephen Menn's Cartesian Augustine: Metaphysical and Ahistorically Modern', *Animus* 3, (1998), pp. 183–210.

— 'Philosophical and Theological Foundations for Augustinian Theology in the Future'. In *Augustinian Spirituality and the Charism of the Augustinians* (ed. John E. Rotelle; Villanova: Augustinian Press, 1995), pp. 32–45.

— *God in Himself: Aquinas' Doctrine of God as Expounded in the Summa Theologiae* (Oxford: Oxford University Press, 1987).

— 'The Place of the Psychological Image of the Trinity in the arguments of Augustine's *De Trinitate*, Anselm's *Monologion*, and Aquinas' *Summa Theologiae*', *Dionysius* 3 (1979), pp. 99–110.

Harding, Brian, *Augustine and Roman Virtue* (Continuum Studies in Philosophy; London: Continuum, 2008).

Harmless, William (ed.), *Augustine in His Own Words* (Washington, DC: The Catholic University of America Press, 2010).

— *Augustine and the Catechumenate* (Collegeville: Liturgical Press, 1995).

Harnack, Adolf, *History of Dogma* (trans. Neil Buchanan; vol. 5; Boston: Little, Brown and Company, 1902).

Harrison, Carol, 'Taking Creation for the Creator: Use and Enjoyment in Augustine's Theological Aesthetics'. In *Idolatry: False Worship in the Bible, Early Judaism, and Christianity* (ed. Stephen C. Barton; London: T&T Clark, 2007), pp. 179–97.

— *Rethinking Augustine's Early Theology: An Argument for Continuity* (Oxford: Oxford University Press, 2006).

— 'The Assault of Grace in St. Augustine's Early Works', *StudPat* 43 (2006), pp. 113–18.

— '"Not Words but Things": Harmonious Diversity in the Four Gospels'. In *Augustine: Biblical Exegete* (ed. F. van Fleteren and J. C. Schnaubelt; Bern: Peter Lang, 2001), pp. 157–73.

— *Beauty and Revelation in the Thought of Saint Augustine* (Oxford Theological Monographs; Oxford: Clarendon Press, 1992).

Harrison, Simon, *Augustine's Way into the Will: The Theological and Philosophical Significance of De libero arbitrio* (Oxford: Oxford University Press, 2006).

Hart, David B., 'The Hidden and the Manifest: Metaphysics after Nicaea'. In *Orthodox Readings of Augustine* (ed. A. Papanikolaou and G. Demacopoulos; Crestwood, NY: St. Vladimir's Seminary Press, 2008), pp. 191–226.

Hazlett, W. Ian P., 'Calvin's Latin Preface to His Proposed French Edition of Chrysostom's Homilies: Translation and Commentary'. In *Humanism and Reform: The Church in Europe, England and Scotland, 1400–1643* (ed. J. Kirk; Oxford: Basil Blackwell, 1991), pp. 129–50.

Healy, Nicholas J., 'Henri de Lubac on Nature and Grace: A Note on Some Recent Contributions to the Debate', *Communio* 35 (Winter 2008), pp. 535–64.

Hebblethwaite, Brian, *The Christian Hope* (Oxford: Oxford University Press, rev. edn, 2010).

Hellebrand, Johannes (ed.), *Augustinus als Richter* (Res et signa 5; Würzburg: Augustinus-Verlag, 2009).

Hengel, Martin, *The Septuagint as Christian Scripture: Its Prehistory and the Problem of Its Canon* (trans. M. E. Biddle; Edinburgh: T&T Clark, 2002), pp. 57–74.

Hennings, Ralph, *Der Briefwechsel zwischen Augustinus und Hieronymus und ihr Streit um den Kanon des Alten Testaments und die Auslegung von Gal. 2, 11–14* (Supplements to Vigiliae Christianae 21; Leiden: Brill, 1994).

Hermann, Rudolf, *Luthers These 'Gerecht und Sünder zugleich'* (reprint edn; Darmstadt: Wissenschaftliche Buchgesellschaft, 1960, [originally 1930]).

Hick, John, *Evil and the God of Love* (Basingstoke: Macmillan, 1977).

— *Death and Eternal Life* (London: Collins, 1976).

Hochschild, Paige, *Memory in Augustine's Theological Anthropology* (Oxford Early Christian Studies; Oxford: Oxford University Press, 2012).

Holl, Karl, *Gesammelte Aufsätze zur Kirchengeschichte. Vol. 1: Luther* (6th edn; Tübingen: J.C.B. Mohr, 1932 [1st edn, 1921]).

Hollerich, Michael J., 'John Milbank, Augustine and the "Secular"', *AugStud* 30/2 (1999), pp. 311–26.

Hollingworth, Miles, *The Pilgrim City: St. Augustine of Hippo and His Innovation in Political Thought* (London: T&T Clark, 2010).

Hölscher, Ludger, *The Reality of the Mind: Augustine's Philosophical Arguments for the Human Soul as a Spiritual Substance* (Studies in Phenomenological and Classical Realism; London: Routledge, 1986).

Holt, Laura, 'A Survey of Recent Work on Augustine', *HeyJ* 49 (2008), pp. 292–308.

Holte, Ragnar, *Béatitude et sagesse. Saint Augustin et le probléme de la fin de l'homme dans la philosophie ancienne* (Paris: Institut d'études augustiniennes, 1962).

Hombert, Pierre-Marie, *Nouvelles recherches de chronologie augustinienne* (Paris: Institut d'études augustiniennes, 2000).

— *Gloria Gratiae: se glorifier en Dieu, principe et fin de la théologie augustinienne de la grâce* (Paris: Institut d'études augustiniennes, 1996).

Houghton, Hugh A. G., *Augustine's Text of John: Patristic Citations and Latin Gospel Manuscripts* (Oxford: Oxford University Press, 2008).

Hunter, David, 'Augustine and the Making of Marriage in Roman North Africa', *JECS* 11/1 (2003), pp. 63–85.

— 'Augustinian Pessimism? A New Look at Augustine's Teaching on Sex, Marriage, and Celibacy', *AugStud* 25 (1994), pp. 153–77.

Hwang, Alexander, 'Augustine's Interpretation of 1 Tim 2:4 in the Context of His Developing Views of Grace', *StudPat* 43 (2006), pp. 137–42.

Ignatius, *Trall.* 3. In *The Apostolic Fathers* (trans. Bart D. Ehrman; Loeb Classical Library; vol. 1; Cambridge, MA: Harvard University Press, 2003).

Inglis, John, *Spheres of Philosophical Inquiry and the Historiography of Medieval Philosophy* (Leiden: Brill, 1998).

Jackson, Belford D., 'The Theory of Signs in St. Augustine's *De doctrina Christiana*', *REtAug* 15 (1969), pp. 9–49.

Jeanmart, Gaëlle, *Herméneutique et subjectivité dans les confessions d'Augustin* (Monothéismes et philosophie; Turnhout: Brepols, 2006).

John, Helen James, *The Thomist Spectrum* (New York: Fordham University Press, 1966), pp. 17–24.

Johnson, David, 'The Myth of the Augustinian Synthesis', *Lutheran Quaterly* 5/2 (1991), pp. 157–69.

Johnson, Timothy, *Bonaventure. Mystic of God's Word* (Hyde Park: New City Press, 1999), pp. 152–66.

Julian, *Revelations of Divine Love* (trans. Clifton Wolters; New York: Penguin, 1966).

Kähler, Ernst, *Karlstadt und Augustin. Der Kommentar des Andreas Bodenstein von Karlstadt zu Augustins Schrift* De Spiritu et Littera (Halle: Max Niemeyer, 1952).

Kahnert, Klaus, *Entmachtung der Zeichen? Augustin über Sprache* (Bochumer Studien zur Philosophie 29; Amsterdam: B. R. Grüner, 2000).

Kany, Roland, *Augustins Trinitätsdenken. Bilanz, Kritik und Weiterführung der modernen Forschung zu 'De trinitate'* (Studien und Texte zu Antike und Christentum 22, Tübingen: Mohr Siebeck, 2004).

Karfiková, Lenka, *Grace and the Will According to Augustine* (Supplements to Vigiliae Christianae 115; Leiden ; Boston: Brill, 2012).

— 'Memory and Language: Augustine's Analysis of Memory in Confessions X'. In *Strategies of Remembrance* (ed. Lucie Doležalová; Newcastle: Cambridge Scholars, 2009), pp. 93–102.
Kaufman, Peter I., 'Christian Realism and Augustinian(?) Liberalism', *JRE* 38 (2010), pp. 699–724.
— *Incorrectly Political: Augustine and Thomas More* (Notre Dame: University of Notre Dame Press, 2007).
Keech, Dominic, *The Anti-Pelagian Christology of Augustine of Hippo, 396–430* (Oxford Theological Monographs; Oxford: Oxford University Press, 2013).
Kelly, John N. D., *Early Christian Doctrines* (New York: Harper & Row, 2nd edn, 1977).
Kennedy, Robert, P., Kim Paffenroth and John Doody (eds), *Augustine and Literature* (Lanham: Lexington, 2006).
Kenney, J. Peter, *The Mysticism of Saint Augustine: Rereading the Confessions* (London: Routledge, 2005).
Kenny, Anthony and Jan Pinborg, 'Medieval Philosophical Literature'. In *The Cambridge History of Later Medieval Philosophy* (ed. N. Kretzmann, Anthony Kenny and Jan Pinborg; Cambridge: Cambridge University Press, 1982), pp. 11–42.
Kent, Bonnie, *Virtues of the Will. The Transformation of Ethics in the Late Thirteenth Century* (Washington, DC: The Catholic University of America Press, 1995), pp. 1–38.
King, Peter, 'Augustine's Encounter with Neoplatonism', *The Modern Schoolman* 82 (2005), pp. 213–26.
Kinnamon, Michael and Brian E. Cope (eds), *The Ecumenical Movement: An Anthology of Key Texts and Voices* (Geneva: WCC Publications, 1997).
Kirwan, Christopher, *Augustine* (London: Routledge, 1989).
Kloos, Kari, *Christ, Creation, and the Vision of God : Augustine's Transformation of Early Christian Theophany Interpretation* (Bible in Ancient Christianity 7; Leiden: Brill, 2011).
Kolbet, Paul R., *Augustine and the Cure of Souls: Revising a Classical Ideal* (Notre Dame: University of Notre Dame Press, 2010).
Komonchak, Joseph A., 'Augustine, Aquinas or the Gospel *sine glossa*? Divisions over *Gaudium et Spes*'. In *Unfinished Journey: The Church 40 Years after Vatican II: Essays for John Wilkins* (ed. Austen Ivereigh; London: Tablet, 2003), pp. 102–18.
Kotila, Heikki, *Memoria mortuorum. Commemoration of the Departed in Augustine* (Studia Ephemeridis Augustinianum 38; Rome: Institutum Patristicum Augustinianum, 1992).
Kotsko, A., 'Gift and Communio: The Holy Spirit in Augustine's *De Trinitate*', *SJT* 64/1 (2011), pp. 1–12.
Kotzé, Annemaré, 'Augustine, Jerome, and the Septuagint'. In *Septuagint and Reception: Essays Prepared for the Association for the Study of the Septuagint in South Africa* (ed. Johann Cook; Leiden: Brill, 2009), pp. 245–60.
— *Augustine's Confessions: Communicative Purpose and Audience* (Supplements to Vigiliae Christianae 71; Leiden: Brill, 2004).
Kronenberg, Maria E., 'Albertus Pighius, Proost van S. Jan te Utrecht, zijn Geschriften en zijn Bibliotheek', *Het Boek* 28 (1944–46), pp. 125–58.

La Bonnardière, Anne-Marie, *Biblia Augustiana* (7 vols; Paris: Études augustiniennes, 1960–75).
— *Recherches de chronologie augustinienne* (Paris: Études augustiniennes, 1965).
Ladner, Gerhart, *The Idea of Reform* (New York: Harper Torchbooks, 1967).
— 'St. Augustine's Reformation of Man to the Image of God'. In *Augustinus Magister. Congrès International Augustinien Paris, 21–24 septembre 1954* (vol. 2; Paris: Etudes Augustiniennes, 1954), pp. 874–75.
Lam, Joseph C. Q., *Theologische Verwandtschaft: Augustinus von Hippo und Joseph Ratzinger/Papst Benedikt XVI* (Würzburg: Echter, 2009).
— 'Die Menschwerdung des Gottessohnes – christliche Identitätsfindung sowie ihre theologisch-gesellschaftlichen Konsequenzen nach Augustinus von Hippo', *Augustiniana* 59 (2009), pp. 227–46.
— *Die Menschheit Jesu Christi in den Werken des Augustinus, Bischof von Hippo* (Studia ephemeridis Augustinianum; Roma: Instititutum Patristicum Augustinianum, 2007).
— 'Der Einfluss des Augustinus auf die Theologie des Papstes Benedikt XVI', *Augustinianum* 56 (2006), pp. 411–32.
— 'Der Religionsbegriff bei Augustinus und Kant. Augustinus von Hippo und Immanuel Kant zum 1650. Geburtstag bzw. 200. Todestag', *Augustinianum* 45 (2005), pp. 549–70.
— 'Die Menschheit Jesu Christi und die Gottesschau in Augustins Werk de Trinitate', *Augustiniana* 54 (2004), pp. 417–30.
Lamberigts, Mathijs, 'Jerusalem and Babylon: Augustine's Two Cities in Context', *Concilium: International Review of Theology* 5 (2011), pp. 71–81.
— 'Augustine on Marriage: A Comparison of *De bono coniugali* and *De nuptiis et concupiscentia*', *Louvain Studies* 35 (2011), pp. 32–52.
— 'Augustine's Use of Tradition in the Controversy with Julian of Aeclanum', *Augustiniana* 60 (2010), pp. 11–61.
— 'Competing Christologies: Julian and Augustine on Jesus Christ', *AugStud* 36 (2005), pp. 159–94.
— 'Augustine on Predestination: Some *Quaestiones Disputatae* Revisited', *Augustiniana* 54 (2004), pp. 279–305.
— 'Julian and Augustine on the Original Sin', *Augustiniana* 46 (1996), pp. 243–60.
— (ed.), *L'Augustinisme à l'ancienne Faculté de théologie de Louvain* (Bibliotheca Ephemeridum Theologicarum Lovaniensum 111; Louvain: Peeters, 1994).
Lancel, Serge, *Augustine* (trans. Antonia Nevill; London: SCM Press, 2002).
Lane, Anthony, 'Calvin, John (1509–64)'. In *Oxford Guide to the Historical Reception of Augustine* (ed. Karla Pollmann and Willemien Otten; Oxford: Oxford University Press, 2013 [forthcoming]).
— 'Anthropology: Calvin between Luther and Erasmus'. In *Calvin – Saint or Sinner?* (ed. H. J. Selderhuis; Tübingen: Mohr Siebeck, 2010), pp. 185–205.
— 'Calvin'. In *Augustin-Handbuch* (ed. V. H. Drecoll; Tübingen: Mohr Siebeck, 2006), pp. 622–27.
— *John Calvin: Student of the Church Fathers* (Edinburgh: T&T Clark, 1999).
— 'Justification in Sixteenth-Century Patristic Anthologies', in *Auctoritas Patrum. Contributions on the Reception of the Church Fathers in the 15th and 16th Century* (ed. L. Grane, A. Schindler and M. Wriedt; Mainz: Philipp von Zabern, 1993), pp. 69–95.

— 'Bondage and Liberation in Calvin's Treatise against Pighius'. In *Calvin Studies IX* (ed. J. H. Leith and R. A. Johnson; Davidson, NC: Davidson College and Davidson College Presbyterian Church, n.d.), pp. 16–45.

Lang, August, 'Recent German Books on Calvin', *Evangelical Quarterly* 6 (1934), pp. 73–6.

Lange van Ravenswaay, Jan M. *Augustinus totus noster. Das Augustinverständnis bei Johannes Calvin* (Forschungen zur Kirchen- und Dogmengeschichte 45; Göttingen: Vandenhoeck and Ruprecht, 1990).

Laporta, Jorge, 'Les notions d'appétit naturel et de puissance obédientielle chez saint Thomas d'Aquin', *Ephemerides theologicae Lovanienses* 5 (1928), pp. 257–77.

Lawless, George, *Augustine of Hippo and His Monastic Rule* (Oxford: Oxford University Press, 1987).

Legaspi, Michael C., *The Death of Scripture and the Rise of Biblical Studies* (Oxford Studies in Historical Theology; ed. D. C. Steinmetz; Oxford: Oxford University Press, 2010), pp. 3–26.

Lemmens, Leon, *Foi chrétienne et agir moral selon Saint Augustin* (Studia ephemeridis Augustinianum 120; Rome: Institutum Patristicum Augustinianum, 2011).

LeMoine, Fannie and Christopher Kleinhenz (eds), *Saint Augustine the Bishop: A Book of Essays* (New York: Garland, 1994).

Leyser, Conrad, *Authority and Asceticism from Augustine to Gregory the Great* (Oxford: Oxford University Press, 2000).

De Libera, Alain, *La philosophie médiévale* (3rd edn; Paris: Presses universitaires de France, 1998), pp. 404–6.

Lienhard, Joseph, 'Augustine on Dialectic: Defender and Defensive', *StudPat* 33 (1997), pp. 162–66.

— 'Reading the Bible and Learning to Read: The Influence of Education on St. Augustine's Exegesis', *AugStud* 27 (1996), pp. 7–25.

Lienhard, Joseph T., Earl C. Muller and Roland J. Teske (eds), *Augustine: Presbyter factus sum* (Collectanea augustiniana 2; New York: Peter Lang, 1993).

Lison, Jacques, 'L'esprit comme amour selon Grégoire Palamas: une influence augustinienne?' *StudPat* 32 (1997), pp. 325–31.

Loewen, Howard J., 'The Use of Scripture in Augustine's Theology', *SJT* 34 (1981), pp. 201–24.

Löhr, Winrich A., 'Augustinus und sein Verhältnis zu Pelagius: eine Relecture der Quellen', *Augustiniana* 60 (2010), pp. 63–86.

Lohse, Bernhard, *Der Durchbruch: Neuere Untersuchungen* (Stuttgart: F. Steiner, 1988).

— *Der Durchbruch der reformatorischen Erkenntnis bei Luther* (Darmstadt: Wissenschaftliche Buchhandlung, 1968).

Lombard, Peter, *Sententiae in IV Libris Distinctae*, tom. 1, part 2 (ed. Ignatius Brady; Grottaferata: Collegium S. Bonaventurae, 1971).

— *The Sentences Book 2: On Creation* (trans. Giulio Silano; vol. 2; Toronto: Pontifical Institute of Medieval Studies, 2008).

Lossky, Vladimir, *Éssai sur la théologie mystique de l'église d'orient* (Paris: Aubier, 1944).

Lössl, Josef, 'Augustine, "Pelagianism", Julian of Aeclanum, and Modern Scholarship', *JAC* 11, (2007), pp. 129–50.

— 'Augustine on Predestination: Consequences for the Reception', *Augustiniana* 52 (2002), pp. 241–72.
— 'A Shift in Patristic Exegesis: Hebrew Clarity and Historical Verity in Augustine, Jerome, Julian of Aeclanum and Theodore of Mopsuestia', *AugStud* 32/2 (2001), pp. 157–75.
— *Intellectus gratiae. Die erkenntnistheoretische und hermeneutische Dimension der Gnadenlehre Augustins von Hippo* (Supplements to Vigiliae Christianae 38; Leiden: Brill, 1997).
— 'Autorität und Authentizität. Augustins Lehre von den Lebensaltern in "De vera religione"', *Wissenschaft und Weisheit* 59 (1996), pp. 3–19.
— 'Wege der Argumentation in Augustinus, "De libero arbitrio"', *Theologie und Philosophie* 70 (1995), pp. 321–54.
— '"The One". A Guiding Concept in Augustine, "De vera religione"', *REtAug* 40 (1994), pp. 79–103.
— 'Religio, philosophia und pulchritudo: ihr Zusammenhang nach Augustinus, "De vera religione"', *VC* 47 (1993), pp. 363–73.
Louth, Andrew, 'Love and the Trinity: Saint Augustine and the Greek Fathers', *AugStud* 33 (2002), pp. 1–16.
De Lubac, Henri, *Augustinianism and Modern Theology* (New York, NY: Crossroad Herder, 2000).
— *The Mystery of the Supernatural* (trans. Rosemary Sheed; New York, NY: Crossroad Herder, 1998).
— 'The Mystery of the Supernatural'. In *Theology in History* (San Francisco: Ignatius, 1996), pp. 296–97.
— *Catholicism: Christ and the Common Destiny of Man* (trans. Lancelot C. Sheppard and Elizabeth Englund; San Francisco: Ignatius, 1988).
— *Augustinisme et théologie moderne* (Théologie 63; Paris: Aubier, 1965).
— *Surnaturel: Études historiques* (Paris: Aubier, 1946).
Ludlow, Morwenna, *Universal Salvation: Eschatology in the Thought of Gregory of Nyssa and Karl Rahner* (Oxford: Oxford University Press, 2000), pp. 136–50.
Lütke, Karl-Heinrich, '*Auctoritas*' bei Augustin, mit einer Einleitung zur römischen Vorgeschichte des Begriffs (Stuttgart: Kohlhammer, 1968).
Lyotard, Jean-François, *The Confession of Augustine* (trans. R. Beardsworth; Stanford: Stanford University Press, 2000).
MacCurry, Jeffrey M., 'Towards a Poetics of Theological Creativity: Rowan Williams Reads Augustine's "De Doctrina Christiana" after Derrida', *Modern Theology* 23 (2007), pp. 415–33.
Mackey, Louis, *Faith Order Understanding: Natural Theology in the Augustinian Tradition* (Toronto: Pontifical Institute of Mediaeval Studies, 2011).
Madec, Goulven, *Portrait de saint Augustin* (Paris: Desclée de Brouwer, 2008).
— *Lectures Augustiniennes* (Collections des Études Augustiniennes, Série Antiquité 168; Paris: Institut d'Études augustiniennes, 2001).
— *Le Dieu d'Augustin* (Paris: Cerf, 1998).
— (ed.), *Augustin Prédicateur (395–411): actes du Colloque International de Chantilly (5–7 septembre 1996)* (Paris: Institut d'Études augustiniennes, 1998).
— *Introduction aux 'Révisions' et à la lecture des œuvres de sain Augustin* (Paris: Institut d'Études augustiniennes, 1996).

Manchester, Peter, 'The Noetic Triad in Plotinus, Victorinus and Augustine'. In *Neoplatonism and Gnosticism* (ed. Richard T. Wallis and Jay Bregman; Studies in Neoplatonism 6; Albany: State University of New York Press, 1992), pp. 207–22.

Mandouze, André, *Saint Augustin: l'aventure de la raison et de la grâce* (Paris: Études augustiniennes, 1968).

Manetti, Giovanni, *Theories of the Sign in Classical Antiquity* (trans. C. Richardson; Advances in Semiotics; ed. T. A. Sebeok; Bloomington: Indiana University Press, 1993).

Mann, William E. (ed.), *Augustine's Confessions: Critical Essays* (New York: Rowman & Littlefield, 2006).

Mannermaa, Tuomo, *Christ Present in Faith: Luther's View of Justification* (ed. K. Stjerna; Minneapolis: Fortress, 2005).

Marenbon, John, *Medieval Philosophy: An Historical and Philosophical Introduction* (New York: Routledge, 2007), pp. 230–32.

De Margerie, Bertrand, *An Introduction to the History of Exegesis 3: Saint Augustine* (trans. P. de Fontnouvelle; Petersham, MA: Saint Bede's Publications, 1991).

Marion, Jean-Luc, *Au lieu de soi: l'approche de saint Augustin* (Paris: Presses universitaires de France, 2008).

Maritain, Jacques, 'St. Augustine and St. Thomas Aquinas'. In *St. Augustine: His Age, Life and Thought* (New York: Meridian Books, 1957).

Markus, Robert, 'Donatus, Donatism'. In *Augustine through the Ages: An Encyclopedia* (ed. Allan D. Fitzgerald; Grand Rapids: Eerdmans, 1999), pp. 284–87.

— *Sign and Meaning: World and Text in Ancient Christianity* (Liverpool: Liverpool University Press, 1996).

— *Conversion and Disenchantment in Augustine's Spiritual Career* (Villanova: Villanova University Press, 1989).

— *Saeculum: History and Society in the Theology of St. Augustine* (Cambridge: Cambridge University Press, 2nd edn, 1989).

Marrone, Stephen P., *The Light of Thy Countenance: Science and Knowledge of God in the Thirteenth Century* (2 vols; Leiden: Brill, 2001).

Marrou, Henri-Irénée, *The Resurrection and Saint Augustine's Theology of Human Values* (Villanova: Villanova University Press, 1966).

— *Saint Augustin et la fin de la culture antique* (Paris: E. de Boccard, 3rd edn, 1958).

— *Augustine and His Influence through the Ages* (New York: Harper, 1957).

Marshall, Michael, *The Restless Heart: The Life and Influence of St. Augustine* (Grand Rapids: Eerdmans, 1987).

Martin, Thomas F., 'Augustine, Paul, and the *Ueritas Catholica*'. In *Tradition and the Rule of Faith in the Early Church: Essays in Honor of Joseph T. Lienhard, S.J.* (ed. Alexander Hwang and Ronnie Rombs; Washington, DC: The Catholic University of America Press, 2010), pp. 173–92.

— *Rhetoric and Exegesis in Augustine's Interpretation of Romans 7:24–25A.* (Lewiston: Edwin Mellen, 2001).

Mathewes, Charles T., *The Republic of Grace: Augustinian Thoughts for Dark Times* (Grand Rapids: Eerdmans, 2010).

— 'The Liberation of Questioning in Augustine's *Confessions*', *JAAR* 70 (2002), pp. 539–60.

Matthews, Gareth B., 'Augustine on Reading Scripture as Doing Philosophy', *AugStud* 39/2 (2008), pp. 145–62.

— *The Augustinian Tradition* (Berkeley: University of California Press, 1999).

— *Thought's Ego in Augustine and Descartes* (Ithaca: Cornell University Press, 1992).

Mayer, Cornelius P. (ed.), *Scientia Augustiniana: Studien über Augustinus, den Augustinismus und den Augustinerorden. Festschrift Adolar Zumkeller zum 60. Geburtstag* (Würzburg: Augustinus-Verlag, 1975).

— *Die Zeichen in der geistigen Entwicklung und in der Theologie des jungen Augustinus* (2 vols; Würzburg: Augustinus-Verlag, 1969–74).

Mayer, Cornelius P. and Karl Heinz Chelius (eds), *Internationales Symposion über den Stand der Augustinus-Forschung 12.-16. April 1987 im Schloß Rauischholzhausen der Justus-Liebig-Universität Giessen* (Würzburg: Augustinus-Verlag, 1989).

— *Homo spiritalis: Festgabe für Luc Verheijen, OSA, zu seinem 70. Geburtstag* (Würzburg: Augustinus-Verlag, 1987).

McEvoy, James, 'St. Augustine's Account of Time and Wittgenstein's Criticisms', *Review of Metaphysics* 37/3 (1984), pp. 547–77.

McGrath, Alister, *Iustitia Dei: A History of Christian Doctrine of Justification* (New York: Cambridge University Press, 1998), pp. 178–79.

McNamara, Marie A., *Friendship in Saint Augustine* (Fribourg: University Press, 1958).

McSorley, Harry J., *Luther: Right or Wrong?* (New York: Newman and Minneapolis: Augsburg, 1969).

McWilliam, Joanne (ed.), *Augustine: From Rhetor to Theologian* (Waterloo: Wilfrid Laurier University Press, 1992).

Meconi, David V., *The One Christ: St. Augustine's Theology of Deification* (Washington, DC: The Catholic University of America Press, 2012).

Van der Meer, Frederick, *Augustine the Bishop: The Life and Work of a Father of the Church* (trans. B. Battershaw and G. R. Lamb; London: Sheed & Ward, 1961).

Meijering, Eginhard P., *Calvin wider die Neugierde. Ein Beitrag zum Vergleich zwischen reformatorischem und patristischem Denken* (Nieuwkoop: de Graaf, 1980).

— *Augustine über Schöpfung, Ewigkeit, und Zeit: Das elfte Buch der Bekenntniste* (Philosophia partum 4; Leiden: Brill, 1979).

Menn, Stephen P., *Descartes and Augustine* (Cambridge: Cambridge University Press, 1998).

Mettepenningen, Jürgen, *Nouvelle Théologie – New Theology: Inheritor of Modernism, Precursor of Vatican II* (London: T&T Clark, 2010).

Meslin. Michel, *Les Ariens d'Occident. 335–430* (Paris: Editions du Seuil, 1967), pp. 44–58.

Merdinger, Jane E., *Rome and the African Church in the Time of Augustine* (New Haven: Yale University Press, 1997).

Meynell, Hugo A. (ed.), *Grace, Politics and Desire: Essays on Augustine* (Calgary: University of Calgary Press, 1990).

Milbank, John, *The Suspended Middle* (Grand Rapids, MI: William B. Eerdmans, 2005).

— *Theology and Social Theory: Beyond Secular Reason* (Oxford: Blackwell, 1990).

Miles, Margaret R., *Augustine and the Fundamentalist's Daughter* (Eugene: Cascade Books, 2011).

— *Rereading Historical Theology. Before, during and after Augustine* (Eugene: Cascade Books, 2008).
— 'Sex and the City (of God): Is Sex Forfeited or Fulfilled in Augustine's Resurrection of Body?' *JAAR* 73/2 (June 2005), pp. 307–27.
— *Desire and Delight: A New Reading of Augustine's Confessions* (New York: Crossroad, 1992).
— *Augustine on the Body* (AAR Dissertation Series 31; Missoula: Scholars Press, 1979).
Moltmann, Jürgen, *The Coming of God: Christian Eschatology* (London: SCM, 1996).
Mondin, Battista, *Il pensiero di Agostino: filosofia teologia cultura* (Roma: Città nuova, 1988).
Monti, Dominic, *St. Bonaventure's Writings Concerning the Franciscan Order* (St. Bonaventure: The Franciscan Institute, 1994), pp. 39–56.
Morgenstern, Frank, *Die Briefpartner des Augustinus von Hippo: prosopographische, sozial-und ideologiegeschichtliche Untersuchungen* (Bochumer historische Studien 11; Bochum: Universitätsverlag, 1993).
Muller, André, 'Trinitarian Theology and the Shape of the Christian Life: The Prolegomenon to Augustine's *De Trinitate*', *AugStud* 40/1 (2009), pp. 121–37.
Nash, Roland H., *The Light of the Mind: St. Augustine's Theory of Knowledge* (Lexington: University Press of Kentucky, 1969).
Nauroy, Gérard and Marie-Anne Vannier (eds), *Saint Augustin et la Bible. Actes du colloque de l'université Paul Verlaine-Metz (7–8 avril 2005)* (Recherches en literature et spiritualité 15; Bern: Peter Lang, 2008).
Nichols, Aidan, 'Henri de Lubac: Panorama and Proposal', *New Blackfriars* 93/1043 (January 2012), pp. 3–33.
Nightingale, Andrea, *Once Out of Nature: Augustine on Time and the Body* (Chicago: University of Chicago Press, 2011).
Nisula, Timo, *Augustine and the Functions of Concupiscence* (Supplements to Vigiliae Christianae 116; Leiden: Brill, 2012).
— 'Continuities and Discrepancies in Augustine's View on Concupiscence and Baptism (410–30)', *StudPat* 49 (2010), pp. 21–5.
Oberman, Heiko A., Frank A. James and Erik L. Saak (eds), *Via Augustini: Augustine in the Later Middle Ages, Renaissance, and Reformation: Essays in Honor of Damasus Trapp, O.S.A.* (Leiden: Brill, 1991).
O'Connell, Marvin, *Critics on Trial: An Introduction to the Catholic Modernist Crisis* (Washington, DC: Catholic University of America Press, 1994).
O'Connell, Robert J., *Images of Conversion in Saint Augustine's Confessions* (New York: Fordham University Press, 1995).
— *St. Augustine's Confessions: The Odyssey of Soul* (New York: Fordham University Press, 1969; reprint, 1989).
— *The Origin of the Soul in St. Augustine's Later Works* (New York: Fordham University Press, 1987).
— *St. Augustine's Early Theory of Man, A.D. 386–391* (Cambridge, Belknap, 1968).
O'Daly, Gerard, *Augustine's 'City of God'* (Oxford: Oxford University Press, 1999).
— *Augustine's Philosophy of Mind* (Berkeley: University of California Press, 1987).
O'Donnell, James J., *Augustine: A New Biography* (New York: HarperCollins, 2005).

— 'The Strangeness of Augustine', *AugStud* 32/2 (2001), pp. 201–06.
— 'Bible'. In *Augustine through the Ages: An Encyclopedia* (ed. A. D. Fitzgerald; Grand Rapids: Eerdmans, 1999), pp. 99–103.
— 'Augustine's Idea of God', *AugStud* (1994), pp. 23–34.
— (ed.), *Augustine: Confessions* (3 vols; New York: Oxford University Press, 1992).
— 'The Authority of Augustine', *AugStud* 22 (1991), pp. 7–35.
— *Augustine* (Boston: Twayne, 1985).
O'Donovan, Oliver, *The Problem of Self-Love in St. Augustine* (New Haven: Yale University Press, 1980).
Ogliari, Donato, *Gratia et Certamen: The Relationship between Grace and Free Will in the Discussion of Augustine with the so-called Semipelagiansm* (Bibliotheca Ephemeridum Theologicarum Lovaniensium 149; Leuven: Peeters, 2003).
O'Meara, John J., *Studies in Augustine and Eriugena* (ed. Thomas Halton; Washington, DC: The Catholic University of America Press, 1992).
— *The Young Augustine: An Introduction to the Confessions of St. Augustine* (London: Longman, reprint 1980).
— *The Young Augustine: The Growth of St. Augustine's Mind up to His Conversion* (London: Longmans, Green, 1954).
Van Oort, Johannes, 'Augustine's Manichaean Dilemma in Context', *VC* 65 (2011), pp. 543–67.
— *Augustinus' confessiones: gnostische en christelijke spiritualiteit in een diepzinnig document* (Turnhout: Brepols, 2002).
— *Jerusalem and Babylon. A Study into Augustine's City of God and the Sources of His Doctrine of the Two Cities* (Supplements to Vigiliae Christianae 14; Leiden: Brill, 1991).
Van Oort Johannes, Otto Wermelinger and Gregor Wurst (eds), *Augustine and Manichaeism in the Latin West* (Proceedings of the Fribourg-Utrecht Symposium of the International Association of Manichaean Studies, Nag Hammadi and Manichaean Studies 49; Leiden: Brill, 2001).
Opelt, Ilona, *Die Polemik in der christlichen lateinischen Literatur von Tertullian bis Augustin* (Bibliothek der klassischen Alterumswissenschaften 2, Reihe, Bd. 63; Heidelberg: C. Winter, 1980).
Ormerod, Neil, 'Augustine's *De trinitate* and Lonergan's Realms of Meaning', *TS* 64 (2003), pp. 773–94.
Pacioni, Virgilio, *Agostino d'Ippona: Prospettiva storica e attualità di una filosofia* (Milano: Mursia, 2004).
Paffenroth, Kim, *The Heart Set Free: Sin and Redemption in the Gospels, Augustine, Dante, and Flannery O'Connor* (New York: Continuum, 2005).
Paffenroth, Kim and Kevin L. Huges (eds), *Augustine and Liberal Education* (Aldershot: Ashgate, 2000).
Paffenroth, Kim and Robert P. Kennedy (eds), *A Reader's Companion to Augustine's Confessions* (Philadelphia: Westminster John Knox, 2003).
Pani, Giancarlo, 'L'*Opera omnia* di S. Agostino in Lutero e nei Riformatori', *Augustinianum* 40 (2000), pp. 519–66.
Partoens, Gert, Anthony Dupont and Mathijs Lamberigts (eds), *Ministerium sermonis: Philological, Historical, and Theological Studies on Augustine's Sermones ad populum* (Turnhout: Brepols, 2009).

Paronetto, Vera, *Augustinus: Botschaft eines Lebens* (Würzburg: Augustinus-Verlag, 1986).
— *Agostino: Messagio di una vita* (Rome: Studium, 1981).
Pecham, John, *Registrum epistolarum fratris Johannis Peckham, archiepiscopi cantuariensis* (ed. Charles Trice Martin; vol. 3; London: Longman 1882–85).
Pecknold, Chad C., 'Beyond Our Intentions: An Augustinian Reading of Hanna's Child'. *Pro Ecclesia* 20/3 (2011).
— 'Theo-Semiotics and Augustine's Hermeneutical Jew, or, "What's a Little Supersessionism between Friends?"', *AugStud* 37/1 (2006), pp. 27–42.
Pelikan, Jaroslav, *The Christian Tradition: A History of the Development of Doctrine, vol. 1: The Emergence of the Catholic Tradition (100–600)* (Chicago: University of Chicago Press, 1975), p. 330.
Pépin, Jean, *Les confessions de Saint Augustin: leurs antécédents et leur influence* (Paris: Librairie C. Klincksieck, 1964).
Perissinotto, Luigi (ed.), *Agostino e il destino dell'Occidente* (Rome: Carocci, 2000).
Peter, Rodolphe and Jean-François Gilmont, *Bibliotheca Calviniana. Les oeuvres de Jean Calvin publiées au XVI siècle* (vol. 2; Geneva: Droz, 1991–2000).
Petersen-Boring, Wendy, 'St. Bonaventure's "Doctrine of Illumination": An Artifact of Modernity'. In *Dreams and Visions. An Interdisciplinary Enquiry* (ed. Nancy van Deusen; Leiden: Brill, 2010), pp. 137–66.
— 'Revising Our Approach to "Augustinian Illumination", a Reconsideration of Bonaventure's *Quaestiones disputate de scientia Christi IV*, Aquinas's *Summa Theologiae* Ia.84, 1–8, and Henry of Ghent's *Summa Quaestionum Ordinarium*, Q. 2, art. 1,2', *Franciscan Studies* 68 (2010), pp. 39–81.
Pinkaers, Servais-Theodore, 'The Sources of the Ethics of St. Thomas Aquinas'. In *The Ethics of Aquinas* (ed. Stephen J. Pope; Washington, DC: Georgetown University Press, 2002).
Piret, Pierre, *La destinée de l'homme: la Cité de Dieu. Un commentaire du "Ce Civitate Dei" d'Augustin* (Collection IET 12; Brussels: Éditions de l'Institut d'Études Théologiques, 1991).
Pizzolato, Luigi F., Julien Ries and José M Rodriguez (eds), *'Le Confessioni' di Agostino d'Ippona* (4 vols; Palermo: Augustinus, 1984–87).
Plumer, Eric, *Augustine's Commentary on Galatians: Introduction, Text, Translation, and Notes* (Oxford Early Christian Studies; ed. G. Clark and A. Louth; Oxford: Oxford University Press, 2003), 92–3.
Pollmann, Karla, '*Alium sub meo nomine:* Augustine between His Own Self-Fashioning and His Later Reception', *ZAC* 14 (2010), pp. 409–24.
— *St. Augustine the Algerian* (Göttingen: Duehrkohp & Radicke, 2nd edn, 2007).
— *Doctrina Christiana: Untersuchungen zu den Anfängen der christlichen Hermeneutik unter besonderer Berücksichtigung von Augustinus, 'De doctrina christiana'* (Paradosis: Beiträge zur Geschichte der altchristlichen Literatur und Theologie 41; Freiburg: Universitätsverlag, 1996).
Pollmann, Karla and Meredith J. Gill (eds), *Augustine beyond the Book: Intermediality, Transmediality, and Reception* (Brill's Series in Church History 58; Leiden: Brill, 2012).
Pollmann, Karla and Willemien Otten (eds), *The Oxford Guide to the Historical Reception of Augustine* (Oxford: Oxford University Press, 2013).

Pollmann, Karla and Mark Vessey (eds), *Augustine and the Disciplines: From Cassiciacum to Confessions* (Oxford: Oxford University Press, 2005).

Polman, Andries D. R., *The Word of God According to St. Augustine* (Grand Rapids: Eerdmans, 1961).

Przywara, Erich, *Analogia Entis* (trans. John Betz; Grand Rapids: Eerdmans, forthcoming 2013).

Quillen, Carol E., *Rereading the Renaissance: Petrarch, Augustine, and the Language of Humanism* (Ann Arbor: University of Michigan Press, 1998).

Quinn, John Francis, *The Historical Constitution of St. Bonaventure's Philosophy* (Studies and Texts 23; Toronto: PIMS, 1973), pp. 17–100.

— 'Chronology of St. Bonaventure (1217–1257)', *Franciscan Studies* 32 (1972): pp. 168–86.

Quinn, John M., *A Companion to the Confessions of St. Augustine* (New York: Peter Lang, 2002).

Rahner, Karl, *The Trinity* (London: Herder & Herder, 1970).

— 'Remarks on the Dogmatic Treatise De Trinitate'. In *Theological Investigations* (trans. K. Smyth; vol. 4; Baltimore: Helicon Press, 1966), pp. 80–2.

Ratzinger, Joseph, 'Conscience and Truth'. In *On Conscience* (San Francisco: Ignatius Press, 2007), pp. 11–41.

— 'The Holy Spirit as Communio: Concerning the Relationship of Pneumatology and Spirituality in Augustine', *Communio* 25/2 (1998), pp. 324–39.

— *Milestones: Memoirs: 1927–1977* (trans. Erasmo Levia-Merikakis; San Francisco: Ignatius Press, 1998).

— 'Glaube, Geschichte und Philosophie. Zum Echo auf *Einfuehrung in das Christentum*', *Hochland* 61 (1969), p. 543.

— *Volk und Haus Gottes in Augustins Lehre von der Kirche* (Münchener Theologische Studien 2. Systematische Abteilung 7; München: Zink, 1954).

Rebillard, Éric, 'A New Style of Argument in Christian Polemic: Augustine and the Use of Patristic Citations', *JECS* 8 (2000), pp. 559–78.

Remy, Gérard, 'Augustin converti: dialogues philosophiques et mystères dela foi', *Augustinianum* 57 (2007), pp. 281–320.

Reuter, Hermann, *Augustinische Studien* (Gotha: F. A. Perthes, 1887).

Rigby, Paul, 'The Role of God's "Inscrutable Judgments" in Augustine's Doctrine of Predestination', *AugStud* 33/2 (2002), pp. 213–22.

— 'Paul Ricoeur, Freudianism, and Augustine's *Confessions*', *JAAR* 53 (1985), pp. 93–114.

Rist, John M., *Augustine: Ancient Thought Baptized* (Cambridge: Cambridge University Press, 1994).

Robertson, Charles D., 'Augustine and Vatican II: A Broadening Conception of the Church', *StudPat* 48 (2010), pp. 431–36.

Rombs, Ronnie, '*Unum Deum . . . Mundi Conditorem*: Implications of the Rule of Faith in Augustine's Understanding of Time and History'. In *Tradition and the Rule of Faith in the Early Church: Essays in Honor of Joseph T. Lienhard, S.J.* (ed. Alexander Hwang and Ronnie Rombs; Washington, DC: The Catholic University of America Press, 2010), pp. 232–50.

— *Saint Augustine & the Fall of the Soul: Beyond O'Connell & His Critics* (Washington, DC: The Catholic University of America Press, 2006).

— 'St. Augustine's Inner Self: The Soul as "Private" and "Individuated"', *StudPat* 43 (2006), pp. 233–38.
Rose, Seraphim, *The Place of Blessed Augustine in the Orthodox Church* (Platina: St. Herman of Alaska Brotherhood, 1996).
Rostock, Nigel, 'Two Different Gods or Two Types of Unity? A Critical Response to Zizioulas' Presentation of "The Father as Cause" with Reference to the Cappadocian Fathers and Augustine', *New Blackfriars* 91 (May 2010), pp. 321–34.
Rottmanner, Benedictine Odilo, *Der Augustinismus* (Munich: J. J. Lentner, 1892).
Rousseau, Philip, 'Language, Morality and Cult: Augustine and Varro'. In *Transformations of Late Antiquity: Essays for Peter Brown* (ed. Philip Rousseau and Manolis Papoutsakis; Farnham: Ashgate, 2009), pp. 159–75.
— 'Christian Culture and the Swines' Husks: Jerome, Augustine, and Paulinus'. In *Limits of Ancient Christianity: Essays on Late Antiquity and Culture in Honor of R. A. Markus* (ed. William E. Klingshirn and Mark Vessey; Ann Arbor: University of Michigan Press, 1999), pp. 172–87.
— 'Saint Augustine: Ascetical Theology', *Canadian Catholic Review* 5 (1987), pp. 136–40.
— 'Augustine and Ambrose: The Loyalty and Single-Mindedness of a Disciple', *Augustiniana* 27 (1977), pp. 151–65.
De Ru, G., *De Rechtvaardiging bij Augustinus, vergeleken met de leer der iustificatio bij Luther en Calvijn* (Wageningen: H. Veenman, 1966).
Du Roy, Olivier, *L'intelligence de la foi en la trinité selon saint Augustin: Genése de sa théologie trinitaire jusqu'en 391* (Paris: Études augustiniennes, 1966).
Ruokanen, Miikka, *Theology of Social Life in Augustine's De civitate Dei* (Göttingen: Vandenhoeck & Ruprecht, 1993).
Russell, S. H., *A Study in Augustine and Calvin of the Church Regarded as the Number of the Elect and as the Body of the Faithful* (Oxford: Oxford University DPhil thesis, 1958).
Rydstrøm-Poulsen, Aage, *The Gracious God: Gratia in Augustine and the Twelfth Century* (Copenhagen: Akademisk, 2002).
Saak, Eric L., *Creating Augustine: Interpreting Augustine and Augustinianism in the Later Middle Ages* (Oxford: Oxford University Press, 2012).
— 'The Episcopacy of Christ: Augustinus of Ancona OESA (d. 1328) and Political Augustinianism in the Later Middle Ages', *Quaestio* 6 (2006), pp. 259–75.
— *High Way to Heaven: The Augustinian Platform between Reform and Reformation, 1292–1524* (Leiden: Brill, 2002).
Sestili, Gioacchino, *In Summam theologicam S. Thomae Aquinatis Ia. Pe., Q. XII, A. I: De naturali intelligentis animae capacitate atque appetitu intuendi divinam essentiam: theologica disquisitio* (Rome: A. et Salvatoris Festa, 1896).
Schindler, Alfred, *Wort und Analogie in Augustins Trinitätslehre* (Hermeneutische Untersuchungen zur Theologie 4; Tübingen: J.C.B. Mohr, 1965).
Schindler, David C., 'Freedom beyond Our Choosing: Augustine on the Will and Its Objects', *Communio* 29 (Fall 2002), pp. 618–53.
Schlapbach, Karin, *Augustin Contra Academicos Buch I. Einleitung und Kommentar* (Patristische Texte und Studien 58; Berlin: Walter de Gruyter, 2003).
Schmitt, E. Émile, *Le mariage chrétien dans l'œuvre de saint Augustin: une théologie baptismale de la vie conjugale* (Paris: Études augustiniennnes, 1983).

Schnaubelt, Joseph C. and Frederick Van Fleteren (eds), *Augustine, Second Founder of the Faith* (Collectanea Augustiniana; New York: Peter Lang, 1990).

Schramm, Michael, 'Taufe und Bekenntnis: Zur literarischen Form und Einheit von Augustinus' Confessiones', *JAC* 51 (2008), pp. 82–96.

Schultheiss, Jochen, *Generationenbeziehungen in den "Confessiones" des Augustinus: Theologie und literarische Form in der Spätantike* (Hermes Einzelschriften 104; Stuttgart: Steiner, 2011).

Schulz-Flügel, Eva, '*Der lateinische Bibeltext im 4. Jahrhundert*'. In *Augustin Handbuch* (ed. V. H. Drecoll; Tübingen: Mohr Siebeck, 2007), pp. 109–14.

Schumacher, Lydia, *Divine Illumination: The History and Future of Augustine's Theory of Knowledge* (Challenges in Contemporary Theology; Oxford: Wiley-Blackwell, 2011).

Schwab, Wolfgang, *Entwicklung und Gestalt der Sakramententheologie bei Martin Luther* (Frankfurt: P. Lang, 1977).

Scott, Kermit T., *Augustine: His Thought in Context* (New York: Paulist Press, 1995).

Shanzer, Danuta, 'Latent Narrative Patters, Allegorical Choices, and Literary Unity in Augustine's *Confessions*', *VC* 46 (1992), pp. 40–56.

Sieben, Hermann-Joseph, *Studien zum Ökumenischen Konzil: Definitionen und Begriffe, Tagebücher und Augustinus-Rezeption* (Paderborn: Schöningh, 2010).

— 'Die "res" der Bibel: Eine Analyse von Augustinus, *De doctr. christ.* I-III', *REtAug* 21 (1975), pp. 72–90.

Siecienski, A. Edward, *The Filioque: History of a Doctrinal Controversy* (Oxford: Oxford University Press, 2010).

Smith, Warren, J., 'Augustine and the Limits of Preemptive and Preventive War', *JRE* 35/1 (2007), pp. 141–62.

Smits, Luchèse, *Saint Augustin dans l'oeuvre de Jean Calvin* (2 vols; Assen: Van Grocum, 1956–58).

Smyth, Marina, 'The Body, Death and Resurrection: Perspectives of an Early Irish Theologian', *Speculum* 83 (2008), pp. 531–71.

Snell, Farley W., *The Place of Augustine in Calvin's Concept of Righteousness* (New York: Union Theological Seminary ThD thesis, 1968).

Solignac, Aimé, 'Doxographies et manuels dans la formation philosophique de saint Augustin', *RechAug* 1 (1958), pp. 113–48.

Speigl, Jakob, 'Der Religionsbegriff Augustins', *Annuarium Historiae Conciliorum* 27/28 (1995–96), pp. 29–60.

Stark, Judith C., *Feminist Interpretations of Augustine* (University Park: The Pennsylvania State University Press, 2007).

Van Steenberghen, Ferdinand, *La Philosophie au XIIIe Siècle, Deuxième édition, mise à jour* (Louvain: Éditions Peeters, 1991).

Steinhauser, Kenneth, 'Augustine Laughed: De beata vita'. In *Tradition and the Rule of Faith in the Early Church: Essays in Honor of Joseph T. Lienhard, S.J.* (ed. Alexander Hwang and Ronnie Rombs; Washington, DC: The Catholic University of America Press, 2010), pp. 211–31.

— 'Augustine's Autobiographical Covenant: A Contemporary Reading of His *Confessions*', *Perspectives in Religious Studies* 18 (1991), pp. 233–40.

— 'Creation in the Image of God According to Augustine's *Confessions*', *The Patristic and Byzantine Review* 7 (1988), pp. 199–204.

Steinmetz, David, *Luther and Staupitz* (Durham, NC: Duke University Press, 1980).
Stock, Brian, *Augustine's Inner Dialogue: The Philosophical Soliloquy in Late Antiquity* (Cambridge: Cambridge University Press, 2010).
— *After Augustine: The Meditative Reader and the Text* (Philadelphia: University of Pennsylvania Press, 2001).
— *Augustine the Reader: Meditation, Self-Knowledge, and the Ethics of Interpretation* (Cambridge: The Belknap Press, 1996).
Stone, Harold S., *St. Augustine's Bones: A Microhistory* (Amherst: University of Massachusetts Press, 2002).
Stone, Martin W. F., 'Michael Baius and the Debate on Pure Nature'. In *Moral Philosophy on the Threshold of Modernity* (ed. Jill Kraye and Risto Saarinen; European Science Foundation; Dordrecht: Kluwer Academic, 2005).
Studer, Basil, 'Veritas Dei in der Theologie des Heiligen Augustinus', *Augustinianum* 46 (2006), pp. 411–55.
— *Augustins De Trinitate: eine Einführung* (Paderborn: Schöningh, 2005).
— 'Geschichte und Glaube bei Origenes und Augustin', *Cristianesimo nella Storia* 25 (2004), pp. 1–24.
— 'Zur Bedeutung der Heiligen Schrift in Augustins De Trinitate', *Augustinianum* 42 (2002), pp. 12–47.
— 'Augustinus und Tyconius im Licht der Patristichen Exegese', *AugStud* 29/2 (1998), pp. 109–17.
— 'History and Faith in Augustine's *De Trinitate*', *AugStud* 28 (1997), pp. 7–50.
— *The Grace of Christ and the Grace of God in Augustine of Hippo: Christocentrism or Theocentrism* (trans. M. J. O'Connell; Collegeville: The Liturgical Press, 1997).
Stump, Eleonore and Norman Kretzmann (eds), *The Cambridge Companion to Augustine* (Cambridge: Cambridge University Press, 2001).
Suárez, Francisco, 'De ultimo fine hominis ac beatitudo', in *Opera Omnia* 4 (Paris: Vivès, 1856), pp. 1–156.
Svensson, Manfred, *Theorie und Praxis bei Augustin: Eine Verhältnisbestimmung* (Alber-Reihe Thesen 36; Frieburg: Verlag Karl Alber, 2009).
Swift, Louis J., 'Augustine on War and Killing: Another View', *HTR* 66 (1973), pp. 369–83.
Tanner, Norman P. (ed.), *Decrees of the Ecumenical Councils* (London: Sheed & Ward, 1990).
Tappert, Theodore G., *The Book of Concord: The Confessions of the Evangelical Lutheran Church* (Philadelphia: Fortress Press, 1959).
Taylor, Charles, *Sources of the Self: The Making of Modern Identity* (Harvard: Harvard University Press, 1989).
Taylor, Chloë, *The Culture of Confession from Augustine to Foucault: A Genealogy of the 'Confessing Animal'* (Studies in Philosophy; New York: Routledge, 2009).
Taylor, Jerome, *The Didascalicon of Hugh of Saint Victor: A Medieval Guide to the Arts* (New York: Columbia University Press, 1991), p. 8, n. 22.
Taylor, Richard C., David Twetten and Michael J. Wreen (eds), *Tolle Lege: Essays on Augustine & on Medieval Philosophy in Honor of Roland J. Teske, SJ* (Milwaukee: Marquette University Press, 2011).
TeSelle, Eugene, *Augustine the Theologian* (London: Burns and Oates, 1970).

Teske, Roland. J., 'Augustine's Appeal to Tradition'. In *Tradition and the Rule of Faith in the Early Church: Essays in Honor of Joseph T. Lienhard, S.J.* (ed. Alexander Hwang and Ronnie Rombs; Washington, DC: The Catholic University of America Press, 2010), pp. 153–72.
— *To Know God and the Soul: Essays on the Thought of St. Augustine* (Washington, DC: The Catholic University of America Press, 2008).
— 'Saint Augustine as Philosopher: The Birth of Christian Metaphysics', *AugStud* 23 (1992), pp. 7–32.
— 'The *De libero arbitrio* and Proof for God's Existence', *Philosophy and Theology* 2 (1987–88), pp. 124–42.
— 'Augustine, the Manichees and the Bible'. In *Augustine and the Bible* (ed. P. Bright; The Bible through the Ages 2; Notre Dame: University of Notre Dame Press, 1986), pp. 208–21.
Thomson, Francis J., 'Economy: An Examination of the Various Theories of Economy Held within the Orthodox Church, with Special Reference to the Economical Recognition of the Validity of Non-Orthodox Sacraments', *JTS* 16 (1965), pp. 402–12.
Thompson, Phillip, M., 'Augustine and the Death Penalty as the Balance of Mercy and Justice', *AugStud* 40/2 (2009), pp. 181–203.
Tianyue, Wu, 'Augustine on Involuntary Sin: A Philosophical Defense', *Augustinianum* 59 (2009), pp. 45–78.
Trapé, Agostino, *S. Agostino: L'uomo, il pastore, il mistico* (Fossano, Esperienze, 1976).
Trapp, Damasus, 'Augustinian Theology of the 14th Century: Notes on Editions, Marginalia, Opinions and Book-Lore', *Augustiniana* 6 (1956), pp. 146–274.
Trelenberg, Jörg, *Das Prinzip 'Einheit' beim frühen Augustinus* (Beiträge zur Historischen Theologie 125; Tübingen: Mohr Siebeck, 2004).
Torchia N. Joseph, 'Creation, Finitude, and the Mutable Will: Augustine on the Origin of Moral Evil', *ITQ* 71 (2006), pp. 47–66.
— 'St. Augustine's Critique of the Adiaphora: A Key Component of His Rebuttal of Stoic Ethics', *Studia Moralia* 38 (2000), pp. 165–95.
—'Creatio ex nihilo' and the Theology of St. Augustine (American University Studies; Series VII, Theology and Religion; New York: Peter Lang, 1999).
— 'The Significance of the Moral Concept of Virtue in Saint Augustine's Ethics', *The Modern Schoolman* 68 (1990), pp. 1–17.
— 'St. Augustine's Treatment of *Superbia* and Its Plotinian Heritage', *AugStud* 18 (1987), pp. 66–79.
Toom, Tarmo, 'Was Augustine an Intentionalist? Authorial Intention in Augustine's Hermeneutics', *StudPat* 54 (2012).
— 'Augustine on the Resurrection of *totus homo*'. In *Resurrection and Responsibility: Essays on Scripture, Theology, and Ethics in Honor of Thorwald Lorenzen* (ed. K. Dyer and D. Neville; Eugene, OR: Pickwick Publications, 2009), pp. 59–75.
— 'Augustine on Ambiguity', *AugStud* 38/2 (2008), pp. 407–33.
— 'The Potential of a Condemned Analogy: Augustine on *logos endiathetos* and *logos Prophorikos*', *HeyJ* 48 (2007), pp. 205–13.
— 'The Necessity of Semiotics: Augustine on Biblical Interpretation', *StudPat* 43 (2006), pp. 257–62.

— 'Augustine on the "Communicative Gaps" in Book Two of *De doctrina Christiana*', *AugStud* 34/2 (2003), pp. 213–22.
Trout, Dennis E., 'Augustine at Cassiciacum: *Otium honestum* and the Social Dimensions of Conversion', *VC* 42 (1988), pp. 132–46.
Truax, Jean A., 'Augustine of Hippo: Defender of Women's Equality?' *Journal of Medieval History* 16 (1990), pp. 279–99.
Uhalde, Kevin, *Expectations of Justice in the Age of Augustine* (Philadelphia: University of Pennsylvania Press, 2007).
Unterseher, Lisa A. *The Mark of Cain and Jews: Augustine's Theology of Jews and Judaism* (Gorgias Dissertations in Early Christian Studies 39; Piscataway: Gorgias Press, 2009).
Vaggione, Richard P., (trans. and ed.), *Eunomius: The Extant Works* (Oxford Early Christian Texts; Oxford : Oxford University Press, 1987).
Vannier, Marie-Anne, *'Creatio','conversio','formatio' chez s. Augustin* (Paradosis 31; Fribourg: Éditions universitaires, 1991).
— 'Saint Augustin et la création', *Augustiniana* 40 (1990), pp. 349–71.
Vannini, Marco, *Invito al pensiero di Sant'Agostino* (Milan: Mursia, 1989).
Vassallo, Antonio, *Inquietum cor: con Agostino alla ricerca di Dio* (Quaerere Deum 5; Palermo: Edizioni Augustinus, 1988).
Vawter, Bruce, *Biblical Inspiration* (London: Hutchinson, 1972).
Verbraken, Pierre-Patrick, *Études critiques sur les sermons authentiques de saint Augustin* (Steenbrugis: 'In abbatia S. Petri', 1976).
Verheijen, Luc, *La Règle de saint Augustin* (2 vols; Paris: Études augustiniennes, 1967).
Vessey, Mark, 'Opus imperfectum: Augustine and His Readers, 426–35 AD', *VC* 52 (1998), pp. 264–85.
— 'Conference and Confession: Literary Pragmatics in Augustine's *Apologia contra Hieronymum*', *JECS* 1 (1993), pp. 175–213.
Vessey, Mark, Karla Pollmann and Allan D. Fitzgerald (eds), *History, Apocalypse, and the Secular Imagination: New Essays on Augustine's City of God: Proceedings of a Colloquim Held at Green College, The University of British Columbia, 18–20 September 1997* (Bowling Green: Philosophy Documentation Center, 1999).
Visser, Arnoud S. Q., *Reading Augustine in the Reformation: The Flexibility of Intellectual Authority in Europe, 1500–1620* (Oxford Studies in Historical Theology; ed. David C. Steinmetz; New York: Oxford University Press, 2011).
— 'Reading Augustine through Erasmus' Eyes: Humanist Scholarship and Paratextual Guidance in the Wake of the Reformation', *Erasmus of Rotterdam Society Yearbook* 28 (2008), pp. 67–90.
Vogelsang, Erich, *Die Anfänge Luthers Christologie nach der ersten Psalmenvorlesung, insbesondere in ihren exegetischen und systematischen Zusammenhänge mit Augustine und der Scholastik dargestellt* (Berlin and Leipzig: de Gruyter, 1929).
Walls, Jerry R. (ed.), *The Oxford Handbook of Eschatology* (Oxford: Oxford University Press, 2008).
Watson, Francis, 'Hermeneutics and the Doctrine of Scripture: Why They Need Each Other', *IJST* 12/2 (2010), pp. 118–43.
Warfield, Benjamin B., *Calvin and Augustine* (Philadelphia: Presbyterian and Reformed Publishing Company, 1956).

Weaver, Rebecca H., *Divine Grace and Human Agency: A Study of the Semi-Pelagian Controversy* (Patristic Monograph Series 15; Macon: Mercer University Press, 1996).
Webster, John, *Holy Scriptures: A Dogmatic Sketch* (Current Issues in Theology; ed. I. Torrance; Cambridge: Cambridge University Press, 2003), pp. 17–30.
Weissenberg, Timo J., *Die Friedenslehre des Augustinus. Theologische Grundlagen und ethische Entfaltung* (Theologie und Frieden 28; Stuttgart: Kohlhammer, 2005).
Wendebourg, Dorothea, 'Taufe und Oikonomia: Zur Frage der Wiedertaufe in der Orthodoxen Kirche'. In *Kirchengemeinschaft – Anspruch und Wirklichkeit* (ed. Wolf-Dieter Hauschild, Dorothea Wendebourg and Carsten Nicolaisen; Stuttgart: Calwer Verlag, 1986), pp. 97–103.
Wenning, Gregor K., 'Erkenntnislehre und Trinitätsspekulation bei Augustinus', *Augustinianum* 50/1 (2010), pp. 189–232.
Wetzel, James, *Augustine's City of God: A Critical Guide* (New York: Cambridge University Press, 2012).
— *Augustine: A Guide for the Perplexed* (London: Continuum, 2010).
— 'Splendid Vices and Secular Virtues. Variations on Milbank's Augustine', *JRE* 32/2 (2004), pp. 271–300.
— *Augustine and the Limits of Virtue* (Cambridge: Cambridge University Press, 1990).
— 'The Recovery of Free Agency in the Theology of St. Augustine', *HTR* 80/1 (1987), pp. 101–25.
White, Carolinne, *The Correspondence (394–419) between Jerome and Augustine of Hippo* (Lewiston: Edwin Mellen, 1990).
White, Hayden, *Tropics of Discourse: Essays in Cultural Criticism* (Baltimore: The Johns Hopkins University Press, 1978).
Wicks, Jared, 'Applied Theology at the Deathbed: Luther and the Late-Medieval Tradition of the *Ars moriendi*', *Gregorianum* 79 (1998), pp. 345–68.
— '*Fides sacramenti – fides specialis*: Luther's Development in 1518'. In *Luther's Reform: Studies in Conversion and the Church* (ed. Jared Wicks; Mainz: von Zabern, 1992), pp. 117–42.
— *Man Yearning for Grace: Luther's Early Spiritual Teaching* (Washington and Cleveland: Corpus Books, 1968).
Williams, Michael S., *Authorised Lives in Early Christian Biography: Between Eusebius and Augustine* (Cambridge Classical Studies; Cambridge: Cambridge University Press, 2008).
Williams, Rowan, '"Good for Nothing?" Augustine on Creation', *AugStud* 25 (1994), pp. 9–24.
— 'Language, Reality and Desire in Augustine's *De doctrina*', *Literature and Theology* 3/2 (1989), pp. 138–50.
— *Politics and the Soul: A Reading of the City of God* (Milltown Studies 55; Dublin: The Milltown Institute of Theology and Philosophy, 1987).
Wilken, Robert L., 'Is Pentecost a Peer of Easter: Scripture, Liturgy, and the Proprium of the Holy Spirit'. In *Trinity, Time and Church: A Response to the Theology of Robert W. Jenson* (ed. Colin E. Gunton; Grand Rapids: Eerdmans, 2000), pp. 158–77.
Willis, Geoffrey Grimshaw, *Saint Augustine and the Donatist Controversy* (London: S.P.C.K., 1950), pp. 36–92.

Wippel, John F., 'Thomas Aquinas and the Unity of Substantial Form'. In *Philosophy and Theology in the Long Middle Ages. A Tribute to Stephen F. Brown* (ed. Kent Emery Jr., Russell L. Friedman and Andreas Speer; Leiden: Brill, 2011), pp. 117–54.

Wilson, Gordon A., 'The Critique of Thomas Aquinas's Unicity Theory of Forms in John Pecham's Quodlibet IV (Romanum)', *Franciscan Studies* 56 (1998), pp. 423–31.

Wolfson, Harry A., *The Philosophy of the Church Fathers* (Cambridge: Harvard University Press, 1956).

Wood, Christine E., 'The Metaphysics and Intellective Psychology in the Natural Desire for Seeing God: Henri de Lubac and Neo-Scholasticism' (unpublished PhD diss., Marquette University; March 2011).

Wright, David F., '*Non posse peccare* in this life? St. Augustine, *De correptione et gratia* 12:33', *Studia Patristica* 38 (Leuven: Peeters, 2001), pp. 348–53.

Yannaras, Christos, *Elements of Faith: An Introduction to Orthodox Theology* (trans. K. Schram; Edinburgh: T&T Clark, 1991), pp. 154–55.

Yates, Jonathan P., 'Augustine and the Manicheans on Scripture, the Canon, and Truth'. In *Theology and the Quest for Truth: Historical- and Systematic-Theological Studies* (ed. Mathijs Lamberigts, L. Boeve and T. Merrigan; Leuven: Peeters, 2006), pp. 11–30.

— 'Was There "Augustinian" Concupiscence in Pre-Augustinian North-Africa?' *Augustinianum* 51 (2001), pp. 39–56.

Young, Frances, 'The Confessions of St. Augustine: What Is the Genre of This Work?' *AugStud* 30/1 (1979), pp. 8–16.

Zizioulas, John, *Eucharist, Bishop, Church: The Unity of the Church in the Divine Eucharist and the Bishop during the First Three Centuries* (trans. Elizabeth Theokritoff; Brookline, MA: Holy Cross Orthodox Press, 2001).

Zumkeller, Adolar, *Augustine's Ideal of the Religious Life* (New York: Fordham University Press, 1986).

— 'Die Augustinerschule des Mittelalters. Vertreter und philosophisch-theologische Lehre (Übersicht nach dem heutigen Stand der Forschung)', *Analecta Augustiniana* 27 (1964), pp. 167–262.

Index

Adam 92, 151, 154, 169, 189–91
Adams, Marilyn McCord 98, 109, 243
Aegidius Romanus (Giles of Rome) xiii, 197, 200–4, 211–12, 221, 245
  In secundum librum sententiarum quaestiones 201
  Ordinatio 201
  Primus Sententiarum 201
Ahn, In-Sub 194, 243
allegory 139, 145, 182
Althaus, Paul 173, 243
Ambrose of Milan 37, 53, 76, 269
  De Fide 4
Anselm of Canterbury 139, 140, 150, 243
  Proslogion 133, 135
anthropology 21–2, 31, 104, 179, 213, 215, 223, 234, 243, 257, 260
Aquinas Thomas xiii, 32, 35, 71, 113, 114–30, 131–7, 148, 170, 197, 199, 201–7, 210, 212, 215, 218, 220, 222, 229, 249, 250, 252, 253, 254, 256, 259, 263, 267, 275
  Quaestiones disputatae De malo 218
  Quaestiones disputatae De veritate 199, 218
  Summa theologiae 71, 114, 135, 170, 199, 218, 256, 267
  Super Boetium De Trinitate (Q. 5: *De divisione speculativae scientiae*) 218
Aristotle/Aristotelianism 31, 114–16, 126, 132, 135, 145, 147–50, 155–6, 160, 199–200, 239, 248, 249
  Nicomachean Ethics 148, 155
Arius/Arianism 3, 231, 246
asceticism 183, 261

Athanasius 3, 232
Augsburg Confession 166, 170
Augustine/Augustinianism xi, 114, 116–21, 129, 131–8, 148, 158, 171, 186, 189, 192, 200–2, 205, 208, 210, 212, 221, 246, 248, 251, 255, 262, 269
  Ad Cresconium 84
  Ad Simplicianum 84
  Adnotationes in Iob 183
  Adversus Iudaeos 183
  Confessiones 21–30, 34, 85, 120, 136–7, 170, 172, 197, 199, 234, 236, 245, 246, 248, 250, 251, 252, 254, 258, 259, 263, 265, 266, 267, 268, 270, 271, 275
  Conlatio cum Maximino 184
  Contra Academicos 163, 250, 254, 269
  Contra duas epistulas Pelagianorum 183
  Contra Fortunatum 184
  Contra litteras Petiliani 57
  Contra Secundinum 184
  Contra sermonem Arianorum 37, 53, 183–4
  De anima et eius origine 184
  De baptismo 59
  De beata vita 163, 183, 270
  De bono viduitatis 184–5
  De catechizandis rudibus 115
  De civitate Dei xii, xiv, 24, 30, 37, 39, 42–6, 60, 91–102, 104, 106, 109, 115, 123, 126, 136, 163, 177, 182–3, 198, 222, 249, 265, 266, 269, 273, 274
  De consensu Evangelistarum 80, 85
  De continentia 184–5
  De correptione et gratia 181, 183, 275
  De dialectica 183

Index

De disciplina Christiana 183
De diversis quaestionibus 14, 39, 185, 253
De divinatione daemonum 184
De doctrina Christiana 78, 81, 82–6, 89, 137, 162, 243, 258, 262, 267, 273
De dogmatibus ecclesiasticis 184
De excidio urbis Romae 184
De fide sanctae trinitatis (= *Sermo 38 de tempore*) 184–5
De Genesi ad litteram 14, 182–3
De Genesi ad litteram imperfectus liber 14
De Genesi adversus Manicheos 183
De gratia et libero arbitrio 183
De immortalitate animae 183
De libero arbitrio 163, 179–81, 188, 193, 257, 262, 272
De magistro 183, 248
De moribus 163
De musica 183
De natura boni 183
De nuptiis et concupiscentia 170–1, 260
De octo quaestionibus ex Veteri Testamento 183
De patientia 184–5
De perfectione justitiae hominis 161
De praedestinatione et gratia 184–5
De praedestinatione sanctorum 183
De rhetorica 183
De sancta virginitate 183
De spiritu et anima 184–5
De spiritu et littera 154–7, 166, 192, 258
De symbolo ad catechumenos 184
De Trinitate 3–19, 20–5, 35, 69, 88, 99, 136–7, 141, 163, 227, 229, 232, 237, 243, 244, 246, 249, 255, 256, 258, 259, 260, 265, 266, 268, 271
De unico baptismo 184
De utilitate jejunii 183
De vera et falsa poenitentia 184
De vera religione 14, 262
Enarrationes in Psalmos 38, 63, 252, 253
Enchiridion 39, 146–7, 183

Expositio Epistulae ad Galatas 76, 85
Gesta cum Emerito 184
Hypognosticon 184
In Johannis evangelium tractatus 46
Psalmus contra partem Donati 183
Quaestiones in Genesim 182–3
Quaestiones in Matthaeum 183
Retractationes 68, 77, 181, 183
Sermo ad Caesariensis ecclesiae plebem 184
Sermones 107, 215 and 236 184
Speculum 77, 183
Super epistolam ad Romanos 126
Augustinus Hibernicus,
  De mirabilibus sacrae Scripturae 138
authority x, 77–9, 84, 87–8, 117, 124, 132, 140–50, 174–7, 181–2, 185–6, 194, 198, 238, 253, 261, 266, 273
Ayres, Lewis 19–21, 34, 233, 243

Babcock, William 38, 244
Babylon 260, 266
Backus, Irena 142, 150, 175, 180, 187, 244, 246
Bainton, Roland 154, 172–3, 244
Baius, Michael 171, 201, 205, 271
baptism 54–74, 161, 166, 170–1, 179, 186, 194, 221, 247, 253, 265, 269
Barnes, Michel R. 3–4, 21, 226, 244
Barnikol, Hermann 190, 192, 244
Bartholomew of Urbino 88
  Milleloquium veritatis S. Augustini x
Basil of Caesarea 3, 186, 230–2
Battles, F. Lewis 174–7, 185, 248
Bauerschmidt, Frederick C. v, 113–30, 199, 240
Baum, Guilielmus 182
Bavaud, Georges 191, 244
Bazàn, Bernardo C. 140, 244, 251
Beckmann, Joachim 191–2, 244
Bede 77, 88
Benson, Joshua C. v, 131–50, 240, 245
Berengar of Tours 115
Bernard of Clairvaux 139, 150, 162, 179
Besse, Georges 181, 245
Bieringer, Reimund 79, 245
Blanchette, Oliva 117, 245

Index

Blondel, Maurice 117, 119–23, 128, 221, 245
body 21, 29, 39–40, 45, 48–50, 60–71, 83, 91–2, 98–109, 122, 127, 138, 146–7, 198, 243, 248, 250, 254, 265, 270
Boehner, Philotheus 133
Bogaert, Pierre-Maurice 84, 245
Bonaventure v, xiii, 116, 131–50, 245, 246, 250, 256, 258, 265, 267, 268
  Apologia Pauperum 138
  Breviloquium 132, 142–8, 150
  Commentaria Sententiarum 137, 140, 145–8
  De reductione artium ad theologiam 138, 245
  Epistola de tribus quaestionibus ad magistrum innominatum 136
  Quaestiones disputatae de scientia Christi 148
  Sermons [sic] *de diversis* 149, 245
Bonner, Gerald 37, 246, 251
Book of Concord, The 166, 170, 271
Bougerol, Jacques-Guy 142–3, 149–50, 245, 246
Boureau, Alain 131
Bouyer, Louis 122
Braaten, Carl E. 157, 173, 246
Bradshaw, David 239
Braine, David 215, 222, 246
Brecht, Martin 154, 173, 246
Breviarium Hipponense 84
Breyfogle, Todd 97, 246
Bright, Pamela 75, 82, 90, 243, 247, 272
Buber, Martin 120
Bultmann, Rudolf 94–5, 247
Burns, J. Patout 43, 190, 247
Burr, David 136, 248
Burrus, Virginia 102–3, 108, 248
Bynum, Caroline Walker 103, 248

Cajetan Thomas (De Vio Gaitanus Tomasso) 166, 202, 205–13, 220
Calvin John xiii, 6, 98, 172, 174–95, 243, 244, 245, 248, 253, 257, 260, 261, 264, 267, 269, 270, 273
  Acta Synodi Tridentinae, cum antidoto 179

Articuli a facultate Parisiensi determinata, cum antidoto 179
De aeterna Praedestinatione Dei 185
Defensio sanae et orthodoxae doctrinae de sevitute et liberatione humani arbitrii 193
Iacobi Sadoleti epistola. Ioannis Calvini responsio 175
Institutio christianae religionis 172, 174, 177, 185, 248
Psychopannychia 184–5
Ultima admonitio ad Ioachimum Westphalum 179
Cameron, Michael 75, 83, 248
Canon 77, 79, 83–6, 251, 254, 257, 275
Cappadocians 225–7, 230–3, 238
  see also Basil; Gregory Nazianzen; Gregory Nyssa
Cary, Phillip v, xi, xiii, 20, 23, 82–3, 151–73, 235, 239, 240, 248, 249
Cassiciacum 268, 273
Cassiodorus,
  Institutiones 84
celibacy 258
Chenu, Marie-Dominique 122–3, 125, 128–9, 249
Chesterton, Gilbert K. 34
Christology 17, 20, 36–53, 78, 139, 143, 224, 243, 250, 259
Chrysostom John 125, 182, 257
church iv, xii, xiv, 36, 43, 53, 54–74, 75, 78–81, 86–9, 93–6, 121–4, 126–8, 130, 165–6, 170, 173, 175, 179, 182, 186–7, 189–90, 194, 212, 219, 223–4, 237, 239, 243, 244, 246, 247, 252, 255, 257, 259, 264, 268, 269, 270, 271, 272, 274, 275
Cicero 75, 98
  Hortensius 36, 163
Clark, Gillian 85, 249, 267
Cohen, Will vi, xiii, 223–39, 240
concupiscence 42, 44, 126, 146, 162, 170–1, 180, 265, 275
Congar, Yves 69, 72, 74, 122, 209, 249
conversion 16, 22, 30, 37, 58, 165, 170–1, 173, 192–3, 243, 245, 251, 254, 263, 265, 266, 273, 274

279

Index

Cope, Brian E. 73, 259
Cornwall, Susannah 105–8, 249
councils 70–1, 271
  Carthage 84
  Constantinople 56
  Hippo 84
  Lateran IV 24
  Nicaea 56
  Trent 80, 86, 180
  Vatican II 70, 121–2, 209
Cox Miller, Patricia 102
creation xii, 6, 14, 23, 28, 30, 32, 85–6, 92, 96, 123, 126–7, 136, 143–6, 189, 197, 199, 213–14, 220, 244, 252, 257, 259, 261, 270, 272, 273, 274
Cross, Richard 203–4, 250
Cullen, Christopher 137–8, 150, 250
Cunitz, Eduardus 182
curiosity 136–7
Cyprian of Carthage 55–6, 59, 66, 84, 178
Cyril of Alexandria 37

Daley, Brian E. 37–8, 40–3, 47, 53, 99, 109, 230, 250
Damasus I (Pope) 84
Daniélou, Jean 122–4, 128, 250
Dankbaar, Willem F. 191, 250
Dante Alighieri 172, 266
D'Arcy, Martin C. 129
Dauphinais, Michael 114, 130, 250
Davis, Stephen T. 21, 244
De Broglie, Guy 202–4, 206, 208, 211, 221, 247
De Chardin, Teilhard 123
De Jonge, Henk J. 84, 251
De la Mare, William 134
De Libera, Alain 134, 261
De Lubac, Henri vi, xiii, 122, 196–222, 239, 243, 244, 246, 257, 262, 265, 275
  Augustinianism and Modern Theology 212, 262
  Catholicism: Christ and the Common Destiny of Man 33, 262
  Mystery of the Supernatural, The 209, 212, 262
  Surnaturel: Études historiques 210–12, 262

De Margerie, Bertrand 90, 263
De Régnon, Théodore 226–7, 230, 244
De Ru, Gerrit 191, 269
De Soto, Domingo 204
De Wulf, Maurice 132–3
death 34, 37, 42, 59, 68, 88, 92–3, 97–8, 106, 117, 127, 138, 146, 158, 160, 163–4, 167–9, 172–3, 188, 236, 257, 261, 270, 272, 274
Della Mirandola Pico 205
Delorme, Ferdinand 136, 250
Demacopoulos, George 230, 238, 250, 257
Demmer, Dorothea 164, 251
Denys the Carthusian 210
Descoqs, Pedro 208, 220, 247, 251
desire 22, 25, 28, 93, 96–7, 119, 126–7, 151, 153, 159, 162–3, 197–222, 235, 248, 249, 253, 264, 265, 274, 275
devil 42
Dieter, Theodor 155, 160, 251
Diocletian persecution 56
Dionysius the Areopagite 114, 134, 139, 150, 214, 256
discipline 70, 102, 117, 140, 148, 179, 268
Donatism 56–7, 247, 263
Dorival, Gilles 84, 251
Dossetti, Giuseppe 129
Douie, Decima L. 131, 251
Doyle, Dominic 121–2, 251
Drecoll, Volker H. 87, 174, 242, 252, 260, 270
Du Roy, Olivier 20–1, 269
Duffy, Eamon 172–3, 252
Dulles, Avery 38, 48–52, 89, 252
Duns Scotus 196–7, 203–8, 210, 219, 250
  Ordinatio 203

ecclesiology 54–7, 61, 67–70, 74, 167, 194, 224, 243, 252
election 93, 191, 248
Emery, Gilles 115, 252
Erasmus Desiderius 179, 184–5, 189, 260, 273
eschatology xii, 91–109, 194, 262, 265, 273

Index

eternal life/eternity 17–18, 23–9, 39, 41, 46–7, 49, 51–2, 59, 62, 82–3, 93–5, 98–9, 105, 108–9, 139–41, 147, 149, 161–4, 171, 185, 257
ethics 97, 114, 125, 134, 155–6, 162–3, 213, 244, 247, 248, 249, 267, 271, 272
Eugippius 77, 88
Eunomius 3, 6, 273
Evans, Gillian R. 61, 74, 140, 243, 252
evil 65, 68, 97–8, 109, 117, 146, 159, 162–4, 173, 193, 218, 235–6, 243, 248, 252, 257, 260, 272
exegesis 21, 75, 86–7, 90, 99, 177, 181–2, 194, 244, 248, 261, 262, 263

Facin, Domenico 135, 252
Faggioli, Massimo 121–2, 124, 252
faith xi–xiii, 3, 11, 22–4, 27, 36, 43, 45, 49–50, 53, 61, 64, 70–2, 77, 80, 87, 95, 100, 118, 122, 127, 129, 134, 136, 139–40, 143–8, 150, 153, 155–61, 163–70, 173, 174, 178, 184–5, 206, 208, 221, 223, 230, 233, 235, 243, 246, 247, 249, 253, 262, 263, 268, 270, 271, 272, 275
fall 92–3, 97, 100, 146, 191, 251, 268
A Fanna, Fidelis 140, 252
   Ratio novae collectionis operum omnium sive editorum sive anecdotorum Seraphici Eccl. Doctoris S. Bonaventurae 140, 252
Father (God the) 4–8, 10, 13–14, 18–19, 23–8, 38–50, 62–3, 114–15, 139, 141, 166, 173, 224–33, 237, 269
fault 58, 85
Faustus of Milevis,
   Capitula 75
Feingold, Lawrence 197, 207, 212, 215–18, 222, 253
Feldmann, Erich 53
Ferguson, Everett 55–6, 253
Filioque 228, 270
Finan, Thomas 76, 253
Fitzer, Joseph 191, 253
Fitzgerald, Allan D. xi, 19, 40, 56, 74, 83, 96, 242, 253, 263, 266, 273
Flogaus, Reinhard 226, 254

Florus of Lyons 77, 88
Fredriksen, Paula 98, 109, 254
Fridemann, Russel 148, 254
friends/friendship 264
Friethoff, Caspar 190, 254
Froehlich, Karl 76, 254
Fulgentius of Ruspe 147

Gallagher, Edmon L. 84, 254
Garrigou-Lagrange, Réginald 206–7, 209, 216, 220–1, 254
Giles of Rome *see* Aegidius Romanus
Gilmont, Jean-François 178, 267
Gilson, Étienne 15, 117–21, 124, 132–7, 255
Gioia, Luigi v, xii, 3–19, 20, 23, 240, 255
God *see* Triune God
good works 154–6, 161, 167, 169, 171, 173
goodness/good 17, 22, 25, 28, 34, 59, 71, 96, 121–2, 126–7, 151–2, 156, 162–3, 167, 193, 197, 220
Grabowski, Stanislaus J. 69, 74, 255
grace xii, 13, 22, 25, 28, 30, 36, 38, 42, 44, 46, 50, 53, 54, 58, 93, 114–16, 118–22, 126, 128, 143, 146, 151–71, 178–80, 186, 189–94, 197–222, 248, 249, 257, 258, 263, 264, 266, 271, 274
grammar 249
Grane, Leif 157, 186, 255, 260
Gregory Nazianzen (Nazianzus) 232
   Orationes 49
Gregory of Nyssa 3, 95, 262
Gregory the Great 114, 261
Grillmeier, Aloys 38, 41
Grosseteste, Robert 146, 256
guilt 57, 71, 154, 172, 190
Gunton, Colin E. 6, 95, 237, 256, 274
Gutiérrez, David 200–1, 256

habit 45, 141
Haight, Roger 38, 48–53
Hamel, Adolf 156, 256
Hammond, Jay 138, 256
Hanby, Michael v, xii, 20–35, 240, 256
Hankey, Wayne 27, 97, 114, 247, 256
Harrison, Carol 85, 257
Hart, David B. 232, 257

281

Hauschild, Wolf-Dieter 56, 274
Hazlett, Ian P. 56, 274
Healy, Nicholas 212, 218–22, 257
heaven 34, 44, 63, 82, 92–6, 99, 101, 104, 107–8, 127, 141, 173, 269
Hebblethwaite, Brian 94–6, 257
Hedley, Douglas 97, 247, 256
hell 93–4, 97–9, 108–9, 126, 146–7, 155, 163, 172, 189, 243
Hengel, Martin 85, 257
Henry of Ghent 116
  Summa Quaestionum Ordinarium 135, 267
Heresy 56, 60, 70, 147, 247
Hermann, Rudolf 170, 257
Hermeneutics 77, 89, 95, 256, 272, 273
Hick, John 97–8, 109, 257
Hilary of Poitiers 3, 7
history xi–xii, 13, 23–6, 48, 51, 55–6, 84, 89, 95–7, 108, 122–5, 145, 197, 209, 223, 250, 253, 262, 263, 268, 271, 273
Hofmann, Fritz 74
Holcomb, Justin S. 82, 90, 247
Holl, Karl 159, 257
Hollerich, Michael J. 96, 258
Holy Spirit 4–13, 17–19, 23, 26–8, 37, 57–9, 62–4, 73, 76, 79–81, 85, 143, 149, 154, 166, 193, 224–5, 227–33, 237, 259, 268, 274
Huby, Joseph 208, 221
Hugh of St. Victor 139–40, 150, 271
Hütter, Reinhard 222
Hwang, Alexander 43, 247, 253, 258, 263, 268, 270, 272

Ignatius of Antioch 38–9
  Trallians 55, 258
illumination 125, 133–6, 140, 214, 267, 270
incarnation 5–6, 11–13, 28, 40, 44, 51–3, 62, 67, 89, 95, 103, 139, 143, 251
infant baptism 58
Inglis, John 134, 258
Innocent I (Pope),
  Epistula 'Consulenti tibi' 84
Isidore of Seville 198–9

Jackson, B. Darrell 89, 258
Jenson, Robert W. 157, 173, 237, 246, 274
Jerome of Stridon 246, 259, 262, 269, 274
  Epistula 79–80, 84, 87
Jesus of Nazareth xii, 28, 36–53, 37, 39, 57, 63, 73, 76, 85–6, 95, 127, 149, 152–3, 164, 167, 171–3, 174, 229, 254, 260
Jerusalem 243, 260, 266
Jews, Judaism 87, 254, 257, 267, 273
John Chrysostom 125, 182, 257
John, Helen J. 118, 258
John the Baptist 57
Johnson, Robert A. 190, 261
Johnson, Timothy 149, 258
Jonas, Hans 29
Julian of Eclanum 87, 98, 248, 251, 260, 261, 262
Julian of Norwich,
  Revelations of Divine Love 172, 258
Junillus,
  Instituta regularia divinae legis 84
justice 23, 109, 146–7, 152, 155–6, 163, 202, 211, 213–14, 247, 272, 273
justification 151–73, 174, 178, 186, 191, 204, 232, 244, 260, 263, 264

Kähler, Ernst 166, 258
Kany, Roland 19, 258
Karlstadt, Andreas 165–6, 258
Kasper, Walter 223
Kelly, John N. D. 225–6, 259
Kendall, Daniel 21, 244
Kenis, Leo 79, 245
Kenny, Anthony 140, 259
Kent, Bonnie 134, 259
Kerr, Fergus 21
Kierkegaard, Søren A. 123
Kilwardby, Robert 131
Kinnamon, Michael 73, 259
Kirk, James 182, 257
knowledge 9–10, 12, 14–19, 22–4, 29–30, 33, 45, 83, 100, 118–19, 125, 134, 135, 139–42, 145, 148, 149–50, 179, 200, 203, 206, 208, 220, 230, 247, 256, 263, 265, 270, 271

Komonchak, Joseph A. 122, 129, 130, 259
Kotsko, Adam 237, 259
Kraye, Jill 205, 271
Kretzmann, Norman 140, 259, 271
Kronenberg, Maria E. 188, 259

La Bonnardière, Anne-Marie 77, 84, 90, 260
Laberthonnière, Lucien 117
Ladner, Gerhart 14, 29–30, 260
Lamberigts, Mathijs 35, 79, 245, 247, 260, 266, 275
Lane, Anthon vi, xiii, 174–95, 240, 260
Lanfranc of Canterbury,
   De corpore et sanguine Domini adversus Berengarium 115
language 36, 53, 59, 62–3, 66–70, 73, 77–84, 94, 127, 148, 168–9, 185, 192–3, 197, 213, 219, 248, 254, 259, 268, 269, 274
Laporta, Jorge 204–6, 261
Legaspi, Michael C. 88, 261
Leget, Carlo 124
Leith, John H. 190, 261
Lenfant, David,
   Biblia Augustiniana 77
Leo XIII (Pope) 79–80, 86, 135, 206
Leporius,
   Letter of Aristeas 85
   Libellus Emendationis 39
Levering, Matthew 114, 130, 250
Lienhard, Joseph T. 19, 53, 245, 247, 253, 261, 263, 268, 270, 272
Lison, Jacques 226, 261
Liturgy 55, 87, 237, 253, 274
Loewen, Howard J. 90, 261
Lohse, Bernhard 156, 261
Lonergan, Bernard 122, 266
Lossky, Vladimir 225–6, 261
Lössl, Josef 87, 248, 261
Louth, Andrew 85, 230, 262, 267
love 9–19, 22–9, 32, 34, 37–8, 44, 48, 61–2, 66, 73, 82–3, 93–4, 97, 109, 126–7, 129, 151, 154–9, 162–5, 167, 172, 192, 220–1, 224, 230, 236, 243, 248, 249, 251, 252, 255, 257, 258, 262, 266

Ludlow, Morwenna v, xii, 91–112, 240, 262
Luther Martin v, xiii, 77, 80, 86, 89, 151–73, 179, 182, 190–1, 243, 244, 246, 249, 250, 251, 255, 256, 257, 258, 260, 261, 263, 264, 269, 270, 271, 273, 274
   1535 Lectures on Galatians 152, 155
   Against Latomus 171–2
   Babylonian Captivity of the Church, The 166, 170
   'Brief Instruction on What to Look for and Expect in the Gospels' 152, 168
   Commentary on Psalm 51 152
   Freedom of a Christian, The 152, 167
   Heidelberg Disputation 155, 157, 171
   'How Christians Should Regard Moses' 152
   Large Catechism 170
   'On Three Kinds of Righteousness' 169
   'On Two Kinds of Righteousness' 167, 169
   Preface to Romans 152, 155
   Preface to the New Testament 152
   Sacrament of Penance, The 166
   sermon on Christmas day 1519 A 153
   Table Talk 152, 165
   Theses on Faith and Law 167
lying 79, 126, 255

McGrath, Alister 204, 264
Mackey, Louis 134, 150, 262
McNeill, John T. 177, 185
McPartlan, Paul 239
McSorley, Harry J. 190, 264
McWilliam, Joanne 53, 264
Madec, Gulven 37, 46, 53, 262
Mandonnet, Pierre 132–3
Manetti, Giovanni 89, 263
Mani/Manicheism 75–6, 86, 98, 109, 123, 126, 183, 198, 243, 245, 250, 254, 266, 272, 275
Mannermaa, Tuomo 168, 173, 263
Mansini, Guy 222

Index

Marenbon, John 134, 263
Maritain, Jacques 117–21, 263
Marius Victorinus 3
marriage 258, 260
Marrone, Stephen P. 134, 263
Mary 41, 46
Maximinus 3
Maximus the Confessor 214
  Mystagogia 230, 233, 250
Mayer, Cornelius 53, 242, 253, 254, 264
Meijering, Eginhard P. 189, 264
Melanchthon,
  Apologia Confessionis Augustanae 166, 170
memory 9–10, 15–17, 25–6, 31, 88, 114, 183, 187, 243, 257, 259
Menn, Stephen 20, 27, 256, 264
Meslin, Michel 4, 264
Mettepenningen, Jürgen 120, 264
Milbank, John 96–7, 109, 212–15, 218–20, 222, 258, 264, 274
Miles, Margaret R. 99, 103–5, 108, 248, 258, 264
mind 3, 9–10, 15–16, 18, 22–4, 26, 29, 45, 47, 78, 85, 102, 114, 116–17, 119, 121–2, 125, 141, 234, 235, 258, 265
Moltmann, Jürgen 96, 265
Monica 251
Monti, Dominic 136, 142–4, 146, 148, 150, 265
Mooi, Remco J. 176–7, 179–80, 183–4, 195
Muller, Earl C. 53, 261

Nauroy, Gérard 84, 245, 265
Neoplatonism 41, 114, 243, 259, 263
Nestorius 37
Newton, John T. 40
Nicene Creed 4
Nicholas V (Pope) x
Nichols, Aidan xii, 221, 265
Nicolaisen, Carsten 70, 274

O'Collins, Gerald 21, 244
O'Connell, Marvin 36, 117, 265, 268, 271
O'Daly, Gerard 93–4, 100, 109, 265

O'Donnell, James J. 83, 265
Optatus of Milevis 55
Origen 40, 98–9, 214–15, 271
Original Sin 43, 127, 146, 169, 189–90, 250, 260
orthodoxy 6, 131, 223, 244
Owens, Joseph 27

Paffenroth, Kim 167, 247, 249, 251, 259, 266
Pagans, Paganism 39, 42, 45, 60, 67, 99, 123, 127, 149, 249, 255
Palamas Gregory 226, 254, 261
Palladius 3
Papanikolaou, Aristotle 230, 239, 243, 250, 257
Pascal, Blaise 117, 123
Paschasius Radbertus 214
Patte, Daniel 89
Paul, the Apostle 57, 62, 64, 75–6, 82, 85, 98, 100, 106, 109, 149–50, 152, 154–5, 164, 174, 244, 248, 250, 254, 263
Pecham, John 131–2, 137, 251, 275
  Registrum epistolarum fratris Johannis Peckham, archiepiscopi cantuariensis 267
Pecknold, Chad C. v–vi, xiii–xiv, 196–222, 240, 267
Pelagius/Pelagianism 25, 28, 36–7, 68, 98, 109, 146–8, 152, 154, 181, 183–4, 197–9, 214, 246, 248, 254, 259, 261
  Libellus fidei ad Innocentium papam 184
Pelikan, Jaroslav x, 267
Peter Lombard,
  Sententiae 115, 144, 146–7, 153, 162, 261
Peter, Rodolphe 267
Petersen-Boring, Wendy 134–6, 267
Petilian 56, 65
Philo of Alexandria,
  Vita Moysis 85, 87
Pighius Albert 184, 186–8, 190–3, 259, 261
  Controversiarum 188
  De libero hominis arbitrio et divina gratia 179–81, 193

Index

Pinborg, Jan 140, 259
Pinkaers, Servais 114, 267
Pius VI (Pope) 201
Pius X (Pope) 135
Planoudes 88
Plato/Platonism 6, 20, 23, 77, 82–3, 88, 98, 102, 114, 118, 149, 219, 239, 244, 248, 249, 251
  Meno 22
Plotinus 27, 235, 263
  Enneads 82
Plumer, Eric 85, 267
pneumatology 224, 233, 237–8, 243, 244, 255, 268
Pollmann, Karla xi, 96, 174, 195, 260, 267, 268, 273
Polman, Andries D. R. 80–1, 90, 268
Pope, Stephen J. 114, 267
Porphyry 98, 245, 249
Possidius,
  Indiculum 77
  Vita Augustini xii–xiii
predestination 93, 178–9, 185, 190–1, 194, 260, 262, 268
pride 11, 122
Prosper of Aquitaine 88
  Epistula ad Rufinum 75
Protestant Reformation(s) xi, 201, 256
Przywara, Erich 213, 268
Pseudo-Dionysius *see* Dionysius the Areopagite

Quinn, John Francis 132–4, 149, 150, 268

Rahner, Karl 6, 38, 41, 48–52, 95, 122, 225–6, 262, 268
Ramsey, Boniface 39
Ratzinger, Joseph (Pope Benedict XVI) xii, 20–1, 25, 31, 34, 48, 120–2, 129, 212, 221, 237, 245, 260, 268
Reid, John K. S. 175, 185
resurrection 12, 91–5, 98–108, 138, 181, 248, 263, 265, 270, 272
Reuss, Eduardus 182
Reuter, Hermann 68, 268

Richard of St. Victor 139, 148, 150
  De Trinitate 20
Robbins, Tom 129
Rombs, Ronnie v, xii, 36–53, 240, 247, 253, 263, 268, 270, 272
Root, Michael v, xii, 54–74, 241
Rose, Father Seraphim 239, 269
Rostock, Nigel 230–1, 269
Rule of Faith 43, 143, 174, 243, 247, 253, 263, 268, 270, 272
Russell, Stanley H. 194, 269

Saak, Erik L. 116, 265, 269
Saarinen, Risto 205, 271
sacraments 54–7, 59–65, 67, 69–73, 115, 143, 153, 179, 191, 250, 272
Sadolet Jacob 174–5
Sagovsky, Nicholas 74
Satan *see* devil
Scheel, Otto 37, 53
Schillebeeckx, Edward 122
Schindler, David C. 28, 35, 269
Schism 55–6, 58–61, 64–71, 247, 249
Schmaus, Michael 53
Schnaubelt, Joseph C. 85, 253, 254, 257, 270
scholastic/scholasticism xiii, 25, 31, 132–3, 135, 140, 142, 150, 152–3, 155, 168–70, 197, 199, 201, 203–4, 206, 208–10, 216, 220, 225–6, 246, 254
Schulz-Flügel, Eva 87, 270
Schumacher, Lydia 135–6, 270
Schwab, Wolfgang 165, 270
Scola, Angelo 21
scripture xii, 4–5, 7–8, 23, 75–90, 113, 139–45, 149, 161, 174–5, 181–2, 186–7, 201, 208, 237, 243, 245, 247, 252, 253, 254, 257, 261, 263, 272, 273, 274, 275
Selderhuis, Herman J. 179–80, 194, 195, 243, 244, 260
Seneca,
  De clementia 192
Sestili, Gioacchino 201–4, 206, 210–11, 221, 269
sexuality 21, 99–100, 103–8, 249, 258, 265

285

Sieben, Hermann-Josef 83, 270
Siecienski, A. Edward 228, 270
Simon Magus 57
sin 11–12, 16–18, 29, 38, 41–5, 58–9,
    63–4, 71, 92, 121, 126–7, 136–7, 143,
    146–7, 151–5, 158–67, 169–72, 174,
    178–80, 189–90, 235–6, 244, 250,
    260, 266, 272
skeptics/skepticism 76, 250
Skillrud, Harold C. 77
Smits, Luchesius 176–7, 179–80, 183–4,
    188, 192, 195, 270
Smyth, Marina 138, 270
Snell, Farley W. 191, 270
soteriology 11, 17, 37–8
soul 23, 27, 29, 34, 39–40, 48–50, 59, 62,
    76, 92, 98, 101, 109, 118–20, 125,
    127, 131, 133, 136, 139, 146, 167,
    169, 172, 198, 202, 206, 219, 230,
    235, 237, 243, 250, 251, 254, 258,
    259, 265, 268, 269, 272, 274
Steinmetz, David C. x, 75, 88, 167, 261,
    271, 273
stoics, stoicism 47, 272
Stone, Martin W. F. 205, 271
Studer, Basil 23, 36–41, 44, 46, 53, 271
Suárez Francisco 197, 206, 208, 211,
    215, 217, 220–1
    *De ultimo fine hominis ac
    beatitudo* 207, 271
Sullivan, John E. 14

Tanner, Norman P. 70–1, 271
Tappert, Theodore G. 166, 170, 271
Taylor, Charles 20, 271
Taylor, Jerome 140, 271
Teresa of Avila xiv
Tertullian 280
    De baptismo 55
TeSelle, Eugene 40, 191, 271
Teske, Roland 53, 75, 261, 271, 272
Theodore of Mopsuestia 87, 262
Thomas of Strasbourg 201
Thomson, Francis J. 56, 272
Toom, Tarmo v, xii, xiv, 75–90, 241, 272
Torrell, Jean-Pierre 130
tradition x–xi, xiii, 4, 22, 37–8, 41, 43,
    48, 71, 77, 79, 84, 86, 94, 98, 102,
    107, 134–6, 140, 144, 150, 155,
    167, 169–70, 172–3, 174, 190, 192,
    196–7, 199–201, 203, 205, 209–15,
    218, 220–1, 223, 226, 228, 234, 238,
    246, 247, 248, 250, 252, 253, 254,
    255, 260, 262, 263, 264–7, 268, 270,
    272, 274
Trinity 3–19, 20–5, 27, 29–31, 34–5, 39,
    40, 44, 53, 114, 136–7, 143, 148, 178,
    224–30, 232–3, 237, 239, 243, 244,
    252, 256, 262, 268, 274
Triune God xii, 3–19, 20–1, 148, 221,
    243
truth 3, 8, 11, 17–18, 20, 23–5, 33–4, 45,
    71–2, 76, 78–9, 85, 88, 97, 118, 120,
    122, 133, 139–43, 145, 150, 189, 199,
    210, 218, 220, 223, 245, 247, 256,
    268, 275
Twomey, Vincent 76, 253
Tyconius 55, 244, 271

Vaggione, Richard P. 6, 273
Van Bavel, Tarsicius 19, 21, 35, 37, 40,
    53, 74, 244, 247
Van der Meer, Frederick 125, 264
Van Fleteren, Frederick 85, 253, 254,
    257, 270
Van Geest, Paul 81, 124, 255
Van Ravenswaay, Lange 195, 261
Van Steenberghen, Ferdinand 132–4,
    136, 270
Vannier, Marie-Anne 84, 245, 265, 273
Varro 98, 249, 269
Vawter, Bruce 79, 273
Verhaghen, Pieter-Jozef 113, 129
Vessey, Mark 96, 242, 268, 269, 273
Victorinus Marius 3, 263
    Aduersus Arianum 4
virtue 22, 35, 82, 118, 121, 125, 127,
    134, 155–6, 161, 206, 208, 214, 255,
    257, 259, 272, 274
vision 18, 45, 69, 101, 104, 106–7, 119,
    122, 127, 133, 135, 146–7, 172,
    198–200, 202–7, 209–11, 216–18,
    221–2, 254, 259, 267
Visser, Arnoud S. Q. x, 88, 273
Vogelsang, Erich 156, 273
Volusianus 39

Von Balthasar, Hans U. 28, 95, 122, 209, 213, 220, 244
Von Harnack, Adolf 69, 257

Walker, Adrian 32, 35
Walls, Jerry R. 94, 273
war 131, 247, 270, 271
Ware, Kallistos 223
Warfield, Benjamin B. 189, 273
Watson, Francis 77, 273
Webster, John 9, 89, 95, 256, 274
Wendebourg, Dorothea 56, 274
Wetzel, James 22, 35, 274
White, Hayden 113, 274
Wicks, Jared 154, 165, 173, 274
Wilder, Thornton 33–4
will 9–10, 27–8, 35, 73, 78, 97, 109, 114, 119, 126, 134, 151, 154–5, 158–60, 163, 165, 168, 183, 190–9, 204, 207, 218–19, 221, 244, 250, 257, 258, 259, 266, 269, 272
William de la Mare, *Correctorium fratris Thomae* 134
Wilken, Robert 237, 274
William of Tocco 125

Williams, Rowan 19, 21, 24, 35, 262, 274
Willis, Geoffrey G. 70, 274
Wilson, Gordon A. 131, 275
Wippel, John F. 131, 275
Wolfson, Harry A. 225–6, 275
women 101–2, 106–7, 236, 244, 273
Wood, Christine E. 220, 275
Wood, Jacob vi, xiii, 196–222, 241
worship 13–19, 82, 92, 176, 257
Wriedt, Markus 186, 260
Wright, David F. 181, 275

Yannaras, Christos 223, 225, 275
Young, Frances 30, 275

Zizioulas, John xiii, 223–39, 269, 275
  Being As Communion 224–2, 229, 237
  Communion and Otherness 223, 225–6, 229, 231–5
  Eucharist, Bishop, Church: the Unity of the Church in the Divine Eucharist and the Bishop During the First Three Centuries 224, 275
  Lectures in Christian Dogmatics 225